For almost fifty years Joseph Howe was at or near the centre of public affairs, first in Nova Scotia and later in imperial relations and in the earliest years of the new Dominion. He was his province's most articulate spokesman as well as its leading politician and publicist and was pre-eminent in the struggle for responsible government, the introduction of railroads, opposition to Confederation, and in a quixotic advocacy of imperial federation.

In the first volume of this biography, Professor Beck deals with aspects of Howe's life and career comparatively neglected in previous studies, such as the pervading influence of his Loyalist father, which led Joseph, in his early adult life, to defend the existing political system; his relationship with his wife and family; and the "rambles" which gave him a more intimate knowledge of Nova Scotia than any other politician before or since.

Beck describes the events and experiences which played a part in Howe's political education and led to his emergence in middle life as the quintessential "conservative reformer": the editorship of the *Novascotian* which made his name a household word throughout the province and was largely instrumental in creating the Reform (Liberal) party; his triumph over the Halifax establishment in a celebrated libel suit; the ill-conceived coalition with the Tories in 1840–3 followed by his intemperate attacks on the Tory compact and Governor Falkland; and his perceptive assessment of what was needed to realize a Liberal victory in 1847 and thereby win the battle for responsible government.

Drawing on a variety of records including Howe's private papers and the vigorous provincial press of his day, Beck places Howe firmly in the political, social, and intellectual life of colonial Nova Scotia, assessing his contributions to that society and revealing the breadth of both his vision and his influence.

J. Murray Beck is Professor Emeritus, Department of Political Science, Dalhousie University.

Joseph Howe

Volume I
Conservative Reformer
1804–1848

J. MURRAY BECK

McGill-Queen's University Press
Kingston and Montreal

© McGill-Queen's University Press 1982
ISBN 0-7735-0387-0 (cloth)
ISBN 0-7735-0445-1 (paper)

Legal deposit 4th quarter 1982
Bibliothèque Nationale du Québec

Reprinted 1984
First paperback edition 1984

Printed in Canada

This book has been published with the help of a grant from the Social Science Federation of Canada, using funds provided by the Social Sciences and Humanities Research Council of Canada. Publication has also been assisted by the Canada Council under its block grant program.

Canadian Cataloguing in Publication Data

Beck, J. Murray (James Murray), 1914–
Joseph Howe

Includes bibliographical references and indexes.
Contents: v.1 Conservative reformer, 1804–1848.

ISBN 0-7735-0387-0 (v.1, bound) – ISBN 0-7735-0445-1 (v.1, pbk.)

1. Howe, Joseph, 1804–1873. 2. Politicians –
Nova Scotia – Biography. I. Title.

FC2322.1.H68B43   971.6'02'0924   C82-094676-1
F1038.H68B43

The map on pp. 74–5 is reprinted with permission of University of Toronto Press from Joseph Howe, *Western and Eastern Rambles: Travel Sketches of Nova Scotia*, edited by M.G. Parks, and has been adapted for use on pp. 84–5.

Frontispiece Joseph Howe, lithograph by C.G. Crehen, 1854, apparently from a portrait of 1851 by T. Debaussy. Courtesy Nova Scotia Museum

Contents

Preface

Ages ago – it seems to me now – my friend John Wheelock Spurr, then librarian of the Royal Military College of Canada, persuaded me to attempt a biography of Joseph Howe. Both as Nova Scotians and as Canadians we regretted and found strange the inadequacy of his treatment by historians. At most there have been four serious biographies, none based on systematic research, the last in 1935 by a professor of English literature seemingly obsessed with treating him as the protagonist of a Shakespearian tragedy whose fortunes rose steadily to some point in the third act, from which they moved inexorably downwards.

In crucial matters the earlier estimates have tended to be highly adulatory or sharply condemnatory, depending upon the political or religious predilections of the writer; yet modern historians of repute have accepted these judgments – usually the unfavourable ones – without attempting to separate myth from fact. Although my study lays bare, I believe, the warts of Howe in full measure, my conclusion, like that of Premier Angus L. Macdonald, is that Howe was, and is, the greatest Nova Scotian. Critics may suggest, however, that in trying to divorce fact from fiction, I have treated Howe altogether too kindly.

Because Howe was a human dynamo, almost unceasing in his travelling, speaking, and writing, any serious biographer is confronted with a massive amount of material, relating not only to politics but to a wide variety of other subjects. At the risk of cluttering up the book with detail I have attempted to tell the whole story, much of it through Howe's own words. Only in material relating to his private and family life are the Howe papers skimpy. This dearth, true even of the period before 1838, becomes so pronounced in the decade which follows as to turn the later chapters into an almost purely political study. Because he was seldom away from Halifax for long in these years, there are no highly revealing letters to his wife; perhaps, too, some material relating to his private and family affairs was included in the papers which one of his grandchildren is reported to have destroyed in a bonfire in her backyard.

I must thank, first, Dr Phyllis Blakeley, the Provincial Archivist, and the staff of the Public Archives of Nova Scotia, which over an extended period became almost a second home. Here, at least, the personal touch has not given way to bureaucratic rigmarole; no group of people could have been more pleasant, cooperative, and helpful. Special thanks are due to senior archivist Allan C. Dunlop, who provided so many useful bits of information on Howe that I opened a separate Dunlop file.

I am also highly indebted to McGill-Queen's University Press, especially to Professors E.R. Black, Kerry McSweeney, and David Norton, and to Charles Beer who edited the manuscript for the Press, for their efficiency, helpfulness, and congeniality. The Canadian academic community is indeed fortunate that such an institution exists and performs an invaluable function so capably. My thanks, too, to the Research Development Committee of Dalhousie University for a typing grant and to Mrs Mary Skinner for typing the manuscript.

The failings of the book are entirely my own.

John Howe, Sr, father
of Joseph Howe.
Courtesy Public Ar-
chives of Nova Scotia

Jotham Blanchard.
Courtesy Nova Scotia
Museum

Lawrence O'Connor
Doyle, from J.G.
Bourinot, *Builders of
Nova Scotia*

Herbert Huntington,
from J.G. Bourinot,
Builders of Nova Scotia

Joseph Howe
1804–1848

The Hon. James Boyle
Uniacke, about 1835.
Courtesy Nova Scotia
Museum

Lord Falkland, about
1845. Courtesy Public
Archives of Nova Scotia

Overleaf Province
House and Mather's
Church, Halifax, about
1828–9. Courtesy
Public Archives of
Nova Scotia

CHAPTER ONE

"Our Worthy Father"

"If I could be content to go along quietly and peaceably like my neighbours and at the end of some fifty or sixty years tumble into my grave and be dust, I should be happy – very happy." That is how twenty-one year-old Joseph Howe referred to the "restless agitating uncertainty" that was haunting him in 1826. But he would never be rid of the "infernal feeling" that forced him to "pursue ... something ahead ... viewless and undefined,"[1] since it was a basic element of his make-up and distinguished him from most men. Throughout his career he was possessed of an unrelenting drive to see new places, seek out new adventures, or propose new undertakings. Although, after months of frenzied activity, he might welcome a short respite, he would soon be chafing for want of a challenge and before long he would be pressing new proposals or new claims. Even in his later years, when he was taking steps for the entry of the Red River colony into the Canadian federation, he would insist, despite his enfeebled health, on a first-hand view of the province-to-be at an inclement season of the year.

In his unceasing search for challenge and adventure, Joseph Howe stood in marked contrast to his three half-brothers, offspring of the earlier marriage of his father John Howe to Martha Minns. Like their father, all three were fine specimens of manhood, tall, well-built, splendid in appearance. But while they put Joseph at a disadvantage in physical attributes, it was quite another matter in intellectual vigour and personal ambition. The eldest, John, Jr, who succeeded to his father's offices, was entirely satisfied with the status quo and highly displeased with any relative of his who sought to disturb it. William Howe, who lived much of his life in Quebec as assistant commissary general, looking resplendent in the cocked hat and gold epaulettes of his office, seemed content with a continued round of pleasures in which he consorted with governors general and their associates. Excelling in sports, he was easily one of the most accomplished racquet players of his day,[2] invariably beating Lord Dalhousie, the best in the Halifax garrison, when the latter was lieutenant-governor of Nova Scotia. David, the youngest of the half-brothers, failed to secure an entrée into the establishment even in a minor way. For a time he edited a paper in St Andrews, New Brunswick, but unable to maintain a continuing interest in business, he returned to Halifax, and off and on edited nearly all its newspapers for short periods. Reputedly, he composed his editorials as he walked up and down the floor of the printing shop, the compositor putting in type "what he said in this way, his pen being unable to keep pace with the rapidity of his thoughts."[3] But although he was also a fluent speaker, a good tragic actor, a well-read, interesting conversationalist, even a poet of sorts, his ambitions fell far short of his talents, and he came to be known as a drifter, almost a ne'er-do-well. The best that Joseph could say about David was that his son William sympathized with his efforts to bring about political reform, the only member of the Howe family to do so.

In their lack of zeal and their acceptance of the status quo, John, Jr, William, and David Howe resembled their mother's brother, William Minns, who, as a youth, had come to Halifax with his brother-in-law John Howe and set type in the latter's office before starting the *Weekly Chronicle* in 1786. For forty years he continued to publish what was, by the standards of the day, a marginally creditable paper. Occasionally, in the earlier years, he would produce an editorial on such topics as Nova Scotia's relations with the United States, but if the general lack of editorial comment and the complete absence of controversy are an indication, Minns was altogether content with Halifax and Nova Scotia as they were. Year after year he churned out a paper almost unchanged in format and consisting mainly of material appropriated from other sources. One of the best-dressed and best-proportioned men of his day, he got his greatest satisfaction from activities unconnected with his newspaper, particularly as an actor in the theatre that existed during the governorship of Sir John Wentworth early in the century.

Perhaps John Howe's second wife Mary Ede[4] bequeathed qualities to her son Joseph which distinguished him from his half-brothers; perhaps the spirit of adventure which they lacked and he possessed in abundance came from the Capt. William Ede who set sail from the Thames for America in the mid-eighteenth century. Years later, when Howe addressed the Fishmongers' Banquet in London, he glamourized the spirit of adventure that moved his maternal grandfather, picturing him as having been "bred in that old school of seamanship in which Anson and Boscawen, Hawk and Keppel were trained," "familiar with the [Thames] River from the Isle of Dogs to the Forelands," and knowledgeable about "the perils of navigation on the east coast and in the Channel."[5] But although his idyllic account may have borne some relation to the facts, actually he was giving free rein to his imagination, for his knowledge of William Ede was scanty.

In America Ede married Sarah Hilton of Baltimore or its environs, a member of a family that had lived in Maryland for at least three generations. Her husband having been lost at sea, Sarah Ede came to Halifax during the Revolution, accompanied by her two teen-age daughters, Sarah, who had been born in 1761, and Mary, born two years later. If Sarah Hilton Ede was a Loyalist, as the evidence seems to indicate, she was the only member of her family to leave the United States on that account. Apparently she and her daughters lost contact with their relatives in Maryland, and it was not until 1808, on a visit to Washington, that John Howe, Sr, drove out into the country to get from his wife's uncles, John and Abraham, an account of everything that had befallen the family since her departure.[6]

In Halifax Mary Ede married Capt. Henry Austen in 1780, and had five children before he died in 1788. Ten years later she married John Howe, Sr, and bore him Sarah and Joseph. Surprisingly little is known about her, but apparently she was not nearly so indulgent as her second husband. In one of his poems Joseph Howe testifies that, although "ever provident and good," she was "of sterner mood ... who my faults would chide."[7] Joseph's son Sydenham pictured her as "a careful housewife who made the best of small means." While she did not object to her husband's generosity to the needy, she "did not always approve of [his] bringing 'jail birds' to live with them until they could find employment."[8] Except perhaps genetically, she left no lasting mark on Joseph, and it was clearly an understatement for Sydenham to suggest that his father was "not so drawn to her as to his other parent."[9] If the family papers are any indication, she played no more than the part of housewife.

By contrast, John Howe was Joseph's "instructor, ... play-fellow, almost [his] daily companion"[10] for thirty years, and George Monro Grant attributes some of the son's most significant qualities to his father: "that milk of human kindness in him which no opposition could permanently sour; his poetic nature, which if it inclined him to be visionary at times, was yet at the bottom of his statesmanship; his reverence for the past."[11] Joseph Howe sought to trace his father back to the John Howe who was chaplain to Oliver Cromwell. Certainly the two John Howes had one thing in common, an unusual solicitude for the unfortunates who crossed their paths; thus Cromwell is reported to have said to his chaplain: "John, you are always asking something for some poor fellow; why do you never ask anything for yourself?"[12] Although Joseph was unable to establish any definite connection between the two Howes, he did satisfy himself that his father belonged to the fifth generation of a line that could be traced back to the Abraham Howe of Hatfield, Broad Oak, Essex, who settled in Roxbury, Massachusetts, and was admitted a freeman on May 2, 1638. Abraham was one of a number of Puritan Howes who left the central counties of England after 1630 to settle in America, not – according to one biographer of Joseph Howe – "because they loved old England less but because they loved freedom more."[13] Generally they were hardy, vigorous men, with large families, who contributed usefully to the development of their new land. In the accomplishments of both the English and American Howes Joseph took exceptional pride.

A remarkable man in his own right, John Howe of Nova Scotia (1754–1835) was the ninth of fifteen children born to Joseph Howe, a tinsmith of Boston, and the third of his four wives. That this Joseph Howe could devise property worth £30,184 on his death in 1779 indicates that he lived in very comfortable circumstances. He apprenticed his son John to the printing business, a decision which was to affect markedly the career of his grandson, Joseph Howe of Nova Scotia. As a printer's boy, John was "familiar as such lads are, with every nook and cranny of Boston, when the first affray between the people and the troops occurred in 1770."[14] He was just "out of his time" as an apprentice when even more exciting events in Boston were marking the beginnings of the American Revolution. According to his son Joseph, he actually witnessed the scenes of the night of December 16, 1773, when indignant colonists led by Samuel Adams, Paul Revere, and others disguised themselves as Indians, boarded three tea ships in Boston harbour, and threw their cargo into the water.[15]

For their action John Howe had no sympathy. One authority mistakenly suggests that on April 5, 1775, only a fortnight before the fights at Lexington and Concord, he accepted the invitation of Gen. Thomas Gage, the commander of the British troops in Boston, to take part in a scouting mission into rebel territory around Worcester. But actually this was another John Howe, whose own *Journal* indicates that he later supported the American cause and followed it up with smuggling activities.[16] The John Howe who was Joseph's father contributed to the British cause in a different way. When Richard Draper, the publisher of the *Massachusetts Gazette and Boston News*

Letter, died without children in 1774, his widow Margaret determined to maintain the staunch allegiance of that newspaper to the Crown. Accordingly she parted company with her husband's partner, John Boyle, who sympathized with the revolutionary cause, and took on as a junior partner John Howe, whose political convictions were not open to doubt. Howe was performing these duties when Boston was besieged in the autumn of 1775, although his name did not appear in the imprint until the Continental Army encircled the city some time later. When the British evacuated Boston on March 17, 1776, Mrs Draper and Howe moved to Halifax.

He did not remain there long. In December the British occupied Newport, Rhode Island, and there, on January 16, 1777, John Howe published the first number of the *Newport Gazette* in support of the British cause and continued to do so until shortly before the British evacuated the city late in October 1779. While at Newport, in June 1778, he married Martha Minns, the daughter of William Minns of Boston, who had migrated from Great Yarmouth, Norfolk, in 1737. Only sixteen years of age and known for her beauty, Martha Minns Howe accompanied her husband from Newport to New York and eventually to Halifax. There they set up house above a printing office at the corner of Sackville and Barrington streets, from which, on December 28, 1780, John Howe published the first number of the *Halifax Journal,* a paper that was to survive until 1870. For almost fifty-five years, until his death, Halifax was to be his home; yet, according to his son Joseph, he continued to love New England and especially old Boston with "filial regard": "He never lost an opportunity of serving a Boston man if in his power ... He loved his Sovereign, but he loved Boston too, and whenever he got sick in his latter days, we used to send him up [there] to [recuperate]. A sight of the old scenes and a walk upon Boston Common were sure to do him good, and he generally came back uncommonly well."[17]

The precise basis of John Howe's "loyalism" cannot be determined with certainty, although some informed guesses are possible. To understand him, he must be envisaged in the Massachusetts, and especially the Boston, environment of Revolutionary days. Although not many New Englanders supported Britain's position at the start of the dispute with the colonies, more than a few thought a solution was possible without the use of force. When a relatively small number of Massachusetts Whigs resorted to violence to convince the waverers that revolution was necessary, they automatically drove into the opposing camp all who opposed their excesses, especially men of substance who reacted strongly in defence of their property.

Prominent among the latter were members of the Sandemanian

church of Boston, which was characterized by the prominence and the affluence of its adherents.[18] A form of Puritanism, Sandemanianism held, as its principal tenet, that anyone who believed the same truth as the Apostles had unfeigned truth and would assuredly be saved. The practices which set the Sandemanians apart from other Christians included the weekly administration of the Lord's Supper according to the manner of the Primitive Christians; the cultivation of mutual knowledge and friendship through love feasts, in which the members dined together in the vestries of their meeting-houses between morning and afternoon services; the belief in "community of goods, by which each [member] considered the whole of his property liable to the call of the poor and of the church; and the unlawfulness of laying up treasures upon earth, by setting them apart for distant, future, and uncertain use."[19] The Sandemanian Church in Boston, in contrast with its sister congregations throughout New England, did not become embroiled in theological disputes; according to Charles Stayner, it consisted of "a devout group of dignified business men with their equally respectable families [who] seem to have been more concerned with leading Christian lives than with mixing in either religious or political discussions."[20] But since they owned so much property they could not escape attention, all the more so because they were often outspoken against the lawlessness of the Boston "mob." In turn, their opponents labelled them Tories, and often traitors.

Included among the Boston Sandemanians was a Joseph Howe who, while he might have been the brother of John Howe – older than he by one year – was more likely his father, the prosperous tinsmith.[21] Although John Howe himself is not listed in the membership of the Boston Church, he became a Sandemanian before he left Boston, probably with other members of his family. His newfound religion stamped him as a man of peace. Probably his feelings were much like those of his brother Joseph who was arrested in 1776 for not appearing on the Boston Common for drill and who excused himself on the ground that "it was against his conscience to take up arms for any government whatever."[22] This inhibition would not have prevented John Howe from taking up his pen, or venturing on scouting and intelligence missions, in aid of the British cause. The crucial problem is to explain the ardour and vigour he brought to these undertakings, to such a degree that he burned all his bridges behind him, and left himself no choice but to leave Boston – and later Newport and New York – with the British troops, the only male Howe to abandon the thirteen colonies at the time of the Revolution.[23]

But John Howe's pro-British stance was much more than the natural reaction of a member of a comfortably affluent Sandemanian family against the excesses of the Boston mob. Years later his son Joseph referred more than once to his father's determination, at all costs, to live and die under the British flag. Obviously, he found abhorrent the attempt of New Englanders to shake off the British connection by force. Yet, as was true of other New England Loyalists, especially those of Puritan adherence, his pronounced pro-British feelings did not stem from his devotion to the British Crown as such, especially not to King George III, for with these emigrés, or more accurately their descendants, the first monarch to enjoy personal popularity was Victoria.

What counted with John Howe was the British heritage, the contributions that Britons had made to human achievement over the centuries in politics, the arts, science, literature, and the like. Some of his deepest satisfactions stemmed from his membership in a nation whose accomplishments he admired and idealized, and he was determined never to relinquish it. Because his brand of religion emphasized the frailties of man and recognized that human institutions, especially in their practical operation, fell far short of perfection, he could all the more readily regard the difficulties between Britain and her colonies as arising, not from defective political institutions, but from the weaknesses of George III and the deficiencies of the British politicians of the day. Since John Howe put none of his political thinking in written form, it was left to his son Joseph in scattered references over the years, to demonstrate his father's attachment to the British connection and heritage. Perhaps the best clue to John Howe's feelings is the reverential attitude toward the achievements of Britons that Joseph displayed in his first editorials, written at a time when his father had been almost his only teacher.

John Howe's sacrifices were apparent from the very day he arrived in Halifax with his wife and infant daughter Martha. As contrasted with Boston, Halifax was, in the eyes of a fellow-Sandemanian, "a miserable village ... [in which] most of the houses were in a dilapidated state, letting in the bleak winds of the season through manifold chinks, hardly a room having ever known the luxury of being plastered."[24] Many of the Loyalists stayed but a short time, some moving on to Britain, some to Shelburne and Parrtown, and some back to the country of their birth, but for John Howe it was to be home for the remainder of his life. If anyone deserved well of government, it was he, a man who had not merely been loyal, but who had made a positive contribution to the British cause at great cost to himself. However, although most Loyalists expected to be well rewarded for their loyalty, John Howe declined to press his claims, and sought instead to make a living from the *Halifax Journal*. Because of his able reporting of the assembly debates, Col. Thomas Barclay, a fellow Loyalist and member for the township and county of Annapolis, wanted to give him the printing of the House,[25] but Howe declined to usurp one of the prerogatives of Anthony Henry, the incumbent King's printer, and not until 1801, sometime after Henry's death, did he receive the appointment, almost by default. Even then the returns were hardly lucrative, since prior to 1809 the yearly allowances of the office were a meagre £140 and subsequently only £175.

John Howe received even less from the deputy postmaster generalship of Nova Scotia, New Brunswick, and Prince Edward Island, which he assumed in 1803. Somehow he was induced to give the incumbent John Brittain, ailing and supposedly about to die, £200 a year for the good will of the office. But Brittain was to live on for another seven and a half years, and to pocket a total of £1,500 for which he rendered no service. Meanwhile John Howe was receiving a salary of £290 a year, out of which he paid a clerk £100 a year to assist in the conduct of the office. Thus during Brittain's lifetime the net return of the office, for all the effort that Howe and his family put into it, was a loss of £75.[26] Later Joseph Howe would point out that his father's "heavy payment [to Brittain] laid the foundation of debts and sources of perplexity which ran over half his life."[27]

Even as John Howe was accepting the responsibilities of two government offices, he was also taking on the obligations of raising a second family. Martha Minns, his first wife, had died in November 1790, shortly after giving birth to David, her fourth son. Eight years later Howe married Mary Ede Austen, and from this union there were born Sarah, in 1800, and Joseph, on December 13, 1804.

CHAPTER TWO

Education and Training

Joseph Howe was born in a one-and-a-half-story cottage situated on the eastern side of the North-West Arm about 200 yards south of the site on which Pine Hill Divinity Hall would be built.[1] Although the cottage was destroyed by fire even before his son Sydenham was old enough to remember it, for years Joseph visited the spot and drank from the spring described in one of his poems: "Half hid 'neath Blackberries and Roses, / The crystal Spring is yet o'er flowing."[2] Almost two miles from the centre of town, the cottage was in those days well out in the country, a circumstance that would have an important bearing on both his formal and informal education.

The household in which Howe grew up was small in number. David, the youngest of John Howe's children by his first wife, was fourteen at the time of Joseph's birth, had married before the latter was nine, and had left home some years earlier. Mrs John Howe's children by Capt. Henry Austen were likewise on their own before her second marriage, although Joseph later recalled that some of them spent months at the Arm during his boyhood.[3] "My Father," he wrote, "made no distinction between his own and his wife's children so far as I could perceive. He divided among them all that he ever earned by a long life of industry and frugality."[4] Other than his mother and father and himself, the only regulars of the family were his half-sister, Jane Howe, sixteen years older than he, and his sister Sarah, his elder by four years. For the latter, who left home to get married at twenty-two and died several years later, he had none but the fondest memories; for Jane he retained "a life-long affection" which, according to one writer, "bordered ... on the erotic."[5] Once he wrote glowingly that "her native talent and virtue ... spread their influence over the domestic circle, with ... no other ambition than to render [the] home more happy." On another occasion he described her as "my first schoolmistress and pleasant admonisher ... a sister whose every action has taught [me] to love and respect her." After he lost Sarah he wrote, "what I am most in want of is a sister," and over the next twenty to thirty years he turned to Jane even more than before.[6] He let no crisis in his life, domestic or political, pass by without telling her in minute detail "the secret history" of his trials and conquests.[7] Apparently she had filled the vacuum left in his formative years by the seeming abdication of his mother, and she continued to be his confidante in his later years.

By far the greatest influence on Joseph was exercised by John Howe, Sr. The evidence indicates that he was his father's favourite, perhaps, as Sydenham suggests, "because he was the son of his old age."[8] In turn, Joseph had a respect for his father that he accorded no other man. To the end of his days his speeches and writings frequently referred to John Howe in terms almost of reverence. "He was too good for this world; but the remembrance of his high principles, his cheerfulness, his childlike simplicity and truly Christian life is never absent from my mind."[9] Especially impressed on Joseph was his father's determination to render the highest type of public service without thought of personal gain. Under him the post office "never seemed, as it did in the Canadas, to be imposed on the province. From the beginning it was accepted for what it is: an agency indispensable to the varied activities of a civilized state."[10] John Howe always worked closely with a standing committee of the Legislature in considering applications for post offices and routes, and in determining the subsidy for those routes which produced only scant revenues. Since he put the provision of service first, he was not averse to winking at the principles that governed the operation of the post office, even going so far as to establish new offices and make new contracts without the approval of his superior, the postmaster general in Britain. But because he was held in universal respect and sought nothing for himself, he was always let off with the gentlest of warnings.[11]

Also noted by Joseph, although obviously not until later, was the willingness of his father, "the noblest Briton" of all, to render service to the Mother Country well beyond the call of duty. Because of the acute tension between Great Britain and the United States in 1807 and an accompanying "rattle of arms," the lieutenant-governor of Nova Scotia, Sir George Prevost, was instructed to use his "utmost endeavours to gain Intelligence with regards to the projects of the American Government,"[12] and to that end he sent a "respectable and intelligent Inhabitant of Halifax – John Howe – to the United States.[13] During Howe's first mission, which lasted from April to September

1808, he reported that little had been done to implement plans for fortifying New York harbour; that Fort Mifflin, near Philadelphia, was in "very indifferent repair" because of "niggardly economy"; and that "as far as respects military preparations ... there are none whatever."[14]

By November Howe was back in the United States, this time for about two months. Much of it was spent in observing official Washington at the highest level. With David Montagu Erskine, the British minister, he called on President Jefferson and on James Madison, his secretary of state, whom he preferred to Jefferson. Like Erskine, Howe concluded that Madison, almost certainly to be the next president, did not want war with England and that, if he were left to himself, "things [might] ... ultimately take a better course." But unlike Erskine, he did not adopt a thoroughly alarmist view of the situation. While the minister agreed that war would not break out that winter, it would occur, he believed, as soon as the Americans put their defenceless harbours in a more secure position. Howe was not so certain; after hearing reports of a secret session of the House of Representatives, attending an open session in person, and talking to "many sensible men," he could not "quite subscribe" to the opinion that war was inevitable, even though it might be the safest thing to contemplate. Of one thing Howe was certain: Nova Scotia need fear no attack that winter, and Prevost might safely dispatch troops from Nova Scotia for service in the West Indies.[15]

For these services, Joseph once said ruefully, his father "never received a farthing."[16] The son could not see why this man of talent, who consorted with governors, ambassadors, generals, congressmen, and even a president, should be so self-effacing. Ought he not occasionally to put his great talents to work in "hammering some of our great folks"? Yet, on reflection, Joseph realized that nothing else could be expected from one who thought "this the best of all possible worlds, and the people upon it the best of all possible people."[17] Whatever the reason John Howe remained a quiet sedate man who never meddled in political matters and made no enemies, was seldom ruffled and always kind, unobtrusive, and unambitious.[18]

Indirectly John Howe helped the lieutenant-governors preserve the peace in the first decade of the nineteenth century. Then, for the first time, Nova Scotia had something like a genuine political party, a "country" party unofficially led and directed by William Cottnam Tonge, whom Governor John Wentworth accused of pursuing a course that was destructive of the very foundations of government.[19] In 1806 Wentworth exercised the power, "long unused in Great Britain and without precedent in this province," of refusing to accept

Tonge as Speaker of the assembly.[20] Alexander Croke, judge of vice-admiralty, went even further while he administered the province in 1808–9. By rejecting the annual appropriation bill he caused actual paralysis in government, and his exalted view of the prerogative might have "thrown a province less well ordered than Nova Scotia into complete turmoil."[21] Although the assembly strongly denounced Croke's conduct, the public remained largely in the dark about his strong-handed action.

True, the Speaker had authority to print the resolutions, but authority was one thing, power another. He tried the Gazette office, the journal of John Howe and Son, but the senior Howes were made of different stuff from the one who afterwards became so famous in Nova Scotia; they declined to print the resolutions. Other persons were applied to with a similar result; no printer had the ambition to become a martyr for his country's cause.[22]

Until the *Acadian Recorder* made its appearance in 1813 the Howe family had a complete monopoly of the Halifax press. In addition to owning the *Halifax Journal,* John Howe published the *Royal Gazette* as King's printer, while his brother-in-law owned and published the *Weekly Chronicle.* But Howe accepted things as they were without comment, not because he was a Tory in the usual sense of the term, nor because he approved the actions of authoritarians like Wentworth and Croke, but rather because he refused to become embroiled in the politics of what he thought would always be an imperfect world and imperfect people. Yet despite the absence of newspaper support the country party won a major victory over the prerogative-conscious Wentworth and Croke, one which resulted in a substantial departure from "a known and established principle of the british constitution" and left a later governor general aghast. Relating to the procedures for making expenditures on roads and bridges, it meant that, after the council and assembly had agreed on the total amount of money to be spent for these purposes, the assembly usurped the normal function of the executive and not only determined the specific allocation of the money but also nominated the commissioners to spend it. Since the rural assemblymen had won their major demands, it was hardly surprising that the Nova Scotia political scene quieted down and remained largely unruffled for two decades.[23]

At the time Joseph was too young to appreciate the successes and tribulations of the country party. As he got older he was exposed to the personal sketches of these and earlier times with which his father "used to enliven our family circle," but almost ashamedly he admitted to giving them only passing attention, since he "thought of nothing but play." Later in life he sometimes got his father to reminisce over a glass of wine, but then he was so caught up in family and business cares that he hardly had time to listen. In the end John Howe left "not a trace of a pen that could connect his children and grandchildren with the age in which he lived," perhaps because he thought it "unfair to preserve even friendly notices of his contemporaries." But to Joseph it was regrettable since his father knew "a great number of people who were worth knowing, and saw a great many that either at the time or afterwards, became eminent for something."[24]

Joseph did remember something of what his father said about Nova Scotians like Strange, Deschamps, the elder Inglis, and Tonge, none of whom he ever saw. Indelibly impressed upon his mind was a picture of Tonge as "an accomplished and fascinating fellow, that neither man nor woman could resist."[25] Obviously he had an undisguised admiration for Tonge despite, or perhaps because of, his failure to observe the usual proprieties, political and moral. Naturally John Howe had drawn the lesson that it was Tonge's indiscretions and vices that laid him open to his enemies and helped drive him from the province. But Joseph recited with relish the story of Tonge sleeping with a girl disguised as a naval officer at Dimock's in Newport, and of Squire Dimock objecting to "a whore in [his] house ... and bundl[ing] them both into the roads."[26]

Of all these things the boy Howe growing up along the Arm was quite unaware at the time; instead, according to Dr J.D. Logan, his days were fully occupied in following the tenets of his father's "theory of education" which, although not nearly as formalized as Logan suggests it was, emphasized reading, reflection, and romping. "In [an] environment of wild beauty Joseph Howe grew up with Nature and became her daily companion. His first love and walks and talks were with Lady Beauty in her free and joyous haunts on the North West Arm – and Lady Beauty made him a poet."[27] Later he would recall his style of life in those years:

'Midst Trees, and Birds, and Summer Flowers,
   Those fleeting years went by;
With sports and books the joyous hours,
   Like lightning seemed to fly.

The Rod, the Gun, the Spear, the Oar,
   I plied by Lake and Sea –
Happy to swim from shore to shore,
   Or rove the Woodlands free.[28]

To the end of his days Howe would remember with affection "the dear old place, so quaint and queer, our home for many a pleasant year," with its lilac hedge "that wandering lovers used to rifle," and "the old red Cow that gave us syllabubs and trifle"; where "north the Currants formed the hedges" and "south the Maples worshipped God."[29] These surroundings, suggests George Johnson, nurtured the poetry in Howe's soul, and led to "his speeches, his editorials, his literary essays [being] beautified by a lively imagination which even in the arid controversies of party politics brightened his oratorical efforts."[30] Certainly the outdoor life helped to develop the robust constitution that was to serve him in good stead. Assisting in his physical development was a retired service man who, for a time, acted as a servant in the Howe household and who taught the boy to box, fish, and swim. On one occasion his new prowess almost cost the young Howe his life. One evening, while swimming in the Arm, he got a cramp and felt he would never reach the shore. But in the words of his son Sydenham, "happening to glance upward his eye caught the gleam of the firelight through the window of the old cottage and the thought of the sorrow his death would cause … nerved him to greater effort and he struggled on till at last he regained the beach."[31]

Not as much is known about the other side of Joseph's education, but several accounts picture him and his father spending the long winter evenings reading and reflecting on "the two great wells of English undefiled, the Bible and Shakespeare."[32] Howe himself attributes his "fondness for reading" and his "familiarity with the Bible"[33] to his father, and attests to their influence in shaping his career. Both his speeches and his writings are replete with apt allusions from Shakespeare and the Bible, and his speeches in the legislature indicate that they were often extemporaneous, part of a well-stocked repertoire that he could draw upon at will to meet almost any circumstance.

Because he lived so far from town, Howe received no formal instruction until his eleventh or twelfth year when, for parts of two sessions, he attended the Acadian School, established by Walter Bromley, a half-pay soldier, on the Lancaster model.[34] Scanty evidence suggests that it had little to offer him; since he was "thoroughly grounded in his father's 'Three R's … the rusty regime or 'grind' of the day school was a waste of time: and he, with his mind on higher things than arithmetic and accounting, naturally paid little attention and was acclaimed a dunce at school."[35] More than once he played truant. One evening, at home, he described how that afternoon his father's brother-in-law William Minns had been accidentally knocked off his half-brother's sailboat and might have drowned if another member of the party had not held on to his pigtail as he was dragged through the water. When Joseph finally got around to telling how he had helped pull Minns on board, he was sternly checked by his father: "why were you not at school my son?"[36]

At the Acadian School Joseph was known as a "tease" and for his homely appearance. Much later a woman who had been a schoolmate said of him: "he had a big nose, a big mouth, and a great big ugly head; and he used to chase me to death on my way home from school."[37] George Monro Grant described his appearance in early manhood more explicitly: "He never had a very handsome face; his features were not chiselled, and the mould was not Grecian. Face and features were Saxon; the eyes light blue, and full of kindly fun."[38] Clearly his inheritance in looks from his mother fell considerably short of those bequeathed to his half-brothers by Martha Minns. Yet later on, while his enemies were saying he had a "common look," his friends thought of him as "a splendid-looking fellow." Grant felt that both were right in some sense:

... when he filled and rounded out, he had a manly, open look, illumined always by sunlight for his friends, and a well-proportioned, burly form, that well entitled him to the name of a man in Queen Elizabeth's full sense of the word. And when his face glowed with the inspiration that burning thoughts and words impart, and his great, deep chest swelled and broadened, he looked positively nobly and kingly ... Very decided merits of expression were needed to compensate for his total absence of beard, and for his white face, into which only strong excitement brought any glow of colour.[39]

During 1818, probably just before his father relinquished his two offices to his son John, Joseph Howe entered the printing office of John Howe & Company. Old John Howe had concluded that his youngest son would gain little from further formal education, and he wanted, while he remained active in the business,[40] to assist Joseph in preparing to earn his livelihood as a printer. Obviously, he could provide no other assistance, since, unlike so many other Haligonians, the Howes had not profited financially from the War of 1812. In those years Halifax harbour had been "the temporary home of the ships of war, and the place where their prizes were brought and disposed of ... Trade was active. Prices rose. The fleet increasing, provisions were in great demand ... Rents of houses and buildings in the town were doubled and trebled."[41]

Under these circumstances the families of some of Joseph Howe's later political associates had done exceedingly well. Attorney General Uniacke, whose sons were to be friends and assailants of Howe, had reaped handsome emoluments in his capacity as advocate general of the Admiralty Court, which was also a Prize Court, and put by the sum of £50,000 during a two-or-three-year period.[42] John Young, shortly to become "Agricola," had come from Scotland to Halifax in 1814, and was "a superior classical scholar, frustrated in his choice of a profession by an unyielding father and seeking compensation and financial independence in the inferior role of a merchant, with the ultimate view of *otium cum dignitate.*"[43] Assisted by his sons William and George, the latter a mere child, he had, in addition to putting himself in a strong financial position by his trading operations at Castine in 1814–15,[44] left an indelible mark on his two sons, both of whom were to be political colleagues of Joseph Howe. Not merely was he able to provide them with a kind of education that John Howe could not, but he impressed upon them, as a first priority, an ambition for fame and fortune that was entirely foreign to John Howe's philosophy of life.

In contrast with the Uniackes and the Youngs, the youthful Joseph Howe knew next to nothing about Halifax society and its ways. Until his eleventh year his picture of the town had come largely from trotting behind his father to and from the Sandemanian church; two short terms at the Acadian School had done little to fill it out. As Charles Stayner points out, those who read tales of the Halifax of these days must wonder "at the apparent absence of a middle class society. The story-tellers have made it appear there were only two kinds of Haligonians: the world of fashion on the one side, and the demi-monde of the waterfront on the other."[45] The first world was reflected in the grand spectacle that took place in St Paul's Church of England, Halifax, on Sunday mornings. To one youthful observer it "presented a coup d'œil ... far more impressive than that in [his] manhood days, many years afterwards, when [he] occupied a seat in St. George's Chapel, Windsor, where the Queen, Prince Albert and some of England's most illustrious Nobility worshipped beneath the same roof."[46] Few persons, "not to the manor born," he said, occupied pews below the galleries in St Paul's, Halifax. Here, next to Government House itself, was the grand pivotal place, where the great congregated in their specially designated seats – the governor and his suite, the bishop and the judges, the higher-ranking officers of the garrison in their scarlet, the heads of departments and the leading merchants. Of this many-splendoured affair, Howe was altogether unaware.

He knew little more, although he would soon learn, about the upper street along the base of Citadel Hill which had come to be known as "Knock him Down" Street because of its brawls and even murders. Writing of life in this area during the War of 1812, the first archivist of the province stated that "no person of any character ventured to reside there, nearly all the buildings being occupied as brothels for the soldiers and sailors. The streets of this part of the town presented continually the disgusting sight of abandoned females of the lowest class in a state of drunkenness, bare headed, without shoes, and in the most filthy and abominable condition."[47] Perhaps these conditions were only to be expected in time of war "with eight or ten thousand soldiers, sailors, and paroled prisoners on the loose," but they changed very little over the next couple of decades.

John Howe and his family were part of a third world that most historians have tended to ignore: the New England Puritans and their families, the largest group in the town. Charles Stayner, himself a descendant of Sandemanians, pictures them as "content to lead their own lives, [ignoring] both the wild life at Government House and the depraved orgies of the dives in Barrack Street. These were the people who did the real work of Halifax, and after business hours, retired to their own firesides and left to the two extremes of society the task of providing those sensational and romantic legends that have been handed down to us as typical of Halifax life."[48] For thirteen years the sheltered life of a Sandemanian home well removed from the town had insulated Joseph from the day-to-day life of Halifax and all its undertones. His own basic nature and the kind of duties he was about to assume would soon remedy his want of knowledge.

Although he worked mainly in the printing establishment, he also helped out in the post office when the need arose. It had once been "the great centre of intelligence and lounging place for the whole Town,"[49] where his father had talked familiarly with the prominent men of the province, and it was still performing the same role in a lesser degree. Even in these days, perhaps because of his own humble upbringing, Joseph found it fascinating to observe the ways and note the foibles of the great, storing it all within the confines of a capacious memory. Before being apprenticed, he had seen Governor Sir John Coape Sherbrooke more than once and appreciated the attention he gave to the needs of the poor and friendless.[50] Though of tender years, he was highly amused at Sherbrooke's teasing of the venerable treasurer of the province, Michael Wallace, who had been one of the commissioners for building Government House, the home of the lieutenant-governor. While no one else dared take liberties with that grim, foreboding figure, on rainy days Sherbrooke would "send for him in great haste, when there was a leak, and greet him with 'Wallace, here's this bantling of yours making water again'."[51]

Although Howe also remembered Sherbrooke's successor, Lord Dalhousie,[52] as a familiar sight in the town, the first governor upon whom he attempted a personal judgment was Sir James Kempt, whose régime lasted from 1820 to 1828. Kempt, who had seen Napoleon's roads on the continent and studied McAdam, brought to Nova Scotia the seemingly obvious idea of going around rather than over the hills, and won full marks from Howe as a road-builder. But Kempt had his debits too. Normally courteous and gentlemanlike, he could at times be brusque and peremptory. Once he rode to the post office window, and John, Jr, being absent, bullied his father about some matter and made Joseph almost "mad enough to knock him off his horse."[53]

The young apprentice also discovered that Government House was "not the most moral place in the world" during the days of Kempt. Perhaps because the governor was a bachelor, much was overlooked or forgiven. As a mere stripling, Joseph was sent to Government House in the middle of the night with the governor's mail bag that had just arrived from England. He had a hard time rousing anyone; finally, Colonel Yorke, one of Kempt's aides, descended in his shirt, and exclaimed, thinking it was Lord Frederick Lennox, another aide: "Damn it, Lennox, when you go to see that girl of yours why the devil don't you take the key?"[54] Even more calculated to impress upon the young Howe the pattern of behaviour in a world remote from his own were stories of the gay parties in Government House, in which the centre of attraction was a voluptuous Mrs Logan "with a dark, elongated, and dangerous eye."[55] The daughter of an artillery officer, she could operate freely because her husband was the captain of an Indiaman who was usually gone on long voyages. At Sir James's numerous parties the fast men habitually clustered around her, and not a few sowed their wild oats. Years later, the always observant Howe, noting a lovely girl, the image of Mrs Logan, in the town of Shelburne, discovered that her maintenance had been regularly paid for by someone since childhood. "Who her father was I never learnt, but nobody could mistake the maternity."[56]

Meanwhile Howe's education was proceeding in many directions and he was developing warts of his own. From the beginning of his apprenticeship he found more than enough to do; indeed, "after the first month ... I made myself too useful to be often spared."[57] Among other things, "he learned to set type by hand, [and] work the slow and cumbersome screw presses of the time," even as he mastered "the forms, ritual, jargon and content of government documentation." He soon found that "the setting of type – picking the tiny lead characters from their individual compartments and arranging them on a grooved 'stick' to form line after line of type – was an exacting and wearying performance, requiring superhuman concentration, somewhat complicated by the fact that to verify your type you had to read it in mirror image, upside down and backward." But setting the type was mere child's play compared with redistributing the used type which, for every page of the *Gazette*, meant putting "thousands of tiny pieces of metal, each with its character moulded in relief – [again] upside down and backward," into more than 100 compartments, ready for re-use.[58]

While Howe mastered these skills, he was learning other things not nearly so edifying: he was becoming "one of the boys." Cast suddenly from the most sheltered of existences into the rough and boisterous life of an apprentice, he quickly picked up the coarseness and vulgarities of his companions. While in later life he always acquitted himself well in refined and elegant circles, he could in other circumstances readily stoop to the ways and manners of the commonest of people. Also, probably in 1824, he became the father of an illegitimate child, Edward, whose mother's identity is uncertain and who in his early years was apparently cared for in the Howe household.[59] By December 1824, only twenty, but already past his apprenticeship and acting as foreman of the Howe printing establishment, he appears a self-assured, almost brash individual, not averse to engaging in sharp practices to serve the ends of his family.

That picture emerges from a legal action in which the Howes sought to recover the services of an apprentice, Edward Sentell, who had left them to work for George Renny Young as he prepared to publish the *Novascotian*. Some ancillary evidence presented to the Court of Sessions indicates that Joseph Howe, noting an exchange of letters between Young and James Pierce,[60] and suspecting that they dealt with an offer of employment, sought through a mutual acquaintance to dissuade Pierce from accepting it. While Howe testified that the wrong inference was being drawn from his action, the *Acadian Recorder* suggested that he had used "representations of a singular nature,"[61] and there is more than a suspicion that his principal motive was to put difficulties in the way of establishing another newspaper and not to protect Pierce's interests. The later inability of Howe to establish a rapport with the Youngs, even though they were leading members of the same party, may have stemmed partly from this incident. In his testimony Sentell stated that, although the older Howes, to whom he was distantly connected by marriage, had always treated him well, Joseph Howe had, by his continued harassment, made his life miserable. When William Bliss, the lawyer for the Youngs, asked the alleged tormentor somewhat superciliously what position he held, the reply was prompt: "the same as you seem to hold here, that of chief devil."[62] Not only was the young man not abashed, but even at the age of twenty he was already showing signs of a gift of repartee.[63]

While Howe was being trained in the practical arts, he was educating himself along other lines. Because the post office and printing shop occupied all his time during the day, he feared that his "stock of ideas would receive but precious few additions," and so he followed the "maxim of borrowing from the night," generally reading a book until 12 or 1 a.m., sometimes later if the book was amusing and the fire did not go out.[64] Previously he had devoted himself to the Bible and Shakespeare, and since "his memory was like sticking-plaster,"[65] he knew them thoroughly. Now he read avidly anything he could lay his hands on, and although he thought the books were few in number, the allusions to them in his writings and speeches suggest that they were numerous and the choice eclectic. But if he "read voraciously, he also appears to have read uncritically, picking out the bits and kernels his mind needed for sustenance and seemingly oblivious to the chaff."[66]

George Stupka describes Howe's reading, both during his apprenticeship and the decades that followed, as "a life-long curriculum in the humanities – above all, in the poets."[67] He made his way through Homer, Ovid, Juvenal, and Dante's *Inferno*, common in the stock of pedlars throughout the century. He delved into the works of earlier English poets like Chaucer, Spenser, Milton, Dryden, Samuel Butler, Pope, and Samuel Johnson. He was familiar with such modern poets as Byron, Coleridge, William Cullen Bryant, Thomas Campbell, Felicia Hemans, and Thomas Moore, and he found especially congenial Burns, Thomson of *The Seasons*, and the little-known Anna Laetitia Barbauld, but apparently there are no allusions in his own work to Shelley, Keats, or the earlier Wordsworth.[68] He had some acquaintance with the legal commentaries of Grotius, Coke, Mansfield, Marshall, and Story, much of it acquired as he prepared himself for his libel suit in 1835. He read the novels of Bunyan, Defoe, Swift, Goldsmith, Scott, and the early Dickens; the plays of Congreve, Otway, and Sheridan; the essays of Addison and Lamb; the economic treatises of Adam Smith (Howe rightly claimed to be a disciple of Smith); and the writings of colonial authors such as Roger Williams and Benjamin Franklin.

In history he turned to old masters like Tacitus, Thucydides, and Plutarch, and to such British historians as Gibbon and David Hume. But "for political history he preferred the horse's mouth": the speeches of Chatham, Fox, the younger Pitt, Burke, Sheridan,

Grattan, and Canning; the letters of "Junius"; and the speeches of the Americans Patrick Henry, Daniel Webster, and Edward Everett. "By whatever means, Howe acquired an intimate knowledge of the minutiae of three centuries of English parliamentary history, from which, throughout his political career, he seemed always to be able to draw, effortlessly and at a moment's notice, the apt parallel, the precise analogy, or (another of Howe's favourite tactics in debate) the citation that hit the point 'just beside the point'."[69] Certainly this knowledge was not got up specially for the occasion, but exuded from him naturally, giving a charm all its own to his ordinary conversation.[70]

In addition to his reading, Howe also found time to write a few lines of poetry. In January 1821 "A Youth" somewhat timorously asked William Minns, proprietor of the Weekly Chronicle, to publish a "grateful tribute ... to a kind and indulgent Parent." Minns obliged the sixteen-year-old Howe and printed the ten-line poem "My Father," which portrays John Howe as "God's noblest work, an honest man."[71] Two years later Howe published a longer poem, "To the Mayflower," in the same paper: "Scotia ask'd, and Flora gave her, Precious boon, her fairest child."[72] George Stupka has suggested that Howe's immersion in poetry, earlier and modern, proved anything but a boon to his own ventures into verse, since it led him to work "within a convention of diction as exacting as the structural convention of the sonnet." Thus his poetry abounded with hardy chestnuts like "rocky strand," "manly bosom," "dauntless course," and "winged Hope," and occasionally he resorted to lines that were almost ludicrous: "The gay moose in jocund gambol springs."[73] Clearly it was unfortunate for Howe that Wordsworth did not appear earlier as an exemplar.

Already poet of sorts, printer, post office clerk, boon companion of rough fellows, Howe had, by mid-1824, begun to contemplate his future prospects, and until the matter was finally decided late in 1826, the "infernal feeling" which was always agitating him kept pressing him ahead towards something "viewless and undefined."[74] As he told Jane, 1824 was his year of suspense. "I am something like a poor devil of a traveller who finds himself at the entrance of three or four roads – hardly knowing which to adopt, but determined to prosecute one or the other vigourously whenever his starting time may come."[75] For the present politics was not one of the roads. Howe later observed that "there were no politics in those days"; certainly he had no interest in the proceedings of the legislature, even though he was continually carrying proofs of the Journals to James Boutineau Francklin, the aged clerk of the assembly. Because the legislative sessions were the busiest time of the year for John Howe & Son,[76] Joseph had little opportunity to see the assembly in action, and on the only occasion on which he was given a holiday to hear a debate Judge John George Marshall, the member for Sydney county, spoiled it with a long-winded speech that lasted the whole afternoon.[77]

For more than one reason Howe had doubts about remaining in his half-brother's establishment. Above all, he was determined not to stand in the way of John's children. The recession following the War of 1812 persisted, leaving its mark on the printing business as on all other businesses, and, in addition, the Howes suffered more than others from a built-in restriction. Because they were the servants of government, they could not expand their concern by taking the popular side on the questions of the day; even worse, they did not enjoy freedom of expression and were not "infrequently subject to the caprice of men in office – this, while a boy, I never liked, and now when a man I never could put up with."[78] Accordingly, early in 1824, Howe had almost made up his mind to go to South America which, he believed, offered excellent opportunities for young men of industry. Personal factors made him decide, for the moment, that the precise location would be Lima. His half-sister Jane had moved to Saint John after her marriage in 1816, and while on a visit there his sister Sarah had met and later married Samuel Langshaw. When he suffered business reverses early in 1823, Langshaw and his wife moved to Liverpool, England,[79] and later decided to go to Peru, where they thought they might quickly pay off their debts. It was only natural that, if Joseph were going to South America, it would be to Lima, and old John Howe, who had stoutly resisted the idea of his leaving Halifax at all, was less opposed when it meant joining Sarah.

By the end of 1824, however, it was much less certain that Joseph would go to South America, much less to Peru. By that time John was conducting negotiations with the British authorities that might permit him to extend his business. He had almost persuaded Joseph to continue working for him, if the negotiations were successful, and study law at the same time. While Joseph had already acquired the prejudice against lawyers that he would retain throughout his life, he believed that, by engaging in another business at the same time, he might remain "above the low chicane and unprincipled petty foggery of the profession."[80] But he was also keeping some other options open, like setting up a printing office in New Brunswick or Canada, admittedly "another Air Castle," or going to the Brazils, if Lima proved unpropitious. A little earlier he had started, with some assistance, to study French and he could now read Marmontel's *Moral Tales* and Le Sage's *Gil Blas* with tolerable ease; in anticipation of going to South America, he had also begun to teach himself Spanish, since he had been unable to find a tutor.[81] Of one thing he was certain:

he would not spend another summer of idleness in Halifax. His days of apprenticeship over, he had little to do once the legislative printing had been completed early in the year.

But like it or not, he was fated to spend another two years unproductively when all his plans did turn out to be air castles and nothing more. His sister was lost, apparently on the sea voyage to Peru,[82] after which old John Howe would not hear of his going to South America. His half-brother John had got nowhere in his correspondence with his superiors in England, and although Joseph kept urging him to "go home and get a decided answer to his claims,"[83] the prospects were gloomy. The incident serves to illustrate the contrast between Joseph and his half-brother since, in effect, the twenty-year-old was assuming the leadership of the family by default. More than once Joseph told John that the sooner they "quit the path which he and my father have trod to so little purpose,"[84] and threw themselves on their own resources, the better it would be for all of them.

While Joseph still awaited answers, he tried his hand at verse in more ambitious fashion than before. Early in January 1826 the *Weekly Chronicle* published anonymously his "Melville Island," which followed the measure and metre of Goldsmith's "Deserted Village."[85] It was almost too well received, the first number of the *Acadian Magazine or Literary Mirror* declaring that it needed "no commendation to render it immortal in the land that gave birth to its author."[86] In time, all sorts of stories developed around it as part of the Howe mythology. It was said that, since the lieutenant-governor, the earl of Dalhousie, liked it, it afforded Howe an entrée into Government House. But Dalhousie had left the province seven years earlier, and his successor, Sir James Kempt, was interested in roads and partying, not in literary works. It was said that the aged chief justice went out of his way to congratulate Howe, but in the latter's own words Sampson Salter Blowers did "nothing to stimulate the general intellect of the country – suggested nothing new and left nothing written behind him, that I ever heard of, but his legal decisions."[87] The judge who did recognize "Melville Island" was W.H.O. Haliburton, father of Thomas Chandler Haliburton and first justice of the Inferior Court of Common Pleas for the Western District. According to Howe, he "talked even greater nonsense" than his own friends, who were trying to convince him it was his duty to continue with creative writing. But while he admitted he had been pursuing "a kind of warfare with the Muses," he had determined not to neglect business to "commit the sin of rhyme," and the success of "Melville Island" had not changed his mind.[88] Besides, he had finally made the decision about which he had been agitated for so long. "I am partial to the printing business, and am convinced that I can always provide for myself by starting a paper either here or elsewhere, which, if they determine at home to send us no relief I will immediately do."[89] As it turned out, he would not have to await a decision in England.

CHAPTER THREE

A Trial Balloon

On January 5, 1827, Halifax got the news that its third-oldest paper[1] was to appear in a new guise. Twenty-two-year-old Joseph Howe and nineteen-year-old James Spike announced that they had purchased the copyright of the *Weekly Chronicle* and would change its name. For Howe it was one of the major decisions of his life, and, as has been seen, not an easy one. Fortuitous circumstances helped him make up his mind. The *Weekly Chronicle*, which his step-uncle William Minns had been publishing since its founding, had been deteriorating as cancer of the throat took its toll of the publisher.[2] Hence it seemed a happy arrangement from everyone's point of view for Howe and Spike to take it over. To the Minns family it offered an opportunity to realize something from a dubious asset; to Spike, distantly related to the Howes and apparently apprenticed to them, it permitted a youth with meagre financial means to make an early start on his own; to the Howes it meant that Joseph might establish a place for himself in Halifax, something that old John Howe wanted above almost anything else; to Joseph Howe it provided the means to pursue the printing business in an independent capacity, unbeholden to government or anyone else, and to keep his resolve not to put a burden on the Howe business or to limit the opportunities of his half-brother's children.

Yet Howe's "ballon d'essai"[3] presented a formidable challenge since his family provided him with no financial assistance. "I worked from 13 to 23 for the support of all concerned, and then commenced life without one pound, of many hundreds which I had earned and cheerfully threw into the common stock."[4] Spike was even worse off because he had not even the moral encouragement that the Howe family offered his partner. Still, the paper had a compelling consideration for entrepreneurs without capital. Debilitated though it was, it was a going concern, and the Minns family would let it go for £350, to be paid in equal instalments over seven years. For Howe and Spike it was the *Weekly Chronicle* or nothing at all. So they took over its printing press and its subscription list, and established themselves in rented premises near the Long Wharf at the foot of Sackville Street.[5] Limited because of lack of capital, they made only one change of substance: to shed the lack-lustre image of the *Weekly Chronicle* and make a fresh start, they decided to call their paper *The Acadian and General Advertiser.*

The youth and inexperience of the proprietors cast more than a few doubts on the undertaking. While practically they formed a partnership, legally it was not, since Spike was too young to enter into one.[6] Almost cheerfully the partners admitted to their deficiencies in the first number: "none of our years have been devoted to the calm retirement of a college, or to the systematic acquirement of knowledge and information"; yet they hoped that their readers would "overlook [any] errors with an eye of friendly indulgence."[7] A partnership in name, the *Acadian* was hardly one in editorial direction. All the evidence supports Howe's estimate of Spike: "My partner ... is a steady, slow going [fellow] – with no talent and little or no energy – but he is always in the office and takes the greater part of the charge and labour of the printing part of it off my hands and is, so far, very useful."[8] This left Howe all the more time for purely journalistic activities, including a free hand in determining the content of the *Acadian.*

From the outset he stamped unmistakable qualities of his own on the paper. By taking his readers into his confidence he quickly established the close rapport which would always characterize his relations with them. Once he let them into the secret of how leading articles are made, "because by so doing, we escape the necessity of making one ourselves."[9] Sometimes he told them with regret that he had had to "lift a lid of [his] Balaam Box to deposit a heavy article." To this "gloomy receptacle" he consigned in a single week Silvio's "Sonnet to a Blue Bird" and the *Sighs of Sensibility*, "a Tale, in 32 pages of Bath Post," by Miss F —.[10] Occasionally, when both domestic and foreign news was scant, he begged his readers' indulgence for having to cook his weekly *olla podrida* with less spice than usual.[11]

The *Acadian* would have been burden enough for any man. Yet he could not give it the attention it deserved early in the year because of his half-brother's extended absence in England. He hoped, "when John comes [back] and takes the anxieties, and his share of the labour of his own concerns, upon his back, ... to make my paper more useful and interesting."[12] But it did not turn out that way for, as he ruefully confessed, "while we were connected with the Acadian, by far the greatest portion of our time was devoted to a Government Office."[13] Nevertheless he contrived to make himself a journalistic jack-of-all-trades. "When tired of Editorial restraint and its attendant cant and humbug, I put on the reverend wig and sober phiz of Fred Maple and ramble along in my own way – perhaps mount Pegasus and gallop a distance of four or five verses which you may occasionally see signed with four stars."[14]

The gallop with Pegasus led to eight poems bearing the Howe trademark, six of them early in the year.[15] Fred Maple provided homely philosophizing on a wide variety of subjects. He might comment gravely on Burns's aphorism that "vituperation is to the mind, what phlebotomising is to the body,"[16] or affirm light-heartedly that "for headaches ... and above all for that most terrific of feminine maladies, the Vapours ... there is nothing so certain to cure as plenty of exercise."[17] Sometimes he betook himself to the outlying settlements of Halifax, where Chizencook – "thou peaceful and happy hamlet" – so fascinated him that it occupied his attention for three successive weeks.[18] Undoubtedly mouthing the sentiments of Howe, Fred would console himself for being unable to set off on an extended journey; it was, after all, far better that "he study the characters of [his] fellow Provincialists, peep into their hearts, and take part in their sympathies and affections, than ... travel to the pole with Parry for the sake of seeing an Esquimaux."[19]

Elsewhere in the *Acadian* Howe elaborated his views of the functions of a newspaper and its editor. He had no use for an editor who was largely "a clipper of items or a condenser of telegrams," and who merely chronicled "the receipt of big potatoes or immense cabbages."[20] Since a paper was primarily a purveyor of news, it should carry all the local topics that were worthy of general consideration, and furnish the latest intelligence from Great Britain and other parts of the world. But it should also open its columns to useful discussion as long as it was conducted with decency and decorum, and not perverted to private scandal or the disturbance of domestic tranquillity. Seldom did Howe refuse the use of the *Acadian* on any grounds, and only once did his liberal policy give rise to contention.

In this instance Howe's opponent – the first of his career – was Edmund Ward, the publisher of the Halifax *Free Press*. Although Ward was many years his senior, Howe could never take him seriously, and periodic sniping marked their relations until the *Free Press* went out of business in 1834. They first exchanged pleasantries after Howe published the letter of "a Protestant," who advised his coreligionists not to join the Catholics in pressing for the removal of the oaths against popery and transubstantiation that were required of assemblymen; why, he asked, be liberal to a church whose catechism held that none outside its field could be saved?[21] This was too much for Ward, who denounced the publication of the letter for being "at variance with those principles, by which Public Journalists should be actuated."[22]

If Ward expected Howe to knuckle down to the voice of authority, he was quickly disappointed. After demonstrating that the letter of "a Protestant" fell within none of the grounds he had laid down for denying publication, Howe turned on Ward, "that self appointed judge of Public Journalists, and preacher of peace and good will to men." Was he not the man who so singed his neighbours left and right that he could best be compared to "one of the firebrands which Sampson tied between the tails of the Foxes?"[23] Responding in his most patronizing manner, Ward warned the young men on the *Acadian* they could not make themselves or their paper respected by scattering firebrands in a peaceful community.[24] Whereupon Howe replied that he was quite satisfied with his juvenility after Ward had so amply demonstrated that "years do not always bring wisdom, or age put a period to folly."[25] That ended the exchange, but not before Howe had made it abundantly clear that he would not be trifled with because of his youth.

In addition to being a medium for news and other people's views, Howe contended, a Nova Scotian newspaper ought, above all, to foster the spirit of industry and strengthen and perpetuate the British connection. Thirty years later they were still foremost among his objectives. The second function, and duty, was hardly surprising and was only to be expected of a son of old Loyalist John Howe. In the *Acadian* it showed itself in his uncritical acceptance of the actions of British statesmen and his reverential attitude towards the British constitution. His first venture into foreign affairs was to praise George Canning's measures for the defence of Portugal against Spain; the foreign secretary was simply following the sage advice of Polonius to "beware of entrance to a quarrel, but being in, bear't that the opposer may beware of thee."[26] Three months later the serious illnesses of Canning and Lord Liverpool caused Howe to reflect on Westminster Abbey and "Britannia's Mighty Dead! ... those rare and choice spirits – which give life and energy to the world ... at whose word, Nations quake, and old ocean trembles through her coral caves!"[27]

How fortunate was the position of British statesmen as compared with that of President John Quincy Adams of the United States. There Congress had risen without dealing with the commercial troubles between Britain and the United States, leaving it to the president to "untwine the Gordian knot of difficulty which was woven by their hands." While the Americans might put forward their Utopian theories as models, their governmental scheme suffered badly in contrast with the British system, "hallowed as it is by the experience of ages, tried as it has been in many a fearful ordeal, and weighed so often in the balance and never found wanting."[28] Yet, despite the soundness of its institutions, Britain might be plunged at any time into war with the United States because its statesmen suffered from a lack of correct information. It was up to the colonial press to rectify this deficiency and dissipate "the vapours of insidious delusion ... before they settle[d] into a cloud too dense for the eyes of British Statesmen to penetrate."[29] Howe's acquaintance with the functioning of British and American political institutions may have been superficial, but nonetheless he wrote with assurance and conviction.

With equal confidence he plunged into the murky political waters of Lower Canada. There the business of the legislature had come to a halt after Lord Dalhousie, the governor general, had rejected the assembly's choice of Louis Joseph Papineau as its Speaker. The *Acadian* of May 4 and 11 took up those matters in letters which, although signed "A Nova Scotian," were clearly the work of Howe.[30] In them he took special aim at Papineau's insistence that the salaries of every officer of government should be subject to an annual vote of the assembly. Concede this, and Papineau would soon be demanding that all the power which the law of the land divided among three branches should be exercised by the elective branch alone.

The letters then went on to apply Howe's conception of the British constitution to Nova Scotian and colonial conditions. Every Englishman had the right to insist that no law affecting his person or property should be passed without the concurrence of his sovereign and both Houses of Parliament. While Nova Scotia lacked the materials to create a perfect replica of "this noble structure," it had established its humble institutions on the same principles and it had not yet, "thank Heaven ... [placed] the rights and privileges of Her Majesty's subjects in America ... at the disposal of any one body politic, be it sole or aggregate." The Nova Scotian practice, like the British, was not to provide temporary salaries for permanent offices. Although the assembly might debate vigorously the need to create a specific office, once the measure was carried, its opponents would never dream of making the appointee dependent on an annual vote from which either branch might withhold its assent. This accorded with the British constitution, and should Papineau disagree he had but one course to follow: "honestly declare yourself a Democrat, and let your Constituents decide whether they concur in your political sentiments." Put simply, the question at issue was:

Shall the Inhabitants of Canada retain a Constitution which the wisest Statesmen and the soundest Philosophers have pronounced to be the best preservative of civil liberty; shall they retain those checks and counterpoises by which the three *independent* Branches preserve the people from the effects of arbitrary power, or shall they allow these three Branches virtually to merge in one, and thereby substitute an actual Democracy for the mixed Government under which British subjects have hitherto lived in peace and security?[31]

Howe thought he was done with Papineau. But on May 18 "A Nova Scotian" was back with a third letter that for sheer vigour went beyond anything else that Howe wrote in the *Acadian*. His outburst resulted from a number of proposals for the redress of grievances which appeared in the radical *Canadian Spectator* of Montreal and which he linked directly to Papineau.[32] Among them were the organization of committees in every parish and county, the establishment of a central committee, and the sending of commissioners to other provincial assemblies. Aghast, Howe accused Papineau of laying the foundations of revolution: "For shame, for shame, rash man; blinded as you may be by party zeal, intent as we must suppose you upon personal aggrandizement ... [surely] you must have known ... the horrors of the French revolution; ... look, I beseech you, to the scenes of misery which are passing in South America, and ask yourself if you are willing to take the awful responsibility of risking the introduction of such horrors into your native Land."[33] Did Papineau not understand the danger of convening public bodies which had no constitutional authority? Did he not know that they invariably became infatuated with the power they assumed and in time refused to submit to those who created them? If commissioners were sent to Nova Scotia they would be told that Lord Dalhousie, when governor of Nova Scotia, guarded rather than violated the rights of Nova Scotians, and that Lower Canadians, if they abstained from aggression, could enjoy the same peace and happiness under his governorship that Nova Scotians had previously experienced. But the Nova Scotia Assembly would also be careful to add that "we have no desire to interfere with your internal concerns, and we request that there may be no interference on your part with ours."[34]

"A Nova Scotian" got his reply, not from Lower Canada, but from two letter-writers in the *Acadian Recorder*, who told him he had little or no understanding of the situation in Lower Canada. "An Acadian" reminded him that the assembly of that province shared in the disposal of only £15,000 out of total revenues of £92,000; yet none could surmise from his letters that a constitutional question of importance was at stake.[35] "An Observer" demonstrated the complexity of politics in Lower Canada and the impossibility of judging the motives of its public men from a distant vantage point like Halifax. How could any critic with "a few sweeping, general assertions, without reference to facts" condemn "in mass, the whole Assembly of Lower Canada as a set of demagogues."[36] Rather than defend the accuracy of "A Nova Scotian," Howe used his editorial columns to uphold the right of his fellow countrymen to know. Hitherto they had received little more than snippets about the dispute in Lower Canada; hence "A Nova Scotian," by filling a vacuum in the sources of information, had served the province well. Yet, "if his assertions are not founded in fact, and if his reasoning is unsupported by the principles of the Constitution, we shall be most happy to see him combatted and overthrown."[37]

"An Observer" did not limit his criticism to "A Nova Scotian," but broadened its scope to include all the writers in the *Acadian*, especially its chief editorial writer. If they wished to make the paper more respectable, they ought to replace their pompous, inflated, dictatorial tone with modesty and moderation. While nature did supply capacity, only time, patience, instruction, and attention could ripen the powers of understanding.

We all have to learn much at first, if we would attain to eminence; and ere we can reach the point of distinction, we must undergo the painful though equally necessary task of unlearning much of what we have been taught ... [especially] the errors of prejudices which the peculiar circumstances of our youth or education may have led us into. This is up hill work I confess, but give up high flying, and try my prescription – *Pergite juvenes*.[38]

By his flippant reply Howe almost proved the critic's point; despite the admonitions about speaking in too decided a fashion, he declined to lower his tone:

There may, perhaps, be a frankness and candour about our mode of expression, which he may think offensive. We never say one thing and mean another; when we believe a man a ninny, we freely tell him so, and if he denies it, we prove the fact to demonstration; ... As to our descending a peg or two – What does ["an Observer"] mean, can he wish to bring us to the level of the Recorder?[39]

Actually his critic was not far off the mark, for while at times Howe tried to sound avant-garde, he largely reflected the stereotyped ideas and values implanted in him during his early years. Anyone as close to his father as he could not help becoming an ardent admirer of the British heritage, political and otherwise, but his inacquaintance with the real world of Britain and the practical working of its institutions made the admiration altogether uncritical. He conceived the British governmental system in abstract, theoretical terms that might have come directly from Montesquieu. He did not appreciate that the separation of powers of which Montesquieu wrote in 1748 did not apply fully to Britain even at that time and was even less applicable in 1827. He had no inkling that the House of Commons, far from being perfect, was in the process of change and that it would take the first major step towards democratization within five years. He did not understand that the rights and powers of colonial assemblies were but a pale imitation of those enjoyed by the British Commons. He could not appreciate that it was not the separation of powers that was crucial, but rather the distribution of power within the governmental system. He wrote of the forms, but neglected the spirit of the constitution. "An Observer" put it correctly that, although nature conferred capacity, only knowledge and experience could bring it to fruition.

For the same reason Howe's knowledge of Nova Scotia politics was almost as superficial. His father had led him to believe that the assemblymen were for the most part worthy men with the best interests of the province at heart, but personally he knew them only from serving them across the counter at the post office. The first assembly on which he could pronounce a judgment was the Thirteenth General Assembly, which began its sessions in February 1827. To him it was apparent that its leading members were Samuel George William Archibald, Thomas Chandler Haliburton, and Charles Rufus Fairbanks, all lawyers. Archibald, Speaker of the House in the last two sessions of the previous General Assembly and reelected in the new one, was unexcelled as an orator and used his speaking abilities to advantage whenever the House sat in committee. Though tending to be liberally inclined, he tempered his opinions with prudence. Since Chief Justice Sampson Salter Blowers was eighty-one and Archibald had ambitions, he had no intention of appearing radical in British eyes. As a mediator of sorts between the ultra-conservatives and the moderate advocates of piecemeal change who infrequently enlivened the assembly with their contentions, he performed the function of "softening the collision between these two extremes, and of rendering it harmless."[40]

Although Howe's path seldom crossed that of Archibald, he got to know Haliburton and Fairbanks well. Only time would reveal Haliburton's highly conservative attitudes. For the moment they were largely hidden from view, and he used a lively imagination and generous mind in his stands against bigotry and intolerance. While he far outshone Fairbanks in sheer brilliance of oratory, the latter won more of Howe's respect than any other assemblyman as a liberal-minded man who disdained narrow and petty considerations. Though a lawyer, Fairbanks had familiarized himself with the principles of political economy and he presented the commercial viewpoint with logic and ability.

Among the non-lawyers in the second tier of assemblymen Howe singled out two for special attention. One of them, William Lawson, was a respected Halifax merchant serving in his fifth assembly and widely known for his independence of mind. The other was John Young, the immigrant from Scotland, whose letters on the backward state of agriculture had led to the formation of the Central Board of Agriculture and to his appointment as its secretary. When he published these writings under the title *Letters of Agricola* in 1822, the name stuck to the end of his days. Talented and ambitious, he fell far short of his hopes, largely because he failed to gain the confidence and respect of his associates. "Timothy Touchstone," in the *Colonial Patriot*, somewhat harshly but with not a little truth, said this resulted in part from a suspicion that he was not averse to plagiarism "in a country where the means of detecting literary pilfers" were largely nonexistent. But mostly it was because "his known selfishness, and instinctive tendency to underhand dealing, and pitiful intrigues, totally destroyed all confidence in his disinterestedness and integrity."[41] Howe did not get to know "Agricola" intimately, but his path and those of Young's sons, William and George Renny, were often to cross. There is a more than a suspicion, however, that Howe was repelled by their display of some of the unpleasant traits of their father.

Among the lawyers in the second tier of assemblymen Howe gave attention to three for different reasons. Richard John Uniacke, Jr, the son of the attorney general, was serving in his second assembly but showed little of the ability of other members of his family. "Timothy Touchstone" observed that, although nature had left him without a mind, he still had his use because his harangues provided an occasional relaxation from the fatiguing exercise of serious thinking.[42] A newcomer to the legislature was the young Beamish Murdoch, Fairbanks's colleague for the township of Halifax. Although he would later be called "the Blackstone of Nova Scotia," he would never again be returned to the assembly. In time he would be revealed as a Tory, and when his path crossed that of Howe, it would normally be as an opponent. Another newcomer, Alexander Stewart of Cumberland, started out impressively in debate. Generally liberal at the outset, he was to swing far in the opposite direction and become Howe's inveterate enemy within a decade.

These were the principal actors whom Howe observed from the gallery as the Thirteenth General Assembly began its deliberations. They were to be the leaders in providing the most stirring debates that the assembly had produced since the first decade of the century, especially on three questions: Should the legislature provide a continuing annual grant to Presbyterian Pictou Academy as it had long done to King's College of the established Church of England at Windsor? Should the British government be asked to abandon the right of the Crown to collect quit rents on land, or if the right was to be commuted, what should be the terms? Should the total amount of the imperial duties collected in Nova Scotia be paid into the Provincial Treasury and should the legislature of Nova Scotia assume the full responsibility for the salaries of the customs officials?

Nothing remotely resembling party divisions emerged from these debates. The leading assemblymen of the Thirteenth General Assembly were individualists presenting a purely personal point of view with little thought of ideological considerations. "On quit rents it was Stewart, Fairbanks, and Murdoch against Archibald and T.C. Haliburton; on customs house salaries it was Stewart and Fairbanks against Archibald, Haliburton and Murdoch; while Stewart alone opposed a permanent grant to Pictou Academy."[43] None of them intended an attack on the basic elements of the governmental system; none wished to disturb the compromise between the council and the assembly that had enabled government to be conducted on an even tenor for two decades.[44]

Because of Howe's other duties, he reported in detail only three debates in 1827, and he rose in righteous indignation only once, when the assembly, by a single vote, turned down a bill to encourage the fisheries. It left him aghast that members, with the voters' voice still ringing in their ears, would reach this decision in closed session.[45] Not surprisingly his hero of the session turned out to be John Homer from the township of Barrington, who sponsored the bill on the fisheries. Howe was elated that "the opinions of practical men [were] gathering weight and influence in the Assembly" and that "common sense has not yet been banished from the land, by theoretical mysticism and speculative humbug."[46] As yet, he had no open criticism of the lawyer-assemblymen, but he may have had them in mind when he talked of the political quacks who, in their own interest, scattered dust in the public eye, and who would have less success in the future as other practical, experienced men joined Homer in the assembly.

Despite his outburst on fisheries, Howe found no serious fault in the governmental system in 1827. The acts of the executive, he thought, were prompt, energetic and impartial, while the annual session of the legislature guaranteed the essential liberties of the public. If the assemblymen were unresponsive to the public interest, they could quickly be made aware of the people's attitudes because grumbling was one of the many blessings of the British constitution. But occasional grumbling notwithstanding, "we are a contented and happy People."[47] Thus Howe treated Nova Scotian politics no more profoundly than he had British, American, and Canadian politics. His sheltered existence had denied him a genuine insight into the motive forces in Nova Scotian society, and deprived him of the ability to distinguish the reality from the façade of the decision-making process. It would take him another few years to determine the true wielders of power and the means they used to manipulate the province's institutions to their advantage.

As yet there was no sign of the political animal that Howe was to become. He confessed that the politician would find Nova Scotia a limited and barren field for the exercise of the mind,[48] and lamented jokingly the lack of a standard dish — a doleful grievance — against which newspaper editors might thunder every seventh day. How happy were his Canadian counterparts, whose supply of contention was almost inexhaustible; or the New Brunswick editorial corps, who could always bewail the falling off of the timber trade; or the Americans across the bay, who usually had some half-dozen candidates for office to chase over hill and dale for their amusement. In contrast, he was reduced to magnifying coroners' inquests, describing some new invention like Smollet's machine for cutting cabbages, or swelling molehills into mountains. But actually he did not mind, for it meant that Nova Scotia's political affairs were in a healthy state,[49] and he could employ himself profitably as philosopher and moralist in contemplating the province's other concerns.[50]

Although the young Howe has often been pictured as the gayest of gay blades, his writings more typically manifested the puritanical attributes of his father, and preached industry and frugality as the greatest of virtues. The task to which he devoted the most attention in the *Acadian* was, in his own words, to "call forth [Nova Scotia's] resources – to facilitate the march of improvement – and above all, to mould the Provincial character so as to lay a sure and solid foundation, not only for her future wealth, but for the honorable consideration of her Inhabitants."[51] Howe began the mission that he was to continue throughout his life on March 16 when he published an article entitled "My Country," his first genuine attempt at editorial writing,[52] and the first of many writings which displayed what D.C. Harvey called "the Nova Scotia-ness" of Howe.[53] In it he exulted that his native province was a land of "inexhaustible treasures, which will lead us onward, in the facilitated march of improvement, to opulence."[54]

But advancement would not come about automatically. Throughout 1827 Howe criticized the scribblers who pictured Nova Scotians as being entitled to admiration and respect for the wonders they had performed. On the contrary, he felt they had done little to be proud of despite the bounties of nature. Their greatest need was improvement of the mind, and it would not occur until reading became general. He was not worried about the little aristocracy of wealth because it could meet its own needs. His concern was with the middle and working classes, who were essentially the people. To give the youth of these classes, many of them apprentices, a means of acquiring knowledge was the surest way to lessen the dissipation and vice that first-hand experience told him was all too prevalent among them. The remedy was to establish apprentices' libraries, thereby carrying out Franklin's maxim of giving youth a taste of the Madeira of learning to displace their relish for the small beer of vice.

A second impediment to development especially appalled Howe. He may have been the first – certainly he would not be the last – to criticize merchants who accumulated capital in Nova Scotia only to invest it elsewhere. Since there were many avenues for utilizing funds within the province, "such should be the policy of those *who love Nova Scotia.*"[55] Whenever entrepreneurial activity deserved it, Howe praised it liberally. He hailed in particular the launching of a 400-ton copper-fastened ship for John Bingay of Yarmouth at a time when commerce was temporarily depressed.[56] He also gave his blessing to the builders of the Shubenacadie Canal, especially after they promised to land coal in Halifax from Gay's River at fifteen shillings per chaldron.[57]

For Howe developments of this kind were an indication of steady advances in industry and commerce. He was pleased that the long recession following the artificial prosperity induced by the War of 1812 was at long last dissipating and that the economy was being rebuilt on a more solid foundation. While the average Nova Scotian might not be able to amass wealth, he could, if he practised thrift and industry, gather around him the comforts, although perhaps not the luxuries of life; certainly, at a time when he was striving to provide for his physical necessities he could not be expected to interest himself in "more etherial viands" for the mind.[58] Until recently, therefore, the Nova Scotian press had performed the one-way function of disseminating information and comment. But Howe detected the beginning of change; now "the budding intellect ... springing up within the Province ... returns some of the light that it borrowed from the Press."[59] In effect, Howe was describing some features of what D.C. Harvey has labelled "the intellectual awakening of Nova Scotia."[60] Harvey's general picture is that of Nova Scotians rubbing the sleep out of their eyes after 1812 until by 1835 they were thoroughly awake. In the process they became "thoroughly aroused to the strength and weakness of [their] birth-right, and eager to overhaul the entire ship of state, from the keel of commerce to the captain on the bridge."[61] In succession, their new attitudes were reflected first in trade and industry, then in literary forms, and only lastly in politics.

Howe was right that the press had played a part in laying the foundations of the awakening. But it was clearly not the older Howe press – the *Royal Gazette, Weekly Chronicle,* and *Halifax Journal*[62] – that he had in mind, nor was it Edmund Ward's *Free Press.* Since 1813, however, the *Acadian Recorder* had been making a useful contribution, and since late 1824 George Renny Young's *Novascotian* had been offering encouragement to both entrepreneurial and literary activity. Dr Harvey therefore suggests that, without minimizing Howe's achievement, he must be regarded more as "the embodiment of the spirit of the age" than "as having sprung Minerva-like from the rocks of the North-West Arm."[63]

Like G.R. Young, the Howe of the *Acadian* devoted himself largely to the encouragement of men of industry and letters, rather than to political reform. Although he deposited an occasional item in his Balaam Box, he was more than delighted with the quantity and quality of the letters, articles, and poems that he received. James A. Roy has written favourably of the wide variety of topics from contributors, writing under all sorts of noms de plume: "fantastic little essays suggestive of Steele, with titles such as 'Journal of a Voyage of Discovery of a Dinner, by a Poet'; 'January and May' or 'Age and Youth'; sketches like 'Mid-Day in the Village'; Letters to 'Messrs. Editors' by 'Alister'; a humorous etching of 'The Touchy Lady'."[64] Contributions like these encouraged Howe to believe that the *Acadian* was playing a substantial part in the founding of a provincial literature.

Such was the character of the *Acadian.* Some commentators have spoken of its amateurishness and the meagreness of its contents, but Howe could truthfully say that he had not published merely "a weekly sheet of gleanings from other places."[65] In a day when the worth of a colonial paper was often measured by the proportion of original to borrowed items, the record of the *Acadian* compared favourably with any provincial newspaper, even the much more prestigious *Nova-scotian*. This may explain why, after three months, Howe could report that, "in addition to retaining Mr. Minn's subscribers, with the exception of four, we have already added 120 to our list,"[66] and why, at the end of the year, he could refer to the continued growth of the subscription list.

The *Acadian* had defects, too, and they flowed naturally from traits of the editor that are clearly delineated in its columns. Nor were the weaknesses of style that Howe was striving to overcome the worst of his failings. The Howe of the *Acadian* was a thorough-going conservative, a Burkean of the later years who tended to treat existing institutions as the distilled wisdom of the ages and who thought it dangerous to interfere with the fruits of time and experience. In itself this was not bad, but when it was associated with an imperfect knowledge of the topics he chose for editorial comment and an obvious unawareness of the motive forces in society, it often led to naïvely simplistic discussions of political events. Nonetheless, nothing could put a dent in his self-assurance. Sometimes, perhaps for want of a better alternative, he gave a flippant reply to his critics or chose not to take them seriously. Because of his youth, he may have felt that any admissions on his part would cause him to lose face with his readers. More than once, he left the impression of cocksureness, even brashness, and raised doubts about his open-mindedness. It was unlikely that he would ever have doubts about the beneficence of the British heritage or the potentiality of Nova Scotia. But perhaps, with greater knowledge and understanding, he might modify his views about the essential goodness of the Nova Scotian political system.

CHAPTER FOUR

The Novascotian *of 1828*

By enabling Howe to serve his apprenticeship as editor and publisher much as he pleased, the *Acadian* had contributed notably to his development. Late in 1827, when an even more challenging opportunity presented itself, he accepted it with alacrity. George Renny Young having decided to abandon journalism in order to study law, Howe took over the sole proprietorship of the *Novascotian*. In a variety of ways that decision was to transform his whole way of life. The mere fact that an inexperienced youth of twenty-four had assumed the full responsibility of publishing Nova Scotia's second newspaper, next in circulation to the *Acadian Recorder*, caused raised eyebrows throughout Halifax, even among his own relatives and associates. As usual, old John Howe supported him to the hilt. In his mind there was no doubt that Joseph had "acted judiciously" and that the *Novascotian* would give him "a comfortable and permanent independence."[1] In contrast, John Howe, Jr, became estranged from Joseph for a time, apparently because he objected to the latter's new undertaking.[2] Even while Joseph was at the *Acadian*, he had shared much of the burden of his half-brother's concerns, and John could hardly have looked with favour upon a step that would deprive him altogether of Joseph's services.

Having committed himself inescapably to the newspaper business, Howe felt he was in a position to take on the responsibilities of married life. There are suggestions that he had been having indifferent success with his courtships, and that was certainly the case with Agnes Wallace of Rawdon, Hants county, who, by one account, boarded at the home of John Howe, Sr, in 1825 before returning home early the next year. Howe writes to her in terms which at first suggest a brother-sister relationship, or that of a schoolmaster and his pupil (although she was his senior by two years), in which he helped her with French, composition, and English literature. What progress had she been making in her studies, he asked; what books had she been reading and what did she think of them? Surely she had "a little leisure to devote to the culture of the mind." When, in five months, he had received only a few lines in return, he was desolate. Why was she breaking "every part of our treaty of friendship and amity"? As one of the "high contracting parties" what excuse had she for "this palpable neglect"? Did she even recollect his name? Had the air of Rawdon wrought some mighty change? For his part he was determined never to forget her – as one of those friends "endeared to me by their virtues – or by their talents – who never are named in my hearing without calling up grateful holy recollections."[3]

Rather than those of a brother or a schoolmaster, the sentiments appear to be those of a suitor. Apparently rebuffed, Howe tried his hand elsewhere. More particularly, in the evenings he rowed over to McNab's Island in Halifax harbour and there, with Catherine Susan Ann McNab, "worshipped the fireflies and the moon ... under the trees."[4] Late in 1827, as the formalities of the day required, John Howe wrote Capt. John McNab in his blunt, practical way suggesting that as soon as Joseph could conclude the necessary arrangements for the *Acadian* and the *Novascotian,* "Susan Ann and he better be settled together." While a little surprised that Joseph had taken over the *Novascotian* all by himself, McNab was pleased to have as his son-in-law "a young man of the strictest honor and principle in which I feel more contented than if he possessed wealth."[5] That was all there was to it, and in due course the marriage of Joseph Howe and Susan Ann McNab took place on February 2, 1828. Because of the difficulties that stood in the way of non-Anglican marriages, they – like so many others – followed the line of least resistance and chose St Paul's as its setting.

Susan Ann's paternal grandfather, Peter McNab, had served as a lieutenant in the Royal Navy at the siege of Louisbourg and after the war established himself on McNab's Island. One of his sons – also Peter – lived in some style on the island and was the father of the Hon. James McNab, Susan Ann's cousin and Joseph's long-time political colleague and backer of his notes during the troubled days of the thirties. A second son of the first Peter McNab was John, captain in the Nova Scotia Regiment of Fencible Infantry, or simply the Nova Scotia Fencibles. In 1807, while he was serving with his regiment in Newfoundland, his daughter Catherine Susan Ann was born there. So when Joseph referred to his wife as a Newfoundlander, he was at least technically correct.

Captain McNab had suggested that his daughter's marriage with

Howe offered "every reasonable prospect of happiness" so far as that could be "possible in this variable scene."[6] He would surely have been gratified with his success as prophet. If ever wife was helpmate, it was Susan Ann McNab Howe, despite the fact that being married to Joseph Howe often placed heavy, even inordinate demands upon her. She might be suddenly confronted with dinner guests with nothing to offer them but a mess of smelts. She might, during her husband's lengthy rambles, be required to care for a young family, edit the *Novascotian*, and juggle the creditors' notes. She might, at a time when the family was hard pressed, discover that her husband had been over-generous to someone in distress, or given financial support to a dubious project. Nonetheless, through it all, the understanding, affection, and love of the early years continued unchanged to the day of Howe's death with scarcely a sign even of impatience. When required, Susan Ann could always be counted on to provide the encouragement and stability that was required by a husband who, at times, moved quickly from the heights of optimism to the depths of despair. Posterity has been told of the infidelity of Howe, in fact, of his peopling the hamlets of the province with illegitimate Howes. This is sheer folklore. Certainly Howe charmed the opposite sex, but he appears to have sown most of his wild oats before his marriage.

His early indiscretion might have caused difficulty at the time of his marriage, had his wife not insisted that Edward be brought into their household. After all, she told her husband, "he's as much my son as yours."[7] Accordingly their major problems in starting married life were financial. There was no assurance that Spike could meet the balance still owing on the *Acadian*, and Howe was obligated to pay George Young £1,050 over a period of five years for the *Novascotian*. While Young was only twenty-two when he started its publication late in 1824 and therefore lacked experience, he had some advantages which were denied to Howe. His family saw to it that he had adequate capital for the undertaking; his father John Young ("Agricola") and his brother William were both in a position to assist him with articles of their own; and his father's extensive connections in the eastern part of Nova Scotia and Britain assured him of contributions from correspondents outside Halifax. Not surprisingly, Young quickly established the *Novascotian* as the best all-round paper in the province.

In general philosophy the Young of the *Novascotian* bore a close resemblance to the Howe of the *Acadian*. From the outset Young had eschewed anything that savoured of radicalism and declared his attachment to the British constitution, the forms of British liberty, and the enlightened and liberal character of Britain's colonial policy.

Rather than deal with topics which might offend private feeling or embroil the country in hot disputes, he had declared his intention to take such action as he could to hasten the progress of internal improvement. He was as good as his word, for it was the amount and variety of original material dealing with provincial agriculture, commerce, industry, and the like that gave the *Novascotian* its unique character. On the rare occasions that Young ventured into politics, it was generally to criticize the assemblymen for their failure to do what he thought was requisite for provincial development. Thus, when the electorate returned only twenty of the forty-one old assemblymen in 1826,[8] he was certain that the rejected had paid the penalty for neglecting the fisheries, treating agriculture apathetically, adding unnecessary offices to the provincial civil list, and increasing the duties on West Indian and American commerce, all of which proceedings were calculated to impede provincial growth.[9]

Such had been the paper that Howe brought out for the first time on January 3, 1828. Until he could find premises of his own, he apparently continued to use those of Young on Upper Water Street nearly opposite the Halifax Banking Company, but by February 28 he had established his own office near Boyle's Country Market. In almost routine fashion he assured his readers that he belonged to no party and promised that his paper would not be used to promulgate any one set of opinions.[10] The Howe of the *Novascotian* could not be expected to feel any less satisfied with the province's political institutions than the Howe of the *Acadian*, and within a month he was extolling Nova Scotia as the best of all possible worlds. Unlike Spain, Portugal, and France, Nova Scotians did not have to rely upon the discretion of their rulers for civil and religious freedom. The province did not suffer by comparison even with the United States. Because it was settled earlier, that country clearly surpassed Nova Scotia in material development, but no section of the Union was "richer in all the great essentials to individual and collective happiness" or had "a government which sits lighter on the people, or under which they may enjoy more of rational freedom."[11] Once it had appeared as if Nova Scotia might be better off within the American Republic, but no more. The enlightened measures of the British government, especially its trade policy, and the growing doubts about the stability of republican institutions had removed any lingering desire to join the American Union. Howe insisted he had no wish to picture Nova Scotia as a second El Dorado; admittedly the colony had its cares and anxieties, "but they are the necessary alloys of life – they are felt on the Alps and on the Andes, by the margin of the glassy Rhine, and the flowing borders of the Mississippi and why should we be exempt."[12]

The prospectus which Howe inserted in the *Novascotian* in his first number supposedly summed up his whole political creed as simply "the Constitution, the *whole* Constitution, and *nothing but* the Constitution." Yet no more than in the *Acadian* did he explain specifically what he conceived the constitution to be. He did say, however, that it was the basic function of the press to act as a two-edged sword, defending the constitutional tree both from the misguided zeal of the people and from the dangerous encroachments of their rulers. "We will therefore as steadily defend the Government when its acts are just, as we will boldly warn the People when they are unjust."[13]

Nothing during the session of 1828 disturbed Howe's good opinion of the political system or the legislators. He still looked with pride upon the assemblymen, especially a few of "Home manufacture" who would not disgrace any popular body.[14] He was pleased that Charles Rufus Fairbanks's bill for the incorporation of Halifax had got nowhere. While the police were admittedly inefficient, and while the town was no better informed of the management of town property than of the finances of the Emperor of China, he still preferred to "bear the evils we have than fly to others that we know not of."[15] Certainly he had no wish to have the peace periodically disturbed by the election of civic dignitaries "and by all the mighty nothings attendant on a corporation." As he saw it, the existing machinery was entirely adequate to cure the evils in the government of the town: the magistrates in session could remedy some faults, the grand jury others, while the governor, "by occasionally turning his eye, which never slumbers over public business," might exercise a salutary influence over the whole operation.[16] Apparently it never crossed Howe's mind that some of the magistrates composing the Court of Sessions might have a vested interest in inefficient and expensive government. To him their motives and actions were only a little less pure than those of his own father, who was still unselfishly devoting himself to his duties as magistrate.

A year earlier Howe had not been unduly upset when the council rejected a bill to offer encouragement to common schools. Not so Thomas Chandler Haliburton who, though he had not the faintest desire to disturb the basic political structure, did insist on asserting the rights of the British Commons in this matter and others like it. Bursting with indignation, he scandalized the councillors by referring to them as "twelve dignified, deep read, pensioned old ladies, ... filled with prejudices and whims like all other antiquated spinsters ... Two-thirds of them have never been beyond Sackville Bridge, and think all the world is contained within the narrow precincts of Halifax."[17] Again Howe appeared not to be disturbed when the assembly, under dire threats from the council, formally censured

Haliburton for his remarks.[18] Instead, early in 1828 he published anonymously a pamphlet which not only ridiculed Haliburton's style of oratory: "Othello could not spout more finely,"[19] but attacked his constitutional position. The work of Brenton Halliburton, later to be chief justice, it was reviewed favourably by Howe, in the *Novascotian* of May 15, who thus took the side of the undiluted Tory against the constitutional Tory. Little did he or Brenton Halliburton realize that the whirligig of time would bring them together in quite different circumstances at a libel trial seven years later.[20]

Howe's review of the pamphlet provides the fullest and clearest elaboration of his political theory at this stage of his career. He conceded first that he did not share the alarms of the author of the pamphlet that a dangerous doctrine, or the specific individual who advocated it, could do much harm in Nova Scotia. It was not that his feelings were any more sluggish than others but that, when he turned to the state of the province and the character of its people, he invariably concluded that "there never was a country where one man, or a dozen men (if he or they were so disposed) could do so little mischief."[21] Unlike men in tropical countries who were liable to sudden impulses, Nova Scotia had long winters, and cool morning and evening breezes even in August, to calm the fever of their blood. Unlike Ireland, Portugal, the West Indies, or Canada, Nova Scotia was not divided into two or three classes, religious or political, which might cause mischief. Unlike older countries, Nova Scotia had fewer prejudices and animosities to hand down from father to son. Besides that, a Nova Scotian who had hewn his own little fortune out of the wilderness, had also become accustomed to depend on his own resources and do his own thinking. "He receives the ipse dixit of no man without examination, and builds up his political opinions as he built his fortunes, in his own way, and by the operations of his own mind."[22]

The length of Howe's introduction might appear curious unless it is appreciated that he was calling into play his old theory of checks and balances, or perhaps more correctly, of countervailing power, to explain his disagreement with Haliburton. In appraising the council, the two were not far apart. Both agreed that the councillors who held public office might be confronted with a conflict of interest when they acted as legislators. But the assembly – and again they agreed – had a power over public opinion that the council would never enjoy and could therefore exercise a subtle influence over the upper house that more than counterbalanced any undue power that the latter body might possess.

In turning more specifically to the assembly, Howe treated it much more harshly than Haliburton, himself an assemblyman. In the voting of money Howe contended that the lower house was at its very worst: "hundreds of pounds are granted to clear a few sticks or stumps from a rivulet, or to make a road, when as a witty member last year observed, they ought also to try and *make a passenger.*"[23] All too often log-rolling – "if you give me a vote I'll give you another" – decided the outcome. Like other popular bodies, the Nova Scotia Assembly always contained a few members who could carry any measure no matter how ridiculous it was. While most of them deservedly enjoyed the confidence of the assembly and the people, a few put their own interests first. Would Nova Scotians care to entrust the public purse solely to these men?

Accordingly, Howe rejected Haliburton's proposals that the council forgo its right to reject individual money votes, and that it be content simply to accept or reject the whole appropriation bill. As he saw it, even with the control exercised by the council, the proceedings of the assembly were sometimes deplorable; without it, the scenes of cupidity would be extended throughout the entire session. Within three years the appropriations for roads and bridges would rise from £20,000 to £30,000 or even £40,000, and swallow up almost all the revenue. The council might then face the painful alternative either of having to gratify a popular leader in the assembly or of bringing the public business of the country to an entire halt. Howe also refused to go along with Haliburton's proposal to deprive the council of its power to originate money bills. He gave no reason, other than that the Royal Instructions of 1756 granted the council that right. Seemingly Haliburton would have to produce stronger evidence to justify a change in a provision that had stood the test of time.

At first sight Howe's case appears to suffer from internal inconsistencies. How could he be content with a legislative process that was subject to so many deformities? How could a shrewd and knowing people keep on electing assemblymen who acted so deplorably? In effect, Howe answered these questions by recognizing, more than he had ever done before, the general frailty of men, even of Nova Scotians. Reflecting his father's tolerant and sympathetic appreciation of man's infirmities, he concluded that these weaknesses put serious limitations on the perfectibility of political institutions. Abuses were likely whenever people possessed power, and might be expected equally from the councillors and the popular leaders in the assembly. For that reason "the safety of the People depend[ed] on their placing as little power to do evil in the hands of either [council or assembly] as the practical business of the country [would] allow."[24] Howe had no doubt that any mischief resulting from the council's item veto was not a tithe of the evil that would follow its removal; accordingly he objected to the obliteration of one of the province's legislative landmarks.

Even as Howe was presenting this résumé of his political views, they were being challenged vigorously by the first Nova Scotian newspaper of consequence to be established outside of Halifax. On December 7, 1827, only three weeks before Howe took over the *Novascotian*, the *Colonial Patriot* had its beginnings in Pictou. Little did Howe realize at the time how fateful its presence was to be for him over the next two or three years. Perhaps the highly conservative press of Halifax should have suspected the worst since the *Patriot*'s first editorial proclaimed that "in politics we shall side with the most liberal system." In putting the motto "Pro Rege, Pro Patria" at its mast-head, it contended that "he who pretends to support the dignity of the government and the honour of the Crown at the expense of the general happiness, alike commits treason against the King and his subjects – he betrays the people, and dishonours their Sovereign."[25]

The editor of the *Colonial Patriot*, except for the year following March 15, 1828, was Jotham Blanchard, even though it was not admitted openly. Crippled since youth, and subject to bouts of ill health, he was in no way deficient in intellectual vigour. Over the next few years the interplay between Blanchard and Joseph Howe probably did as much as anything to bring substantial change in Howe's political stance. More than was usual, the *Patriot* relied on letters of substance from correspondents, some of which were those of the editor masquerading under a nom de plume. Although its founders had been students of Thomas McCulloch at Pictou Academy and sided with him against the council and his enemies, they did not support the cause of the academy in extravagant fashion, nor did they make it the primary concern of their paper.[26]

Within weeks the *Colonial Patriot* had been tried in some quarters and found wanting. It had invited trouble in its very first number by pointing out that the persons who embarrassed and ruined all governments were not the bold, manly characters – the true patriots – who pointed out errors in administration and the evils that would follow in their wake. Rather it was the servile men who supported every government measure, no matter how bad. They were the ones who had helped to lose the United States, and who were doing their best to lose Lower Canada. For Papineau, in his struggle against men like these, the *Patriot* expressed every sympathy.[27] Even in Nova Scotia, where much of the administration was good, there was "no scarcity of employment for a few of the Patriots, or as the SERVILES would say, *Radicals* of '99."[28]

Except for an occasional article or letter, the *Patriot* was hardly extreme and certainly not violent. But in the Nova Scotia of that day it was a fresh new breeze, alien to anything in the provincial experience, and the reaction was not surprising. An utter reactionary like Richard John Uniacke, Jr, might even accuse it of treason and demand that its proprietor be hailed before the assembly.

It was by a somewhat circuitous route that Howe was led to joust with the "Pictou Scribblers," as he called them. The radical *Canadian Spectator* of Montreal had published part of a letter from a Nova Scotian which suggested that the hostility to Papineau in Nova Scotia was not as pronounced as its newspapers made it out to be, and concluded that "our papers and our Parliament were servile in the extreme and ought to be given as authority no where except among slaves." Because of a new paper in Pictou, however, "the old managers of the government here will not be able to keep matters so quiet as they have been accustomed to do."[29] These extracts were taken from a letter of Jotham Blanchard to his friend James Leslie, a Montreal assemblyman who supported Papineau, and their publication came as a surprise to Blanchard himself, who did not publicly admit their authorship until 1833.[30] For Howe they were a bitter pill to swallow. Indignantly he asked "The writer of the Canadian Letter," as he came to be called, to point out "one abject sentiment ... one instance of servility" in the files of his newspaper.[31]

The worst was yet to come. Through the *Colonial Patriot* "The writer of the Canadian Letter" addressed a letter to Howe in which he inserted the whole of his former letter, including the sentence: "The Acadian is conducted by a young man connected with the Post Office, and, of course, tied to a party."[32] He also told Howe that in a future letter he would "pull the mask from his face, and exhibit the real feature of the Nova-Scotian." Howe sought, in his reply, to demolish his opponent through scorn and ridicule. In language that had obviously improved and provided a foretaste of what was to come, he vehemently denied that his connection with the post office had tied him to a party:

[This] gratuitous and slanderous conclusion ... shews that the slave cannot understand real independence of mind – that he never felt his breast throb with those feelings which in the Court of Kings or the hut of obscurity may still be enjoyed – and which the voice of authority can never conjure down. Burns was an Excise Officer – to what party did he belong? Franklin was Postmaster-General – did he forget the public welfare? And have not hundreds of the great and the good – the virtuous and the noble, been employed, at some period of their lives, in offices of the Government, but did it follow, "of course," that their minds and their opinions were not as free as the air they breathed?[33]

Jokingly, Howe said he had no objection to removing his mask and revealing himself, starting with "a good broad face," but should not his critic unmask himself too, "and let us see whether you belong to any party, and whether no sinuosities and discrepencies can be found in your own conduct."[34]

Although "The writer of the Canadian Letter" did not identify himself, he proceeded forthwith to unmask Howe as an agent of a longstanding system that was designed to stifle freedom of thought and discussion in Nova Scotia. That system operated on the principle that anyone who thought more of duty than his own interest, and who dared to criticize the managers or management of public affairs, would be "ridiculed or branded as a Patriot – Hampden – Radical – Demagogue – Lighter of the fires of discord – Defamer of the country's institutions – and even Rebel."[35] Into this system Howe fitted perfectly. As proof positive, Howe's critic seized gleefully upon a badly worded sentence in the *Novascotian* which contended that although it was "part of an Englishman's privilege ... to abuse the Government, ... in the Colonies ... we must be content to bear with [the] defects [of the Constitution]."[36] Howe had not intended to deny freedom to attack the government, but this is what he appeared to do, and this is how his critic interpreted it. Had Howe not grossly defamed the British constitution as it should operate in the colonies? Did the right to attack public measures not make Britain the Queen of Nations? Thereupon, since he and Howe had no common ground from which to start debate, "The writer of the Canadian Letter" declined further correspondence until Howe humbly recanted his past.[37]

It was too much to expect that Howe would not be brought into direct collision with the editors of the *Patriot* themselves. For most of May he granted them "editorial clemency," but by the end of the month he had initiated an attack which was to result in vitrolic exchanges, some of which descended to downright nastiness.[38] When Howe said, somewhat loftily, that the Halifax papers possessed means beyond the reach of a county paper, the *Patriot* concurred. Was it not true that, whenever Howe received a British periodical, he cut from it sufficient matter from which to construct a showy editorial? "He then bestows upon it a little dressing, and introduces it to the world as his own well begotten child, and not the son of his adoption."[39] Thus a recent article by Howe on Leigh Hunt and Lord Byron appeared to have been "well cropt and dressed in a new suit" to prevent the discovery that *Blackwood's Magazine* had been consulted in its fashioning.[40] Not so, replied Howe; his article had appeared in print twenty days before the magazine had arrived by packet from England. But, rejoined the *Patriot*, it might have reached Halifax earlier, perhaps via the United States. Howe, who gave as good as he got, replied that the *Patriot's* determination to sit on his throne and pontificate, reminded him of "the fondness of levellers for making themselves kings" and of "the trite saying that 'Pygmies are Pygmies still when perched on Alps'."[41]

These clashes helped to make Howe a master of repartee and invective. Sometimes he was at fault, and sometimes the *Patriot*. When he condemned the *Patriot* as "the mere speaking trumpet of a party," the spokesman for Pictou Academy and one of two religious factions which were tearing Pictou county apart, he was clearly off the mark, since the *Patriot's* major concern could hardly be said to have been Pictou Academy or the anti-burgher position.[42] But when he heaped scorn on the editor of the *Patriot* for referring to "1000 Provincial grievances" and failing to spell them out, he had much the better of it. Was this "windy Patriot" not worse than Don Quixote who, although he had taken windmills for giants and flocks of sheep for troops of cavalry, had at least charged upon them like a true knight?[43] Was it not time to drag the delinquents before the public, or show specific instances in which servility had affected the public good?[44] In the perspective of time it seems astonishing that the *Patriot* could create such a stir before it had got down to specifics. In part, this may have been a natural reaction against the injection of a hostile element into a hitherto staid and tranquil society; in part, an attempt to clip the *Patriot's* wings before it began to apply its abstract radicalism to particular Nova Scotian concerns.

By the end of June, Howe's jousting with the *Colonial Patriot* had come to a close. As it did so, Howe suggested that "about once a month or so, we may ... take up one of these Patriots from his throne, and holding him between our finger and thumb, make the country merry at his expense."[45] But except for a minor exchange of pleasantries in September,[46] he apparently thought better of it. Two years later he is reported to have said, on a visit to Pictou, that "the Pictou Scribblers ... have converted me of the error of my ways."[47] But although this statement has been written into the folklore of the province, there was as yet no evidence to support it. Certainly Howe had given no signs of an increasing respect for the *Patriot* or its editorial direction. In matters political he had conceded nothing to the *Patriot*, but generally remained a staunch and admiring supporter of the status quo. Although he reported about seventy-five columns of debates during the session of 1828, almost his only editorial comment had dealt with quit rents, and there his position – the Crown had the right to collect them, but should abandon its claims on the grounds of expediency – was one that many Tories would have been content to accept.

Obviously Howe could not change his stance while he was engaged in controversy, but he must surely have begun to question some of his assumptions; the *Colonial Patriot* had at least seen to that. He must have asked himself if there was some truth in its charges that the Halifax press served largely to buttress the establishment and remained oblivious to the evils of the governmental system. Was he himself, without being conscious of it, acting in a servile manner? Had he been too content to accept the premises with which he had started adult life and not subjected them sufficiently to critical examination? One shaft of the *Patriot* must certainly have struck home. How, it asked, could an editor who, in replying to "The writer of the Canadian Letter," had praised the general performance of the assembly, make a complete turn-about and only a little later, in reviewing Halliburton's pamphlet, charge the assemblymen with subverting the Appropriation Act to their own interests? Either the articles had been contributed by different authors, or "The writer of the Canadian Letter" had brought about a sudden transformation in the political creed of the editor of the *Novascotian*, or the editor possessed no fixed principles at all.[48] Howe did not answer this argument effectively, and in the light of subseqent events, it may be surmised that he had begun to peer more deeply into the innermost processes of Nova Scotian politics and reexamine the basic premises of his own political beliefs.

In July the first two numbers of the *Novascotian* were particularly run-of-the-mill because the proprietor was off on a ramble to the western counties. The earliest of Howe's journeyings, it served at least three purposes, one specific and two general. Throughout his life he felt a compelling need to escape periodically from the humdrum of everyday life and refresh himself in new surroundings. If he betook himself to other parts of Nova Scotia, he could become acquainted with old subscribers or solicit new ones and, equally important, collect the subscriptions of those in arrears. In the process he would get to know his native province as well as anyone was ever to know it and would prepare himself to write and speak with authority on almost anything of provincial concern.[49]

Fortuitous circumstances made his trip all the easier. Since 1816 Isaiah Smith had been running a coach service to the westward, but only as far as Windsor. By 1828 the road west of Windsor had improved sufficiently to permit an extension of the service, and the legislature granted £300 annually for five years to the Western Stage Coach Company to run stages with at least four horses each, three times a week, between Halifax and Annapolis. While the time of the journey was not to exceed sixteen hours, this turned out to be "an absurd provision,"[50] since it invariably occupied the best part of two days. Because the Western Stage Coach Company did not run its first stage until June 3, Howe was among the first to use the service, and he was more than delighted to "get a look at the country, without having to hire a sorry gelding at the rate of a shilling a day for every ounce of flesh upon his ribs."[51]

Two weeks after his return he began to report his travels in the eleven "Western Rambles" which, except for a lapse of one week, appeared in successive issues of the *Novascotian* between July 23 and October 29. Little escaped his observant eye. Among the passengers he detected a young lawyer "who has been down to town getting his 'licence to plunder'";[52] upon sighting some blacks around the shores of Bedford Basin, he begged his fellow Nova Scotians to have a little patience and "let the leaven of ignorance and idleness work out of these gentlemen of color."[53] Everywhere he went he found something to delight him: Windsor, "the ultima Thule of all peregrinating Tourists";[54] the valley of the Gaspereaux, which beckoned "all true lovers of the Picturesque – all who like to see nature, wild, unsophisticated and sublime, unprofaned by the hand of art, and untouched by the tiny labour of man's ingenuity";[55] the "well favored population" of the Annapolis Valley – "not an ugly female have I seen since I got over the mountain";[56] "the sweet little village of Kentville" and its thirty houses;[57] the hospitable people of Bridgetown with their "disposition to pull together ... in undertakings for the general benefit";[58] and Abbé Sigogne and his flock in the district of Clare, "a simple and affectionate people rising up in usefulness and virtue, and looking to him with reverence and love, as a common parent and guide."[59]

The models for the "Western Rambles" were the *Rural Rides* of William Cobbett, and James A. Roy calls on William Hazlitt's description of Cobbett to demonstrate the latter's "almost startling"[60] likeness to Howe. Both were self-taught men, having the merits and faults common to that breed of person; both were "in the constant hurry and fever of gestation" and their brains "teem[ed] incessantly with some fresh project." On the other hand, both lacked steadiness and were "liable to be led astray by their own sagacity and the overweening petulance of hard-earned and late-acquired wisdom." Common faults and strengths aside, Roy clearly prefers the *Rides* to the "Rambles." He is disappointed because Howe's "more ambitious descriptions are stilted and unnatural," and because "a certain innate lack of good taste leads him too frequently into excesses, where he mistakes maudlin sentimentality for genuine sentiment, and the false for the true sublime." Clearly Roy can produce apt quotations to illustrate these weaknesses; most readers would add that the "Rambles" are excruciatingly dull. In contrast, M.G. Parks, while admitting that Howe lacks discipline in the use of words, overdoes his "occasional flights of florid sentiment," and is sometimes guilty of "heavy-handed ... mannered pretentiousness," maintains that these faults are minor when the "Rambles" are treated as they ought to be, "as consciously conceived and executed literary pieces" demonstrating a "skill well above the reach of ordinary colonial journalism."[61] Roy is certainly mistaken in suggesting that they provide only a glimpse of the real Joseph Howe. In saying that "we are never permitted to forget that it is the editor of the *Novascotian* who is speaking, who takes himself as seriously as he expects to be taken by his readers,"[62] he is actually admitting that he does not understand Howe. Whatever harm it may have done to his literary efforts, and however distasteful it may be to his literary critics, Howe believed that his first mission was to spur provincial development and to improve the provincial character, and he missed no opportunity to moralize along these lines.

So it was on his "Western Rambles." At Windsor his discussion of Miss Tonge[63] and her poetry led naturally to a consideration of the function of women in Nova Scotian society. "Can your intellects take no range beyond the kitchen, or your fancies soar no higher than the garret? and must your minds be forever employed in a perpetual round of gossip?" Surely women ought to serve the higher purpose of giving society an elevated tone. In fact, their obligation to posterity was such that the future destiny of Nova Scotia was in their hands, "and in exact proportion as they are alive to the fact, the intellectual and moral character of the province must be raised."[64] In the township of Wilmot Howe selected as his model Caleb Slocomb, who by steady toil had surrounded himself with comfort and all that made a man truly rich and independent. Surely he was "worth a dozen of your lazy, slow-going fellows, who care not how short the day is, if the task be short also; and who, while a heavy debt is hanging over their heads, will spend an afternoon at a tavern in harvest, or waste evenings ... debating about a horse race, over a tumbler of brandy."[65]

Perhaps Howe was irked most by the people of the township of Cornwallis, where nature was its most bounteous. Because the soil was so productive, men who found that a living could be made with so little labour, thought it could be made with less. So they ran a race with poverty, and "so long as they can keep one length ahead, never think how close Sparebones is upon their rear."[66] Nor was indolence the only evil: "a cursed fondness for dress, and tea parties, and gossippings,which not only lead to the squandering of money, but to the squandering of time, which is the parent of wealth, all serve to make Mortgages grey headed, and if they do not saddle a farm with new incumbrances, are sure to perpetuate the old ones ... The poisoned shirt of Dejanira was not more pernicious to Hercules, than are the jiggery trappings of affected gentility to our Agricultural population."[67] Four times at least Howe interrupted his "Western Rambles" to lecture his fellow Nova Scotians before he finally called a "truce to moralizing and sermonizing." None would have been more surprised than he by Roy's objections. Certainly he had no intention to let his readers forget that it was the editor of the *Novascotian* who was speaking. Clearly he took himself as seriously as he expected to be taken by his readers.

In one special way the *Novascotian* of 1828 attempted to cater to the desire for self-expression that was coming into play at the time. Howe had gathered about him a group of wits, including Thomas Chandler Haliburton, Doctor Grigor, Lawrence O'Connor Doyle, and Captain Kincaid, and sporadically between May 8, 1828, and June 23, 1831, they produced for the *Novascotian* "a collaboration called 'The Club' ... lampooning the follies and foibles of the day, particularly those incident to legislative activities."[68] While the first Club paper bore a strong resemblance to Steele's "Trumpet Call," Roy concludes that the papers were generally done in the manner of Wilson's "Noctes Ambrosianae" in *Blackwood's*. This led to his assertion that "they are derivative and lack individual distinction, owing to a too close imitation of the original,"[69] a criticism he levelled at most early colonial writing. But perhaps little more ought to have been expected in the first stages of development of a provincial literature. In any case, Roy willingly concedes that the Club papers, "under the guise of harmless banter and amusing satire, did much towards the formation of an intellectual public opinion on the main questions of the day."[70] It comes as something of a surprise, therefore, to find the later Howe wondering if there might not have been "too much of personality in these dialogues."[71]

Although the authorship of particular Club papers is sometimes in doubt, clearly Howe makes the bulk of the contributions, and in 1828 they usually parallel his comments elsewhere in the *Novascotian*. Thus, when the Doctor (an original member of the Club) pressed the Editor (undoubtedly Howe) to express an opinion of assemblymen who "chewed the cud of former arguments, and travelled over all the old ground, without adding a new idea," he is repeating one of Howe's pet annoyances. Amusingly satirical, the Editor replied that just as people would have found hidden wisdom in downright absurdities if they had been proclaimed by the oracle at Delphos, so when he found the assemblymen's conduct incomprehensible, he generally "laid all the blame on [his] own want of taste and right apprehension of senatorial wisdom and imagination."[72]

Shortly after Howe defended the prerogative of the council on money bills against Haliburton's attacks, the Major (another original member of the Club) referred to the Councillors

as the "Corinthian Capitals" of the Provincial columns – hewn from the same rock, and when any are detached by the decays of time – to be replaced by the same materials as compose the shaft which supports them – we know their best motto would be

"prodesse quam conspici
vitality rather than ornament"

and we have no misgivings as to its illustration in their practice.[73]

Although Howe had nowhere described the councillors in terms quite as laudatory as these, he clearly agreed with the Major on the general quality of their performance.

One of the Club papers allowed the Lowland Scot and anti-burgher Donald McGregor to make a ludicrous exhibition of himself in a parody on the council's supposedly unsympathetic attitude towards Pictou Academy in which McGregor prophesied an awful fate for the academy if the council had its way: "the Academy will first be stormed and demolished, and the bottles o' lightnin' and the jars o' fermentation, and a' the apparatus for the black art, broken, and in the vera place, whar the Doctor's [i.e., Principal McCulloch's] butterflys are noo pinn't against the wa', his sons and dochters will be stickit wi' bagonets and ither things."[74] But it is almost equally ludicrous to infer from this parody, as Roy does, that Howe was "opposed to the idea of government grants to educational institutions other than those of the Anglican persuasion";[75] the proper conclusion is that Howe objected to the eastern part of the province being thrown into constant turmoil by the unceasing efforts of one faction in the county to secure a permanent grant for Pictou Academy.

The Club papers were part of Howe's continuing effort to render the *Novascotian* "less dependent on foreign aid" for literary works. Periodically he invited Nova Scotians to send him their contributions, and by the end of the year he could pay tribute to "the host of correspondents whose pens have enriched our paper with a great variety of productions, some of them scarcely inferior to any of which the publications of the Mother Country can boast."[76] Although they did not change the character of the *Novascotian* very much in 1828, there were already signs of the growing rapport between the editor and his contributors and readers that was to be the hallmark of the Howe newspaper. So far it seemed to have paid off, for Howe delightedly reported that he had lost few of Young's subscribers and had added a substantial number of new ones.

CHAPTER FIVE

Barry and Brandy

Although Blanchard had given him cause to wonder, the Howe who began his second year with the *Novascotian* outwardly seemed little different in political stance from the Howe of the first year. There was the same resolve to "speak a firm and liberal tone – such as best comports with the spirit of the Constitution," and the same promise to accommodate his paper, not to "the wild and reckless blast," but to "the healthful and invigorating breeze, that refreshes and purifies the earth." There was also the same conviction that government was not primarily responsible for the province's well-being. While the loss of a governor as able as Sir James Kempt was regrettable, it was the people themselves, rather than their rulers, who would preserve the blessings that Nova Scotia enjoyed; so long as they chose suitable representatives and carefully scrutinized their conduct, the province would remain tranquil and happy.[1]

Still, Howe's attitude towards the assembly had something ambivalent about it. On the one hand he described it as a constitutional landmark which demonstrated to the people their power in the governmental system. He also showed signs of a growing fascination with it that would inevitably lead him into its ranks. "We love to hear the free and thrilling tone of debate ringing in our ears, ... we delight to listen to those bursts of oratory, and flashes of imagination, which display the rising genius of our country, and by their electric effect kindle up ardent and patriotic emotions."[2] Yet at the same time he told the assemblymen not to take themselves too seriously since there was "nothing of mighty moment to engage [their] attention"[3] in the well-ordered province of Nova Scotia. It took John Alexander Barry to rouse him with a jolt from this state of contentment.

Barry was one of those representatives who pass across the political stage like a meteor, who cause a stir for a moment and are unheard of again. That momentary stir was to write his name into the folklore of the province as well as contribute directly to Howe's continuing education. Initially defeated in 1826 for the township of Shelburne, Barry petitioned against the sheriff's return, and through the testimony of a host of witnesses brought by schooner from Shelburne in midwinter convinced the assembly committee trying the case that he was entitled to the seat. Thereupon he proceeded to alienate many assemblymen, especially those who were militia officers, by his continued criticism of the administration of the militia laws.[4]

When, in 1829, Barry presented a petition from Patrick Gough of Liverpool asking to be relieved from militia duty, the members for the township of Liverpool and Queens County described Gough as "a radical by principle and a smuggler by practice." Evidently expecting that reply, Barry read to the House part of a letter from Gough to Col. Joseph Freeman, a member for Queens county, which concluded: "I am, sir, your old friend and partner, Patrick Gough." Allegedly he emphasized the word " partner" and turned to the gallery with a laugh as he did so. Colonel Freeman protested against being called "a smuggler," and the House degenerated into an uproar. Although Barry said he was sorry if he had wounded Freeman's feelings, that was not enough for the assembly. On February 26 it ordered Barry's exclusion until he apologized both to Freeman and the House in terms it must have known would be unacceptable to a person of Barry's temperament.

During this stage of the Barry affair Howe offered no editorial comment, but he could not avoid being drawn into its second stage. Barry's next step was to petition, through himself and his constituents, to have his seat vacated and a new election called for the township of Shelburne. On being denied his request, he took his seat in the House on April 4, and on his refusal to make the required apology, he was committed to the custody of the sergeant-at-arms. This was too much for Philip Holland of the *Acadian Recorder* and Edmund Ward of the *Free Press*, both of whom castigated the assembly in their papers. Ward went so far as to suggest that " the treatment bestowed on Mr. Barry, must have originated in motives and feelings, unworthy to have a place, in the breasts of Members of such an august body."[5] On April 8 he and Holland were required to appear at the bar of the House to be reprimanded by the speaker for their breaches of the assembly's privileges. This attack on the press turned Howe, at long last, from the factual reporting of the Barry affair to a decisive expression of opinion. He warned the assembly that "if Editors are brought for offences to the Bar of the House, Legislators may depend upon this – that they will be brought, individually and collectively, to a bitter expiation before the bar of the public."[6] The assembly referred these comments forthwith to its Committee of Privileges.

Barry's capacity to cause mischief had not yet been exhausted. The sergeant-at-arms, in a quandary what to do with him, entrusted him to the care of his wife in his own home. From there he launched a scathing attack on the actions and motives of the Committee of Privileges in an address to his constituents that was published in the *Acadian Recorder* on April 11.[7] Deciding that it had had enough of Barry, the assembly committed him to the county gaol in Halifax. The last act attracted an excited group of people – Howe later described it as a Tory mob egged on by Barry's friends – which released him from his escort. Later the same day, some assemblymen who were to dine at Government House were "hooted and hissed along the streets, pelted with snow, mud, stones and other missiles, and assailed by every opprobrious expression that could be vented by a heedless and unthinking rabble."[8] The military were called out to ensure the safety of the members; Barry surrendered himself almost immediately; the assembly vacated his seat, jailed him to the end of the session, and voted £500 to discover and punish the perpetrators of the violence. The Barry riots were over, but not soon to be forgotten.

Howe had hoped that the affair would cool off before he needed to treat it again, but the proportions it assumed prompted him to intervene a second time before he intended to do so, and in a manner different from his fellow editors. Whereas Ward and Holland continued to show some sympathy for Barry, Blanchard and the *Colonial Patriot* dismissed him with contempt. As Blanchard saw it, the assembly – if it was to maintain its dignity – had no choice but to exact the most ample apology from Barry. Indeed, it ought not to admit him even if he was reelected because of his obvious unfitness to sit in a body which he had treated with contumely.[9] In contrast, Howe decided to review the controversy in the manner of a judge, unravelling its successive developments one by one and pronouncing judgment on each in turn. At the outset he presented his credentials as a judge. On the one hand, he had always been on friendly if not intimate terms with Barry; on the other, he had nothing to fear from the frowns of the assembly and nothing to hope from its favours. "Therefore in forming our decisions we are only influenced by our sense of justice."[10] He was soon to learn that it is sometimes injudicious to attempt to become too judicial.

Seemingly less on the basis of evidence and more as a result of the readiness of the early Howe to ascribe only the best of intentions to his fellows, he assured his readers that the assembly's initial actions against Barry had in no way proceeded from sinister motives. Yet, despite Howe's opinion, there is more than a suspicion that a few of the leading assemblymen welcomed an opportunity to take vindictive action against a man who had rendered himself persona non grata. He himself might have thought differently if, as Barry suggested, he had been permitted "a peep behind the scenes."[11] As it was, he made two admissions which rendered his judgment suspect in supporting the assembly's motives so readily. Why, he wondered, had the Committee of Privileges, after delving deeply into the practices of the British Parliament, advised the Assembly to exact an apology from Barry instead of reprimanding him, as was the usual custom of the House of Commons, and why had the assembly demanded an apology in a specific form on a take-it-or-leave-it basis? Did the assemblymen not have a duty to "leave no measure untried for the honorable adjustment of their [petty squabbles], before they throw a quiet Province like this into a state of uproar and confusion"?[12] In short, Howe adjudged Barry to be the chief culprit, but found the assembly guilty of inept behaviour, although not wilfully so. Yet surely Howe should have recognized the possibility that the assembly had not reached an accommodation with Barry because its leading members did not want one.

Howe had left himself open to criticism, and it was not long in forthcoming. It was bad enough for Barry to tell him that he had "heard many express their surprise at [his] editorial observations ... not knowing *which* part[y], or whether *both*, [he] had really espoused."[13] But what irked Howe most of all was to read in the *Free Press* that, except for "two mercenary and vacillating Journals," the *Acadian* and the *Novascotian*, the press had stood firmly for the liberties of the people at a time when the legislative body had become more corrupt than the executive.[14] "Vacillating," he retorted, came strangely from Edmund Ward, "the veriest weathercock that ever fluttered in a political breeze," who changed almost overnight from "the most flaming of patriots" to "the most grovelling of sycophants." Surely it was not "'mercenary' to do justice to a body from whom we can receive no reward, and to defend men to the great majority of whom we are almost strangers."[15]

Much more perturbing to Howe were the doubts that both Barry and Ward expressed about his independence. Why, they asked, had he been able to threaten the House and get away with it, while Ward and Holland, for lesser offences, were dragged before the bar of the assembly? Barry had two explanations for Howe's seemingly favoured treatment. The first, which he got second-hand from a member of the Committee of Privileges, was that Howe was to publish "*a piece ... in [his] paper next day defending the conduct of the House.*"[16] The second was that Thomas Chandler Haliburton had influenced the assembly not to proceed against Howe. Ward went so far as to say that Haliburton had acted as he did because Howe was publishing his *Historical and Statistical Account of Nova Scotia*,[17] and while Barry himself did not charge Howe either with courting or wanting Haliburton's assistance, he did draw attention to the immense influence that even one lawyer of Haliburton's stature could exercise in the assembly.[18] Naturally Howe denied categorically that his connection with Haliburton had affected his independence. Had not Haliburton been the only assemblyman that the *Novascotian* had attacked since Howe took over its management?[19] Yet his documentation in support of this statement is unconvincing since it indicates that most of the criticism of Haliburton came from the correspondents, and not the editor, of the *Novascotian*. In fact, Howe's only major disagreement with Haliburton had been the one relating to the prerogatives of the council, and this had occurred on a theoretical rather than a personal level.

For the moment Howe was done with the Barry affair. When he came back to it weeks later he had little new to add. By that time Barry had published ninety columns of material justifying his position in weekly instalments in the *Acadian Recorder*, and the editor of that newspaper was begging him to desist so that he might open his columns to other correspondents. By that time, too, Barry had been reelected for the township of Shelburne, and Howe had suggested that he be allowed to take his seat: "He has been imprisoned, expelled, and put to the trouble and expense of a new election – and, (which we take by no means the most trifling part of the punishment) he has been subjected to the labour of poring over the Journals of the House of Commons, and vindicating his conduct in an amount of matter which will certainly fill a book."[20] Barry did resume his seat unchallenged early in 1830, not because Howe advised it, but because the assembly had no intention of running afoul for a second time of his inordinate propensity for trouble-making. Howe himself emerged from the Barry affair with anything but flying colours. In assuming a judge's garb he had tried too hard to make points for and against all the antagonists and he had ended up by pleasing no one. The outcome may have led him to doubt his father's practice of placing the best possible interpretation on men's motives, and to take to heart Barry's advice to "peep behind the scenes." But it exercised its major influence on him more obliquely since it brought Jotham Blanchard into print in such a way as to force him to think more deeply about Nova Scotia society and politics.

When the *Colonial Patriot* was founded, Blanchard had freely admitted the handicap of publishing a newspaper outside of Halifax. To him, an editor who could watch the legislature in action and observe the conduct of public affairs at first hand had incalculable advantages over a country editor in gaining a thorough understanding of the governmental process.[21] Apparently Blanchard had spent part of 1828 in Halifax, prying into the innermost recesses of Nova Scotian politics. So, beginning in April 1829, only a few days after he had resumed the editorship, and extending over a period of more than six months, the *Patriot* presented in weekly instalments the first detailed examination of the practical working of the province's political institutions.

By Blanchard's own account the lessons of the Barry affair had prompted this editorial investigation. Why had he been so insistent that the assembly protect its dignity at all costs in this case? To answer this question he posed a second one. Why did the Halifax mob treat the assemblymen with impunity during the Barry riots? It was not, he thought, out of sympathy for Barry. Rather it was because the assemblymen, through their increasing servility to the council, had gradually lost their respectability in the eyes of the public until "finally, they have been mobbed."[22] Hence there was a good reason to explore the difference in status between the two bodies. Unfortunately the assemblymen could not earn popularity through their enlightened views on matters of substance, but only through the expenditure of a few pounds on "some little two-penny affair" like a by-road, to which their constituents attached more importance than all the rest of the provincial business put together. The result was the degradation of the assembly. If one of its members was to get what he wanted, he had to please the council first. "For the sake of paltry sums, which the Council know how to dispense with discriminating hand, our representatives may be said to have sacrificed their independence ... even boys know their legislative insignificance."[23]

At the same time, wrote Blanchard, there had grown up around the council "a system of grandeism and grasping"[24] that had already transferred almost the whole patronage of the province into its hands. Possessing the major offices as they did, the councillors could extend their influence to every segment of the society. Besides that, the council had other faults. Obviously it had too much to do and was called upon to do things for which it had no talents. How could the lord bishop of Nova Scotia as councillor take on "the care of pickled fish, in addition to the care of souls"? How could H.N. Binney, the collector of impost and excise, manage roads when he perhaps "never saw a public road in his life"? Accordingly, the assemblymen should seek to relieve the council of these duties by pressing for a separate Legislative Council, selected like themselves from all parts of the province. Only then would the country be "delivered from those factions, lay and clerical, which have nestled themselves about our metropolis, and which are ever prepared to shout disloyalty, while their own selfish measures are forcing the community into a state of turmoil."[25]

By the end of May Blanchard had analysed the basic features of the relationship between the council and the assembly. Hence there had been ample time for Howe to read and digest them before July 9, the day on which he started to publish the legislative reviews he had long promised. Stylistically, the contrast between his reviews and Blanchard's articles is startling. Blanchard is partisan and argumentative; Howe is moderate and judicious. Blanchard is enthusiastic and excited; Howe is calm and unhurried. Clearly Blanchard's editorials had not impelled Howe to venture on a crusade of his own, but neither had they induced him to enter into a new controversy with Blanchard despite the latter's harsh indictment of the political system.

Howe's reviews show him at times thin-skinned and a little sorry for himself. How much more pleasant, he said, it would be to write for a party! In that case he would get no support from the one side, but he would expect none; on the other hand, he could always count on the support of his own political faction. In contrast, a person like himself, who followed his own principles, " must expect at times to differ with all; and he will be very fortunate, if by all, in turn, he is not suspected and reviled."[26] Such had been his fate for telling the friends of Pictou Academy that they sometimes injured their cause by their violence, for declaring that the Council, despite its faults, had "some intelligence, virtue, and patriotism," and for defending the assembly against Barry and the intemperance of the Halifax mob. Nevertheless, he would continue to aim for the relationship between an editor and his public that he considered ideal, one in which the editor looked to his readers for support, they looked to him for counsel, and he advised them all the better because he could not be over-awed by the powerful, bought by the wealthy, or frightened by sudden outbursts of popular feeling.

By the time he went to the neighbouring provinces and the United States in August he had completed nine of the twelve reviews. Unmistakably they revealed a steadily maturing Howe, who could write forcefully on a wide variety of subjects. It might be on a matter of purely Halifax concern such as limiting the height of wooden houses as a fire prevention measure,[27] or on a matter of province-wide interest such as the shortage of doctors.[28] Occasionally he might enunciate a general principle he would never abandon: "Trade should be left as free as possible, and taxed no further than may be necessary for the purposes of Revenue."[29]

In two instances in the purely political realm it appeared as if the leaven of Blanchard had begun to work on him and that the Pictou Scribblers were, in fact, turning him from the error of his ways. The first related to the hypothetical questions that he posed in his introduction to the "science of legislation." Suppose that the colonist discovered that his interests were to be unjustly sacrificed or that his "fair participation in the advantages of the national compact," i.e., the compact with Britain, were to be unnecessarily curtailed, what should he do? Obviously he had a duty to resist the loss of his rights by every constitutional device at his disposal, including the submission of his case to the British government and Parliament. But suppose that they found against him. He then had to "consider whether a separation from a government which he cannot approve, will not be more desirable than a submission to the evils that are to be entailed upon him by an act of manifest injustice."[30] The omnipresent Edmund Ward was utterly aghast: this was "a pretty piece of business"; if colonists did not get what they wanted, "then clap arms a-kimbo, order the troops out of the garrison, send the government officers about their business, and let the fullblooded Nova-Scotians set up for themselves."[31] But in its proper context Howe's conclusion was nothing as revolutionary as that, He wrote in the abstract without reference to any particular situation and it was furthest from his mind that his advice could have any application to a well-ordered Nova Scotia and a well-disposed Britain.

On a more specific level Howe was outspoken about official salaries which, excepting that of the governor, he would not have let exceed £600. Surely Nova Scotia should not continue to pay its governor and treasurer three times as much as the corresponding officers in the wealthy state of New York. In his favourite role of social critic, he contended that exorbitant salaries for provincial offices reduced the funds for works of general utility, induced luxurious and baneful habits, and distracted the numerous applicants for these offices from useful labours.[32] But he did it all with calmness and moderation, and without mentioning a single official by name. Jeffery and Binney, Uniacke and Wallace escaped the individual attention that Blanchard would certainly have lavished upon them. None of them would have liked Howe's treatment of the subject, but neither would they have been unduly perturbed.

Perhaps Howe's moderation is best revealed in his attitude towards the regulation of the customs establishment. After years of controversy the assembly finally got control of it in 1829, but only after agreeing to pay out of the duties the lump sum of £6,430 9s. stg. per annum in lieu of all fees, perquisites, and emoluments. Although Howe acknowledged that the salaries guaranteed to the incumbent customs officers were altogether too large, nevertheless, he argued, Nova Scotians should approach the change with a liberal feeling: "if the arrangement is not as satisfactory as we could wish, we think, upon the whole, it is as fair as under the circumstances, we could expect to obtain."[33] Such was the tenor of the first nine legislative reviews. Clearly Howe thought they were much bolder than they actually were, while Edmund Ward, who had moved well to the right on the political spectrum, went him one better and accused him of republicanism.[34] Howe had a ready answer: if republicanism was to be equated with economy in government, he pleaded guilty to the charge; if loyalty to government meant blindness to its ills, he was a republican.[35]

In the three legislative reviews that Howe published on his return from the United States he advanced two new propositions. The first, to reduce the number of lawyers in the assembly and bring them into "a more rational proportion with the other classes,"[36] could hardly have been seized upon as wildly revolutionary, but the second, to constitute an Upper House which excluded the principal officers of government and confined itself solely to legislation, appeared to reflect more than ever before the influence of Blanchard. In fact, Howe's list of complaints about the council might have come directly from the *Patriot*: the councillors were mostly Haligonians and manifestly ignorant of the conditions and needs of the province; those councillors who were major officers could not only vote in one House, but could indirectly influence the other whenever they were subject to its scrutiny; the Anglican bishop was busying himself with legislative duties about which he knew little and neglecting the ecclesiastical duties which should be his chief concern; the judges on the council were administering the very law they had helped to enact.[37]

But although the arguments were like those of Blanchard, the manner and style were decidedly not. Unlike Blanchard, Howe continued to assume the mien of a judge and generally avoided names and specific examples; unlike Blanchard, he weakened his case with reservations and qualifications. Thus he almost exulted that he was not among those men who "trace[d] more evils than ever sprung from the box of Pandora, to the defects of the constitution of our Council," and he gladly acknowledged that, despite the faults in the council, "fewer traces of oppression and bad government are no where to be discerned than within the limits of Nova Scotia."[38] Comments like these led Blanchard to conclude that Howe had not changed his political stance even though for the first time he had given his blessing to a major change in the province's political institutions. The Pictonian acknowledged that he too wanted harmony and that, like Howe, he would much sooner "lounge in a picture gallery, than write political Editorials" that stirred up conflict. But rather than accept a council "composed of men whose sole object is the aggrandisement of themselves and their sons, and their sons' sons ... at the expense of the great body of the people" he would infinitely prefer "an eternal interruption of harmony."[39]

Blanchard's sense of urgency led him to contemplate a remedy that Howe found repugnant. At a time when he was condemning political parties as little more than factions, Blanchard was becoming convinced that the solution to the province's political problems lay in an "organized party against misrule."[40] Because there was no such party, the regularly organized party had an easy time of it. Whenever someone had the effrontery to attack it, its members simply formed themselves into a phalanx, and its opponent soon wearied of acting alone. Until party was marshalled against party, all sorts of stupidities would continue; for example, "our bachelor friends [would] remain unmarried, or be bawled in Church, or submit to an unconstitutional and illegal tax, and to a ceremony which they do not fancy."[41]

This time the differences between Howe and Blanchard did not produce a violent clash, and within weeks they were to adopt a common position on the Revenue Dispute of 1830. That dispute started innocently enough when the assembly sought to correct an error in a revenue law.[42] Four years earlier it thought it had imposed a duty of 2s. 4d. a gallon on foreign brandy, but because of a technicality the collector of excise hade seen fit to collect only 2s. a gallon. When the assembly at long last discovered its mistake and sought to enact its original intention into law, the council flatly refused to sanction it. Why it chose this particular time to disturb its longstanding accommodation with the assembly on money matters is something of a mystery. Although it insisted that it was simply opposing any increase in the burden on commerce, it may actually have intended its intervention as the first stage of a broader plan to arrange the provincial finances to suit its own interests.[43]

During the first two weeks in April a fascinated Joseph Howe looked on as the General Assembly of Nova Scotia reached a pitch of excitement it had not known since the clashes between Governor Wentworth and Speaker Tonge in the first decade of the century. He watched admiringly as S.G.W. Archibald descended from the Speaker's chair to deliver speeches that were, in Howe's opinion, the finest of his career.[44] Essentially, Archibald contended that, by the law and constitution of Great Britain and by the practice of the General Assembly of Nova Scotia, the people's representatives had the sole, inherent, and inalienable right to frame and originate all revenue bills, free from any amendment by the council, and that "such right is one ... which British subjects will never surrender but *with their lives.*"[45] The council replied correctly, though only from a strictly technical point of view, that money could not be wrung from a British subject at the will of a single branch of the legislature, and that, in exercising the rights of a second branch, its members considered themselves responsible, not to the House of Assembly, but to their own consciences.[46]

Howe looked on as the assembly received a message from the council, complaining that the reports of the assembly's debates in the *Novascotian* contained libels against the council, and demanding that the guilty be punished, whether they be assemblymen or printer.[47] He watched the relations between the two bodies worsen to the point that the council refused to receive further messages from the assembly. He was present when the General Assembly was prorogued without its having renewed the revenue laws or passed the appropriation bill. He was delighted that all the assemblymen but three, R.J. Uniacke, Jr, Lawrence Hartshorne, and John Barry, had resisted the warnings about disloyalty, disaffection, and anarchy that had been dinned into their ears, and he praised them for "act[ing] like men."[48] As soon as circumstances permitted, he promised a full justification of their conduct.

For the moment he could offer little in the way of editorial comment because the reporting of the debates fully occupied him. As he pointed out ruefully, his position was not that of a legislative reporter in Britain. There a newspaper might have a dozen reporters who, by relieving each other at short intervals, could write out a limited portion of a speech while the language and sentiments were fresh in their minds. "Here the whole has to be taken down by one hand, and elaborated and filled up by one mind – often at the distance of a week or a fortnight from the time when a debate occurs."[49] Ought he to be blamed, therefore, for not reporting word for word, "the pointless harangues of one of our *fourth* rate speakers"? As it was, his note-taking in the gallery for five or six hours a day throughout the session bore fruit in 160 columns of closely printed debates, the equivalent, according to his calculations, of 480 pages of manuscript.

Obviously these reports would not pass unchallenged by friends of the council. The irrepressible John Barry complained that the account of one of his speeches on the revenue question was so different from the original that he hardly recognized it,[50] only to draw Howe's retort that, because of Barry's "fulsome pomposity of manner ... tiresome array of high sounding words ... [and] a silly intrusion of all the scraps of knowledge he has ever been able to gather together," his speeches were unreportable as they were given.[51] What annoyed Howe most was Barry's charge that his speeches had been deliberately garbled to suit the purposes of "the youthful Editor of the Nova Scotian, to whose very superior abilities, knowledge, experience, and information, the whole population of the Province of Nova Scotia, is, *apparently*, expected to bow."[52] This was to be a recurring theme of Howe's critics as the *Novascotian* steadily extended its influence. For Barry he had a ready answer: having failed to achieve the notoriety of the previous session and having shown himself "a very every day sort of person" when contrasted with Archibald, Young, Stewart, Murdoch, and Fairbanks, he had sought to attribute the obvious inadequacy of his speeches to inaccurate reporting.[53]

For his unfailing critic, Edmund Ward, Howe displayed his usual contempt. Ward had charged him with lending himself to a party and, more specifically, with having thrown open his paper to anything submitted by those whose tool he had become.[54] Nothing more angered the Howe of 1830 than to be charged with belonging to a party. After writing his critic off as "devoid of talent, veracity or principle," he charged him with annually making and breaking his promise to report in full the debates of the assembly. In contrast with the *Novascotian*'s 160 columns of debate, the *Free Press* had published only six columns, and "if it had not been for our reports [on the revenue dispute] the country would not have possessed the means of estimating the merits of the controversy."[55]

Following the session Howe took five weeks to recover from his weariness and ponder the significance of the revenue dispute. By May 20 he was ready to publish a series of four articles on the question, of which the first was incontestably the most important. Blanchard himself would have agreed that Howe had done more than peep behind the scenes, and that he had developed a considerable awareness of the forces operating below the surface in Nova Scotian politics. Although he still measured the worth of a political system in terms of the effective operation of a system of checks and balances, his analysis was now in dynamic rather than static terms. In other words, the specific arrangement of checks and balances was not a constant, but needed adjustment over time. If in a long-established government like Britain the arrangement had not withstood "the multifarious assaults which the evil principles of our nature make upon the commonwealth," how much more care had to be taken in a new country like Nova Scotia to ensure that the legislative and executive arms were kept within legitimate bounds.[56] Howe did not apologize for his marked change in stance since the twentieth number of the *Novascotian* in 1828,[57] since it was the events of the last two years that had put the council's defects in focus and demonstrated that the existing checks and balances were weighted all too heavily in its favour.[58]

Earlier he had felt that the council had no more power than was needed to counterbalance an assembly that could rely on the sympathies of the people. He had not appreciated, however, that "while the patronage, the power and the influence of the Council, are daily and hourly at work in support of their own measures and opinions ... the sympathies of the people cannot always be brought to bear upon matters of minor importance," but only in extraordinary cases such as the revenue question. The council complained that the assembly had usurped the prerogative power to nominate road commissioners, but "right glad are we that they have [that power] – because, in nine cases out of ten, they are the best men by whom the service can be performed."[59] In any case the council had its own devices to rally adherents to its point of view in any conflict with the assembly. Was not the patronage of customs and excise, the bench and the bar, and the Treasury and Land Departments, together with the power to select magistrates, "a fair set off to the humble privilege of nominating commissioners of Roads"?[60] Did not the council also possess the privileges of a dual branch of the legislature? Furthermore, what check was there on councillors; could they be dismissed every seven years like assemblymen?

Admittedly the council had sometimes checked lavish expenditures by the assembly, but it was also guilty of unaccountable acts of omission. Had the councillors prevented the assembly from creating the office of master of the rolls at a cost of £600 per annum? Had they helped the assembly to cut down the expenses of the customs house establishment or get rid of quit rents without cost to the province? Because they had not, Howe concluded that "the great principles of human nature operate as invincibly in one end of a stone building [Province House] as in the other; making men very watchful and patriotic in matters which only concern the public; but singularly indulgent to matters which deeply concern themselves."[61]

In Howe's opinion, the council had two alternatives, both distasteful. It might accept the lesson of other colonies that councils which seem to aggrandize themselves at the expense of the assembly always lose out, advise the governor to summon the legislature forthwith, and seek ways to repair the evil it had done. Or it might advise a dissolution, have its conduct subjected to close scrutiny by many who previously had paid only passing attention to political subjects, and suffer a serious loss in respect and influence.[62] In either case Howe insisted on a remodelling of the council along the lines he had suggested in an earlier legislative review: "the exclusion of public officers from its Board, and the separation of its executive and legislative powers, which now give to it a character as incongruous as it is overwhelming."[63] In this article the directness and aptness of phrase that marked Howe's later writing were coming more and more into evidence. His determined efforts to improve his style were beginning to pay off.

No less elated by the outcome of the revenue dispute than Howe, and certainly more surprised, was Jotham Blanchard. For him it was nothing less than the "Glorious Emancipation of Nova Scotia." For the first time he accepted the opinions of the *Novascotian* and reprinted some of Howe's articles with obvious approval. He even acknowledged that Howe's estimate of the Speaker was more correct than his own. Although he had read law in Archibald's office, he had become suspicious of the Speaker's moderation in later years, especially his attempts to soften the collision between the assembly and the council, and tone down any manifestations of popular feeling against misrule. But Howe had been right, for it was Archibald's reputation for moderation that had encouraged the council to rush into an incredibly stupid act, and later it was that same moderation that had prevented the councillors from raising charges of disloyalty for fear they would be treated with scorn on both sides of the water.[64] Clearly the new cordiality between Blanchard and Howe resulted more from Howe's coming closer to Blanchard's views than the reverse. It had taken an ill-conceived, in fact, an inexplicable, act of the council to convince Howe that Blanchard's criticism of the province's political institutions was not nearly as extravagant as he had once thought. But while the oral tradition is clearly right that Blanchard gave Howe his first impression of liberal politics, there was as yet no certain indication that he had competely converted him from the error of his ways.

By early June Howe was making his way along the South Shore and through the Annapolis Valley, collecting subscriptions as he went, but taking care to sample opinion as well. So far as he could see, there was "one sentiment from Lunenburg to Annapolis" and it accorded with his own. He was especially elated that the last two issues[65] of his paper had "floored the firm supporters the Council might have had – for I have not yet met a man who attempted to defend their measures."[66] Yet he knew he was approved of in the rural parts not for making opinion but for reflecting it. New settlers went to the wilderness with little capital and were dependent for the first few years upon employment by the road commissioners or well-to-do farmers. Until their own land was productive, they earned some ready cash in this way to buy food, clothing, and implements, perhaps even a yoke of oxen to plough the soil and haul logs, or simply to keep up their credit with the country trader. The absence of road work through the legislature's failure to vote supply had reduced some of these settlers to such dire straits that they were compelled to eat the seed grains and potatoes they ought to have put in the ground. Even the older farmers were having their operations harmed by the deterioration of the roads and bridges. In time Halifax itself would feel the effect in smaller country orders and remittances.[67] While Howe's dismal picture may have been a little simplistic, it exaggerated in no way the evils resulting from a loss of £30,000 or £40,000 in road money.

The special circumstances under which Howe made this trip throughout western Nova Scotia led him to realize, more than before, the value of the insights his travels could provide into the attitude of his rural compatriots towards governmental institutions and undertakings, and especially towards the *Novascotian* and himself. He was grateful to find that, because of the independence he had displayed in the revenue dispute, "the character of the Novascotian is now fairly established – and ... a reliance is placed upon it that I did not hope to earn for many years."[68] Only one cloud crossed his horizon during the trip. Susan Ann wrote to him at Annapolis that the council was raising difficulties about something he had written. Indignantly Howe replied that he recanted not one line, warning her at the same time not to let his father or half-brother apologize for him: "they may put what they please in their own or other papers – but not a scrape of a pen into ours."[69] Towards his father, for whom he showed his usual respect and solicitude, he adopted a somewhat different tone, although the conclusion was the same. He assured old John Howe that he would never wittingly do anything that would cause him pain and begged him "not to let the present state of affairs weigh upon [his] mind – depend upon it *the right side will get the better.*" Because the *Novascotian* was on that side, no matter what the other papers did, his father was "*not [to] let any thing like a retraction be put into ours.*"[70] For the Howes in Halifax it was undoubtedly a traumatic experience to have one of their own take a strong stand against an establishment with which their relations had always been harmonious. But Joseph had his way. The *Novascotian* did not recant.

Earlier Howe had said sarcastically that among the many boons the council might confer by its actions were "the distractions and tumults of a general election."[71] With the death of King George IV late in June 1830, an election became necessary for quite a different reason. While Howe agreed with William Young that the province needed an appeal to the people much more on the resignation of a colonial secretary than on the death of a sovereign,[72] the law ordained a dissolution, and for the first time Howe could observe and participate in an election.

Like all his fellow editors, Edmund Ward excepted, he defended the assemblymen to the hilt during the campaign. He dismissed as preposterous the council's suggestion that they had sought to oppress their constituents by an extra tax on brandy. He told his readers that the accusation came badly from a body which had done nothing towards reducing customs house salaries and was prepared to burden the province permanently with an annual payment of £2,000 for the commutation of the quit rents. He pointed out, in contrast, that the assembly had willingly received all the complaints of the people, starting with the petition of Meuse the Indian. He insisted no less strongly that the assembly was not inferior, either in talent or capacity, to the assemblies that preceded it. Had not its debates on customs house salaries, quit rents, and the revenue question been printed with approval in the newspapers of the neighbouring colonies? Had not 30,000 copies of its members' speeches on the Catholic petition been circulated by English Catholics throughout the United Kingdom? "Away [then] with such wholesale and inconsiderate charges of incapacity, oppression, and neglect."[73]

Logically Howe could ask for the reelection of all the assemblymen who had defied the council, and that is what he did. While he admitted that a few of them might be rejected on local grounds, unless there were insuperable objections they should be returned. Otherwise the council might foist some of its own minions on the assembly and gain debating points from its successes. To prevent the incumbent assemblymen from suffering, either in purse or in spirit, Howe also wanted them reelected without opposition,[74] and he singled out Sydney county for special praise when it returned its former members without expense to themselves.[15] Yet, try as he might, he could not maintain his tough line to the end. Perhaps once again reflecting the kindly feelings of his father for all humanity, he put himself in a distinctly equivocal position by his attitude towards Lawrence Hartshorne, one of the four members for Halifax county and one of the minority of three on the brandy question. He simply could not bring himself to believe that a single fault should tarnish or

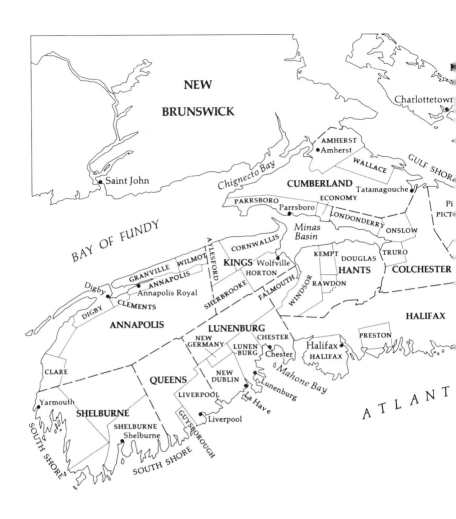

COUNTY AND TOWNSHIP REPRESENTATION

Representation (1830 election) Halifax county 4, Halifax township 2

Total membership 41   Other counties 2, other townships 1

Counties	Townships in each county
Annapolis	Annapolis, Digby, Granville
Cape Breton	None
Cumberland	Amherst
Halifax	Halifax, Londonderry, Onslow, Truro
Hants	Falmouth, Newport, Windsor
Kings	Cornwallis, Horton
Lunenburg	Lunenburg
Queens	Liverpool
Shelburne	Barrington, Shelburne, Yarmouth
Sydney	None

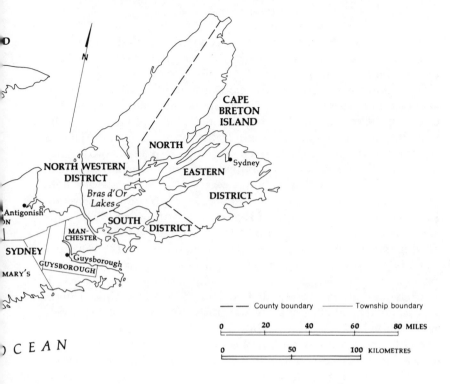

| | County boundary ———— Township boundary |

```
0      20      40      60      80 MILES
├───┬───┬───┬───┬───┬───┬───┬───┤

0            50           100 KILOMETRES
├────────────┬────────────┤
```

Creation of new counties	Addition and elimination of townships with representation
1835 Halifax, Colchester, and Pictou from Halifax county	*Additions*
	1832 Arichat, Sydney
1835 Cape Breton, Richmond, and Juste-au-Corps (renamed Inverness in 1837) from Cape Breton county	1835 Pictou
	1836 Argyle
	1837 Clare
1836 Shelburne and Yarmouth from Shelburne county	
1836 Sydney (renamed Antigonish in 1863) and Guysborough from Sydney county	*Eliminations*
	1851 Onslow
	1859 all others
1837 Digby and Annapolis from Annapolis county	
1851 Cape Breton and Victoria from Cape Breton county	

destroy one whose public conduct generally entitled him to the confidence of his constituents; hence "we should be sorry to see [him] thrown out of our Legislature."[76]

To follow the progress of the elections in the outlying townships and counties, Howe relied on correspondents, but he personally observed the contests in the township and county of Halifax. In the township the merchant Stephen Deblois ran against the sitting members, Fairbanks and Murdoch. Although Deblois put on the garb of a moderate, he was clearly stamped as the nominee of the council. Perhaps because the Howe family was well acquainted with him, Howe again relented a little and expressed regret that the circumstances dictated that he support Fairbanks and Murdoch.[77] The same factor may also have accounted for his appraisal of the outcome. During the polling Deblois boasted of being the son of a Loyalist and described Murdoch as a vain and flippant young man looking for promotion. Irritated to the point of injudiciousness, Murdoch blurted out that many pretended Loyalists had fled the United States to escape their debts, and it was this scum which had largely monopolized the offices of Nova Scotia. Shortly afterwards, Murdoch abandoned the contest and conceded the election to Deblois. Howe attributed the outcome to Murdoch's "unguarded utterances,"[78] but he may have believed what he wanted to believe. Murdoch, who saw the whole influence of the government being exerted against him through all sorts of channels, and who watched helplessly as a powerful section of the mercantile body stooped to every species of trickery to elect Deblois, was certain that these efforts were more than enough to defeat him. There is more than a suspicion that Howe, despite his growing awareness of below-the-surface forces, still underestimated their strength.

The sprawling county of Halifax provided the real drama as it engaged in one of the most celebrated of all Nova Scotian election contests. Because it still included the districts of Colchester and Pictou within its limits, strikingly heterogeneous interests sought, at sundry times and places, to make themselves felt through the electoral process. At the very outset of polling in Halifax the voters clearly identified Lawrence Hartshorne, J.L. Starr, Henry Blackadar, and John A. Barry, who formerly represented the township of Shelburne, as the council's candidates for the four seats. To Howe this was a matter of regret, perhaps because he disliked anything that savoured of party, but mostly because the result was to injure Hartshorne.[79] When he went further and suggested that Hartshorne had not realized he would be regarded as part of a team, he must have stretched the credulity of his readers to the breaking-point.[80]

Opposing the pro-council slate were three of the sitting members for the county of Halifax, S.G.W. Archibald, William Lawson, and George Smith, and a newcomer, Jotham Blanchard of the *Colonial Patriot*. At the outset Howe favoured the return of the four sitting members, even though it meant withholding his support from Blanchard in favour of Hartshorne. As polling progressed, it became evident that three of the four anti-council candidates would be returned, but almost to the end there remained the possibility that Hartshorne would beat out either Smith or Blanchard for the fourth seat. Because of the strenuous efforts of the merchant–official oligarchy, Hartshorne started out well in Halifax, receiving 978 votes to Blanchard's 265. But the contest changed dramatically when the poll moved to Truro, the bailiwick of Speaker Archibald. Howe was there in person, absolutely revelling in what he saw, and forwarding to Susan Ann the latest state of the poll for inclusion in the *Novascotian*. For four days he watched freeholders on horseback, in gigs, or on foot making their way from Gay's River, Musquodoboit, and Stewiacke to the hustings on the parade ground in front of the courthouse. "The spirit of liberty," he wrote, "brought from the most distant portions of the district a collection of yeomanry, which might be compared with any in the world; and whose independent suffrages were neither to be purchased or controlled."[81] How different the results might have been in the township of Halifax if those who had been so conspicuous in that contest had been required to try their powers of persuasion on people of this mettle. Apparently the election was contributing to Howe's own educative process, for he uttered not a lament when Blanchard polled 1,099 votes to Hartshorne's 104 in the district of Colchester and led his opponent by 282 votes.

So far the election had been peaceful. Since Blanchard was a candidate, it was hardly to be expected that it would remain so when the poll moved to Pictou. There the religious differences between Church of Scotland Highlanders and Free Church or Secessionist Lowlanders (anti-burghers) had been carried over into other spheres including politics, and after Blanchard was denied a hearing on the hustings, the contest quickly developed into politico-religious warfare between Tory Kirkmen and Lowland anti-burghers who sided with the assembly.[82] Howe felt that his subscribers were entitled to his first-hand observations on the proceedings, and although Edmund Ward alleged that he had escaped into the woods and had not been heard of since, he was "upon the Hustings a part of every day, and during the whole week moved about in the crowd, among men of both parties, hearing all opinions, and never disguising [his] own."[83] What he saw went well beyond his wildest imaginings. He noted that, even after the hustings were moved outside the court house, there was nothing like free access to the poll. He watched incredulously as a party of sailors, armed with sticks, carrying the banners of the council's candidates, and led by a stout mulatto, marched to the hustings with some of the Highlanders and then to the public houses of their candidates, where they participated in a riot that led to the death of a man called Irvin. Howe was glad to tell Susan Ann that "the wrong side of politics were the originators of the riot."[84] A little later he saw a group of Kirkmen seize the hustings, where they were not to be dislodged until a strong body of George Smith's supporters were landed from a steamboat.[85]

For Howe this was bad enough, but the conduct of the Kirk ministers, as he himself witnessed it, left him absolutely aghast. On the first day of polling three or four of them mounted the hustings or an adjoining wall and repeatedly harangued the people; in the evenings some of them joined John A. Barry in orating to the people in the taverns.[86] Meanwhile the *Colonial Patriot* was denouncing, in much harsher language, this clerical intervention. The leading Kirk minister, the Rev. Kenneth John McKenzie, sought to defend himself and his colleagues in the *Acadian Recorder*,[87] as did "Friend to High-landers" in the *Free Press*, but neither of them was convincing. Howe told McKenzie he had convicted himself out of his own mouth and that in any part of Nova Scotia but Pictou his conduct would lead to his being "hooted out of the Pulpit he had profaned."[88] Like Blanchard, Howe invited McKenzie to prosecute him for libel; or, if he preferred, let him preach in St Matthew's Church in Halifax, and if he did not have empty pews for a congregation, Howe would confess he had done him wrong.[89]

The Pictou Parsons roused Howe as nothing else did in 1830. Hitherto he had lumped Secessionist and Kirk ministers together, and said "a plague upon both your houses," but the Pictou election caused him to see the Kirk clergymen as the chief villains in the politico-religious disputes in that district. The strength of his feeling reflected, in part, his suspicion of organized religions and their ministers that lasted throughout his life. How unchristian the latter seemed to be compared with the lay preachers of the Sandemanian faith of his father; how sad it was that the Kirk ministers should use their powers of vituperation upon any thing "but the devil, who they ought to remember, has a prior claim to their bad language."[90] Yet their efforts were by no means fruitless, since Hartshorne outpolled Blanchard in the district of Pictou by 142 votes. It was not enough, however; Colchester had ensured that Blanchard would be returned, even though it was by a mere 139 votes. Elatedly, Howe wrote Susan Ann from Pictou: "All the popular members – are in – the triumph is too great for utterance."[91]

By the end of October, when the overall provincial results became known, Howe again rejoiced that the orderly and pacific colony of Nova Scotia had shown its neighbours that, when circumstances demanded, it would willingly make resistance a duty.[92] Only one assemblyman, Murdoch, had lost out because he opposed the council on the revenue question; and only one, Deblois, had been elected on a pledge of submission to the council. Even in Hants, where excepting Halifax the council's influence was greatest, David Dill had won for the popular side, although not without a hard fight. None of the three supporters of the council in the last House survived the election. Uniacke had gone to the bench, and Barry and Hartshorne were beaten in the county of Halifax. At least twenty-nine of the new members would maintain the rights of the assembly at all hazards and, so far as Howe knew, only Deblois might not. It was indeed a very great victory.

In part, Howe saw the result as a triumph for "the Liberal side, that is the real intelligence and independence of the country." With anything but becoming modesty, he also saw it as evidence of the success of himself and his newspaper despite the hostility and abuse of his opponents.

As a natural consequence of my mode of life, and the fearless way in which I carry on the war, I have to put up with about half a dozen columns of abuse from some quarter or other every week. This I look out for – read, – answer – laugh at – and bear like a philosopher – satisfied that while some two or three dozen fellows swear, against their consciences, that I am the greatest liar and rascal in the universe – that the great body of our population think me a very worthy and devilish clever fellow, and believe every word they see in the Nova Scotian as religiously as if it were sworn to by five and forty Bishops.[93]

The praise that was heaped upon him as he travelled throughout Nova Scotia may have gone a little to his head, since even at this early date he was manifesting the touch of arrogance that he displayed every now and then throughout his career. He was right, however, in contending that, but for his thorough reporting of the assembly's debates, Nova Scotians would have been left largely in the dark about the details of the revenue dispute; he was also right in maintaining that the *Novascotian* had got a firm hold on the country and had begun to tell on public opinion. But he was altogether wrong in attaching the momentous significance he did to the revenue dispute and its outcome. The election of 1830 was not fought on the merits of the government structure as such, nor even in opposition to a normal use of the council's powers. At issue was the council's injudicious use of a right, admittedly within its legal power, that seriously disturbed the mutual accommodation which had permitted government to be carried on harmoniously for more than twenty years. Howe and his *Novascotian* did much to marshal the freeholders against the council's action, but in perspective they sought no more than to maintain the rather weak position of the assembly in the existing structure, not to introduce bold new constitutional reforms.

Nonetheless, Howe exulted in his new independence. In future, he would have no fear about annoying the anti-burghers or the Kirkmen, or both, as circumstances dictated, since experience had taught him that for every patron he lost for independence of opinion he gained at least a dozen. In any issue, "the party to which we belong is the *Province of Nova Scotia* – and it will puzzle [the critics] to convict us of a slavish devotion to the measures or opinions of any other."[94] What he did not know was that it would take him another eight years to determine exactly what institutional changes were needed in Nova Scotia to establish the kind of political system he wanted.

CHAPTER SIX

Rambling about
Nova Scotia

More than is commonly supposed, Howe's unique rapport with the Nova Scotia public resulted from the personal contacts he made as he rambled about the province for a few weeks each year. While he did not leave a personal account of his travels through the western counties in 1828, in subsequent years his letters to Susan Ann provide not merely a fascinating description of his varied adventures, but also a highly revealing chronicle of his devotion to his wife, his contacts with Nova Scotians in all walks of life, his views on the state of the province, especially as it affected his own undertakings, and, above all, his general philosophy of life.[1]

In 1829 he delayed his departure from Halifax until the third week in August when the first copies of Thomas Chandler Haliburton's *An Historical and Statistical Account of Nova Scotia* were coming off the *Novascotian* press and becoming available for sale.[2] Partly because he had the marketing of the book in mind, he originally intended to include New Brunswick, Prince Edward Island, Canada, the United States, and eventually Britain in his travels. The eventual route he took was a new one for him, to Truro, Pictou, and Charlottetown; back to Truro and on to Amherst, Saint John, and Fredericton; back to Saint John and on to Boston, New York, and Philadelphia. Harried and ailing when he left, he was, as usual, exhilarated by new places, new people, and new adventures, and before long he could say, "I now feel like myself."[3] Starting out by stage, Howe soon decided that he needed another means of transport if he was to dun his old subscribers and solicit new ones to the best advantage. Accordingly, while in Pictou, he invested in a pony and all the concomitant paraphernalia.

... imagine you see me mounted on a little black Pony about half as big again as myself and sallying out of Pictou on [the way to Truro] ... during the greater part of the hundred miles I rode through the rain – had at night to envelope myself in old shirts, trousers, jackets and buskins, and have my own habilements washed and dried for the morning's toilette – and about an hour ago I pruned away the beard which has been growing luxuriously for four days, and strengthened by the genial showers with which it had been continually moistened.[4]

Susan Ann dreaded seeing him go. His previous year's jaunt through the western counties had been a short one, and she might have had him back in three or four days at any time. In 1829 it was supposedly a six-week trip, but even though he abandoned his plans to go to Canada and by-passed Saint Andrews, it was almost three months before he returned. During that time she had to look after Edward, oversee a newspaper, and satisfy the creditors without having the wherewithal to meet their notes.

Through it all she had no lack of solicitude from her husband. In letter after letter he begged his "little Editor" to keep up her spirits, reminding her that they must both conquer their feelings and do their duty. Since her first child, born in May, had lived only a few days, Howe managed, while in Saint John, to persuade his half-sister Jane to let her daughter Sophia spend the winter months in Halifax to console Susan Ann for "having lost our own dear little Babe."[5] Periodically, as at Truro, he consoled her by explaining how valuable the trip was proving to be:

If I were to do nothing more, I should be well paid for my six weeks trip – as I have got in all 43 new Subscribers for the Paper – the most of whom I know to be men, who as old Oxner told Lord Dalhousie, "*have the responsibilities*" ... There is one thing I am not a little proud of – which is that I can now sit a whole day on a horse's back and feel no more wearied than my neighbors. This is a great point gained – as it enables me to see many things which I should otherwise have to pass ... Already the uttermost parts of the earth seem a great deal nearer than they did. Constantinople appears only about a day's ride off and any place to which there is land all the way seems as though it were within the reach of myself and Poney.[6]

From Saint John he sent the good news that he would not have to go to England during the winter and that "in the spring perhaps we may contrive to leave for the old world together."[7] Arriving in Boston and finding her letters a little despondent, he reminded her that they would soon be together for many months, "for wide and beautiful as the world is, and instructive and interesting as the efforts of human ingenuity and industry may be – they have no charm like the little quiet and retired scenes where our heart's affections are treasured, and where we repose on a bosom whose every heave has a lulling and exquisite power to communicate endurance for the trials, and to administer a higher relish to the pleasures and enjoyments of life."[8]

In part, the year's set of letters to Susan Ann, like all the others, could be labelled "how to run a newspaper and publishing business from a distance." Throughout the trip Howe scanned each number of the *Novascotian* with a critical eye. From Pictou he wrote that "the punctuation is bad in some places and there are a few errors – such as 'draw' for 'drain'";[9] he also cautioned "the Boys" in the printing shop not to let the editorial head begin at the foot of a column.[10] To provide something by way of editorial under the Halifax heading, he completed a short article at Pictou which would "do to keep up the series,"[11] but he found it difficult to send an article every week and he soon decided that "being [but] one week in the 5 without an editorial is no great matter."[12] By the time he got to Saint John he had given up the attempt altogether: "you must put some news in the Editorial columns – I cannot now bend my thoughts to writing. As I shall not go away again this winter I can apologize on my return for the lack of originality."[13]

Old John Howe tried, as best he could, to fill the vacuum and generally Joseph was pleased that he did: "tell him to launch out as much as he pleases. A few good paragraphs from him will cover my retreat famously."[14] But there was one reservation: Susan Ann was to warn him not to "crow too much on the side of the Russians ... as our politics have been rather Turkish."[15] When his father did not heed the advice, Susan Ann was asked to tell him a second time that it would "be better to preserve a tone of consistency – you can give him the hint gently."[16] Joseph exhibited no less solicitude for his father when he learned that the ne'er-do-well of the family, his half-brother David, had come back to Halifax: "David's return has not surprised me at all – he is one of those beings who defy calculation – and who if they were stuck in the sky would puzzle, by their eccentric movements, all the almanack makers who ever existed. I trust he will have some mercy upon our poor father whose health and repose require the soothing attention of all his children – rather than their unkind annoyance."[17] One matter Howe could not deal with was the continued sniping of Edmund Ward. Regretfully he told Susan Ann to ignore him: "I will settle scores with him when I return."[18] But he could not help gloating when he secured thirty new subscriptions, mostly in the town of Pictou; certainly Pictonians did not agree with Ward's assessment of the *Novascotian*.

Howe's heavy investment in Haliburton's *History* was a continuing

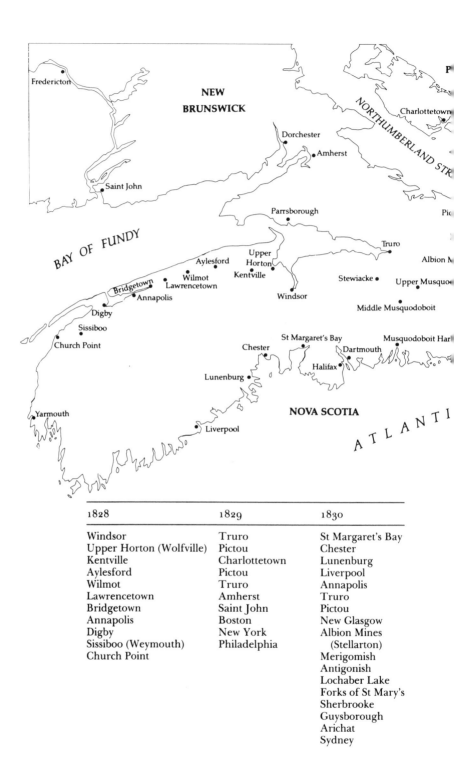

1828	1829	1830
Windsor	Truro	St Margaret's Bay
Upper Horton (Wolfville)	Pictou	Chester
Kentville	Charlottetown	Lunenburg
Aylesford	Pictou	Liverpool
Wilmot	Truro	Annapolis
Lawrencetown	Amherst	Truro
Bridgetown	Saint John	Pictou
Annapolis	Boston	New Glasgow
Digby	New York	Albion Mines
Sissiboo (Weymouth)	Philadelphia	(Stellarton)
Church Point		Merigomish
		Antigonish
		Lochaber Lake
		Forks of St Mary's
		Sherbrooke
		Guysborough
		Arichat
		Sydney

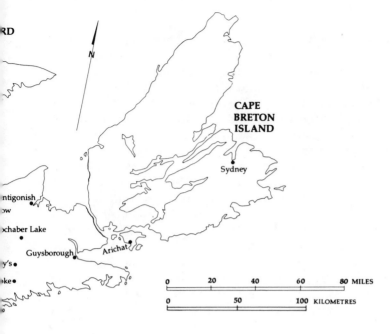

RD

N

CAPE
BRETON
ISLAND

Sydney

ntigonish
ɔw

ɔchaber Lake
•

Guysborough   Arichat

y's •

ɔke •

| 0 | | 20 | | 40 | | 60 | | 80 MILES |

| 0 | | 50 | | 100 KILOMETRES |

OCEAN

JOSEPH HOWE'S RAMBLES 1828–1835

1832	1833	1834	1835
Windsor	Dartmouth	Truro	Musquodoboit Harbour
Kentville	Musquodoboit Harbour	Pictou	Middle Musquodoboit
Bridgetown	Middle Musquodoboit	Charlottetown	Upper Musquodoboit
Digby	Upper Musquodoboit	Miramichi	Stewiacke
Saint John	Forks of St Mary's	Richibucto	Truro
Fredericton	Lochaber Lake	Pictou	Amherst
Dorchester	Antigonish	Merigomish	Windsor
Amherst	Pictou	New Glasgow	Lunenburg
Truro		Antigonish	Liverpool
Pictou		Truro	Windsor
Charlottetown		Amherst	
Pictou		Parrsborough	
		Upper Horton	
		(Wolfville)	
		Kentville	
		Bridgetown	
		Yarmouth	
		Digby	
		Saint John	
		Digby	

preoccupation throughout the trip. At Pictou he told Susan Ann to forward him forty, later fifty, copies to dispose of in that area, but to look around for a cheaper way of sending them since Blanchard, the stage-coach proprietor, had charged him 13s. 2d. for the last box.[19] Later she was to dispatch copies to Liverpool, Windsor, and Cumberland, and to urge Belcher, the binder, to hurry up the books for England, the United States, Canada, and New Brunswick. More than anything else, however, it was the complex transactions surrounding promissory notes that caused both Howe and Susan Ann their greatest concern. At Truro she was to tell him whether her collections were sufficient to meet the bank note; if not, he would make up the deficiency. From Pictou he sent her £15 which, combined with her receipts from other sources, he hoped would permit her to attend to Young's note and the bank's. On his return from Prince Edward Island he forwarded £30 in orders, £2 in gold, and similar instructions. From Saint John he told her to meet a note for £50 by another complex set of transactions; at the same time he exulted that his bank indebtedness would be reduced to £55, not payable until the end of the year.[20] Clearly Susan Ann regarded this manoeuvring with notes as the least pleasant of the burdens placed upon her, but at least she had never a word of complaint from her husband. "I know you will do all for the best, and feel as much satisfied in your judgment as if I were at home."[21]

Howe was to share something of this trip with the general public in the first six "Eastern Rambles," which appeared in the *Novascotian* between December 17, 1829, and February 25, 1830. His readers learned, for example, that the best place to stop for lunch between Halifax and Truro was Hill's near the Stewiacke River, where the traveller would be regaled, not with ham and eggs, broiled fowl, or veal cutlet, but "a fine fresh salmon, that but two hours ago was flashing about through the clear waters of the River"[22] At Truro the place to stay was Squire Blanchard's dwelling with its "bounteous board, handsome accommodation, and a pleasant Veranda, to protect a fellow's head from the evening dews while he puffs his quiet cigar."[23]

But despite an occasional nugget the "Eastern Rambles," like the "Western," are disappointingly dull. The wordy philosophizing does not allow the real Howe to emerge as it does in the warm, affectionate, informative letters to Susan Ann. Thus, in the latter, not in the "Rambles," he discloses how he kept on good terms with both the Kirkmen and the anti-burghers of Pictou. In the morning he went to the Kirk church of the Rev. Kenneth John McKenzie and heard "the famous Mr. Donelly" preach with unpleasing voice, horrible grin, but undoubted fluency; in the afternoon he went to the anti-burgher church and heard the Rev. Mr McKinlay, "dry and pedantic as a pedagogue," preach to a not more numerous but certainly more respectable congregation. With evident satisfaction he told Susan Ann confidentially that Jotham Blanchard "held out the olive branch of peace [at Pictou], if so I can call his five fingers – I of course gave him my hand, and we talked over old offences against each other's tempers and political reputations with the sang froid of a pair of philosophers. I made him confess two things – first, that he did write the Canadian Letter, and secondly that the Patriot was a party paper. This is between you and I remember."[24]

It was on a Sunday, in late May 1830, that Howe started out on the third of his rambles. Because Susan Ann had chided him for travelling on the Sabbath, he sought to convince her in his first letter that the pleasures of that beautiful forenoon did more to strenghten his nobler impulses than any number of pompous sermons might have done. Had he met his worst enemy on the road, perhaps even Edmund Ward, the surliest phrase that he might have drawn from his "bountiful store house of vituperation" would have been a "God speed him."[25] In perhaps the first recorded statement of the depth of his religious feeling he told Susan Ann that

truth – and religion – and philosophy – pass *into the heart* from the constant communing with nature ... my heart was full to overflowing – and sometimes did overflow – with the goodness and mercy of him who created, and has sustained me thus far on the very busy scene of an earthly pilgrimage – amidst many trials and temptations ... and who has crowned these toils and contrives to reward those trials – with a beneficent and bounteous hand – making me every day the object of some mercy, and I trust the humble instrument of some good.[26]

On that Sunday morning on horseback, he continued, he had thought more poetry and concocted more luxurious prose than he could put on paper if he did nothing but write for the next month. "What a pity it is that some apparatus cannot be invented, for catching, without any physical effort, the thoughts and imaginations of the heart, as they rise, at certain times and seasons, with a sort of spring tide exuberance."[27]

Of all Howe's trips through Nova Scotia this was perhaps his longest and most arduous. He started out for Lunenburg by horse, making his way along the shores of St Margaret's Bay, even though it was a route seldom attempted in those days. From the head of the bay to within five or six miles of Chester, he found the road " nothing better than a cow path ... how the Postman gets along in winter the

Lord only knows."[28] On this part of the trip the amenities were no better than the roads. At a house thirteen miles from Chester the only food he could get was a pitcher of milk and some raw cakes, "on which as you may suppose I made a slender repast."[29] At Chester's wretched apology for an inn the smoked salmon would have been tolerable if it had not been for two idiotic children, who kept looking into his face, made all sorts of grimaces, and destroyed his appetite.

From Lunenburg to Liverpool and directly across the province, new territory for him, the journey was much less onerous, although he did apologize to Susan Ann for his handwriting, since "the constant use of the Bridle almost deprives my hand of its cunning in the scribbling way."[30] The roads from Annapolis to Pictou were no mystery for him, but he was again on new ground when he moved further eastward to New Glasgow, Antigonish, and at last Guysborough, where rain, fog, and wind detained him for at least three days. Eventually he was able to make the four hours' boat trip to Arichat and begin his first trip to Cape Breton. Indelibly impressed upon his mind was the condition of the roads on the Island, which he described as "rascally beyond any conception." From Sydney to the Strait, "the horse [was] up to his knees [in mud] the greater part of the way, and sometimes up to his middle,"[31] and he was not surprised when he developed "something of a lumbago" himself.[32]

Through all these wanderings he was, as usual, an acute oberver and learner. Having met a New Brunswick shoemaker with strained ligaments on his way to Lunenburg, "I made him mount my nag ... while I played the pedestrian by the aid of his walking stick. A lame shoemaker is no bad companion on a lonesome road, and one gets stronger insights into life as it is, by such casual companionships."[33] In Lunenburg itself he noted that molasses was used in tea rather than sugar, that women worked like slaves, and that ploughs had two wheels in front, two behind, and were drawn by oxen. At Sydney, where the principal inhabitants gave him a dinner, he noted the presence of Edmund Ward's brother, the sheriff of the Island, and clearly a much more respectable man than Edmund.

As in 1829, Howe cast a critical eye on the *Novascotian* whenever it came to hand. After seeing a copy at Guysborough, he wrote, "I am not much missed,"[34] but at Pictou he was not so congratulatory: "the last two articles [of mine] were wretchedly printed,"[35] and he insisted that any article of his be as "correct as possible – a small error may make parts of it very ridiculous."[36] He continued to find it difficult to keep up a regular flow of articles, and to excuse their absence, he involved Susan Ann in a mild deception: she was to inform the *Novascotian*'s readers that a great variety of interesting selections had been deferred for some time and then fill up the normal editorial space with articles from any source she found fruitful.[37]

Howe's letters to Susan Ann in 1830 were most significant because of the political context in which they were written. During the Brandy Dispute he had prophesied dire results for rural dwellers if they were deprived of the cash payments they received from road and bridge work, but little did he realize how badly he himself would be affected. At Lunenburg he collected only £6 of the £27 he was owed, and although he managed to secure "six good rich Granville farmers to take the place of a few of the bad subjects in Lunenburg,"[38] his collections were well below expectation. Regretfully he told Susan Ann he had no choice but to travel to the eastward. But there his luck was no better even though Priest Grant on the Gulf Shore gave him a bottle of good wine and a promise to have his bill paid in town. "I got into Antigonish after a ride of 50 miles, without collecting a dollar – having only the satisfaction of knowing that my money was perfectly safe – although the want of it for the present subjects me to inconvenience."[39] While his trip to Cape Breton permitted him to add twenty new subscribers to his list, two for every one he knew to be bad, it brought nothing in the way of cash payments. So, "incredibly homesick" though he was, he extended his trip still further and went to Prince Edward Island. Since his meagre collections were all needed for living expenses, he had to devise a strategy for dealing with the two notes falling due at the bank early in July, one for £75 and another for £25. Susan Ann was simply to discount a note he had drawn against Haliburton in the sum of £55, and with the proceeds pay off the smaller of his own notes and apply £25 to the second.[40] But although the financial picture was gloomy, he discovered, as noted earlier, that his articles having silenced the council's few friends, "the feeling in favour of our politics is universal."[41]

Howe's preoccupation with the election of 1830 meant that the last of his sixteen "Eastern Rambles" did not reach the public eye until October 19, 1831. As usual, they provided a wealth of information on all sorts of subjects. If a traveller wanted good accommodation he should stay at a place like Copeland's at French River, which would provide him with "a clean bed, a good cup of tea, a hot johnny cake, and excellent butter with perhaps a saucer of preserves";[42] if he wanted the details of the Seven Years' War or the merits of Frederick the Great, he should put up at Squire Christian Miller's establishment in Guysborough, since its proprietor's knowledge of these subjects was such as was "not stored up in any other head in the Province of Nova Scotia";[43] but if the traveller simply wanted sheer beauty, nothing could rival the quiet loneliness of Lochaber Lake. While the last of the "Rambles" are somewhat less artificial and rhetorical, and much more factual than the earlier ones, in interest and warmth they still pale in comparison with the letters to Susan Ann.

If Howe did any extensive rambling in 1831, the record is silent on that score. By late June 1832, however, he was on his travels again. This time he followed a familiar route which had the merit of permitting the greatest access to old and prospective subscribers – down the Annapolis Valley to Digby, across the Bay of Fundy to Saint John, up the Saint John Valley to Fredericton, then to Dorchester, Amherst, Truro, and Pictou, across Northumberland Strait to Charlottetown, back to Pictou, and home. On none of his rambles did he find the weather more "villainous" than this one, and on more than one occasion he was its victim. At Windsor, having finished his business on a Saturday, he had intended to walk the twenty-five miles to Kentville until Haliburton and Murdoch, both in Windsor at the time, warned him of "the scandal [he] should create by journeying on the Sabbath past half a thousand persons going to and from church."[44] But when he set out on Monday, it began to rain and he had to walk five miles before he found suitable shelter; he ended up beneath a haystack reading the *Athenaeum* and writing twenty lines of a poem to Susan Ann. But the worst weather of all occurred during a schooner passage from Pictou to Charlottetown lasting two nights. In the same boat was Jane Blanchard of Pictou, who had been troubled with indigestion and retchings, and whose friends felt a sea voyage would do her good. As the schooner knocked about on the Gulf, Howe said she was sicker "than I ever wish to see a poor devil again."[45] Yet somehow or other, he managed to finish his verses to Susan Ann during the passage: "They are not perhaps worthy of the subject – but ... some of the poetry is as good as any I have ever written or can write."[46]

Eventually the bad weather and fatigue took their toll even of Howe's robust constitution; on his way back to Truro from Pictou, he fell victim to a "devilish dysentery, which has plagued me beyond measure ... weakening me faster than all the nourishment I took gave me strength."[47] For his ailment he tried several remedies, including a concoction of brandy and sugar, and a prescription of Titus Smith, the land surveyor, that was based on the premise that his sickness was caused by a rich diet taken into an abnormally weak stomach. Because the treatment called for a diet that contained little nourishment but would fill up the stomach, Howe told Susan Ann a little sadly that someone else would have to eat the oysters and custard she had sent him.

Many of Howe's letters to Susan Ann between 1828 and 1836 are undated and are therefore difficult at times to sort out. But those for 1832 are easy to identify because of their repeated references to "Baby." Ellen, the second of his children and the first to survive, had been born in December 1830. Writing from Windsor, Howe told Susan Ann he missed "poor Baby terribly, and [would] give a dollar for a kiss of the dear little soul."[48] Nothing but stern duty forced him to go to Charlottetown and detained him from seeing his "poor little Baby, whose cheerful face I do shortly want to see again."[49] Even seldom-mentioned Edward made two appearances in the letters this year. From Bridgetown Howe wrote: "tell Edward I expect to hear that he has been a very good Boy – make him write me a letter."[50] Later Susan Ann was told to send him, with a small Murray's Grammar and as much clothing as she could get together, to Truro, where there was a teacher who was especially good at a particular branch of knowledge, but she "need not say to any one but Father what is the object of his visit."[51] This suggests that Edward was perhaps becoming hard to handle. Throughout the trip Howe was in constant fear that cholera morbus would make an appearance in Halifax, brought by boat from Europe, and more than once he wrote, "Thank God you are all well – and *no cholera yet*."[52]

Naturally one who was continually in debt to the Halifax Banking Company would await with interest the setting up of a second bank, the Bank of Nova Scotia, but Howe's letters this year showed an almost naïve faith in the virtues of competitive banking: "I wish from my heart they would [open for business], and relieve the country from its troubles."[53] Not till he arrived at Pictou, however, did he learn that the new bank had finally got under way. In the collection of subscriptions, the main object of his ramble, he fared badly at the start. At Windsor he discovered that his agent Bowes had "collected nearly every farthing due, and walked off before I came."[54] In Cornwallis his agent Holland had made hardly any collections at all; in both Wolfville and Bridgetown he borrowed a horse and rode in one direction and another, but gained little other than information. Nevertheless, he decided to "stick to [it] and screw out of them all that can be had,"[55] and, surprisingly, his collections later improved. From Fredericton he sent £20, and it would have been more if he had dared to put it in one bundle; from Truro he forwarded £25; and in Charlottetown he made "a handsome collection," including £29 in Spanish dollars: "do not spend or pay them, if you can help," he told Susan Ann; if she did, she was to demand a five per cent premium: "they are worth that."[56] Above all, she was to husband their resources to take care of other notes that would soon fall due: "do not pay any money to any body but the Bank until I return."[57]

As was his wont, he kept a close eye on the *Novascotian* and the printing business. He was pleased that Bill, one of the shop "boys," had reached the seventh sheet of Beamish Murdoch's *Epitome of the Laws*, which Howe was printing under contract.[58] Perhaps because of bad weather, he was more successful than usual in completing articles on the road. As a result, in three successive numbers of the *Novascotian* starting on July 4, 1832, Susan Ann was able to present his observations on Windsor, Kings county, and Annapolis county. On his return home he added two further articles, dealing principally with New Brunswick and Prince Edward Island. But the five articles, all published under the heading "Letters from the Interior," are almost entirely descriptive, and make little attempt at fine writing or philosophizing, although they do demonstrate that little missed his eye. In Windsor he was fascinated by a freak storm, producing hailstones an inch long, which sent horses scampering in all directions. In Kings county he noted an immense run of fish up the Cornwallis River, and the catching of shad by the thousands and herrings by the million. While he did not want to "impugn the merciful doings of Providence," was it not a pity that "a people ... so bountifully supplied *by land* ... should be sent [these] by water?"[59] In Annapolis county a farmer told him that the buttercups that dotted his fields were not a menace since the butter made from the milk of cows that fed on them had a deep yellow colour that commanded a high price on the market.[60] Although some of this information may have been old wives' tales, he was always adding to the store of knowledge that would give him an advantage over all his rivals, editors or politicians, in the years to come.

In 1833 Howe's rambles were especially significant because they acquainted him with the people of the Musquodoboit Valley who were shortly to play an important role in his life. The beginning of the trip was not auspicious. Some time in September he turned off the Preston highway and found himself battling an absolutely villainous road. For a time it appeared as if the world had once been covered by a sea of granite which had hardened "when the winds were highest and the billows the most turbulent."[61] Later the road became just as soft as it had been hard, and his horse was soon mired, throwing him first upon his neck and then upon his back. In late afternoon he arrived at Stewart's at the lower end of Musquodoboit, and was surprised to discover "the strange fellow," who was a relative of George Renny Young, and whom the Youngs were boarding in this out-of-the-way place to get rid of him. Though urged to stay for the night, Howe decided to press on for another five miles and was "deadly mistaken." Twice his horse went through an old bridge and was extricated with its "shins and thighs ... sadly rubbed and scarified." Eventually he reached a miserable cabin where he "spent the evening listening to the complaints of a peevish old man, and the night in furnishing food to a million of fleas."[62]

In contrast, the next day, Sunday, was one of immense enjoyment. By 10 o'clock he had arrived at Logan's in Middle Musquodoboit, and while Mrs Logan stayed at home to cook a magnificent pair of ducks, her husband drove Howe to the meeting house where he was "a lion for the day." Not only did he meet some old acquaintances and correspondents, but because "our politics agreed" not a few "friends, countrymen and lovers." The pastor of the Presbyterian community was the Rev. John Sprott, who became a continuing correspondent of Howe over the next few decades. "A rough being, of some education and talent," he strayed – at least Howe thought he did – into the "wide ocean of theology without compass or chronometer."[63] Henry Gladwin, who would cross Howe's path politically before long, was absent in Halifax but there was much head-shaking about him. By general agreement he would not succeed as a farmer because he used the English system; in other words, he did no manual work himself.

The next day Howe rode on to Upper Musquodoboit, where he stayed with the Annand brothers, whose commodious, attractive house was matched only by those of Speaker Archibald in Truro and Assemblyman George Smith in Pictou. Their fine farm was just beginning to be profitable, and with proper prudence they were well on the road to being independent. Howe sized up the elder brother, William, with whom he would be associated in business and politics for thirty years, as "an industrious and enthusiastic farmer," while the younger, James, seemed "less fond [of farming] but conforming to the circumstances around him."[64]

Howe had intended to go to St Mary's by the so-called Musquodoboit Road, through thirty miles of wilderness seldom traversed by anyone, and although many laughed at him, he went anyway, after Adams Archibald offered to accompany him half way. The route was as bad as had been prophesied, particularly the last fifteen miles, and for once Howe could neither reflect nor dream because the roughness of the road kept him constantly on the alert to protect himself and his horse. It was with a sigh of relief that he finally emerged on the west branch of the St Mary's River, where he put up at Archibald's establishment at the Forks. Delayed there by bad weather, he got in some fishing and hunting, bringing down six partridge in an hour, three with one shot. "I wish I had been near enough or had [some] conveyance by which they could have been sent to you," he wrote to Susan Ann.[65]

In continuing to Antigonish, Howe made a fascinating diversion by canoe across Lochaber Lake to the home of a former Glasgow man named Brown, uncle of Stayley Brown of Yarmouth. Much about the household interested or pleased him: the remnants of some decent furniture and excellent books and papers; the plastering of the walls with *Novascotians* – a unique way of "perpetuating and extending my words"; the five Brown daughters who filled his pockets with cake and maple sugar as he departed. Although the house was uncomfortable because every room smoked, the Browns were making progress even without money, and they provided a moral for Howe:

You would be astonished to see how the poor settlers in the country live ... and [how they] do without that great indispensible agent of the towns – Money ... Butter, grains, cattle, potatoes, and where they live near brooks and rivers logs are their common mediums ... You may depend I borrow some lessons of content from these people – some inducements to perseverance and activity in a walk of life more laborious to the mind perhaps (although that I doubt) but certainly not so harrassing to the body.[66]

When Howe reached Antigonish and got down to the main purpose of his ramble, he found that economic recession had begun to set in just as in Halifax. "Money," he told Susan Ann, "is as scarce in the country as in town." In Pictou he fared equally badly: "the only thing that reconciles me to all the trouble, is that the little I may get will be of essential service," He sent £5 to Susan Ann in case it was badly needed, "but if you can keep it don't spend or pay one dollar."[67] For once, he thought it useless to prolong his journey; he did not go to Prince Edward Island at all, and made only a short foray into the Annapolis Valley.

Things were to get a good deal worse before they got better, and running through all of Howe's letters to Susan Ann in 1834 is a sense of unease, almost of foreboding, seldom relieved by the light-heartedness of the past. Even the old zest for seeing new people and new places was largely muted. At a time when other businesses in Halifax were collapsing, he pondered the possibilities of a similar fate for his own. In the happier days of 1832 he had established himself in more commodious quarters,[68] but in altered circumstances the heavy mortgage payments became an almost unbearable burden. For a while he had pondered whether he should make the trip at all. It seemed imperative, on the one hand, that he betake himself to the road and gather every penny he could from his agents and subscribers. On the other hand, the complexity of his financial affairs demanded the close personal attention that Susan Ann would find it difficult to give if, at the same time, she was to superintend the publication of the *Novascotian* and look after the family. The latter duty was, in fact, becoming a full-time occupation in itself since a sister for Ellen, Mary, had been born in November 1832, and another child was expected during the summer of 1834.

Nonetheless, Susan Ann agreed that he had no alternative but to go, and towards the end of April he left home for seven weeks in which he pressed himself as on no other trip. In reporting from Truro on May 27, he said he had been in the saddle from 5 a.m. to 8 p.m. the previous day. "I could do more, but the horse must be saved a little."[69] He made sure, too, that his route would take in a large proportion of his clientele: Truro, Pictou, by boat to Miramichi and Prince Edward Island, and back to Pictou; New Glasgow, Antigonish, and back to Truro; Amherst, Parrsborough, and by packet to Horton; down the Annapolis Valley to Yarmouth; across the Bay of Fundy to Saint John and back to Halifax through the Annapolis Valley.

Everywhere his gleanings were slim, compared with the amounts due him. Four days in Miramichi brought him only £3. On Prince Edward Island he collected £4, along with £28 10s. in Island money, which would be difficult to convert without a substantial discount. He did no better in "ransacking" the western counties. "I have fared as miserably to the west as to the east," he told Susan Ann.[70] Even his agents were a matter of no little concern, except for T.C. Allen of Miramichi, who had put £15 or £20 of subscriptions into the hands of lawyers to collect. Elsewhere there were problems: at Richibucto J.W. Weldon had mixed up the £12 he had collected with his post office accounts; at Antigonish R.N. Henry's collections of £20 would not be forthcoming until his son's return; while R. Murray of Merigomish promised him £11 by an early post. More than once Howe inquired anxiously of Susan Ann if she had heard from R.M. Cutler of Guysborough, Thomas Jost of Sydney, or H.G. Farrish of Yarmouth, hoping against hope that they had provided something to meet the obligations that were coming due.

Back of these inquiries was the fear that the Halifax banks might not renew one of his notes or might fail to discount a note drawn in his favour. From Miramichi, whence he could send no remittance – "but for the life of me, I could not help it"[71] – he told Susan Ann that she would have the whole of his father's note for £80 at her disposal. Later he learned with relief that she had renewed this note and others without difficulty. As usual, despite her condition, she proved to be the good steward, so much so that at Bridgetown he told her he would not multiply directions, but leave her to be guided by her experience of his affairs and her own good sense.[72] But because of the succession of business crises in Halifax, he did ask her several times to let him know "all the *on dits* – political or commercial, that I may judge exactly how things are moving."[73]

Yet throughout his letters there runs a feeling of guilt that Susan Ann had been left to "struggle with so much at a time when [she was] so little equal to it."[74] He made no effort to hide his worries resulting from her continued sickness during pregnancy and the common deaths of healthy women. "Some persons would not mention these things to you at all – but we are not children – and our feelings and thoughts have always been too freely communicated, for us to have many that are not shared in common."[75] In whatever way he could he showed his solicitude and sought to allay her fears. When delayed at Miramichi, he composed verses for her: "the poetry may not be very good, but I make no apology for the sentiment."[76] On another occasion he assumed an optimism that he did not feel and that the reality of the situation did not warrant. Learning of the difficulties of Thomson and Fulton, whose note he had backed for a large amount, he told her that both were good men who would not leave him in the lurch. Indeed, when their notes and the small ones he had backed for his half-brother Joseph Austen were settled, he would have little to burden him, for those connected with his own business were comparatively light.

... when I compare my own lot with that of almost any young man whom we know I have great reason to rejoice rather than complain – and even now, notwithstanding all the panic and stagnation around us, if circumstances had not compelled us to do in a shorter time what I proposed to do gradually, we should scarcely have felt the least inconvenience. Though a fagging, and beginning as we did, an anxious business – there is more certainty and less risk in ours than in any I know.[77]

He was more than distressed that Susan Ann was having to bear such a large part of the burden. But before long, knowing what their industry and attention to duty would earn for them, they would look back upon their present anxieties, labour, and separation without regret. "May God in his mercy ever watch over and keep one who has been the dream of my youth, and the Partner and Soother of manhood's cares – and with whom I hope to pass many years of happiness to ourselves, and usefulness to our little country."[78]

Such were the character and spirit of the letters that Howe wrote to Susan Ann between his twenty-fifth and thirtieth years. From them there emerges a picture of an ideal relationship. But they also portray the Howe who at times was forced to endure the rudest of conditions and consort with the most uncultivated and perhaps the most depraved of men. Like his life as an apprentice, these associations may have played their part in developing the less genteel, sometimes vulgar side of a man who adapted his language and behaviour to the company he was keeping. But perhaps the letters are most significant in helping to explain Howe's success in a political career which, at the time, he did not know he was to pursue. Certainly they demonstrate how he got to know every nook and cranny of the province better than any Nova Scotian of his day or perhaps any day. They explain how, in the assembly, he could often speak at a moment's notice and with greater detail than the local member on the roads and bridges of any part of the province. They indicate how he acquired the background that enabled him to talk knowledgeably on the prospects of farming, fishing, mining, or commercial pursuits in every locality in Nova Scotia. They also show how he was able, when he wished, to fill his writings with lyrical descriptions of the beauties of his native province; he had, after all, seen Blomidon, Lochaber Lake, and the Bras-d'or's under all sorts of conditions.

Above all, his rambles were to make it possible for him, later on the hustings, to embellish his speeches with allusions by the score to local events and people, and help to produce the remarkable rapport that developed between him and his audiences. Much later, people who had never seen him would have pointed out to them a spring at which he watered his horse. A large apple tree on the Waterman farm at Pleasant river, Queens county, would come to be known as "the Joe Howe tree," because he liked to sit under it and admire a long stretch of the river,[79] and the story would be repeated many times. As for Howe himself, he was a Nova Scotia patriot even before he saw much of the province. His rambles simply confirmed and reinforced his "Nova Scotia-ness."

CHAPTER SEVEN

Promoting the Spirit
of the Age

The Howe who took over joint ownership of the *Acadian* in 1827 had few of this world's goods, by his own estimate perhaps less than £5. Yet within the year, "having some trust in Providence – and ... a modest reliance on my own head and hands,"[1] he assumed even heavier burdens: an obligation to pay George Renny Young £210 during each of five years for the *Novscotian*, and the responsibilities of a married man. His first year with the *Novascotian* left his optimism undimmed. Because he was unknown to his subscribers, and uncertain of his ability to keep his paper up to its former standard, he feared he might lose a hundred subscribers; instead he gained almost that many. He had also done twice as much job printing as he had expected, and in mid-1829 his confidence knew no bounds: "I have been printing 3,000 copies of Haliburton's History of the Province by which I shall clear a handsome sum, so that, all things considered, I have great reason to be thankful, as I believe few who began with nothing have done more in a year and a half. I now feel no apprehension but what I shall, in a few years, realize a permanent perhaps, handsome independence. I work hard and live frugal and have no debts that I cannot meet when they are due, and none that in good time I cannot extinguish."[2]

From his earliest days on the *Acadian* he had conceived it the duty of a newspaper publisher to promote the rise of a provincial literature. So it was not primarily with the hope of financial gain that he had undertaken the publishing of Haliburton's two-volume *History*. To print and circulate this work was, in his opinion, particularly important because of the abysmal ignorance about Nova Scotia, especially in England. Earlier, in commenting on the *History*, he had told his readers that "the pursuits of Literature cannot for many years be profitable in the Colonies, therefore it behooves us to make them *honorable*."[3] He was therefore delighted that the House of Assembly united to a man in congratulating Haliburton on the eve of publication of his work. Though a duller book is hard to imagine, Howe's natural ebullience led him to unwarranted enthusiasm about its possibilities. His English agent told him frankly it would not sell in Britain, but he preferred to go along with "the very sanguine anticipations" of his friend Richard Smith, who had persuaded him that a large number of copies would be needed in London.[4] So certain was he of its success that he not only assumed the full financial responsibility for printing it, but actually increased the size of the imprint in mid-stream, thereby delaying its publication another month or two.[5]

When Howe left on his second ramble in August 1829, he took with him the first copies off the press, and Susan Ann sent him additional copies as he needed them. In Nova Scotia the sales seemed to be good enough,[6] but by the time he returned from Boston in November, he was "sick with dispepsia, and anxiety."[7] That had been long enough to convince him that there was no market for the work in the United States; a few months later he knew the same was true of Britain, and even of Scotland, where Oliver & Boyd of Edinburgh had sold few copies. "I did suppose that ... a work [about New Scotland] would command an extensive sale in Scotland,"[8] he wrote disappointedly. Admittedly, the *History* was wretchedly bound and the engravings were poor, but that did not account for its failure to sell. Even a cursory examination ought to have sufficed to show that it could have little interest beyond Nova Scotia. Howe himself called it "a ruinous speculation. It cumbered my office for two years, involved me in heavy expenses for wages, and in debts for paper, materials, binding and engraving."[9] In all, he was left with about a thousand copies on his hands, many of them scattered about in Saint John, Boston, New York, Quebec, London, and Edinburgh, almost unsaleable. In most cases the sales did not meet the shipping costs and even when its price was cut to ten shillings, it remained a drug on the market. Towards the end of the thirties Howe made a final accounting of the *History*, and calculated that his total outlay had been £1,173 and his total receipts, including £280 in cash advanced by Haliburton, £855.[10] This was the beginning of the financial difficulties which were to plague him for the rest of his life.

His early ventures with similar works were not so disastrous, although on net he was undoubtedly the loser. In 1831 he printed with pleasure *The Witch of the Westcot; A Tale of Nova-Scotia in Three Cantos; and Other Waste Leaves of Literature*, the work of his friend Andrew Shiels, the Bard of Elenvale, whose poetry he often lauded in the *Novascotian*. In April 1832 he completed publication of the Rev. Robert Cooney's history of northern New Brunswick and the Gaspé with the cryptic comment: "hard work to get money."[11] In the same year and the following one he printed four volumes in two of the *Epitome of the Laws*, the work which was to make Beamish Murdoch "the Blackstone of Nova Scotia." Forced to take notes for £460, he did not receive a final payment until 1850. During the same period he was also printing pamphlets, one of which was a true labour of love, a 77-page *Letter on the Doctrine of Personal Assurance*, the only work of his father ever to see the light of day.[12] Apparently Howe suffered little or no loss on the pamphlets since he printed them under contract. Only once did he think about printing a text book; in 1830 he took a flyer and bought the stereotype plates of Emerson's *Grammar and Arithmetic* at an unstated cost, but he could never use them to advantage.[13]

Howe found other ways of getting into financial difficulties, although not always through his own fault. When James Spike, his partner on the *Acadian*, could not meet his share of the payments, Howe had to assume his indebtedness of £57 to the Minns estate. Howe's letters and records tell the story of his intricate financial dealings with his half-brother Joseph Austen which, although they defy unravelling, were certainly not to Howe's advantage. When Austen failed, his creditor Howe had to take payment in debts owing to him, on which it was difficult to realize anything like their full value. But Howe had no regrets since Austen had backed his note for £250 when he first entered business, and, unlike Harry Austen, had given him his active aid and sympathy on other occasions.[14] Somewhat less explicable was Howe's endorsement of a note for £300, which Messrs Thomson and Fulton of Truro had drawn in favour of Samuel Cunard.[15] Perhaps the best excuse is that both were honourable men who had more than ample means to meet their obligations. But the economic crisis of 1834 was no respecter of persons and Thomson and Fulton were themselves entrapped in its tentacles. On his rambles, Howe kept reassuring his wife that they would be able to pay Cunard, but he was no less worried than the pregnant Susan Ann whose fears he was seeking to allay. "[In the end] I had to assume and pay Thomson and Fulton's note to Cunard for £300," he wrote. "Simple interest on this sum to 1859, 27 years would be £486. At compound interest, which I paid thereafter on the obligations incurred to pay this debt it cannot amount to less than £1200."[16]

As he renewed and renegotiated his notes at the bank, desperately trying to satisfy his creditors and enable him to carry on, he more than once regretted a decision made in the full flush of optimism when the *Novascotian* was on its way to becoming the leading provincial newspaper. In 1832 he had purchased the substantial property of Alexander Murison directly opposite Province House, and in these commodious quarters the *Novascotian* was printed for the first time on December 27. Later Howe would admit that he had moved altogether too precipitately: "1832 ... 27th Dec. of this year took possession of Murison's property on Granville Street – £1500 – expended £824 in all next summer mortgaged it for £1200. Sinking so large an amount in property hampered me for years."[17]

Some critics have suggested that Howe's financial misadventures flowed naturally from his inability to comprehend any figures but figures of speech. In fact, Howe fully understood his financial position at any one time, and rationally calculated his future prospects; further, he possessed some of the major Puritan qualities, especially industry and frugality, which sanctified the acquisitive spirit. But other facets of his make-up sometimes overbalanced these qualities. The ebullient optimism that was particularly characteristic of his early life caused him to purchase the Murison property before he had firmly established himself; his strong feeling that it was the duty of a printer to promote the cultural development of his constituency induced him to publish at his own expense literary works that were high financial risks; his belief in mutual self-help led him to believe that, if he expected accommodation from others in meeting his financial obligations, he must be prepared to return the favour.

Despite these losses, Howe's financial difficulties would have been minimal had he been able to realize on his assets. Thus in 1835 the sum of £3,923 was owing to him in subscriptions, of which he considered only £440 to be uncollectible. During the period of economic distress between 1833 and 1835 he therefore regarded his rambles less as a pleasure jaunt than as a means of putting the screws on subscribers who might not otherwise pay. Occasionally one of his agents would take legal action against the delinquents, but although Howe did not rebuke him, he could not bring himself to follow the same course. When he gave up the *Novascotian*, he placed the unpaid accounts in the hands of lawyer Peter Lynch, instructing him to write those in arrears, but to take no further action without instructions. The outcome might have been anticipated. Delinquents in receipt of letters approached Howe, who would then ask his lawyer to stay proceedings against one because he was "honest but poor," or "too good a fellow to press," another because he "had a large family," and still another because Howe "knew their father or mother, wives, sisters or aunts." "[In the end] I went to see him," wrote Lynch " ... and said to him what's the use of writing to those people you are only

putting yourself to expenses for nothing, and they availing themselves of your good nature. His reply was, Oh don't bother any more
about them. I know the fellows are fooling me but I can't press them ...
If they pay me well and good and if not I can do without it."[18] Probably
it made no difference, for, as Howe himself once said, the more
money he had the better it was for those in need. "A man's poverty, a
woman's tears or a child's impotency ever enlisted his sympathies and
invoked his aid."[19] The son of old John Howe came naturally by it.

By 1832 Howe had established what might be termed his normal
pattern of publication. Early each year he would exult in the
performance of the *Novascotian* during the preceding twelve months;
then, a week or two before the legislature was to meet, he would
present his own views on the major questions of the day. Once the
assembly was in session he had time only to report its debates, but
after prorogation he would turn to the books, magazines, pamphlets,
and newspapers that had been accumulating on his desk, and
compose articles, perhaps more accurately summaries, from the
material which interested him. For a time these activities might be
interrupted by a ramble through Nova Scotia and the adjacent
provinces. Later, after time for reflection, he would review the past
session, singling out its shortcomings.[20] Perhaps over-stating the fact,
one writer has said that with these legislative reviews "the political
literature of Canada begins."[21]

To the reporting of the debates Howe gave a high priority, even
though it was the most arduous of chores. For a while his predecessor
at the *Novascotian*, George Young, had issued a half-sheet twice a
week to provide a full and fresh account of the debates, but later his
reports were only intermittent; the *Acadian Recorder* printed nothing
more than an occasional summary of the assembly's proceedings;
while Edmund Ward of the *Free Press*, said Howe scornfully,
"promised year after year to report the debates, *breaking his word per
annum*."[22] In contrast, Howe's reports were "incomparably the best in
his time and when they first appeared in 1828 broke all precedent for
length."[23] For him it meant almost constant attendance in the
assembly, taking notes under conditions of crowding and jostling,
perhaps using the top of his hat as a desk. Even more onerous were
the long nights he spent in writing out the speeches, partly from
notes, partly from memory, perhaps after an interval of a week or
more. No wonder he was elated when these chores ended for a time,
and he was "no longer constrained like a Tanner's horse, to one
unvarying round."[24]

From the beginning Howe laid down the general rule that he

would "report speeches which are either valuable in regard to matter or felicitous in expression, as accurately and at as great length as our notes and the limits of our paper will allow, but we claim to be the sole judge in this matter."[25] After seven years he willingly admitted all the shortcomings of his reporting: "We do not pretend to say that a tenth part of what was said has been reported, or that all the business done has been regularly noticed – neither do we for a moment wish to convey the impression that what has gone forth is free from error and imperfection. Reports taken by one hand and published in a weekly sheet, must necessarily be meagre and inaccurate."[26] Howe foresaw difficulties from those members, present in all assemblies, "who, from a fondness for the sound of their own voices, would themselves kill a Reporter per week."[27] Clearly he had John A. Barry in mind, and he gave short shrift to Barry's complaints about incomplete reporting. But when Beamish Murdoch alleged that no one, least of all the colonial secretary, could possibly judge the sentiments of members from the garbled reports in the *Novascotian*, Howe's reply was both elaborate and indignant. In his unkindest cut, he suggested that if the colonial secretary had difficulty in determining the real sentiments of Murdoch, it would be due not to faulty reporting but to Murdoch's frequent changes of position, all of which he exposed in detail.[28]

Generally, however, Howe's reporting drew little criticism, even though he continuously increased its volume: from 75 columns in 1828 to 90 in 1829 and 172 in 1834, or 43 entire pages of the *Novascotian*. Since he alone reported the debates systematically he could boast with some reason that, without them, "the country would have been left in almost total ignorance of the measures urged and the sentiments avowed in the Assembly, and have been about as incapable of judging of the conduct of their Representatives, as if they had assembled in the moon."[29] He could also point out that in seven years of reporting he had written as much manuscript as he could carry. At the same time, in educating the public he had been educating himself. By this time no assemblyman knew more than he about the problems that confronted the assembly, and no one appreciated more than he the prevailing ethos of the assembly and the strengths and foibles of individual assemblymen. His sense of history also led him to suggest that his accounts of the debates would provide succeeding generations with "valuable data from which to judge of the character and sentiments of the present age, and of the early habits and condition of the country."[30] In this instance he prophesied even better than he knew.

Throughout these years the *Novascotian* continued to reflect the basic attitudes of the *Acadian* of 1827 and the *Novascotian* of 1828. As the year 1829 began, Howe rejoiced that few Nova Scotians wished they had been raised in another soil, "however diversified and fruitful the surface – or genial the rays by which it may be warmed."³¹ In mid-1831 he expatiated even more eloquently that "at no time since its first settlement, did the Province present an aspect of so much promise as ... at present."³² Agriculture had been crowned with unprecedented plenty and in Halifax every proprietor on the waterfront from the Lumber Yard to the Dock Yard was constructing a stone warehouse or a store of some magnitude. Not surprisingly, he turned with vehemence on any detractors of the province, even on William Cobbett, whose writings had given him the idea for his "Rambles," and whom he still regarded as "one of the wonders of this wonderful age." Cobbett's fault was to characterize British North America as "a barren desert – a howling wilderness, where sterility is the parent of starvation," and to single out Nova Scotia as consisting of "heaps of rocks, covered with fir-trees, for the greater part, with a few narrow strips of clear land in the bottoms of the valleys." This was altogether too much for Howe, who told Cobbett that his disregard of truth, his want of fixed principles, and his glaring inconsistencies, would have made "shipwreck of even a more commanding genius." Was he not aware that "thousands of bushels of corn, such as he is trying to ripen in his garden in England, are grown every year on the worst lands of the bleak and barren North American Colonies."³³

Likewise, his admiration for the contributions of Britain and Britons had in no whit diminished: the language which, "like a noble stream, has come rolling onwards, from the days of the Saxon Heptarchy, down to the present time"; the truths of natural, moral, and political science that were taught by Britain's statesmen and philosophers; the impassioned eloquence of her orators and the lofty inspiration of her poets. For Howe, they were "a free gift from the founders of the British empire ... and are as much the property of a Briton by the banks of the Avon, the Hillsborough, or the St. John, as by the Liffey, the Tweed or the Thames ... long after the [critics of Britain] have gone to their accounts ... Nova Scotia will be still holding her course, by the side of her illustrious parent."³⁴ None was more delighted than Howe when Parliament passed the First Reform Bill of 1832; "the triumph of the Reformers is glorious," he told Susan Ann.³⁵ Two years later, during a period of instability in British politics, he spoke in glowing terms of the bloodless but glorious revolution of the preceding seven years, which had seen the abolition of tithes and the test acts, the emancipation of Catholics, the destruction of rotten boroughs, and the abolition of slavery; surely, then, Britons would not invite the Tories back to govern after the ancient fashion.[36] On occasions like these he would describe his politics as liberal without explaining precisely what he meant. Actually he had too much reverence for the past to be considered a liberal in the usual sense of the term, but that did not prevent him from taking the lead in removing the outworn practices that restricted a wider participation in politics.

His attitude towards the Irish question illustrates this facet of his liberalism. From early adult life he had taken the cause of the Irish of Ireland and Nova Scotia as his own. Even before 1828 when, as he put it, the Irish of Halifax had "the mark of bondage about their necks – the print of slavery upon their brows,"[37] he had attended their meetings at the Exchange Coffee House. He was there when they "gave vent to their feelings of pride and joy"[38] at the passage of the Catholic Emancipation Act of 1828. He was also there, in less happy times in April 1834, to help protest the suppression of the Dublin *Pilot* and the imprisonment of its editor, Richard Barrett, who had dared to publish Daniel O'Connell's letter to the people of Ireland. While seconding the major resolution proposed by Lawrence O'Connor Doyle, he told "those who hate and persecute the Press, [they] might as well try to controul the waves of the Atlantic as attempt to put it down."[39] When he went on to exult that "we dwell in a land where the Press can protect itself,"[40] he little realized that within the year he would stand in a position that might have led to the same fate as Barrett's.

More than once his sympathy for the Irish did not rest well with his readers. Somewhat angrily, "a Conservative" boasted that "any of our great leaders" could have stopped the emancipation bill merely by raising one of his fingers; a no less indignant Howe replied that Britons had "become pretty sick of the Tories and Conservatives," and realizing it, their leaders had supported Catholic emancipation for no other reason than to cling to office.[41] But when the situation warranted it, Howe could be no less critical of the Whigs. That happened in 1833 when they relieved Catholic Irishmen only partially from the payment of tithes to the Church of England. Should anyone have been surprised, Howe wondered, that honourable resistance degenerated into "savage and unjustified revenge," for which the Whigs had no answer but suspension of habeas corpus and trial by jury? His advice to the Nova Scotia Irish was to send an address to the foot of the throne requesting that the Irish of Ireland be put on the same footing as the Irish of Nova Scotia, "where the law makes no invidious distinction, and in which no portion of the people are taxed but for the general benefit of the whole."[42] All unbeknown to Howe at the time, this rapport between him and the Irish was to pay rich political dividends, for in his early political struggles he had no more united group of supporters than the Irish of Halifax. At the same time his opponents would suggest, with thinly disguised innuendo, that he associated mainly with the riff-raff of the town.

Earlier it was pointed out that Howe personified the spirit that was producing an intellectual awakening in Nova Scotia by coordinating activities that were in progress and by vitalizing ideas that were in the air.[43] While "several of his colonial contemporaries published far more titles than he did,"[44] none came close to rivalling his promotion of the awakening. In addition to his personal contributions, he offered editorial encouragement to local poets such as Andrew Shiels, the Bard of Elenvale,[45] and printed small local contributions, both in verse and prose, from a host of local correspondents. Occasionally the performance of this role led to annoyances. Once he discovered that he had published some lines dedicated to Miss George which had been copied from an eight-year-old number of the Halifax *Journal.* Labelling it "a poor, paltry trick," he told the culprit that anyone who would "filch original verses from the Journal, where so very few appear, would plunder a mendicant of his last biscuit."[46] Later he asked "An Old Customer" to pay the postage on his submissions; surely a publisher should not be expected to pay two shillings within as many weeks for "the carriage of his lucubrations."[47] Generally Howe treated those who offered contributions more kindly, especially the younger ones, whom he told, when he rejected a piece, to examine it again and again for inaccuracies and blemishes. "A faithful follower of the muse, must submit to the labor by which her favors, like the favors of less ethereal beings, are to be worn."[48] All in all, Howe was delighted that as time passed his paper could print more and more original contributions by Nova Scotians themselves: "The effusions of our Henrys, Edwins, Albyns, and Alvars, would often have done credit to a London periodical – and have given proof that the day is not far distant when the poetical genius of this country will confer a lustre upon its name."[49]

In fostering the spirit of the age, Howe also promoted any institutions that might contribute to public enlightenment and development. Even at the *Acadian* he had written enthusiastically about establishing a Mechanics' Institute, and in his second year at the *Novascotian* he had prophesied that, within seven years of its founding, a race of men would be produced who, "for scientific knowledge, correctness of method and general intelligence, would transcend, by many degrees, the class by whom they were preceded."[50] With nothing short of elation he reported, late in December 1831, the formation of an Institute in connection with the Mechanics' Library.[51] Two months later he announced that the Institute had already heard able papers on the principles of arithmetic, geometry, algebra, and music, and that every meeting had shown "a vast deal of talent in the Town, that wanted but some impulse to bring it into action."[52] Periodically Howe himself made his own contributions on a variety of topics. For once, his ebullient hopes were realized; over the next quarter of a century, the Institute discussed every phase of literature and science, and it came close to being "the University of Halifax."[53]

In the same spirit, Howe protested against government restrictions that were unsuited to the age, especially when they had been handed down from the hoary past. He became highly indignant when H.W. Crawley was fined for skating on Sunday, even though he had attended church twice the same day, and expressed great satisfaction when, on appeal, the Supreme Court held that the Nova Scotian act, which was based on a British statute designed to cope with levity of manners during the reign of Charles I, could not be used to prohibit innocent recreation. Any other conclusion, he contended, would have been "a direct breach of the religious toleration which we are supposed to enjoy."[54] He protested even more vehemently against a tax on literature – "of all objects of revenue books are the most improper" – and he declined to accept the argument that the tax would preserve the British provinces from the contagion of republicanism: "we cannot believe that the Colonist's situation will be rendered intollerable by contrasts with his republican neighbors ... why should we refrain from gathering the choice flowers of American Literature, for fear there may be some imaginary poison among the leaves."[55]

Howe probably contributed most to the awakening of the province simply through the information that the *Novascotian* provided. Earlier it was noted that he spent a considerable time between sessions in digesting the mass of foreign intelligence that came to him from a variety of sources and presenting it in a manner that was intelligible to his readers. Sometimes he champed at the bit awaiting a packet that never seemed to come: "every body stares at a great bank of fog ... seawards, with the same sort of feeling that we look at the green curtain on the stage – conscious that there must be a vast deal of battle, murder, and sudden death, behind it."[56] As the 1830s advanced his focus of interest changed somewhat and his all-pervading concern was to enlighten his readers on Nova Scotian affairs. But long before then he had concluded that the character of his paper was such as to win general acceptance. Thus he could write in 1831 that "in every county of the Province, the list of its patrons has been considerably enlarged, and in some it had been more than doubled. There is scarcely a settlement where [it] is not constantly read – scarcely a cottage into which it does not occasionally penetrate."[57] The next year he could report that his subscribers in New Brunswick and Nova Scotia alone numbered 3,000, and that although a few people had sought to bring down his establishment by discontinuing their subscriptions, "this formidable body we have found, by the experience of four years, to amount to nearly *twenty*."[58]

To his fellow-editors like Edmund Ward who charged that he had altered the *Novascotian* for the worse, Howe had an easy answer. Why had his subscription list increased so rapidly in three years that his paper was worth one-third more than he paid for it? "Blind and perverse public! ... why do you not encourage some of those deserving periodicals that are continually bewailing our faults."[59] There is in Howe's remarks on this occasion a strain of unctuousness, self-righteousness, and egotism that would become more apparent later. Had he not grappled with every contentious question "without any unmanly fear, or any unworthy designs?"[60] Had he wavered or hesitated when he had to choose between the hirelings who had disgraced the press and the distinguished men who had fought for its liberties?[61] Nevertheless, there was a good deal of truth in the contention that "the *Novascotian* was so comprehensive in its contents, so ably edited, so well written, and so widely circulated" that it had begun to "overshadow all its contemporaries."[62]

CHAPTER EIGHT

A Peep at the Springs of Government

The year 1831 brought political calm to Nova Scotia. Its people in general and Howe in particular welcomed the respite after months of frenzied political activity. Early in the year his pen would have been silent in any event since for six weeks he was struck down with fever after "over-exertion and over-heating" at the garrison Racquet Club. Although at one time his death was expected hourly, his strong constitution pulled him through.[1] For the rest of the year the political convulsions in Europe made him forget domestic affairs. Week after week he waited for the arrival of the packet and another rise of the curtain on the troubled European scene, from which he was certain Nova Scotians could learn by analogy. Above all, should they not limit powers which other people's sufferings had indicated could not be safely entrusted to their rulers?[2]

In a strangely uncharacteristic way Howe caused the greatest stir of the year when he dared to suggest that, if King William IV chose to remove Sir Peregrine Maitland as governor at the end of a three-year term, "it would rank among the popular acts of the new reign."[3] For a son of John Howe to treat the representative of the Crown with disrespect was a new and surprising phenomenon. But when the *Free Press* assumed a guise of shock and horror, the *Novascotian* published the letters of "Junius,"[4] which elaborated on the shortcomings of Maitland, pointing out that he had "done little or nothing – and the little he has done has certainly not redounded much to his honor":[5] irresolution and imbecility in handling the revenue crisis of 1830; delay in having the rightful claimant appointed to the office of attorney general; dismissal from the magistracy of a man who had simply exercised the normal privileges of a freeholder. Perhaps it was an accident that these were the precise ills that Howe had catalogued, but more likely he himself had put on the garb of "Junius." Even with old John Howe looking over his shoulder, that guise would have enabled him to be as critical of Maitland as he wished.

Howe had had his breather; by early 1832 he was telling the assemblymen that the honeymoon was over. While he continued to regard the overweening powers of the council as the principal evil, he was already beginning to attach less and less blame for their continuance to the councillors and more and more to the assemblymen. Again and again he reminded the members that they had been given a special mandate to deal with this vital question.[6] But clearly his interpretation of the election of 1830 was at fault since it had none of the wide-ranging implications that he suggested. He was naïve as well in suggesting that the British government would acquiesce immediately in any assembly resolutions on the question.

The results of the session of 1832 thoroughly disappointed him, since nothing he considered important was brought to a satisfactory conclusion. Worse still, the assemblymen committed a heinous sin in his eye when, because of the length of the session, they voted themselves a fortnight's extra indemnity – £1 a day for each member – at a cost of £650. When he derisively called them "legislative fourteen pounders,"[7] he was led into an open disagreement with Jotham Blanchard which seemed to reverse their earlier positions. Because of failing health, Blanchard had not been making much of a name for himself in the assembly. Brought under the public stigma when Howe published the names of members voting for the additional indemnities,[8] he let loose his frustrations. The town of Halifax and its papers, he wrote, should be the last to complain about higher indemnities since the bill to incorporate the Bank of Nova Scotia, a purely Halifax measure, had taken ten days of the assembly's time. As a spokesman of rural radicalism, he further argued that Haligonians already held too many non-Halifax seats and nothing should be done to discourage country residents from offering as candidates.[9]

Howe's reply was anything but convincing. It was not at all likely that Nova Scotians outside Halifax would derive as many advantages from a second bank in Halifax as he said they would. No more reasonable was his view that a maximum indemnity of £42 was extremely generous, sufficient to allow the country members to live like princes in Halifax and have a bottle of wine a day.[10] Blanchard was right that Howe failed to recognize the financial problems of rural assemblymen, who had to absent themselves from their normal pursuits and incur substantial additional expenses while away from home. It is puzzling that one who had learned so much about rural Nova Scotia would have so little sympathy with the difficulties of its assemblymen.

Because the assembly had not taken a "peep" at the courts as he had suggested, Howe conducted his own inquiry into their operation. To see the great scoundrel who "dashed out [his] neighbours' brains," he discovered that the place to go was the Supreme Court, but to "examine geologically the lower strata of society, or to realize the accuracy of Hogarth's sketches," the proper place was the Court of Sessions. There a great hulking fellow of a man would "lie, and stammer, and shamble about, with the timidity of a hare, and the awkwardness of a Carriboo," while a girl "no bigger than a pint pot" would give evidence with such composure, such quiet glances at the jury, and such tender appeals to the judge that they would need hearts of stone to convict her.[11]

All this was good-natured enough until he came to the Court of Chancery, through which, he said, a man "pursues a Shadow called Equity, until his scrip is empty, and eke his stomach too – till his garments are tattered and his limbs are weary – and he can neither tell how far he has come, nor how far he has to go."[12] Almost the earliest of Howe's legislative recollections – it may have helped produce his phobia regarding lawyers – went back to 1824 when, as he saw it, the leading assemblymen, lawyers all, helped to foist upon the province two courts of dubious value, the Inferior Court of Common Pleas and the Court of Chancery, and then had themselves appointed to the judgeships they had created. The major plum, the post of master of the rolls, had gone to Simon Bradstreet Robie, the Speaker of the assembly. If Robie, in the manner of Lord Brougham, had used his position to point out what should be discarded and what preserved in chancery proceedings, Howe would not have faulted him. Instead he had "wallowed in the luxuries of *old* laws and customs" and "year after year pocketed the public money, for keeping up a body of costly and dangerous absurdities, that he ought long ago to have denounced.[13] Robie's conduct was all the worse because he had pretended to be a reformer and had often railed against petty abuses. Except for Edmund Ward, Howe had heretofore not treated anyone quite as harshly. But he blamed the assembly too, for not taking the initiative in a matter that cried for reform.

This incident serves to illustrate a glaring inconsistency between Howe's articles on Canada and those on Nova Scotia. No matter how hard he was on Nova Scotia assemblymen, he seemed to suggest that the evils in Upper Canada would not last long in his native province, since its politicians possessed the intelligence, the eloquence, and the judgment to cope with them. While he conceded that William Lyon Mackenzie performed satisfactorily in the legislature and catalogued well the absurdities of government in the *Colonial Advocate*, he knew of no colonial who wrote or printed a greater quantity of trash. "He can tear a good passion to pieces, and fritter a strong case away, by an endless reference to detail, and a tiresome array of hints, assertions and personal attacks (with perhaps a single exception) better, than any public character on this side of the Atlantic."[14] Thoroughly impatient with these observations, the Quebec *Mercury* told Howe to abandon a topic about which he knew nothing.[15]

More than anything else, the interrelated bank and currency issues, and to a lesser extent the civil list and quit rent questions, would, over the next two or three years, enable him to peer deeply into the innermost workings of the political process and see the weaknesses of the council and the assembly in their utter nakedness. Prior to 1825 the mercantile interests of Halifax had pressed for the incorporation of a bank, but they had been defeated by the suspicions of the rural members. Eight wealthy merchants and businessmen had then taken matters into their own hands and opened a private bank, the Halifax Banking Company, which "flourished like the green bay tree. Its profits, which were kept secret, were the talk of the town [and the] whole organization was as solid, close, and dominating as the great stone building that housed it."[16] In time it became even more dominating for, although only one of its partners, Enos Collins, had been a councillor in 1825, four others later received that honour.[17]

In 1832 a rival group of Haligonians sought to incorporate a bank through legislative charter, and assemblymen like John Young and Herbert Huntington took pains to protect the public by insisting that it redeem its notes in specie and that its shareholders be subject to double liability. For much less worthy motives, the council wanted even more stringent precautions, including a provision for triple liability. Howe looked on with growing indignation, fearful that the bill would be so much waste paper if the council adhered to its proposals, but convinced, too, that immoderate action on its part would "bring the Province one stage nearer to the attainment of an elective Council."[18] Although the council did not persist in its more extreme amendments, the Bank of Nova Scotia started out in August 1832 with "more safeguards against disaster than any bank of its time in British North America."[19] While Howe was satisfied in the end that the council had "not impair[ed] the value of the bill,"[20] neither he nor anyone else could foresee the thorny issues its amendments would eventually raise.

Despite his criticism of the assemblymen in 1832, Howe addressed them in not unfriendly fashion as the session of 1833 approached. Emphasizing that he looked at change through the eyes of a conservative and wanted nothing of innovation for the sake of innovation, he called on them to deal appropriately with representation and elections. While representation was "not a subject to be tampered [with] from year to year," they ought to arrange it "according to some principle ... which will meet with a general recognition."[21] To prevent the drunkenness, violence, and even bloodshed that characterized voting in Nova Scotia, Howe declared, they ought also to consider the adoption of the ballot and the general registration of voters, even though he knew he would be labelled a republican for suggesting them. For his part, he could see no ill resulting from the ballot equal to the evils that disgraced almost every county and township election.[22]

But his main concerns throughout 1833 were to prevent an inundation of paper money and ensure a sound currency. As early as January the columns of the *Novascotian* abounded with letters bewailing the depreciated state of the paper money, and for this ill the provincial Treasury notes were held chiefly responsible. Normally there had been some provision for their redemption, but in 1828 the assembly had somehow got the council to agree to the issue of £40,000 of nonredeemable notes. The intention was to provide a medium to meet the expenditures on roads and bridges that accelerated at a particular time of year; in turn, the notes were to be accepted by the provincial collectors of impost and excise at their face value. It was "a convenient cycle that guaranteed [the] acceptability [of the Treasury notes] as long as their circulation was limited to a sum roughly equivalent to the provincial revenue."[23] This turned out to be a forlorn hope. Because of a severe shortage of cash and the insistence of the assembly, the issue of Treasury notes was doubled between 1828 and 1833, probably because the council could not stomach the idea of another clash with the assembly on money matters.

The Bank of Nova Scotia was the second villain of the piece. Although it issued only a few of its own notes because it was required to redeem them in specie, and although it accepted only its own notes and specie at its counters, it took notes of the Halifax Banking Company from its shareholders with malicious intent, let them accumulate in the amount of £23,000 and then demanded specie for them. Normally the older bank honoured demands of this kind, but this time it met them only in part; then it suspended payments in specie and henceforth redeemed its own notes in Treasury notes. Partly through the actions of the assembly and partly through the gamesmanship of the banks, the status of the provincial notes had reached a pretty pass. "No longer the equivalent of specie at the old bank, irredeemable since 1828 in their own right, and, after August 1832, unacceptable at the new bank, as they were already at the Imperial Customs and were soon to be at the tea sales of the East India Company, the Treasury notes were now in grave danger of depreciating to the point of being worthless."[24]

In the context of a depreciating paper money, and of deteriorating economic conditions as well, Howe launched a legislative review on the currency question just before the legislature met in 1833. As he would do for the next two years, he denounced "the impropriety of allowing, in any country, an inundation of Paper Currency, which is not responded in the precious metals";[25] in his opinion, the best course was either to fund the Treasury notes at a stipulated rate of interest or to secure gold for their redemption. He was in the assembly on February 20 when it tackled the question, and he remained there for days, reporting a repetitious, often tedious debate. Finally he rebelled and reminded the members that he was the servant of those who read, not of those who spoke. Someone like him, who was wedged in a crowded lobby, had no choice but to listen, but those who were seated before their fireplaces could be more discriminating.[26] Still, the debate gave him a new understanding of the workings of the House. He had expected a discussion couched in terms of the public interest; instead it quickly became a contest between special interests. William Bliss spoke for the Bank of Nova Scotia, Stephen Deblois for the old bank and the council, and from then on the clash between council and assembly, city and country members, and the two banks was seldom far below the surface. Through it all, Howe found the conduct of some members as ncomprehensible as it was appalling.

He was even less satisfied with the outcome of the debate than with the debate itself. To him it was only a small step in the right direction to provide for the redemption of the larger Treasury notes over an extended period,[27] but the country assemblymen would go no further in depriving the province of what was, in effect, an interest-free loan. He was even more indignant that an equally determined council had forced the legislature to deal just as badly with the bank notes; henceforth neither bank would have to redeem its notes in specie, but might respond in provincial paper instead.[28] In his opinion, the legislature had established by law "three manufactories of inconvertible paper." Could a more offensive scheme ever be conceived for a commercial country? "You might as well attempt to uphold the Christian Religion, by appointing *three* Bishops and throwing *the Bible* into the fire."[29]

The session over, Howe, as usual, was "free to frisk and skip over the pleasant fields, and refresh our spirits with the philosophy of nature – the wonders of science – and the graces of poesy and art."[30] Lest the legislators should think their world was everything, he reminded them that other men "in a thousand ways that taste, or genius, or circumstances dictate, are pursuing objects to them as all engrossing and important."[31] But even during the recess he could not divorce himself from politics for long. After taking a peep at politics in the Canadas, he refused to share the alarm of those who feared that their politicians were out to create anarchy. Undoubtedly Papineau was "too apt to indulge in general and indiscriminate censure," but he was confident that the more circumspect John Neilson would treat the British government's concessions as "the earnest of future improvements."[32]

In two separate incursions into provincial politics his ever-hardening attitude was directed towards two men whose paths would later cross his own in a libel suit. Earlier in the year he had condemned the appointment of Brenton Halliburton as chief justice on the grounds that he had "mingled much and warmly in politics" and was considered to be "the head of a party exclusive in its views and violent in its measures."[33] Howe also looked with suspicion upon W.H. Roach of Annapolis, a typical country assemblyman who in the past had offered intemperate opposition to any proposals that might result in additional taxation. Then, in 1833, Howe noted a most curious set of circumstances. First, Roach introduced a flour inspection bill to the accompaniment of rumours he had been promised the inspectorship that it created. Lawyers in the assembly normally hostile to him suddenly changed their stance and supported his bill. A little later, in debating a cheap law bill,[34] the House was treated to the extraordinary spectacle of Roach and the lawyers coquetting "most agreeably over the state of the law [and] expressing for each other's views and intentions the most unbounded admiration."[35] But the cat was let completely out of the bag when the lawyers expressed fears that the flour inspector might not receive adequate compensation. Howe said little editorially on the episode; perhaps he was more effective in simply recording the facts as if they were part of a conspiracy designed to saddle the province with an unnecessary office costing more than £500 a year.

But these matters drew only his passing attention, and the currency question again became his main concern when he began his legislative reviews late in October. Conceding that it was useless to flog the council, but hoping to beat some sense into the assemblymen, he warned the latter they would have to adopt a more determined stance towards the council if they were to solve the currency and other questions. To date they had not yet even tried to remove the worst of abominations, the continued exclusion of the public from the council's deliberations. "Have we gone back to the days of oracular wisdom, and are we to receive without inquiry or dispute the dicta of sages who admit us but to the door of their cave?"[36] Changes for the better in the membership of the council had not altered the basic situation: "who would sleep by Vesuvius, merely because some former explosion had for the moment abated its force?"[37] Howe went on to demonstrate that all his forebodings about the currency had come to pass, since the Bank of Nova Scotia had used to the full its unrestricted right to issue paper, and for aught that anyone knew, there might be "three hundred thousand pounds of paper afloat, for one pound of which, no man can command twenty shillings."[38] To vent his sarcasm against both the legislators and the banks, he resorted to his ample store of mythological allusions. Midas, he said, "by his magic touch, turned everything to gold," but Nova Scotia's bankers and legislators "with a stoke of the pen turned everything to paper. The Titan boasted, in his fetters, that he had taught men the use of the precious metals, our senators aimed at a higher feat when they resolved to teach us to do without them."[39]

How had things come to such a pretty pass? Believing, as he did, in the checks and balances theory, he had strongly supported setting up a second bank, hoping that it would create rival interests and that persons who for years had patiently submitted to the council might adopt a more independent stance. But it had not turned out that way, and perhaps the assembly was most to blame. Although Blanchard had denied that its members were influenced from without on the bank and currency questions, was he not aware that some of them were "moved like puppets by the wires from the other end of the building – and that in no two Sessions had the ancient system of feasting and drenching with Champagne ... been carried to such an extent"[40] as in 1832 and 1833. Reviewing the assembly's conduct during the past two years, Howe concluded that the five bankers on the council moved in mysterious ways behind the scenes their objects to achieve. Speaker Archibald was right not to be surprised at anything the assembly did; clearly it was "an admirable school to teach one the folly of consistency and the value to be placed on the doctrine of chances."[41]

Howe admitted that most assemblymen had come prepared to do the right thing in 1833, but had run afoul of the "old bankers," who followed Cardinal Wolsey's advice to the pope: if the object is to confound the laity, set up one class of learned men to oppose another. Thus the assemblymen were "often so stunned with declamation – so terrified with prophecies, and so perplexed with importunity, that it was difficult to know how to decide."⁴² Even so, by some miracle they had reached the right decision to require both banks to redeem their notes in specie until the council presented an amendment freeing both banks from that requirement. Arguing that if the banks were forced to come to cash payments, they would have to refuse the Treasury notes which had been issued at the assembly's insistence, the council sought to call that body's credibility into question. Would the result not be a further depreciation in the value of these notes, and the wreaking of severe hardship on the poor who, unlike the rich, could not hold them until they increased in value.⁴³

The tactics of the council were no less clever than its arguments. By delaying its amendment until near the end of the session when a third of the assemblymen had gone home and by insisting on adherence to its provisions, it forced the assembly either to accept it or continue an intolerable state of affairs. According to Howe, the assembly took the easy way out,⁴⁴ and, as a result, "destroyed the little of sound currency which we had, and ... made the Province ridiculous in the eyes of all commercial countries."⁴⁵ Even Jotham Blanchard and John Young, of all people, had joined Stephen Deblois in perpetrating the evil. What should be done? Next session, Howe said, the members should come instructed to restore the currency to a sound footing "*though they should have to sit until midsummer, and even though another year's revenue should be the necessary sacrifice.*"⁴⁶ If the council thwarted their intentions, they should let no members return home until they had sent an address to the foot of the throne explaining why they were unable to ensure a sound currency. But was the public sufficiently aroused to demand decisive action from the assembly?

Howe had his answer in January 1834. By that time the economic distress had further deepened, and he attributed it primarily to the debased condition of the currency, and "the total disappearance of every specie of coin – a scarcity of change, delay, vexation and uncertainty."⁴⁷ Rumours having circulated about a public meeting on the subject, the Chamber of Commerce, hoping to have the debate conducted on its terms, intervened by inviting merchants and others to meet on January 16 to discuss the depressed condition of business and trade resulting from "the great increase of illegal traffic and other causes." Howe was flabbergasted by this blatant attempt to "cast into the shade the real and obvious causes of the distress,"⁴⁸ but when the meeting was over, he conceded that things could not have gone better.

Two things especially elated him: the size of the audience, which assured him that "there was an energy and independence still alive in his native town,"⁴⁹ and the refusal of the meeting to let itself be led off on a wild-goose chase. John Williamson, the first speaker, wasted no time on a discussion of smuggling, but proposed a resolution calling for a return to cash payments. When Stephen Deblois attempted a diversion by making the Treasury notes the chief culprit, Howe himself intervened. For him it was a milestone since, for the first time, he was speaking at a general public meeting. Nor was it an ordinary public meeting since it included almost everyone who counted in the business, political, and social life of Halifax. While he willingly conceded that a depreciated currency was not the sole cause of the economic difficulties and that they were partly attributable to those Haligonians who were living beyond their means, he was much more interested in recommendations than causes, and he proposed that the banks be denied the right to issue inconvertible paper and that Treasury notes be allowed to find their own level.

These suggestions demonstrated his growing awareness of the realities of Nova Scotia politics. While he wanted as much as anyone to put the provincial notes on a sound footing, he also knew that the country assemblymen would object until they were taught a lesson. But if the Treasury notes fell sharply in value, as they would if they were the only inconvertible paper, and if the assemblymen received their indemnities in these depreciated notes, they would soon experience a change of heart. "One argument like that addressed to their pockets would be worth a dozen addressed to their minds."[50] Because of his assertiveness, Howe was included with six merchants on a committee that was appointed to draft a memorial for presentation to the assembly. For a thirty-year-old he was indeed in select company, and in a position to exercise influence more directly than usually befell a newspaperman of that day. The committee's recommendation was straightforward: the banks should be compelled to redeem their notes in specie, and a standard should be set for their redemption.[51]

Within a few weeks Howe was closely watching the assembly's treatment of the currency question. Almost at once he saw that the council was on the defensive, too much so even for him. As a result, he pleaded in vain that it delete the assembly's proposal that the banks be limited to issuing notes of £5 and above; to him it was an impolitic restriction at a time when business needed a greater accommodation to relieve the economic distress.[52] Otherwise the legislature conformed closely to the committee's recommendations, and the lesson was not lost on Howe. Above all, it demonstrated to him the effectiveness of public opinion when moved by knowledgeable and skilful leadership. That was to be the key to his political tactics of the future.

By mid-June Howe's prophecy that the assemblymen would be taught a lesson for their failure to deal with the Treasury notes had been more than realized. Forced to respond to their notes in specie, the banks had no choice but to restrict their dealings in Treasury notes. The Bank of Nova Scotia declined to accept them on any terms, the Halifax Banking Company only for debts contracted before June 1. Even the provincial government recognized a depreciation of ninepence in the pound. The situation gave Howe the opportunity to moralize. "We hold it to be sound doctrine, that a Sovereign or a Legislature has almost as much right to pollute the air, or poison the springs of a country, as to debase its currency."[53] Himself a loser by the depreciation, he felt he might as well be philosophical about it. "The Banks ..." he told Susan Ann, "can't put [the provincial paper] lower than 18/ – but that will be a severe loss to the holders – we must bear our share of it with the other evils of the times."[54] To his surprise Howe found himself attacked by "Senex" in the *Recorder*, in the style of Jotham Blanchard four years earlier, for being willing to "lend [himself] to a party, bent on securing their own interest, at the expense of the public."[55] In reply, he denied he had any hope of gain from any of the three parties to the currency dispute, and explained that the party to which he belonged was a growing one, made up of intelligent and independent persons not afraid to maintain sound principles at the risk of inconvenience to themselves, and unwilling to let themselves be "ground down beneath the great wheel of state."[56] Basically, that was the reply he had given to Blanchard in 1830 and would continue to give throughout the thirties.

The summer and autumn of 1834 were bad ones for Nova Scotia, made even worse by the outbreak of Asiatic cholera. Hence it was a sorry picture that Howe painted, late in July, of a town in which business had come almost to a standstill.[57] A little earlier he had begun a series of articles on the state of the province in which, like the honest physician, he sought to "cut out the gangrene with unsparing hand, that health and strength may be restored."[58] He found at least three basic causes of the distress. The failure of the crops for two successive seasons had impoverished the rural districts, and whenever the country was poor large balances always existed on the wrong side of the ledger in Halifax. On the other two causes, the debasement of the currency, and the idleness and extravagance of the people, he could hardly have said much that was very new, but he did elaborate the second more fully than ever before.

Nova Scotia, he argued, was an excellent poor man's home, but it had no place for the gentleman farmers, gentleman merchants, and gentleman mechanics who had lately made their appearance. "Our Merchants like those of Tyre, would fain be 'Princes' – our Mechanics and Farmers fine gentlemen – while a 'profession' [like that of law] has often been supposed to add licence to plunder, and to give dignity to idleness, poverty and profusion."[59] Howe quoted sections of Adam Smith that demonstrated the effect of frugality on the accumulation of capital, and argued that the expenditures of the British and local governments in Halifax should have contributed to that end. Instead, they were being used to destroy moral energy and independence, the more so as they were associated with a military society which naturally favoured habits of idleness, dissipation, and expensive living. Many young Nova Scotians, in associating with the captains and colonels of fortune, failed to acquire their graces, but did learn their disregard of time, their expensive habits, and their contempt for the low pursuits of business. The high salaries of the public officers affected no less injuriously the general tone of the society. A vacancy in a major office produced such a scramble that it left the capital in a state of turmoil for a month. No society, said Howe, assailed its industrious classes with more temptations than did Halifax.

Even in the rural districts he found the same baneful influences at work. Each village had its knot of traders, lawyers, and public officers, through whom the fashionable follies of the capital were reflected upon the country. A farmer who visited a village might become dissatisfied with rusticity, or perhaps his wife, sons, or daughters would find the temptations irresistible. A ruinous credit system, by enabling these desires to be met, let the farmer's family slide almost unknowingly into extravagance. "The master is never without his brandy – the mistress her tea and tea parties – Sam and Dick their broad cloth coats, and Sally and Mary their ribbons and flounces."[60] The outraged Howe suggested that articles of finery bought on credit, instead of being considered as ornaments, should be treated as badges of disgrace. Once more he appeared as a whipper-into-line of public morality, this time as a means of ridding the province of economic distress.

In November, when the assembly met several months earlier than usual to tackle the problem of the Treasury notes and the funded debt, he again used his persuasive talents to the full. While he doubted if a majority of its members could be induced to accept any workable remedy, he suggested it should "gradually withdraw a part of the paper, and establish beyond all cavil, such portion as should still remain in circulation."[61] Whether or not he deserved any of the credit, the legislature actually followed the course he proposed by funding £20,000 of Treasury notes over a two-year period. Nothing more was needed since, after the circulation of Treasury notes was brought into rough equivalence with the revenues from provincial duties, they were able to maintain their face value without difficulty.[62]

For Howe the long-drawn-out currency issue was a disillusioning experience. He had learned that even in idyllic Nova Scotia the machinations of individuals in their own interest took the same form and manifested the same subtlety as in more complex societies, and that the assemblymen themselves became part and parcel of the process, however much they might rationalize their conduct in terms of the public good. He had seen, as J.S. Martell suggests, that "many people in the country in these last few years had learned to put more faith in the judgment of the editors than in that of their representatives,"[63] and that in some cases at least public opinion, when aroused by the press, could force the legislature to take constructive action. He had discovered that he could hold his own with the mighty of the land, both on the public platform and in committee. Above all, 1834 was a watershed year in convincing him that the assembly needed leadership of a different kind if it was to perform its functions as he conceived it should.

The transformed Howe is best reflected in his abandonment of major attacks on the council – why waste energy in activity destined from the outset to be unproductive? – and in his harsher criticism of the assembly, and of assemblymen whom he had earlier admired. But he was always careful not to stray beyond what he regarded as fair comment and thereby get into the bad habit of the Canadian newspapers. Late in 1834 he expressed horror at "the ultra tone which characterizes all [the Canadians] say and do with reference to public men and measures."[64] Because the Upper Canadian newspapers so often swept away the landmarks of truth and reason by torrents of abuse he normally threw away their files in disgust. Sometimes the Lower Canadian press was equally bad, especially when *la Minerve* and *Vindicator* called the governor general a Nero and a Pharaoh for not taking steps to prevent the spread of cholera. Did Lord Aylmer deserve the title Nero for not being able to keep away a disease that had ravaged half the world? Should he be blamed for not advancing money on his own responsibility when the assembly left him without a sixpence and refused to make good the sums he had already spent in coping with the disease?[65]

But although he avoided the "ultra tone," he was severe enough when he tackled the assemblymen on several minor and two major issues which, in addition to the currency question, occupied him in 1834. On representation he told them that they had tried to "shape their camels so as to pass them through the needle's eye."[66] Why should the older townships of Windsor, Falmouth, and Newport in Hants county, whose freeholders he could visit within a week, elect their own members as well as participate in the election of a county member, while the newer townships with larger populations were denied the privilege? Two years earlier he had written mildly on representation, but the tone of 1834 was not that of 1832.

He also expressed himself much more strongly on the conduct of elections, especially the practice of open voting, which permitted wealthy candidates to buy up loads of fishermen, or even gangs of ruffians, and lead them to the polls. "Is this the freedom of election [that is] the corner stone of British liberty? ... Of all the men in the Assembly, who pretend to represent the liberal party ... is there not one who will have the hardihood to propose the adoption of the Ballot?"[67] Apparently there was none, but Alexander Stewart, still regarded as a liberal, proposed resolutions that the council open its doors, that it be divided into Executive and Legislative Councils, and that the latter be selected on a province-wide basis and not from Halifax alone.[68] The assembly approved the resolutions and Howe was pleased. He would have been much less pleased had he known what was taking place behind the scenes. Two years earlier Lord Goderich, the colonial secretary, had authorized the splitting of the council in New Brunswick, and had instructed T.N. Jeffery, the collector of customs, who was then administering Nova Scotia, to consult his council and report on the advisability of a similar change in his province.[69] Taking evasive action, Jeffery replied that the innovation did not appear to be giving satisfaction in New Brunswick, and awaited further instructions.[70] If he expected his letter to be a delaying device, he was right, and Howe waited in vain for a decision that he believed would be favourable. Had he known of Jeffery's intervention, he might not have given him a "well done, thou good and faithful Servant" when he retired as administrator of the province.[71]

Rivalling the currency problem as the leading issues of 1834 were the interrelated civil list and quit rent questions. In one form or another, the negotiations for a civil list lasted from 1825 to 1848, and, as D.C. Harvey has pointed out, the parties to the question realized its constitutional implications from the beginning.[72] By 1830 all the revenues of Nova Scotia, except the casual and territorial revenues of the Crown, had come under the control of the provincial legislature. Further, almost all the expenditures that had once been borne by the British parliamentary grant had been transferred to the casual revenues which, in effect, were being used to maintain a few higher officials who, the British government felt, should be independent of the annual votes of the assembly. During the thirties the colonies sought full control over these revenues, but the colonial secretaries were reluctant to surrender them until the assembly had first made permanent provision for these officials in a civil list.

Under heavy pressure to reduce the parliamentary grant, Lord Goderich managed to remove Nova Scotia from it altogether in 1832, but only by overloading the casual revenues to such an extent that the salaries which they supported were soon in arrears.[73] Nonetheless, he proposed an increase in the salaries of the law officers and the judges, and to get the money he offered to commute the quit rents for £2,000 per annum.[74] The assembly replied that once it had secured control of the casual revenues it would willingly maintain the civil establishment of the province.[75] Goderich's successor, E.G. Stanley, then offered to give up the casual revenues for £4,500, £3,500 for the governor and £1,000 for the provincial secretary, and to make a separate arrangement for the judiciary through the surrender of the quit rents.[76] Howe first interested himself in these proposals in March 1834, when the assembly took them under its consideration. After five days he could scarcely contain himself and he took time off from reporting the debates to warn the assemblymen not to be "led into direct and angry collision with the people themselves." Everything he had heard them propose had been based on "*profuse*, and *unsound*, and *impolitic* principles." Surely they would not lay their "independence at the feet of a grasping and ambitious [legal] profession – and the two or three interested persons, who, from behind the scenes, attune the wires upon which it plays such costly music."[77]

The next week of debates shocked Howe even more. Although the assembly rejected Charles Rufus Fairbanks's scale of salaries for the judges, which he considered little short of preposterous, it gave tentative approval to a second one which he found only slightly less obnoxious.[78] By this time the publicity he had helped to create was bringing him help from another quarter. At the end of March William Lawson presented a widely signed petition from Halifax reminding the assembly that the vested rights of officials must take second place to the right of the people to be economically governed, and that the right to enjoy enormous salaries was much the same as the right to buy and sell legislative power which the holders of rotten boroughs in England had until recently possessed. Lawson had his own test for determining that the public officers were altogether too well paid: "look through this Town ... and see who keep carriages – who sport their equipages, but the Public Officers?"[79] Howe wondered what "even the lavish people of England [would] say, if [they knew] ... that a Legislature, pledged to public opinions, and at a time of deep distress, voted to *one* public officer, an income *four times greater* than the richest farmer in the whole landed interest of the country enjoys."[80]

Eventually the assembly agreed to Alexander Stewart's motion to put the bill over to the next session, although only by a single vote.[81]

Lewis Morris Wilkins of Windsor attributed this reversal of position to the public pressures set in motion by Howe's editorials. Indignantly he chastised the assemblymen for behaving, not like representatives who made up their own minds, but like delegates who bent before every breeze. So much had Stewart and Howe seemed to be in collusion that he would have called Howe to the bar of the House if he had not known that Stewart was an honourable man.[82] Howe, who heard and reported Wilkins's speech, felt it would "not be a bad advertizement" for the *Novascotian* if he needed one; at the same time he warned Wilkins that "he *had better let us alone*."[83] Meanwhile Fairbanks had declared, also in Howe's presence, that the press had misled the public and that the Halifax petition was based on opinions unsupported by fact. Howe replied that, although he still respected Fairbanks, "we have a duty to perform" and no more than Fairbanks could he let himself be "swayed from what we believe to be just and right."[84] D.C. Harvey has suggested that, although the assembly's bill differed substantially from the colonial secretary's proposals, Stanley would likely have accepted it had the bill become law.[85] If that is so, Howe more than anyone had prevented the settlement of the civil list question in the spring of 1834, since the *Novascotian* was primarily responsible for the hostile attitudes that led to the shelving of the bill. Although the *Acadian Recorder* felt much the same as Howe, it printed no more than two or three paragraphs on the subject,[86] while the *Colonial Patriot*, only an insipid imitation of its former self, barely deemed the question worthy of its attention.[87] For Howe it was further evidence of the influence he could exert through the *Novascotian*.

But he was not yet done with the civil list. Shortly before the assembly met in November, he started a new series of articles in which he adopted his severest tone to date, warning that the same assemblymen who "nine months ago, meditated the most daring and selfish sacrifice of the interests" entrusted to their care, might be attempting it a second time. "Cunning hands will doubtless prepare another curiously compounded, but equally dangerous draught ... fortified no doubt with as many threats and dispatches from the Colonial Office, as the intrigues and correspondence of the past summer, may have produced."[88] So it was up to the people to emancipate themselves from the "insidious grasp of office holders and trading politicians." Let them rise as a man on the subject and let a petition be forwarded to Halifax from every township in the province.[89] More and more Howe was invoking grass roots support to settle basic political problems.

Showing a complete lack of interest in ideological considerations, he continued to rely, not on some constitutional argument that the province had an inherent right to control the expenditure of all its revenues, but on grounds of economy and common sense. In Nova Scotia, he pointed out, even the most prosperous farmer found it difficult to clear £100 a year, and excepting perhaps ten, all would gladly give up their farms for an office paying £300 annually.[90] Yet the incumbent provincial secretary received almost £2,000 from all sources and the chief justice £1,500, even though the wealthy state of New York was paying its corresponding officials only £375 and £500. Indeed, the little province of Nova Scotia paid its chief justice more than the chief justice of the United States received, and its provincial secretary more than any American official other than the president. Further, if the conditions of the two countries were compared, the people of England did not pay "half so much to their public servants, as we should pay, if we gave to our chief officers a salary of £500." Yet this was "the Colony to which Lord Goderich and Mr. Stanley send despatches, complaining of parsimony."[91]

For all his efforts Howe was to be defeated, in part by a change of strategy in Britain. In April Administrator Jeffery had told the colonial secretary there was no chance of settling the casual revenues question "at least for some years to come."[92] Accordingly Stanley instructed Sir Colin Campbell, before he left England in July 1834 to become governor, not to make further efforts to commute the casual revenues. Instead he was to insist on the collection of the quit rents unless the legislature, at an early session, agreed to commute them for £2,000 per annum, which would be applied to the salaries of the lieutenant-governor, the provincial secretary, and the judiciary.[93] Campbell's strategy, worked out in an interchange of dispatches with T. Spring Rice, Stanley's successor, was a simple one. By convincing the assemblymen he would start collecting the quit rents forthwith, he hoped they would give way without fuss, since the action would be highly unpopular with the landowners, their chief constituents, and for "whatever annoyance or irritation might be caused ... the odium would rest with the Assembly alone."[94]

Howe had gloomy forebodings as the assembly prepared to debate the issue, fearing there were "not the materials in the House to meet the difficulties of the times."[95] He advised the members to make moderate provisions for all the officers "without reference to vested rights and half legalized robberies" and offer them to the Crown upon the surrender of all the revenues. "We do not believe that Mr. Spring Rice would dare go into Parliament and say that he had refused such an offer, and attempted to coerce the people by collecting the Quit Rents"; if he did, an agent should be sent to Britain to "expose the iniquity of the whole affair" before the House of Commons.[96] Yet, although Howe had come to believe that he was living in anything but the best of all possible worlds, he received even less assistance than he had expected.

The *Acadian Recorder* again supported him, but only to the extent of a paragraph or two.[97] A township meeting in Onslow condemned the exorbitant salaries dictated by the colonial secretaries, but no other township chose to adopt a mode of self-expression seldom used in Nova Scotia.[98] When John Young begged his fellow assemblymen not to "let ... Nova Scotia be the first Colony under the British Crown, where these [quit] rents shall be purchased or enforced," he drew rounds of applause from the gallery,[99] but the support of only nine other members.[100] Even Herbert Huntington of Yarmouth, later to be the "sea-green incorruptible of Nova Scotia Reformers," went along with his constituents' wishes and voted to get rid of the repeated annoyances that would result from the antiquated quit rent claim.[101] Alexander Stewart aptly posed the assemblymen's dilemma: to decide whether it was better to be assailed for giving extravagant salaries, or for letting the tax-gatherer loose among the people when £2,000 a year might set the claims at rest forever.[102] To avoid the worst of the ills, he proposed, and the assembly agreed, that all the commutation fund be made applicable to the governor's salary "so that it cannot be given to support a dominant religion, or to increase the pay of any man, judge or otherwise."[103] Undoubtedly relieved, the governor and the colonial secretary accepted his proposal without argument.

Although defeated on quit rents, Howe had the consolation that the major battles on the civil list question were still to be fought. But the clash between Howe and Stewart arising from their differences over quit rents was to be highly significant for Nova Scotia politics. Before 1830, when Howe was termed a "mild Tory," Stewart was known as a friend of popular causes. During the early 1830s he took the same side as an increasingly liberal Howe did on most matters. But his own Whiggish attitudes were beginning to rebel against the idea that assemblymen should be regularly subjected to the pressures of the electors. Thus he reacted strongly against a group of his own constituents who, in November 1834, formed a political union in Amherst to "bring the general mind of the County ... home to the House of Assembly" and secure the "great and beneficial reforms" that similar unions had helped to bring about in England.[104] Guessing, perhaps not without reason, that the union was a contrivance directed largely against him, he and his friends packed its next meeting and forced through a resolution stating that freeholders did "not require the aid of Societies ... to instruct them how to maintain their rights, or form their opinions on the conduct of their members."[105] Stewart found no less distasteful the continuing insinuations that the lawyers in the assembly thought in terms of places of preferment for themselves rather than the public good. Since Howe was a major exponent of both sets of ideas, it is understandable that Stewart felt less and less kindly disposed towards him.

All of Stewart's pent-up resentment burst into the open when he discussed quit rents in the assembly on December 11. Whatever the lawyers in the House did, he was certain they would be greeted with "contumely and abuse"; indeed, all the members of the assembly had been "inconsiderately attacked by its natural protectors and supporters" so often that it now lay "prostrate in the dust, its power ... gone." Yet its own constituents, "the madmen," continued to heap criticism on it at every opportunity.[106] Even as Howe reported the speech, he knew he would have to reply since Stewart left no doubt that "the natural protectors and supporters" who had failed the assembly were the newspapers, especially the *Novascotian*. He got his chance on December 26 at a public gathering called to discuss another matter. Unlike his speech in January, this one was well planned and rehearsed, even though the time of year prevented him from trying it out beforehand in a secluded grove as he was sometimes to do later. His aim, he said, was to let the meeting pronounce upon the charges made recently by some assemblymen against the press and the public, apparently to excuse their own ill-conceived acts.[107] One after the other he recited the shortcomings of the assembly over the preceding three years and, meeting no opposition, he got the gathering to agree that "if ... the House of Assembly is prostrated and degraded, the causes are to be found in their own acts and sentiments, rather than in the misrepresentations of the Press or the madness of the people."[108]

The speech indicates that Howe's unceasing efforts to improve his style had been successful and that he had largely rid himself of the forced artificiality of his earlier days. In form and substance, it bears a close resemblance to those he would shortly be giving in the course of effecting substantial changes in the province's political institutions. At one juncture he stated that, if he had a profession to choose and could blot out his past sentiments, he would almost certainly become an attorney. He followed with a cynical description of the progress in store for a lawyer who fell in line with the real rulers of the province; it was, in fact, an account of Alexander Stewart's past career and a prophecy, remarkably prescient, of his career to be.[109] Needless to say, the relations between the two men were never the same again.

Howe also took pains to emphasize that, even if Nova Scotians did not automatically acquiesce in the dictates of British statesmen, they could nonetheless be loyal.

My father left his home in the old Colonies ... that he might preserve, in a comparative wilderness, his allegiance to the British Crown. I honour him for the act; and so far as lies in my power, I will pay back the debt of gratitude I owe, by purifying the Institutions and promoting the prosperity of the land which he has made my home ... the best way to prove our loyalty to Britain, is to show that we duly appreciate the struggles in her history, and the glorious principles they conferred ... let us never permit any body of men to make the country too hot for its inhabitants, by selfish infractions upon its peace, and daring inroads on its constitution.[110]

Thus, as he would often do at a crucial stage in his career, Howe invoked his father's loyalty to Britain to demonstrate that he had both a right and a duty to press vigorously for the reform of provincial institutions so as to bring them into line with the British model. About the same time he was taking even bolder steps that were intended to reform the institutions of local government in his native town.

CHAPTER NINE

"A Fool for a Client":
The King *v.* Joseph Howe

January 1, 1835, was to be memorable both for Howe and Nova Scotia. On that day the *Novascotian* published a letter signed "The People," which alleged that "from the pockets of the poor and distressed at least £1000 is drawn annually, and pocketed by men whose services the country might well spare," and that "during the lapse of the last thirty years, the Magistracy and Police have, by one stratagem or other, taken from the pockets of the people, in over exactions, fines, etc. etc., a sum that would exceed in the gross amount of £30,000." In his wildest imaginings Howe could not have foreseen the wide-ranging repercussions of this act, even though the letter was part of a planned campaign against the abuses of the local government of Halifax, and even though he was challenging, as no one before him had done, the men who conducted that government.

The First General Assembly of the province had adopted the Virginian rather than the New England system of municipal government. So, instead of having the functions of local government performed by town meetings and the officials whom they elected, they were entrusted jointly to the justices in sessions (or magistrates), who were selected by the governor and council, and the grand juries, which were composed of substantial proprietors chosen by lot.[1] Over the years, the tendency developed to "subtract from the authority of the grand jury, itself no democratic institution, and to add to that of the even more undemocratic sessions."[2] The upshot of it all, in D.C. Harvey's words, was that "Nova Scotia, like Tudor England, made the Justice of the Peace its man-of-all-work."[3] By the 1820s "the Halifax grand jury's power had declined to the point where the magistrates imposed taxes as they saw fit and ignored nominations which they deemed inappropriate. Although the jurors occasionally protested against magisterial arrogance, they made no concerted effort to improve their subordinate position [in] the civic administration."[4]

David Sutherland has demonstrated that in the 1830s the local governmental functions of Halifax were being performed on a highly stratified basis. At the top was the council, the preserve of the most prestigious merchants and the senior officers of the civil government, who, with the governor, could intervene substantially in local government through both their statutory and prerogative powers. At the second level were the justices or magistrates, possessing "substantial wealth (e.g., an annual income of at least £500), a 'respectable' occupation, and certain genteel social graces," having the proper family connections and religious affiliations, and tending to become more and more of a merchantocracy.[5] The justices in sessions by no means exercised all their powers directly, since a goodly number of largely autonomous boards had been set up to supervise the Bridewell, the public markets, the police department, and other public institutions. Local government in Halifax had, according to Professor Sutherland, "developed into a complex bureaucratic maze where officials were only responsible to themselves or their immediate associates."[6] Nonetheless, those in authority constituted an interlocking oligarchy consisting largely of magistrates, often acting in their individual capacity, and their relatives and hangers-on. Though neither of the John Howes was in receipt of the normal income, both were magistrates in the early thirties, and old John Howe was the senior magistrate in point of service. The two were, of course, eminently respectable, and, perhaps more to the point, neither was likely to disturb the existing order.

If the magistracy was largely upper middle-class, the grand jurors came from the middling ranks of the middle class, in other words, those who could meet a steadily increasing property qualification which stood at £300 in 1833.[7] As proprietor of the *Novascotian*, Howe easily met the required test and was drawn for grand jury duty in 1832. He quickly discovered that the office was not a sinecure, since the grand jury of Halifax met not only in Quarter Sessions but also in numerous special sessions, to make presentments to the magistrates in both civil and criminal matters. Early in the year Howe was indefatigable in his attendance;[8] later, because of his rambles and other business, he was sometimes absent, but he was always there when matters of substance were under consideration. In entering upon these duties, he still held, no less strongly than in 1828,[9] that his objective should be to eliminate the comparatively minor ills of the existing system rather than introduce the greater evil of local elective institutions. But when he took a peep beneath the façade, he quickly realized that much was not well in this supposedly best of all possible worlds.

In the past the grand juries had hardly examined, much less pressed, the recommendations of their predecessors. The one on which Howe sat was of entirely different mettle, and it kept the magistrates in hot water throughout the year. Many of the leading Reformers of Halifax received their early political education as grand jurors, and for Howe the experience was a vital part of his continuing education. While the minutes of the grand jury of 1832 are anything but revealing of the actions of specific jurors, it seems certain that he played a leading role in the initiatives it assumed. By March the jury had noted earlier criticism of William Cleaveland, the clerk of licences, for his inability to account for his returns from fees and liquor licences, and decided to probe into his accounts in his second capacity as county treasurer. Having found nothing but confusion and unintelligibility, it declined to renominate him as treasurer, but when it proposed Edward Pryor, Jr, in his place,[10] the sessions rejected him by a vote of six to three. Neither of the older Howes was present, the majority of six including those magistrates who over the next two or three years rejected all proposals for change.[11] In June the grand jury again nominated Pryor, but this time its recommendation was ignored altogether and Cleaveland continued in office.[12]

The grand jury found it even more galling when others of lesser stature managed to have Cleaveland removed as clerk of licences. It was an indication of the awakening of the middle and even the lower middle classes that the grocers of Halifax had taken their case against the administration of the licence laws to the assembly in January, contending that "hundreds of the Canaille and most worthless Characters in the Town," including the keepers of Brothels, obtained licences as readily as the most respectable dealers and distributed "poison ... in their filthy sinks of iniquity ... [even] on the Sabbath."[13] Having got nowhere, the same group, now calling itself the Grocers' Society, complained by petition to the governor that thirty persons were selling liquor without licences and even had signs advertising their wares attached to their houses without hindrance from Cleaveland.[14] A committee of council having found him to be "an inattentive careless officer,"[15] he was relieved of his duties forthwith.

The immediate outcome was a division within the Howe family. When Cleaveland protested against being deprived of his livelihood, he had the support of eleven magistrates, including the elder Howes, who could not turn down the pleas of a long-time acquaintance. Not so Joseph Howe, who was entirely sympathetic to the well-documented complaints of the grocers, partly because he regarded the middling classes as the backbone of society, and partly because, as an entrepreneur himself, he naturally sided with fellow entrepreneurs who were suffering from a government official's inefficiency. At about the same time he was making it explicit that his only differences with his father related to "the propriety of hammering some of our great folks – he, as you know, thinks this the best of all possible worlds, and the people upon it the best of all possible people. I do not give them credit for so much, and in order to make them better have resort to the lash occasionally."[16]

Howe readily joined the grand jury in applying the lash in its final presentment of the year. This time the sessions received an out-and-out lambasting for permitting the county's accounts to be left "in such a confused and unsatisfactory condition, that it was impossible for any Jury ... to attain a clear view of the state of the revenue and expenditures of the Town." After attributing these ills to "the inefficiency of the officer ... continued in office, in opposition to the presentment of the Grand Jury,"[17] it took the strongest action it could be refusing to levy an assessment for 1833 on the grounds that if economies were introduced and back taxes collected, more than sufficient revenues would be available to carry on the country's business. The puzzling feature is that Howe, though deeply immersed in these proceedings, made so little effort to publicize them. Perhaps he feared that any strong, sustained attack on the sessions would, in effect, be an attack on his half-brother and more especially on his father, for whom he continued to display the greatest solicitude.

The luck of the draw saved the sessions from continuing embarrassment in 1833, since the men who dominated the grand jury were a different breed than those of 1832. A year later, however, it presented quite a different face since it contained associates of Howe like James Leishman, Edward Kenny, and Hugh Bell, all to be identified before long with the Reform party. But basically the motive forces that impelled the grand jury to strong action in 1834 were not men but circumstances. The general awakening in Nova Scotia played its part, but even more important were the continuance and deepening of the recession. Howe, himself severely affected, attributed the primary blame to the bankers' manipulation of the assembly and the consequent failure of the legislature to take the strong action that the situation required. But the ills in local government were also having an unfortunate impact on him, since it was notorious that some large property-holders in Halifax managed to avoid paying their assessments, and to that extent increased the burden on the smaller property-owners. Hoping to press the issue, Howe had declined to pay his own taxes, but succeeded only in having legal action taken against himself, while the abuse still flourished.[18] But perhaps more than anything else, the immediate propellant to taking decisive action against the sessions was their laxity in coping with cholera morbus. In mid-September both the *Acadian Recorder* and the *Novascotian* were depicting conditions in the town in dismal fashion: "The silence of night was not unbroken; the chaise of the Doctor rolled in one direction, the car of the sick and the truck of the dead in another; and, alas! for our nature, the tongues of the prostitutes and of the drunkard, with none to check them, were not unheard, rising in the silent air as if invoking a still heavier scourge on the community which they disgraced."[19] Both papers alleged that the health and police services of the town were collapsing at a time when they were most needed; "as far as [health wardens] were concerned, the poor might lie and die unnoticed, nuisances might exist, purifications and fumigations be neglected, and in short ... matters might proceed as if nothing at all were wrong in their districts."[20]

For good reason, then, the first concerted attack on the establishment in Nova Scotia came at the local level in the town and county of Halifax. Here the ills of the existing system were experienced most harshly in the latter part of 1834; here middle-class frustrations were most concentrated; and here two newspapers were ready to act as a cogent vehicle for their expression. By November Howe had concluded he would have to forgo the inhibitions arising from the membership of his father and half-brother in the Court of Sessions. In conjunction with the more militant members of the grand jury, especially his friend James Leishman, he had determined that this time the sessions would not escape. In a moderate editorial on November 6, he told his readers that he was beginning a campaign against the abuses in local government and warned that, unless these ills were rectified, "a large part of our population are nearly prepared ... to resist."[21]

Two weeks later Howe followed up this editorial with the first of two letters signed "The People," but actually the work of his friend George Thompson, which elaborated his earlier points more fully and sounded a clarion call for action. The recent success of reformers in England, it said, had thrown "a halo of promise over the once gloomy features of Colonial affairs." But Nova Scotians could not hope to rectify colonial abuses until they first reformed the local ills within their control.[22] From then until January 1 Howe remained on the sidelines, except to publicize the memorials and presentments of the grand jury. That was sufficient, so sweeping was its indictment of the magistrates in sessions. On November 14 it approved a memorial to the new governor, Sir Colin Campbell, requesting some method – it could not decide between incorporation of the town or some other device – that would "give the people a greater control over the funds raised from their labor, and over the persons entrusted with the expenditure of those funds for their benefit." Governments, it said, were "made for the people, and not the people for Governments," and it was therefore "a fair inference, that *places indispensably necessary,* should be filled by persons unquestionably eligible, and not places *made,* or filled to accommodate persons, as has been too much the case in many of our public appointments."[23]

Three days later it drew up a presentment to the sessions, expressing perturbation that £552 in taxes were still owing for 1832, and suggesting remedies for dealing with the delinquents. For some unexplained reason it was not until December 2 that the grand jury forwarded these documents to their recipients; a week later it requested Howe to publish both documents in the *Novascotian.* In each case the response was immediate: the sessions replied in terms that the grand jury described as "lame, unintelligible, and unsatisfactory,"[24] while the governor appointed a committee of council to investigate the complaints in the memorial.[25] Meanwhile the grand jury was taking a hard look at the public institutions of Halifax and discovering, among other things, that W.H. Roach, assemblyman, magistrate, flour inspector, and acting commissioner of Bridewell, had systematically perverted that institution, its keepers, and its inmates for his own personal profit.[26] In effect, it was amassing the information that Howe would use during his trial for libel to heap scorn on Roach.

Not surprisingly, when the grand jury got round to making its final presentment on December 16, it declined to accept the Bridewell account "as being incorrect and totally inadmissable," refused to audit the county treasurer's account because it was "incomprehensible," and ended with a warning that "nothing but a thorough reform can prevent ... worse consequences, every succeeding year."[27] Indicating once more its close collaboration with Howe, it asked him to publish its final presentment in the *Novascotian.* Because these documents of the grand jury took up so much space, Howe was unable to print the memorable second letter of "The People" until New Year's Day, 1835.

In publishing this letter, Howe threw down the gauntlet to the sessions, leaving them only two choices, both unpleasant. They might ignore it and, by implication, plead guilty before the bar of public opinion; or they might demand legal action against him and run the certain risk of unpleasant, even damaging revelations. Within a week they had asked the governor to take immediate steps to prosecute the person who had made the charges.[28] Howe might still have escaped prosecution had he been willing to divulge the name of the letter-writer, but he was not asked to do so, and on February 4 Attorney General Archibald informed him of his intention to proceed against him on a charge of criminal libel. For some of the magistrates there must have been gloomy foreboding following Howe's prophecy that, even if they gained a victory, they would not "bear their banners unsullied from the field."[29]

Howe quickly discovered he had any number of willing helpers. When "Justice" wrote to the *Acadian Recorder* asking its readers to supply any information that might help him to contend against "the phalanx of corruption,"[30] the response was overwhelming. "The next day," he said, "I could not get into my office; it was crammed and the passage leading to it, with people, every one of whom had suffered some exaction, had some complaint to expose, or had had justice denied or delayed."[31] Even the magistrates, led by Richard Tremain, next to John Howe, Sr, the ranking member of the sessions in years of service, appeared before Chief Justice Halliburton, requesting that Howe be afforded every facility to substantiate the charges.[32] But to Howe this was a cynical, hypocritical act and he wondered that they could perform it "with [such] amazing power of face."[33]

The suggestion that Howe could not get a lawyer to take his case has no basis in fact. What is true is that every lawyer whom he consulted told him he had no case. "I went to two or three lawyers in succession, showed them the Attorney-General's notice of trial, and asked them if the case could be successfully defended? The answer was, *No*: there was no doubt that the letter was a libel; that I must make my peace, or submit to fine and imprisonment."[34] As the law of libel then stood they were right, for although there was no positive law in England or Nova Scotia defining libel, it was libellous to publish any matter calculated to degrade the persons at whom it was aimed or disturb the public peace.[35] Further, at common law a publisher could not defend himself by demonstrating the truth of his publication, and his motive or intent, especially whether or not he acted from malice, was to be inferred only from a reading of the published matter. To allow evidence of intention to be given in any other way was unknown to the law of the day.[36]

Nonetheless, Howe borrowed books from the lawyers, read libel law for a week, and then told Susan Ann – but no one else – that if he "had the nerve and power to put the whole case before a Jury, as it rested in [his] own mind, and they were fair and rational men, they must acquit [him]."[37] Still, on a stroll to Fort Massey the night before the trial, he confessed his doubts to her. He was worried because he had not had time to commit to memory anything more than the two opening paragraphs of his address to the jury. Other questions also crossed his mind: could he get out of his head what he had put into it, or would be break down because of the novelty of the situation and the want of practice?[38] When he entered the courtroom the next morning, the scene, he said, beggared all description. The room was "crammed to over-flowing, and as hot as a furnace." While he noted the presence of a goodly representation of the Halifax establishment, including some of the magistrates under attack, he saw many more of the "middling" members of the society, whose cause had been his cause, and upon whose sympathies he relied. Indeed, he was confident that, except for the magistrates and their immediate friends, "all ranks and classes, from the highest to the lowest, were in [his] favour." He also knew that they feared – because the charges against the sessions were "so glaring and so gross" – that he would be convicted; yet he was aware too that they were prepared to "console [him] during a 3 months' imprisonment and to pay from £100 to £300 of a fine, which would have been done in two hours, by subscription."[39]

Howe had little to rejoice about in the principal officers of the court. It was not a trial with a single judge and jury, but "a trial at bar before the whole bench of judges and a [special] jury."[40] Presiding over the court was Brenton Halliburton, the chief justice, whose conduct Howe had more than once criticized, and whose appointment he had condemned because Halliburton had "mingled much and warmly in politics."[41] Acting as chief prosecutor was Attorney General Archibald, who, while he still called Howe a friend, could hardly have been pleased by the latter's attacks on an assembly over which he presided and in which he did much to set the tone. Nevertheless, Howe had some advantages. By mid-January the committee of the council had confirmed many of the charges of the grand jury,[42] and this meant that the sessions already stood condemned in the eyes of the public by a body which could in no sense be said to be biased against them. Of even greater significance was the composition of the jury. Five of the jurors had served with Howe on the militant grand jury of 1832,[43] and one of them, Edward Pryor, Jr, had been kept out of the county treasurership by the arbitrary action of the sessions. Howe must surely have realized that these men were unlikely to agree to his conviction.

The Crown did not take long to present its case. James F. Gray, who was assisting Archibald, outlined the position of the prosecution and then called his only witness, Hugh Blackadar of the *Acadian Recorder*, to establish the publication of the alleged libel. When Blackadar hesitated about testifying against a fellow newspaperman, Howe made all the admissions that were required. The prothonotary read the letter signed "The People" into the record and the Crown rested its case. Howe called no witnesses and started his address to the jury forthwith.[44]

If the law had been as it once was, he might as well have given up at this stage. Formerly the jury had simply established the fact of publication and the judge had determined the existence of a libel, but both these functions had now become the prerogative of the jury.[45] Hence, whatever the chief justice thought about the publication, it was of no consequence if Howe could convince the jury otherwise. Although he had been reminded of the old maxim that "he who pleads his own case has a fool for a client," his wisdom in acting on his own behalf was now apparent.[46] Any lawyer who took his case would have been restricted by the court to reading excerpts from the letter in an attempt to show that it was not calculated to degrade the magistrates or disturb the peace, and therefore not a libel. Howe, on the other hand, might come up with an unorthodox defence and, as a layman, be given wide leeway to use it.

Certainly he missed not a trick, even to the point of being utterly irrelevant. In the normal language of the indictments of that day, he was accused of "wickedly, maliciously, and seditiously contriving, devising, and intending to stir up and excite discontent and sedition among His Majesty's subjects."[47] This gave him the opportunity to quote at length from one of his "sermons on sedition," the article entitled "England and her Colonies," which, as previously noted, had been published in the *Novascotian* five years earlier and has seldom been bettered in its professions of loyalty.[48] Howe continued: "While I sat in my office penning these passages, which were to excite disaffection and rebellion, some of their worships were plundering the poor; and others, by their neglect, were tacitly sanctioning petty frauds and grinding exactions; and if His Majesty sat upon that bench ... [he] would tell them that he who robs the subject makes war upon the King; ... he would tell them they were the rebels, and that against them and not against me, this bill of indictment should have been filed."[49]

Sometimes in his preliminary remarks he was anything but fair to his prosecutors. Scornfully, he referred to Richard Tremain and the magistrates piously asking the chief justice to allow him every opportunity to substantiate his charges, even though they knew they had put him in a strait-jacket from which no judge could remove him. But even he would have had to admit that the magistrates' course of action was severely limited. Only if they had proceeded against him in a civil action would he have had the opportunity to justify the charges against them. But the charges were against the whole body of magistrates, and there was no way under the existing law that a public body could vindicate itself in a civil action.[50] As it was, Attorney General Archibald had taken every precaution to ensure that Howe could not allege unfair treatment. He might have proceeded through an ex officio information or a bill of indictment, and had decided against the former since it would have denied Howe the right to have the charges against him considered in the first instance by a grand jury.[51] But neither method would have permitted Howe to demonstrate the truth of the charges, and for him it was just as well they did not. He would then have had to prove wrongdoing against everyone who had served on the sessions in Halifax over the preceding thirty years, something he neither was able nor wanted to do.

Howe raised the most merriment, heaped the greatest scorn, and enjoyed his fullest success when he managed, through the back door, to introduce material supporting his charges that no judge would have admitted by the front door. He told the jury that, if he read the law correctly, the court could not permit him to demonstrate that the charges in the letter were true. But as he understood the law relating to motive and intention, he was permitted to show that, when he published the letter, he was thinking in terms, not of tempting others to a breach of the peace, but of restoring and preserving the peace. So repeatedly throughout his address he asked the jury if he would not have failed in his duty of maintaining the peace had he not acquainted the public with the facts in the letter. Thus he was able to examine the ills of local government much as he willed under the guise of conforming to his own views of motive and intention.[52]

In developing his case, Howe turned first to the ills he attributed to the magistracy as a whole. Here there was little that was new. Howe simply repeated the complaints of earlier grand juries, many of which had been confirmed by the committee of the council, that the method of collecting taxes was partial and unjust, and that the burden was borne by only a part of the community, instead of being equally distributed among the whole. He contended that, if taxes had been collected on all the ratable property at the prevailing rate, the total yield would have been £4,500 even though only £700 to £800 per annum was required. On that basis he concluded that his charges that the method of raising the taxes had in itself wrought injustice in the amount of £1,000 a year were conservative, and that his accusations of over-exactions of £30,000 in thirty years were fully justified.[53]

In his blanket indictment Howe included all the magistrates. "The law makes a looker-on at a felony a participator in the crime. These men looked on for years [and declined to] take any step to produce a reform till driven to it by the refusal of grand juries any longer to assess."[54] In turning to specific magistrates, Howe largely made use of the evidence which had been collected first-hand by the grand juries, particularly that of 1834,[55] and which was never successfully refuted. First on Howe's list was magistrate W.H. Roach, the acting commissioner of Bridewell and inspector of flour, who, according to the grand jury, had used the Bridewell, its employees, and its inmates as if they were his own property. Its woodhouse had become a stable for his horse, the wood being piled out in the yard; one of its cells contained his celery packed in earth, another the rest of his vegetables. The under-keeper inspected his flour; one prisoner manufactured buckets for him; another made boots and shoes for his relatives and his friends; other prisoners fed and watered his horse, or banked his house. "He was in truth," said Howe, "like the ruler in Scripture, who said to one 'go, and he goeth; and to another do this, and he doeth it.'" What, Howe asked, would be "the moral effect of all this upon the poor petit larceny wretches confined in Bridewell ... for the purpose of reformation"?[56]

Next Howe turned to Richard Tremain, who for many years had been one of the commissioners regulating the Poor Asylum, and who, contrary to law, Howe said – more on hearsay and personal knowledge than hard evidence – had furnished supplies, often of an inferior quality and at an exorbitant price, to an institution he helped to regulate. "What would not a man do, who would thus wring a profit from an establishment dedicated to the comfort of the poor and destitute; who would thus filch from mendicants to put money in his purse?"[57] Finally Howe turned his attention to the operations of the so-called brick-building, where the business of the clerk of the peace, the police office, and the commissioners' court was conducted. Here he pointedly asked one unnamed magistrate why there never was any accounting of the fees and fines, and why the fines were "levied by fits and starts in an arbitrary and desultory manner, by which the law is made onerous, and yet contemptible?"[58] Through all his recital of specific ills Howe never failed to interject a question explanatory of his motive: "Now, gentlemen, with this evidence before me ... could I have dared to refuse publication to that letter?"[59]

Howe was done with the magistrates. He concluded with an appeal to the jurors, asking them to do what an English jury might be expected to do in similar cases. "Will you, my countrymen, the descendants of these men, warmed by their blood, inheriting their language, and having the principles for which they struggled confined to your care, allow them to be violated in your hands?"[60] But even if he were convicted he would not desert his principles, but toil on in the hope of better times. "Yes, gentlemen, come what will, while I live, Nova Scotia shall have the blessing of an open and unshackled press."[61] Howe had previously spoken only once or twice in public, but he now emerged, almost overnight, as a full-blown orator. On this occasion his oratory displayed all the characteristics that were to play a substantial role in his later political success. He himself realized how effective he had been; indeed, as he watched the tears flowing copiously down the cheeks of an elderly juror, he knew beyond all doubt that he could not be convicted.[62] But although it was magnificent, from the point of view of the law it was magnificently irrelevant. Furthermore, for all his skill, had he made a tactical error? By speaking six hours and a quarter he had so extended the sitting of the court that it was found necessary to adjourn for the day. In the interval not only might the Crown "reconstruct [its] case,"[63] but the effect of his speech might be dissipated.

Actually the events of March 3 were an anti-climax. Attorney General Archibald, in a calm, unemotional manner, told the jury that Howe had "stated a great variety of things which could not be evidence, which are mere hearsay, and which the court would not have permitted counsel to use,"[64] and suggested that the law was so definite and Howe's power of reasoning so clear that, were he a member of the jury, he might be persuaded to convict himself. Then it was the chief justice's turn. Clearly Halliburton had been in an extremely difficult position throughout the trial, especially because he was trying one who had subjected him to attack and who had the sympathy of most of the spectators in the court room.[65] Accordingly he had followed the line of least resistance as the course best calculated not to damage his position as a judge. Early in Howe's speech he had reached an understanding with the spectators that, while they might laugh at Howe's "occasional corruscations of humour,"[66] they were not to applaud; he had also decided to permit Howe any amount of irrelevancy without intervention. In concluding his charge to the jury, he simply said: "In my opinion, the paper charged is a libel, and your duty is, to state by your verdict that it is libellous. You are not bound by my opinion ... If you think that this is not a libel, as a consequence, you must think that it bears no reflections injurious to the complaining parties. If this is your opinion say so; I leave the case in your hands."[67]

It was in the jury's hands barely ten minutes; that was all the time it needed to decide to take its view of libel, not from Archibald, not from Halliburton, but from Howe, and bring in a verdict of "not guilty." For a moment there was a breathless silence, then shouts of approbation from the crowds in and around the court house. For the rest of the day and the next most of Halifax celebrated. All the sleds in town turned out in procession to serenade Howe. Everyone joined in the festivities, wrote the *Recorder*, except those who, if they had been able to confine him in prison or mulct him to their satisfaction, might have made "the exposure of abuses ... a dangerous amusement."[68] Every newspaperman in Halifax hailed Howe's success, even his old enemy Edmund Ward, formerly the editor of the *Free Press* and now of the *Temperance Recorder*, who wrote that the verdict was "received with an expresion of feeling never before witnessed in this community, and a universal satisfaction seemed to enliven every countenance."[69] Nova Scotians beyond Halifax got a full account of the trial, first in the *Novascotian* of March 12, which published the speeches verbatim, and later in a pamphlet that was sold at county newspaper offices throughout the province.[70]

In the first issue of the *Novascotian* after the trial, Howe boasted that "the press of Nova-Scotia is Free," and it is often stated that Howe established the freedom of the press through his acquittal in 1835. This is a myth that has little basis in fact. Howe had, in effect, convinced the jury that the law applicable to the case was "an ass." But, as Sir Joseph Chisholm has pointed out, "the law is not changed by the verdict of juries [even though] it is sometimes disregarded by juries in their verdicts."[71] In the matter of civil libel, Howe was to learn at close hand that the press of Nova Scotia was not free when, in December 1843, Richard Nugent, his successor as proprietor of the *Novascotian*, was forced to give up the newspaper and actually suffered imprisonment because he was unable to pay the damages awarded against him in a series of actions for libel taken against him by the Tories.[72] In the matter of criminal libel, there would not be freedom of the press until the truth of the libel could be used as a defence. Not until 1843 did the British Parliament enact a statute which permitted that defence, if it could be shown that the publication of the alleged libel was for the public benefit.[73] But obviously there was no connection between Howe's libel suit in 1835 and the action of the British Parliament eight years later.

The immediate outcome of the trial was to create a shambles in the local government of Halifax. W.H. Roach and Matthew Richardson resigned from the sessions within two days of Howe's acquittal, and Roach also relinquished the commissionership of the poor. Even stronger evidence of the traumatic shock experienced by the magistrates was the resignation of four other justices, all identified with the highly conservative wing of the sessions. James Tidmarsh was unwilling to retain an office in which he found neither "*Comfort, Respect,* or *Character*";[74] Joseph Starr got out because "the very name of Magistrate [had become] a byword & reproach in the place, and they are treated with insult by all classes from the highest to the lowest."[75] The worst was still to come. To meet the emergency in the sessions, the governor and council appointed thirteen new magistrates on March 11, only to produce a reaction that was unprecedented in Nova Scotia. Within a day six of their designates had refused the office, and within a week three others. Most of them said that the pressure of their own concerns forced them to decline, but they may have been less forthright than the merchant Lawrence Hartshorne, who gave as his reason, "the result of the late trial, by which it appears that the Editor of a licentious News Paper may, with impunity, first libel the whole Bench of Magistrates, and then in the face of a Court attempt to brand with impunity one of that body [Tremain] who had been on the Commission of the Peace upwards of thirty years, and in my humble opinion conducted himself honorably and zealously."[76]

Simultaneously with the gazetting of the new magistrates, William Q. Sawers, a Halifax lawyer who was already serving as custos rotulorum and judge of the Inferior Court of Common Pleas of the Eastern District, was also appointed custos rotulorum or ranking magistrate of the district of Halifax, and concomitantly the supervisor of its police establishment.[77] To Howe the appointee was notoriously deficient in order and regularity, wont to mingle in street affrays, and had no redeeming virtue of which he was aware,[78] and the *Times*, in no sense friendly to Howe, agreed that the failure to fill up the Halifax magistracy resulted partly from objections to Sawers's appointment as custos rotulorum.[79] A little later some residents of Pictou in the Eastern district also denounced Sawers for his irregular conduct.[80] To say the least, he did not seem suited to leading Halifax into a new era in local government, and to Howe his appointment was clear proof that Governor Campbell was still in the clutches of men who had no desire to remedy the abuses in the county's affairs. During the next year he was at long last to give up any thought of reforming the sessions and think only in terms of elective local institutions.[81] Nothing illustrates the character of Howe the conservative reformer better than this sequence of events. Even after his trial and his forceful demonstration of the frailties of the sessions, he still saw no need to effect any basic changes, provided that the existing system of checks and balances was permitted to function properly. He had no doubt that the grand jury could do its part in checking the sessions if the governor and council used wisely their power to appoint magistrates. But when Governor Campbell made a mockery of local government by riveting a man of Sawers's qualities upon the sessions even a conservative reformer saw the need for fundamental change.

Other repercussions of the trial were to draw Howe into conflict in an even more personal way in defence of his father. During the trial he had taken special care to exempt the old man from his general criticism of the magistracy: "He never carried the municipal bag; he never took a shilling of the fees to which he was entitled; he had nothing to do with their dirty accounts and paltry peculations ... if he had a fault, it was that, being an honest man himself, he could not believe that there was a scoundrel on the face of the earth."[82] Two or three years earlier Joseph had said that his father was performing "the duties of magistrate as ably, and energetically as ever."[83] But there had been a marked change in old John Howe's mental processes since that time. Always friendly to the poor, he had become obsessed with the idea that he ought to devote the remaining portion of his life to improving their condition. Accordingly, he was seeking to settle as many of them as possible on a large tract of land on the Dartmouth side of Halifax harbour. To that end he placed orders for ploughs, harrows, and spinning wheels, and he would have incurred large obligations if the younger John Howe had not prevented his orders from being carried into effect.[84]

In 1832 John Howe, Sr, had presided over a court in which Sawers, acting as counsel for the defence, had assailed some of the institutions and values that the old man held most dear, even daring to suggest that a governor could not place sentries wherever the King's service required them. At the same time he not only charged the court with tyranny and injustice, but so abused the members of the jury which convicted his clients that its foreman felt obliged to ask the protection of the court. John Howe was outraged, but no more so than his fellow magistrates, who, Richard Tremain alone dissenting, condemned Sawers's actions and declined to let him practise before them until he had made a public apology.[85]

Nonetheless, late in March 1835, someone signing himself "G" inserted a letter in the *Novascotian* unabashedly defending Sawers's appointment and crediting him with being the first to point out the ills of the judiciary.[86] The next issue of the paper contained a reply by John Howe, Sr, in which the eighty-one-year old man, bursting with indignation, stated it was nothing less than monstrous to picture Sawers as a reformer of the courts; rather, he should have been castigated for making "a lawless and impudent attack upon a Court which was fairly and impartially performing its duties."[87] The old man's action was all the more astounding, coming as it did from one of the most respected members of the community, who had avoided partisan controversy like the plague during all his adult life, and had seldom if ever written a letter to a newspaper.[88] It was almost as surprising that Joseph permitted it to be published, knowing as he would that it might lead to ferocious attacks on the man he most revered.

Perhaps because there was nothing irrational about the older Howe's letter, Joseph hoped it would escape rough treatment, but if he did he was quickly disillusioned, for Sawers and his friends reacted violently to the statement that "not many ... have the least confidence in the person, to whom, it appears, its most important affairs have been committed."[89] The outcome was a rancorous two-month debate, carried on largely by correspondents in the *Acadian Recorder*, and later the *Times*, in which for the first time in his life John Howe was the target of angry, bitter criticism, allegedly because he had allowed a pitiful squabble at the Court of Sessions to colour his judgment and cause him to proceed malevolently against Sawers. In the *Acadian Recorder*, "Nemo" told him that he had long been an encumbrance to the sessions and that its younger members respected his age, but pitied his imbecility.[90] In the *Times*, "Investigator" wrote that his letter did "not manifest the disposition of a follower of the meek and lowly Lamb,"[91] while "Inquirer" suggested that his "language and style would far better suit the mouth of a Billingsgate fish wife" than a devout Christian.[92]

For a time Joseph Howe kept his peace, even though one of the letter-writers asked why "the keen mind of the son had not prevented instead of laying to the public gaze a parent's failing."[93] But in the end, as Howe himself put it many years later, "I had ... to take up my pen, and clear the decks of these scribblers which I did, giving Sawers some deserved hard knocks in return for those given to my father."[94] In three separate editorials, he lashed out at "the little knot of brainless boobies" who were criticizing the newspapers' treatment of Sawers. If the people of Halifax had foisted upon them "as their Chief Magistrate a man known to them only by his vices ... to whom can [they] look but to the Press?"[95] With these editorials Howe was done with Sawers, and he was content to let "Richard Rabblehater" and "Philo Booby" continue the controversy without reply.[96]

Old John Howe's letter led to a second controversy because of its statement – only partially correct – that the sessions had refused to sit with Tremain until he had taken steps to clear his name.[97] Naturally Tremain was indignant that the "Father of the Bench" had written something so much at variance with his professions, and asked pointedly: "If he took any part, should it not rather have been to breathe peace and good will among men," or at least to reconcile his two sons on these matters.[98] At the same time he told Governor Campbell that the two Howes were conducting a vendetta against him, warning him forcefully that, because of the outcome of the trial, no magistrate, however pure his conduct, could hope to launch a successful action against an editor: "If Public men are to seek the approval of Editors of Newspapers, instead of the Government from whence their authority is derived, soon will they become the master power, and great & small must court their countenance."[99] Tremain also defended his thirty-year stewardship in local government at length in the *Halifax Journal*.[100] But since he failed to address himself to the specific accusations against him, Howe told him to do one of two things: either to institute proceedings against him, or to have a full public discussion of his conduct, during which Howe would admit any errors on his part, but also show Tremain where his defence was weak and where he needed to provide further information. "Let him take the choice of the two courses – we are prepared for either."[101] Whatever the reason, Tremain chose not to reply.

Amidst all the acrimony there was one pleasant note: Howe appeared in the long room of the Exchange Coffee House on March 30 to receive a piece of plate from his fellow-countrymen in New York for his defence of the freedom of the press.[102] Because of the repercussions of the trial, not until late June could he set out on the kind of ramble that, since 1829, had had the effect of an invigorating tonic and restored his normal zest for action. For three weeks he made his way through the Musquodoboit and Stewiacke valleys to Truro and Amherst; across the Bay of Fundy to Windsor, Lunenburg, and Liverpool; back to Windsor and home. As usual, he spared neither himself nor his horse, and by the time he reached Windsor the horse's back was so chafed that he was forced to leave it behind until he returned from the South Shore.[103] The further he went the more he appreciated the dangers he had incurred in risking a heavy fine for libel. Everywhere recession had laid its heavy hand on the land, and the debts on his books remained almost uncollectable. At Truro he dunned doctors and lawyers all morning, but collected not a pound. From Amherst he reported that he had ridden between two and three hundred miles in eight days, and had only £7 to show for his efforts.[104] If anything, his finances were in a worse snarl than usual, and his instructions to Susan Ann on the best way to manipulate his outstanding notes so as to ensure the continued accommodation of the two Halifax banks are bewildering beyond description. "I do not by any means despair of getting through," he told her, "although the prospect seems cloudy enough."[105]

However inhospitable the weather and the roads, and however

poor the collections, Howe's reception in the towns, the hamlets, and the countryside exceeded anything he had anticipated:

the trial has given me a lift and a hold upon the hearts of the population that I could not have dreamed of. I believe from my heart that I could beat [S.G.W.] Archibald in a contest for Colchester without an hour's canvas. But Musquodoboit which will belong to the new County of Halifax[106] will vote for me to a man before any other candidate that may offer – there will be no election, however, until next year, of which I am very glad.[107]

Here, perhaps for the first time, he was making it clear that he intended to run in the next general election; here too he let it be known that he had established a special kind of rapport with many of his countrymen:

If I meet a man in the very depth of the forest – or men under a shed out of the rain – persons I never saw or heard of, the moment they find out my name, greet me with good wishes, and talk about the trial – ... the New York Present – and do me any service in their power. Please God, if I once get [into] my hands a little force, I will endeavor to do something much more worthy of all this than any thing I have done yet.[108]

The trial and its aftermath left its mark on Howe, and indirectly on Nova Scotia, in more ways than one. Above all, it convinced him that his countrymen would not secure the rights of Englishmen at either the provincial or the municipal level through newspaper writing alone. He was now prepared to take the next step and let himself be nominated for the assembly.

CHAPTER TEN

The Road to the Assembly

The trial and its aftermath were to make Howe a much more active advocate of reform. Yet it is difficult to disentangle the elements that made up Howe the reformer since he at no time attempted to examine the basis of his reformist beliefs. Clearly part of it rested on the middle-class values of which he was so eloquent a spokesman. If men of the middle class were permitted an appropriate share in government, they would see to it that the waste and excessive expenditures which characterized the existing order and penalized small businesses were eliminated. No less important, these men would give a new orientation to government and public opinion that would alter substantially the very ethos of the society.

There was also the Howe who took pride in his liberal but by no means democratic views. They might lead him to advocate the removal of Catholic disabilities, provision of equal rights for Irish Catholics, or reform of an archaic system of representation, but whatever course they induced him to pursue, he equated the liberal way with the rational way; it was a good guide because it accorded with his own sense of reasonableness. Yet these two features of his reformism must be understood in the context of the mild toryism that characterized his early adult years and left its mark on his later years. It meant that he was unlikely to proceed to outright radicalism and that change would have to make a good case for itself before he could support it. His toryism also meant a degree of compassion for the unfortunates of society that is not ordinarily associated with nineteenth-century laissez-faire liberalism, but was a natural inheritance of a son of old John Howe. On balance, it makes good sense to treat Joseph Howe as a conservative reformer, even though that description does not take fully into account the complexity of his ideological make-up.

This was the man who, despite his own financial troubles, became more and more self-assured and ebullient in the closing months of 1835. He always felt that way when he faced a strong challenge and thought he knew how to meet it. In his new exuberance he was more confident than he had been for a long time about the future of Halifax and Nova Scotia. Dismissing "the croaking, foreboding, and apathy" of the day as mainly the product of a business recession that seemed to be dissipating,[1] he prophesied that Nova Scotia would progress no less than in the past, and that, if its people changed their habits and improved their government, it would become "what it should become, a busy hive – crowded with wealth, activity, order and intelligence."[2]

During October and November he suggested a few enterprises that might provide profitable opportunities for the investment of capital and substantial employment for the labouring class. In first place he put a railroad from Halifax to Windsor, which he supported altogether too extravagantly in three lengthy articles.[3] A railroad built across the thirty miles of bad land between Halifax harbour and the Ardoise Hills of Hants county would enable Halifax to command all the trade of Minas Basin and let it advance in wealth as the midland counties progressed. "An old woman in Windsor might fill her baskets with vegetables, and, coming down on the railway, reach Halifax as early in the day, as the blacks from Preston get here with their berries. A Fisherman, who found the Halifax market supplied, could take the contents of his flat to Windsor, and return [in] time enough to row himself home to Ferguson's Cove."[4] As a complement to the railroad, Howe also advocated the establishment of a large well-conducted hotel in Halifax "to attract as many ... wealthy travellers ... as possible ... [from the United States] into Nova Scotia."[5]

But political occurrences having a bearing on progress drew most of his attention. Perturbed by rumours that dispatches were passing across the Atlantic exploring the possibility of a political union with New Brunswick, he categorically opposed "any attempt to destroy [the provinces'] institutions ... and divert their industry from tried and appropriate channels, into others of doubtful advantage."[6] Even more worrisome to him was the drift of events in Canada. Although he wished to portray the Reformers of Lower Canada in as favourable a light as possible, he continued to bewail the violent spirit of party in their newspapers.[7] To him it appeared as if the time was fast approaching when the British government would have to decide once and for all either to conciliate or coerce the Papineau party.[8]

In a letter to H.S. Chapman Howe declined outright to be associated with any actions of the Lower Canadians. Chapman, who had been deputized by the Lower Canada House of Assembly to support its petition to the House of Commons and explain its case to the liberal press in London, had sought through Howe to get the Nova Scotia Assembly to forward an accompanying petition; in return, he offered to publicize Nova Scotia's case in London.[9] Howe did not mince words in his reply: two-thirds of the Nova Scotia House of Assembly would not support the kind of petition that Chapman wanted; further, if Lower Canadians precipitated a struggle for independence for which they were unprepared either by education or resources, they would not be supported by the lower colonies.[10] Howe's letter did not become public knowledge at the time, but when it did he was criticized, strangely enough, for not being sufficiently positive in rejecting the advances of the "disloyal" Canadians.[11]

Howe was still confident that Nova Scotia could perfect its political institutions through negotiations with the Colonial Office, but first it must put its own house in order by electing the right kind of assembly. For much too long it had left the choice of members to chance and had not taken enough care to secure candidates of talent and integrity. As a result, the merchant had used his ledger to get himself elected, the publican his rum cask, the lawyer his writs, and the others "a vile system of deception and chicane, backed by a profuse outpouring of bad rum and porter,"[12] the outcome being to rivet the rottenness of Denmark upon the province. Only the supineness of the people stood in the way of an enlightened assembly. Instead of letting half-a-dozen candidates "as ignorant as horses ... and presuming on their own wealth, or personal or professional influence"[13] throw themselves upon the constituency at the last moment, the freeholders should assemble well in advance of the elections, choose suitable candidates, and indicate to them that they had been chosen because of their principles and would be replaced if these were deserted.

That was the message which Howe never wearied of repeating over the next year or two. Thus when he wrote to Jotham Blanchard in October 1835, he pointed out that, although the ordinary people had the advantage of numbers, they were lacking in discipline, knowledge, and leadership. Hoping that Blanchard would supply the leadership, he had counted on serving under him for many years. Yet since the election of 1830 Blanchard had seemingly become "a covert enemy to public measures," or at least "a very suspicious and languid supporter"[14] of principles he had long advocated, and at times Howe had treated him unkindly. For that he was now sorry, since he had only recently learned that Blanchard's health had deprived him of the energy that the times demanded.[15]

Howe's decision to play a more forceful role in politics drew the attention of both critics and friends. Letter-writers in the *Times* wondered if he aspired to speak for Nova Scotians just as the *Vindicator* spoke for Lower Canadians, and, if he did, to "let us distinctly know whether we are to fight under the banner of Papineau or Old England."[16] While Howe told such critics they would not like anything the editor of the *Novascotian* wrote, he took much more seriously the advice of friends like Thomas Chandler Haliburton not to embark on an active political career. He had been seeing more of Haliburton since he had begun to print weekly instalments of *The Clockmaker* in the *Novascotian*. Almost in the same breath that Haliburton told Howe to "*mind the spelling of [Sam] Slick's nonsense, the dialect is half the wit,*"[17] he was also warning him that he would not advance his own interest by going into the assembly: "I fear your paper (always enough on one side of politics) will be thought after your election ... a party paper altogether – I fear you will hurt it, and it will hurt you, and like a gig that runs over a cow, it kills the animal and breaks the carriage. I say consider well, cypher like Slick, set down the advantages on one side, it will make a damn small column, and put the disadvantages on the other, and strike the balance – do this carefully and then decide."[18] Yet Haliburton admitted he was not unduly alarmed since Howe was an old navigator and knew his way, even though "you do crowd on sail like the devil sometimes."[19]

Howe did not seize the first opportunity to be elected, notwithstanding the fact that his opponents had long interpreted every act of his as being motivated by a desire to get into the assembly. "I could not go out to shoot a Partridge in the woods, or catch a Trout in the streams, without being suspected of canvassing for the next election."[20] In November, however, he refused to run against Hugh Bell for the vacant seat[21] in the township of Halifax largely because he was satisfied with both the candidate and the means used to choose him. Bell, neither a lawyer nor an Anglican, espoused much the same principles that he did; further, he had been chosen, not by a small clique of public officers and wealthy merchants, but by a public meeting of the middle class, "which in all Countries should possess the power, as they usually do the industry and intelligence [but] which in our elections have been scarcely consulted at all."[22] Howe hoped it was the dawning of a new day in which public officers and bankers would no longer control the council, nor lawyers the assembly. Certainly it was high time that "a profession embracing some 80 or 90 persons, should [not] enjoy more political power and influence than the other 170,000 persons, who compose our population, put together."[23]

For a short time in December Howe forgot about politics. Throughout the year there had been a further deterioration in his father's mental health. Philosophically, Howe accepted "a most embarrassing circumstance," simply saying it "must be got over."[24] He debated with his half-brother John the possibility of limiting their father's activities, but they could not bring themselves to this distasteful course, even though the old man was a constant source of worry. In the end fate lent a helping hand. On a Sunday late in December old John Howe presided over a Sandemanian service at the home of his friends, the Reeves, on the eastern road near Dartmouth. That night, still at the Reeves, he died in his sleep. For Howe the passing of "our worthy father" did not produce the traumatic shock it once might have done; indeed, it brought a sense of relief. But for years his speeches continued to make nostalgic references to the "venerable figure" who had left such a deep impact upon his thinking and behaviour.

Howe's new buoyancy continued to manifest itself when the legislature met in January 1836. No matter what the assembly did he refused to become excited over a body composed as it was. Only once did he let his temperature rise a little. That was when the council and the assembly, through disagreement, let a temporary law expire and left the country without any fixed standard of value.[25] Still, he saw some signs that public opinion was finally beginning to act upon the legislature. The council, hoping to ride with the breeze it could not control, had at long last begun to print its journals and exchange them with the assembly, while the assembly, on its own, had forwarded an address to England protesting that the fees exacted by the judges were illegal and unconstitutional.[26] Howe was even delighted that Governor Campbell's speech closing the session was made up largely of regrets: "it is of less consequence to displease the Executive than to displease the people."[27] He feared nonetheless that changes of substance would be opposed with such "pious horror" in Nova Scotia and the other colonies that, unless more determined assemblymen were elected, "a century hence ... these Provinces [would not] have ... half the control over their own funds and their own affairs, that is constantly exercised by an English corporation."[28]

For three months Howe's reports of the debates had crowded out everything else in the *Novascotian*. Finally, in mid-May, he revelled in being able to "blow a blast ... through [his] own trumpet"[29] and expressed particular delight in the rapport that had developed between him and his readers: "We sit in our Editorial Chair as if in the midst of a family circle – we take up our pen, as though we were about to pour out thoughts, without disguise or restraint, to those who take the same interest in our welfare that we do in theirs – and the severity of whose criticism is certain to be tempered by old recollections and growing confidence."[30] His message to his family of readers was an optimistic one: the prices of country produce were good; imports of foreign goods were likely to be large; Halifax was, in fact, recovering from stagnation and paralysis.[31] No less gratifying, the Mechanics' Institute he had helped found was succeeding beyond all expectations, so much so that a little earlier, when Principal Thomas McCulloch came from Pictou to lecture on chemical affinities, fifty persons had to be turned away.[32]

Howe had plans for other institutions that would benefit the community. One proposal was a House of Industry, similar to that at Boston, which would relieve Halifax of the crowd of beggars who assailed the passer-by at every step. "A man might walk Boston streets for a month, and not see a beggar. Here, if he be charitable, he may be called on to give away as much as would pay his board."[33] He also favoured undertakings which, by uniting persons of all political colours, would demonstrate that those who disagreed on some subjects need not differ on all. To that end he resurrected his idea of a Horticultural Society[34] and in this instance his hopes were soon realized.[35] But he had no success in getting money to survey a railway line from Halifax to Windsor even though, at his request, J.B. Uniacke had sought £300 from the assembly for that purpose.[36] Howe still insisted, nonetheless, that if Nova Scotia could develop its resources by internal communications, "she will be better worth fighting about. There will then be, even in our political contentions, a dignity and pride which sometimes they may not possess."[37]

Meanwhile his weekly publication of Haliburton's satirical sketches under the title *The Clockmaker* was proving so popular that some readers wanted them published as a book. Haliburton offered to forgo any return for himself; "if there be any little emolument, it belongs of right to him, who has already had the trouble of publishing a great part of them gratuitously."[38] Accordingly Howe agreed to publish the sketches already in print, together with the rest of the series, in "a nice little volume of about 200 pages; prices in boards, 5s." Another of his attempts to encourage native literary talent, he hoped he would do better with it than he had with Haliburton's *History*.

Almost before he knew it, Howe was again immersed in politics. While the assembly had another year to run, he knew that Governor Campbell wanted to dissolve it for fear it would be even more intractable in what was certain to be a pre-election session. But he also realized that a dissolution was unlikely until the colonial secretary had assented to an act of the legislature which erected each of the districts of Halifax – Halifax, Colchester, and Pictou – into separate counties and provided that both the new county of Halifax, as well as the township of Halifax, would elect two members. Howe left no doubt about his desire to run for the county seat, which included the Musquodoboit Valley. His rambles among its settlements, the visits of its residents to his newspaper office, and his frequent exchange of correspondence with the Rev. John Sprott had convinced him that reform feeling was as pronounced there as anywhere in the province.

Following his views that the electors must act on their own, he made it clear he would "solicit no man's vote – waste no money – and only act in the matter in obedience to the wishes of the people publicly expressed."[39] Hence he was altogether delighted when, without his being present, the freeholders of Middle Musquodoboit met on May 26 and agreed to support only those candidates who pledged themselves to measures of essential reform, and to nominate as their candidates Joseph Howe and the local resident, H.A. Gladwin. Howe, who had more than once enjoyed Gladwin's hospitality, told him he was "by far the most likely person in Musquodoboit to obtain support in [the town of] Halifax,"[40] only to discover that, when the freeholders of Upper Musquodoboit met on June 6, they substituted the name of William Annand for that of Gladwin.

Nevertheless, Howe expressed great satisfaction with the new direction in politics when, at their request, he met the residents of the three Musquodoboit settlements on June 16. Formerly, he told them, prospective candidates had ridden about the county for a month, "thrusting themselves into every man's house ... and telling as many lies as would, were they correctly recorded, overwhelm a man of spirit with shame";[41] now the freeholders were making a deliberate selection of candidates after the latter had openly declared their sentiments and principles. But Howe was also learning that open meetings had their drawbacks, for although all the 300 freeholders at the meeting supported his candidature, they were badly divided in choosing between Annand and Gladwin, and neither of the two would withdraw. Thoroughly perturbed, Howe warned Gladwin that the division might prevent either resident of Musquodoboit from being elected and lead to the return of an anti-reform candidate.[42]

Immediately after the dissolution in mid-October Howe read another lecture to his fellow countrymen. What use would it have been for him to have spent "seven years in fault finding and acrimonious criticism, if [the people] will not spend seven days in securing a House that shall truly represent them?"[43] Let them remember that their right to elect one branch of the legislature was "almost the only privilege" they had, and that between elections they were "*never consulted at all.* From end to end of Nova Scotia, there is not one office in the gift of the people but that of Member of the

Assembly. They cannot choose a Health Warden or a Fire-warden – or even a Scavenger."[44] Nonetheless, the members of the last assembly ought not to be rejected out of hand, but be judged on their overall behaviour as it had been manifested in his reports of the debates. For the seventh or eighth time he told the freeholders to consider the claims of prospective candidates in open meeting. "In the great majority of instances, ... the popular cause [would gather] strength from their preliminary discussions and deliberations."[45]

Howe was, in fact, preparing the way for an election, the like of which Nova Scotians had not seen before. Even at this stage he was elated at the change of tone in the election cards that the candidates were inserting in the newspapers. Hitherto they had contained little more than the candidates' promise to behave well if elected, but more typical in 1836 were cards stating the principles that the candidates would follow on questions of importance. In Colchester, Isaac Logan ran against S. G. W. Archibald on a platform calling for the ballot, triennial parliaments, a reformed council, and provincial control of the casual and territorial revenues.[46] In Cumberland, Gaius Lewis and Andrew McKim offered, if elected, to "travel every road in [the] County or Township, [and] take minutes ... respecting its state and length."[47] In Kings, Augustus Tupper promised to be "the Working Men's Representative" and warned: "Farmers and Mechanics: If you desire wretchedness and degradation, sleep on"[48] Perhaps Samuel B. Chipman of Annapolis summed it up rather neatly in announcing, "I am for a General Reform."[49] Throughout Nova Scotia many candidates were making a pitch for the votes of the middling classes whom Howe had been exhorting for some years. "This," he said, "is as it should be, and proves that the intelligence and public spirit of the people are in future to be taken into the account."[50]

Howe was no less pleased that many prospective candidates were being judged at public meetings. He took special note of meetings in Bridgetown and Lawrencetown, since Annapolis county, of all counties, needed to "curb and control the little official clique that has so long lorded it over their local affairs."[51] He was delighted that these meetings did not even deign to consider the claims of the sitting member for Annapolis, W.H. Roach, the flour inspector. Particularly anxious to have his own name submitted to a broader cross-section of the electorate than the voters of Musquodoboit, he got his wish when the sheriff convened a meeting in the long room of the Exchange Coffee House in Halifax on November 9, and he seized the occasion to offer a kind of personal testament.[52]

While he respected the fears of friends who doubted the advisability of his going into active politics, Howe declared, he rejected outright the objections of those who for the first time seemed solicitous for his welfare. There were some who said that as an assemblyman he would be unable to write freely and the *Novascotian* would lose its independence. Such people, he said, had "better make some inroad upon the rights or interests of the people, and perhaps they may have cause to regret having hazarded the experiment." Others of his pretended friends feared his business might suffer. "One ... who, beginning life without a shilling, has worked his way along in such a community as this, is not very likely to become suddenly negligent of his private affairs ... Gentlemen, I tell you plainly that I cannot afford to neglect my own business, to attend to yours; but, if elected, I will give to your interests all the little leisure which my own profession yields." However, if after a few years he lost the people's confidence, he would gladly return to his books, and "spend the little leisure which business affords, with the Poets, Philosophers and Historians; who, as they delighted and informed [his] youth ... [had] a charm to cheer and solace [his] old age."

Howe emphasized that his aim was a majority in the assembly that would insist on a program of rational reform. "If suitable materials for forming and combining that majority were more abundant, I should not have ventured out of the ordinary paths of my profession." To get the kind of majority he wanted would be all the more difficult since his opponents knew he would start at the mountains and not the molehills of corruption. "I want to wrestle with the big ones – to take from those who have far more than they require – to save, where it can be done by hundreds." Because of the opposition of these interests, he was not sanguine about securing a majority in the next assembly. In that case, "I shall be content to battle in a minority for the next six years – to follow, where others are willing to lead – to lead, where they may fall short of what I think is required for the general good."

As usual, he unfolded his innermost thoughts to Jane as he sought election to the assembly. On the one hand there was the Howe with the strong sense of duty, who believed that anyone who was under obligation to thousands of people as he was "ought not to shrink from any sacrifice of time and labor to pay the debt."[53] On the other, there was the more self-interested Howe who thought he could not afford to miss being educated in such an admirable school as the assembly. Lacking a formal education, he had had to pick up one as he went along. "Circumstances teach one better than books – and to learn to reason and think and act with clearness and energy – a man should put himself into situations that compel him to do all these as often as possible." By weighing and balancing his powers against the clever men in the assembly, he hoped, not only to determine what was in him, but also to make it more fit for use. "If my mind gets better my business can't well get worse, for intellectual effort is at the foundation of the whole."[54]

Howe's formal entrance into politics took place at the courthouse in Halifax on Monday, December 4, when he was officially nominated to contest the county election. Following the practice of the day, he addressed the assemblage, indeed at such length that the sheriff asked him to curtail his remarks so that balloting might begin. In his speech there were further signs of the unctuousness that was later to become more marked: "Did I quail before [my political enemies]? Did I give up a particle of my own views? Did I flinch from the assertion of which I believed to be right?"[55] Yet the speech outlined his idea of responsibility in government more clearly than ever before:

In England, one vote of the people's representatives turns out a ministry, and a new one comes in ... here, we may record five hundred votes against our ministry and yet they sit unmoved ... in England the people can breathe the breath of life into their government, whenever they please – in this Country, the Government is like an ancient Egyptian mummy, ... dead and inanimate – but yet, likely to last forever. We are desirous of a change – not such as shall divide us from our brethren across the water, but will ensure to us what they enjoy ...

Gentlemen, all we ask is for what exists at home – a system of responsibility to the people, extending through all the Departments supported at the public expense.[56]

Howe's attractiveness to the electors far exceeded his own expectations; throughout the polling he outdistanced the next candidate by almost two to one. As the poll was about to be moved from Halifax to Margaret's Bay, his success caused him to break down and weep like a child. "Gentlemen," he told the freeholders, "I was taught by the venerable Being [old John Howe] who has passed away, to respect my fellow creatures, and endeavour to do them good, – I hope I have not forgotten, and shall never forget the lesson."[57] At this stage the Reformer Thomas Forrester was also well ahead in the township vote, but the Reformers Bell and Annand trailed Starr and Lawson for the remaining township and county seats.[58] At Margaret's Bay, however, the issue was not long in doubt, since only a handful of freeholders chose to vote for Starr and Lawson. The county election had still to move to Musquodoboit, where the poll opened on December 13 in a barn jammed to the rafters with freeholders, but soon moved to the Presbyterian meeting house because of the cold. Since the opposing candidates did not put in an appearance, a single vote was taken for Howe and Annand, and an hour allowed to elapse without anyone coming to the poll. Then they were declared elected and Halifax had returned four popular members to the assembly.

Surveying the province Howe noted other results that elated him no less. Hoping to get rid of the stigma resting on him, W.H. Roach had been injudicious enough to offer for the county of Annapolis, but he soon had enough of it and retired after polling only 123 votes to Robichau's 535. In Cumberland the radical program of Lewis and McKim apparently proved attractive, for the former led the poll and the latter lost so narrowly to Alexander Stewart that he demanded a scrutiny of the vote. Perhaps most surprising of all was the serious challenge to Speaker Archibald in Colchester. In the *Novascotian* "a Patriot" taxed him with such questions as: "have you ever raised your voice against unnecessary expenditures of the provincial Revenue?";[59] while in the *Acadian Recorder* "Joe Warner," who was John Young ("Agricola") in disguise, so exasperated Archibald that he finally exploded: "my name shall remain ... when [his] shall be rotten as his compost, and stink like his dung hill."[60] Clearly a new and much less pleasant day was dawning for the greatest eminence in the Nova Scotia House of Assembly.

When all the results were in, Howe wondered if the cause of reform had obtained a majority. He was somewhat doubtful, for he expected that "the seductive influences of the Capital [would be] brought to bear on the wavering and undecided." Yet the more he examined the list of new members the more convinced he was that there would be "at least a pretty strong fighting minority – who [would] see that the Officials and their defenders [did] not have things all their own way."[61] Only the convening of the General Assembly would make known for certain the magnitude of the changes in its composition he had done so much to effect.

CHAPTER ELEVEN

Freshman Assemblyman

For Howe the fanfare that opened the Fifteenth General Assembly on the last day of January 1837 was nothing new. He had seen it all before: outside Province House a guard of honour of the 83rd Regiment; inside, lining the hall and stairs, the Rifle and Drum Companies of Militia; within the Council Chamber "His Excellency seated on the throne, surrounded by an array of female splendour, and military gorgeousness."[1] What was new for him was that, as an assemblyman, he had advanced from beyond the pale to a vantage point near the throne. He had also seen to it – or so he thought – that he could perform his new duties without putting an added burden on himself, since he would, in effect, be paying over his sessional indemnity to faithful John Thompson, who would act as legislative reporter for the *Novascotian.*[2] Within a few days of the assembly's opening – on February 14 – Howe's mother died following "a lingering illness." She remained as much a mystery in death as in life, for Howe made no reference to the event in his writings and the only attention it received was a two-line obituary notice in the *Novascotian* and other newspapers.

The new group of reforming assemblymen were largely inexperienced in legislative ways and clearly in need of leadership. From the outset they found it in Howe and his friend Lawrence O'Connor Doyle, who brought with him the expertise he had gained in pressing the cause of his Irish compatriots both in Ireland and in Nova Scotia. Neither Howe nor Doyle had any objection to the re-election of S.G.W. Archibald as Speaker, nor to the retention of the incumbent clerk and assistant clerk. But when it came to reappointing the Rev. R.F. Uniacke of the established Church of England chaplain of the assembly, they thought it high time to demonstrate that the old order was no longer to prevail.[3] As Howe put it, "we are commencing a race of improvement which renders ... references [to old establishments in England] inapplicable; and seeing how abuses have accumulated at home, we should be careful to avoid unjust inequalities at the outset."[4] Despite charges of godlessness Howe and Doyle carried their motion to dispense with the services of a chaplain by twenty-eight to eighteen. Not in the least deceived by this success, however, they were fully aware that their real strength would be determined on more substantive issues.

Their chance to gauge the general sentiments of the House came a few days later on Doyle's bill to reduce the duration of the assembly from seven to four years. Howe's first major speech, a rebuttal of the redoubtable Alexander Stewart's support of the status quo, demonstrated how effectively he could use the kind of shorthand he had developed over the years as a legislative reporter. From notes he had made, he sought to demolish, point by point, all of Stewart's arguments. When he had finished, there was little left unanswered. By this time Stewart was well advanced on the road from liberal to Whig to extreme Tory. Almost contemptuously he had asked, "if four years be good – why will not one be better?" Howe replied with a homely analogy that was to become almost a trade mark with him: "If that Gentleman's coat would wear well for four years, where would be the necessity for getting a new one every Spring? But if it would not last seven, why should he wear it for three years after it became shabby and defaced?"[5] When Stewart challenged those who condemned the last assembly to make good their charges, he was thoroughly discomfited by Howe's phenomenal knowledge of previous assemblies. After documenting their past history, chapter and verse, Howe concluded: "I am desirous to make the Legislation of this House as little like theirs as possible."[6]

Stewart had one argument which he felt Howe could not answer: Could anyone who extolled the British exemplar as strongly as he did support a change unhallowed by the British experience?[7] Howe replied simply that the change would increase the analogy between Nova Scotia and Britain, where few Parliaments lasted longer than four years. But in any case,

I have not that pious horror of innovation with which some Gentlemen are imbued. I do not think that the Colonial Legislatures should always shrink from the adoption of a sound principle, till the Imperial Parliament sets them the example ... I admit, that innovations should not be hastily pressed in any Country. I will not advise pulling down and changing merely for amusement

– but am anxious that this House should, without reference to what may be done in other Countries, or said across the water, ascertain where the shoe pinches *us*, and having done so, with a firm hand remove the evil.[8]

While Howe wanted Stewart to continue devoting his powerful mind to the business of the country, "whether he stands beside me, or fights in the ranks of the opposition,"[9] he had clearly abandoned any hope of his support in the cause of reform, and he focused his attention upon more fruitful prospects. To lukewarm supporters of reform who argued that they had no mandate to vote for the quadrennial bill he replied that it was sometimes no less the duty of the House to lead the public than it was the duty of the latter to instruct the House. But he was careful not to press his views too strongly and intimated that there might be some who, although they voted against him on this bill as a matter of conscience, would "go hand in hand with him in other matters of equal importance."[10] Whether or not Howe's three speeches on the subject had any effect, the House divided on the quadrennial bill much as it had on the chaplaincy question.[11]

These questions barely touched the major objectives of the reforming assemblymen. When, at the urging of Doyle and Howe, the house adopted resolutions condemning the council for excluding the public from its deliberations in its legislative capacity, they were getting closer to the root of their complaints.[12] What they got from the council was a refusal to discuss with the assembly a matter touching the internal regulation of the council,[13] and an implied intimation that it was all too easy to keep the assembly in its place. In the past the council might have got away with it; indeed, even on this occasion John Young moved two resolutions that were designed to be conciliatory, and to prevent open collision with the council. These resolutions, like the Youngs themselves, constituted a dilemma for Howe. The father and the two sons, William and George Renny, had attached themselves to the popular cause, partly at least, because it seemed advantageous to their own interests. Perhaps because their self-seeking was a little too obvious, they did not secure the recognition they felt they merited, and their letters to each other periodically lamented this failure.[14] Even during the session of 1837 Howe developed a much closer rapport with the Tory J.B. Uniacke than with John and William Young.

Like other assemblymen he had boiled with indignation at the council's reply to the "temperate and respectful remonstrance" of the assembly. "Then it was that the conviction flashed on my mind that the time was come – earlier it is true than I had expected – when we would be compelled to revise our local government, and mould it to a form more consistent with the rights and liberties of the People."[15] Accordingly he moved to replace John Young's resolutions with his own Twelve Resolutions,[16] the first of which proposed that a committee draw up an address to the Crown embracing the substance of the eleven which followed. *The Times*, once neutral in politics, but now showing its Tory colours without as yet resorting to personal invective, compared Howe's resolutions to Papineau's Ninety-Two, and with tongue in cheek stated that "the supporters of the famous twelve ... promise at no distant time, by cultivating their talent assiduously, to rival the Canadian democrat."[17] Basically the resolutions contended that the composition and modus operandi of the Council of Twelve had led to gross injustices that the assembly was powerless to prevent. Nothing else could be expected so long as it contained eight members of the established Church, including its bishop; or "two family connections embrace[d] five Members of the Council [and] five others were Co-partners in one mercantile concern"; or the council's members included a chief justice who was generally regarded as the head of a political party.

By the eleventh resolution Howe had reached "the root of all our evils ... that gross and palpable defect in our local Government, I mean the total absence of all responsibility to the Commons ... I ask ... for nothing more than British Subjects ought to have ... I appeal to [anyone] to say whether we have anything but a mockery of the British Constitution. An Englishman would consider himself no better than a Russian or a Turk if he had no other guards for liberty than these."[18] How was effective responsibility to be secured? In the twelfth resolution Howe rejected the proposal of the Upper Canadian Reformers to convert the Executive Council into a ministry of the British type, which would hold office only as long as it retained the confidence of the country. "I am afraid that ... this Province, is scarcely prepared for the erection of such machinery – I doubt whether it would work well here."[19] Accordingly, even though he called for either "an elective council ... or such other reconstruction of the local Government [as would] ensure responsibility to the Commons," he clearly wanted the former alternative. The executive, he said, would find it difficult to resist the demands of two popularly elected bodies, but that was as far as the principle of responsibility could be carried under the circumstances that existed in 1837. Clearly he was much less optimistic than Robert Baldwin in Upper Canada about the possibilities of fully introducing the British analogy in Nova Scotia. Reversing a position he had held since 1830, he also rejected the idea of separating the Executive from the Legislative Council; it would, he argued, be like "cutting a rotten orange in two, in order to improve its flavour."[20]

Howe knew that his call for an elective council would evoke cries of republicanism, but where, he asked, was the danger? By having the legislative councillors elected at a different time and for a different term than the assemblymen, they would, in effect, represent another class of voters. But even if the two bodies set themselves up in opposition to the Crown, were there not sufficient checks? All bills would still be subject to review by the Governor and the Crown officers, perhaps even by the Board of Trade or the Privy Council. Furthermore, if the people did not approve of the actions of the new Legislative Council, the latter would be subjected to the same type of salutary influence that operated on the assembly. "This ... is the simple machinery I propose, to redress our more prominent evils."[21]

It was one thing for Howe to introduce the Twelve Resolutions; it was another to have them adopted by the assembly. In pressing their acceptance he was to have the sort of opportunity to develop skills in legislative management that is seldom presented to a freshman parliamentarian. On peripheral questions he had no difficulty. Thus Uniacke's motion to send the entire batch of resolutions to a committee was turned down by twenty-six to twenty,[22] a division that reflected as accurately as any the state of opinion in the assembly. But on more substantive matters he could not be nearly as certain of success. Nine members whom he regarded as supporters deserted him when William Young, still smarting because of the elimination of his father's resolutions, sought to remove a reference in the second resolution to councillors "who had a direct interest in thwarting the views of the Assembly"; as a result, Young's amendment carried on the deciding vote of the Speaker.[23] Again, seven members who generally thought as he did could not stomach his assertion in the sixth resolution that the established church's dominance at the council board led to "a general and injurious system of favouritism and monopoly ... creating invidious distinctions and jealous discontent," and he had to be satisfied with a watered-down statement that the preponderant influence of one denomination had "a tendency to excite a suspicion, that, in the distribution of patronage, the fair claims of the Dissenting Population, ... are frequently overlooked."[24]

That was all Howe had to concede. He easily put down L.M. Wilkins's attempt to strike from the seventh resolution the assertion that the bankers on the council had defeated "the efforts of [the] Assembly to fix a Standard of Value, and establish a legal Currency in the province."[25] He also defeated, by a vote of thirty to twelve, Uniacke's effort to remove an allusion in the tenth resolution to "the disposition evinced by some of [the councillors] to protect their own interests and emoluments at the expense of the public"; surely if the members "really meant to accomplish any thing, they should make use of language that would shew they were in earnest ... small shot was frequently ineffectual, when a larger material would be found useful."[26] Finally, he got approval of the resolution calling for an elective council by the decisive majority of twenty-six to sixteen.

Then, only three days later, on March 7, the blow was struck: an ultimatum by the council suspending further business with the assembly until that body had rescinded the tenth resolution and the aspersions it cast upon some councillors. The *Acadian Recorder* caught something of the perturbation that gripped the assembly: "What was to be done? Must the interests of the Province suffer? – Must the Revenue (*upon which none of His Majesty's Council depend ..*) *be sacrificed!* This was a fearful question to be put to the breasts of members. Shall the Road and Bridge service – those essential objects – be neglected? ... We never remember to have witnessed a scene, wherein the agents seemed to feel under the influence of deeper emotion: They manifested in the tone and manner of the speakers a disheartening consciousness of *their own and the People's impotence.*"[27]

At stake in Howe's first crisis as an assemblyman was nothing less than his credibility as unofficial leader of the reform group. His decision was to rescind the Twelve Resolutions in their entirety, knowing full well he would have to face criticism from both sides of the House. From Wilkins and Uniacke there came taunts of lack of courage. He replied that his nerves had not yet failed him in critical times, and he did not expect they would in the future.[28] Naturally he was worried about the disunity that his action might cause among his own supporters. Hugh Bell, a brewer who, for reasons of business if nothing else, wanted to maintain good relations with the council, and had voted against any resolutions which cast aspersions on the councillors, referred scornfully to "those who bluster but shrink back,"[29] apparently with Howe in mind. He wanted to do nothing more than remove the words which the council found objectionable, something that Howe rejected as being equivalent to an apology. In contrast, Doyle felt so strongly about the withdrawal of the resolutions that, if the law had permitted him to resign his seat, he would have retired at once from "a place of deep humiliation." Howe sympathized with him, but could not "reconcile it to [his] conscience to inflict deep injury on the country, – to let the Revenue go down – and withhold aid from [the] Roads and Bridges."[30]

In the end there was no rift. Bell took pains to make it clear he had been misinterpreted, while Doyle, after his initial misgivings, also fell into line. Howe argued that the council had got into a trap of its own making since, by demonstrating the degraded condition to which the assembly had been reduced, the incident would do more to "arouse the public mind, than hundreds of Speeches and Resolutions."[31] Above all, his supporters should not be despondent. The council "ask us to rescind; we do so, but we do not sacrifice our address. Do Gentlemen suppose for a moment that I would consent to rescind these Resolutions, if they were not to rise again in another shape?"[32]

The same day that Howe moved to rescind the resolutions he also gave notice of motion for the appointment of a committee to prepare an address to the Crown on the state of the province. He also made certain that the committee did not get down to work until the revenue bills were safely secured. When it finally reported on April 13 it presented an address that was in most respects a carbon copy of the Twelve Resolutions in their amended form.[33] But there were two changes of substance. As a possible alternative to an elective Legislative Council, it was proposed to separate the Executive from the Legislative Council, introduce some assemblymen into the former body, make the latter more representative, and by otherwise securing "responsibility to the Commons, confer upon the People ... what they value above all other Possessions, the blessings of the British Constitution."[34] Part of this proposal is more than a little curious unless Howe had come to believe that cutting a rotten orange in two would improve its flavour. In the absence of any explanation all that can be said is that Howe's views on the most appropriate means of remedying colonial ills were still in a state of flux.

The second change was to delete the words of the tenth resolution to which the council had objected. When the address was adopted by thirty-eight to four, the *Novascotian* gloated that it had passed "nearly word for word as reported,"[35] but it neglected to say that the offending words had not been included from the start. Clearly the council's supporters had some point in arguing that, if the sponsors of the Twelve Resolutions had not insisted on incorporating personal reflections on the councillors, they could have had their address without heated controversy or waste of legislative time. For his part, Howe was certain that nothing but good would follow when the *Journals* of the assembly reached Britain and revealed the council's original reaction to a truthful proclamation of its failings. In turn, the council defended itself with an address accompanied by a long series of "Observations," which Howe laughingly summarized: "Nova Scotia is a quiet Colony, where there are no grievances; we are the best

Council in the world; and form the only bulwark ... against the designs of the rebellious and evil disposed – therefore, have a care how your Majesty disturbs us, or interferes with the existing state of things."[36] Then he proceeded to ignore the existence of the "Observations." Howe's behaviour on this occasion clearly illustrates the contrast between his approach to reform and that of the Canadians.

During the session of 1837 all the ingredients that went into Howe the reformer came into play.[37] Tory Howe, with his compassion for ordinary folk, could not stomach the social distinction that was reflected in the wooden partition which separated persons of high and low estate in the gallery of the assembly. To him, "the partition was no test of respectability ... because ... his pocket had been picked on the [side], which was considered the most genteel."[38] Liberal, rationalist Howe, even while supporting a grant of £300 to Horton Academy, promised to show later that the practice of establishing colleges in villages where the population did not exist was ridiculous and absurd.[39] Little did he realize that, when he took a firm stand on this question, it would profoundly affect not only his political position but provincial politics generally. Most of all, there was the middle-class, petit bourgeois Howe, who wanted additional moneys for roads, bridges, and other public improvements to be secured through cuts in the over-sized customs and judicial establishments, and the abolition of "the ridiculous farce of the militia."[40] In distinguishing this assembly from its predecessors, he noted the "greater regard to economy – a more sensitive appreciation of the importance of retrenchment, in the management of the public funds."[41] If the assembly had done no more than arrest the growing tide of expenditures, it might have congratulated itself, "but this Assembly has not stopped here – they have gone much further,"[42] and by Howe's reckoning cut costs by at least £3,519.

Accordingly he reported favourably to his subscribers on the session of 1837. He had not expected the Reformers to have their way on any important question after only one election, and was agreeably surprised to find that they almost always had an actual although not a large majority. Nevertheless, they still did not possess that commanding influence that was needed to let them press their principles with authority either in Nova Scotia or Britain. One-third of the House, including some of its ablest members, were decidedly opposed to them. Even worse, they were "not infrequently at the mercy of that section of the members, which is made up of the men of no decided leaning – no fixed principles – the lovers of peace at all hazards – the timid or the indifferent,"[43] in other words, those whom he would later dub "loose fish." By letting his readers know the true state of affairs, he hoped they might "make the best possible use of their power of purgation"[44] whenever another election occurred.

As usual, Howe made known his own estimate of his performance in the assembly to his half-sister: "I had to battle the watch with many able fellows in the House and have to read a page or two of abuse from some of the enemy every week – but my principles have gained ground – my position is stronger – and the cause in which I embarked has been largely benefited by the experiment, while I believe there are not many counties that would not give me a seat tomorrow if one was wanted."[45] In identifying the Reform cause and struggle so largely with himself, he was letting signs of immodesty show through again. Yet his portrayal of the situation was not far off the mark. That there was a large reforming element in the assembly was substantially his doing; that it acted primarily under his direction and guidance during the session of 1837 none would have denied. Doyle's speaking talents proved highly useful to a group generally unused to public speaking, but the mercurial Irishman lacked the balance, moderation, and prudence that the situation demanded of a leader; Herbert Huntington was not yet in a position where his consistency and integrity would permit him to exercise a kind of moral leadership, and he would never be able to persuade and enthuse others by his oratory; William Young could not erase the impression that he would never let his support of reform estrange him completely from the establishment in Halifax or interfere with his hopes of preferment for himself. In contrast, it would have been difficult to conceive of anyone more suitable as a leader than one who had, day in and day out, watched the assembly in action for almost ten years; who had heard debated ad nauseam the pros and cons of every provincial issue; who, through his rambles, correspondence, and a constant stream of visitors to the *Novascotian* office, knew the province and provincial attitudes as no one else; and who, largely through his own efforts, had secured the election of a large bloc of assemblymen oriented towards his views.

The session over, Howe as usual devoted some time to personal and nonpolitical objects. This year he pressed the theme that, if meetings could rouse persons to political action, why should they not be used to promote public improvements? Recently, through the intervention of Governor Campbell and a small expenditure of money, a carriage road had been built from Freshwater Bridge to Point Pleasant, permitting Haligonians a ride or ramble on the most pleasant road on the peninsula of Halifax. But why should they not be able to continue their walk or ride up the margin of the North-West Arm? "Why, as a Community, we could do the whole thing without

contributing more than we would freely give to a Yankee Carravan –
or to see two or three villainously bad plays."[46] Even if his fellow
townsfolk preferred another object that was all to the good; "we are
desirous to see them get at something – to commence somewhere –
and to organize some plan of public improvement, that will ultimately
displace the cloud of apathy and indifference."[47] He was even more
expansive in the autumn following a "hasty ride" through the western
counties to Digby, crossing over to Saint John and returning by
steamboat to Windsor. Once again he found highly gratifying "the
growth of population and extension of culture" in the whole tract of
land from the Shubenacadie to Digby Gut. Because of its lumbering
and shipbuilding operations, New Brunswick might present a more
bustling appearance than Nova Scotia, but it had left the supplying of
the necessities of life chiefly to the western counties of Nova Scotia
"and who shall say that, on a fair balancing of the account, we have not
largely the advantage."[48]

Howe was stressing the development of western Nova Scotia
mainly to provide a basis for renewing his advocacy of a railroad from
Halifax to Windsor. Both the legislature and the public, he said,
should remember that "so sudden and unexpected are often the
transitions, that the apparent absurdity of to-day becomes the fact of
to-morrow."[49] Ten years ago Hamilton had carried the mail to
Annapolis on horseback, or in a little cart "with a solitary passenger
beside him, who looked as if he was going to the end of the world."
Who could ever have believed that within a year or two there would be
a stage coach, drawn by four horses, running three times a week on
the same road? Ten years ago Stewart had carried the mail to Pictou
in his jacket pocket, shooting partridges for sale along the way. Could
anyone have imagined that he would now travel over the same route
in a coach and four, carrying a ton of mail with him?

But miracles were taking place on an even larger scale. Had not the
English firm of Rundell & Bridge leased the mines of Pictou, and was
it not prepared to sink shafts and install steam engines, with the
intention of exporting 70,000 chaldrons of coal a year? Had not three
British banks each with a million pounds of capital commenced
business in the large towns of British North America during 1837?
Had not the Avon River Bridge, about which there had been doubts
even two summers ago, already been completed, and would it not pay
four per cent on the invested capital in the very first year? But what
had all this to do with a railway to Windsor? According to Howe, "as
much as the volume of water in the great lakes had to do with the
River St. Lawrence – as much as the growth of an egg has to do with
the birth of a chicken – as much as an accumulation of gass has to do

with the explosion of a mine."[50] Had his review of the resources and prospects of every part of the western counties from Rawdon to Yarmouth not demonstrated that the factors were "already in active operation" which would make a railway necessary?

Howe's exhilaration carried over to his own business, which was prospering no less than business generally. Early in 1837 a new series of the *Novascotian* appeared, "printed with a new and clear type, and on a very superior paper"; at the same time Howe stated his intentions of introducing further improvements in keeping with a widening circulation.[51] With another of his ventures he had struck a snag. Late in 1836 he had published *The Clockmaker* as his own speculation, and he was doing well with it. Then, while making arrangements to have it published in England, he discovered it had been pirated and was already in print in that country. Not only that, it had run through four editions in six months, an unprecedented degree of popularity for a colonial work with a local setting. Howe adopted the soft line; assuming that the English publisher Richard Bentley had not known that the colonies were protected by the Copyright Act, or that the work had not appeared first in the United States, he told him that he would much prefer to arrange compensation through mutual agreement than be forced to sue in the courts.[52] But he threatened in vain; once again he had fallen victim to one of the unpredictable perils of the publishing trade.

It was not until November that the *Novascotian* again immersed itself in politics. In the interval the *Times* had alleged that the Reformers' main desire was to abolish all the bulwarks of constitutional monarchy, especially the Church and the prerogatives of the Crown. "We hold the Radicalism of Nova Scotia, to be the Radicalism of Papineau and Bidwell, in the Canadas; the Radicalism of Hume, Roebuck and O'Connell in Britain; and a radicalism but a few removes from that which provoked the attempts of Fieschi, Alibaud and others in the French metropolis."[53] When Howe deigned to take notice, it was not so much to reply as to give reasons for not replying.[54] Since the people had permitted him to deal with issues in the assembly, he did not feel that "a whole year's Newspaper agitation – a fighting of old battles over, and new ones by anticipation – was necessary ... to the success of the popular cause."[55] He was certain that once the assembly's address reached London the game would be up with the council and the old church-and-state dynasty would be as dead as Julius Caesar, "although the old warrior set an example of decency in dying which was not likely to be imitated by the Council of XII."[56] He was no less optimistic in his belief that Governor Campbell had too much sense to be led astray by the old influences that normally operated behind the scenes in these instances.

Had he been able to read Campbell's dispatches to the colonial secretary he would have been much less confident. In March Campbell had told Lord Glenelg that since the division of the council could not be delayed much longer without causing dissatisfaction, he would shortly be in a position to make nominations.[57] But in May, making a complete change of stance, he asked Glenelg to examine his councillors' objections to distinct councils. He himself preferred "things to remain nearly as they are" since he had "every reason to be satisfied with the conduct of my Council" and "any material change in the constitution of that Body ... would not diminish the dissatisfaction which at present exists."[58] Even when the colonial secretary insisted on the division of the council, Campbell argued still. Because the colonies did not possess material for anything like a House of Lords, he thought it best to have the legislative and executive power united in the most influential and respectable members of the community; placed between the representative of the Crown and the representatives of the people, they would act as "a check to the democratic influence which is rapidly growing here." Otherwise, the governor would have to bear all the odium for resisting the views of the assembly, "however wild these views may be."[59] Thus, despite Howe's optimism, the old influences had operated upon Campbell and he had succumbed.

Unable to make his views prevail, Campbell called Howe into informal discussion late in October on the possible composition of the two councils should a division take place.[60] Suspecting that such a course had, in fact, been ordered, Howe was all the more convinced that Glenelg was paying attention to the address of the assembly. Told by Campbell that he had been advised there were insufficient materials to operate two distinct councils, Howe showed how it might be done without discarding any of the incumbent councillors, and so as to provide representation for all the important interests of the country. When Campbell noted that he had omitted his own name, Howe replied that "he wanted nothing for himself."[61]

As troubles deepened and ripened into rebellion in the Canadas in November and December, it was only to be expected that the Nova Scotian Reformers would be contrasted with their counterparts in the upper provinces. In August the *Times* had written disparagingly of "those among us, who if they had the power as they have the will, would lead Nova Scotia into the same snare" as Canada.[62] Probably anticipating this kind of comment, Howe had devoted one of his few political editorials of the summer months to the state of affairs in Lower Canada.[63] Prior to 1828, he said, few would have denied that "in the main Papineau and his friends were right." But when Britain altered its policy in that year, the Lower Canadians would have done better to follow a course of temperate firmness rather than one designed to precipitate a crisis that might end in separation. Yet Howe was willing to make large allowances for men who had fought their country's battles for twenty years and had been little more than the plaything of indecisive colonial policy and ignorant or arbitrary colonial secretaries.

After rebellion broke out in Lower Canada in November a public meeting was convened in Halifax to condemn the "misguided" rebels, and raise funds for the families of the soldiers marching through the wilderness to preserve order. Howe seized the occasion to defend himself and his friends:

I have been called the Papineau of Nova Scotia, ... and a connection is attempted to be shown between the Reformers of this Province, and the agitators of Canada ... It has been said that we have been holding treasonable correspondence with traitors in Canada; and so many tales have been invented, that some old women I really believe apprehend, that when the last company of soldiers marches out of town, the standard of insurrection is to be raised.[64]

Clearly Howe exaggerated the number and character of his detractors since no one of prominence associated him with disaffection. For a time it was even doubtful if he would be given a chance to answer his accusers, real or imaginary. Stephen Deblois said that no one had accused him of anything, while T.N. Jeffery took the position that since he had "declared his opinions, his word is enough." Only when Alexander Stewart insisted that "in a meeting of Nova Scotians, a gentleman of Mr. Howe's character, who wish[ed] to vindicate himself, [should not] be denied a hearing,"[65] was he permitted to explain in detail his correspondence with H.S. Chapman in 1835. "This is the way," he said, "in which I have spread disloyalty! ... In these matters, my feeling has ever been ... keep the peace, never break it, use the means within the law and the Constitution, – and these, after patient perseverance, will procure every needful reformation."[66] To make his position doubly clear, he also published the Chapman correspondence in the *Novascotian* with an accompanying article in which he sought to demolish by ridicule those who accused the Reformers of disaffection. They were like the English bishop who, when threatened with a loss of income, replied, "but what will become of religion?" Similarly his detractors, when confronted with reform and retrenchment, raised the bogey of the British connection.[67]

The assembly opened its sittings in 1838 before an excited gallery.

On instructions from Britain Governor Campbell had divided the council into two distinct bodies and had included four assemblymen, including the Reformer Huntington, in the Executive Council. Naturally the gallery was crowded to observe "the first appearance of their New Members, ... some of them recently called to honors and influence – others perhaps shorn of a little of the old."[68] Without delay, on January 29, the governor submitted the dispatches on which the new order was to be based. Howe had some objections to the scale of salaries that Glenelg demanded for the surrender of the casual revenues and he was disappointed that the colonial secretary was opposed to granting Crown lands without charge to actual settlers.[69] But with everything else he was delighted. Tongue in cheek, he said that Queen Victoria and Lord Glenelg had demonstrated themselves to be Nova Scotia Reformers and were fully entitled to be "denounced as Rebels by the Tories of Halifax."[70]

To demonstrate his delight, Howe published the dispatches in full in the *Novascotian*, italicizing those parts he found especially significant.[71] In particular, he underlined Glenelg's statement that previous colonial secretaries had not appreciated the unrepresentative character of the council; otherwise they would have realized that "distinctions so invidious [could] not [but] be productive of serious discontent." Equally pleasing to Howe were Glenelg's remedies: avoidance even of the appearance of favouritism towards the Church of England in the appointment of councillors; exclusion of the chief justice and all other judges from the Executive Council; and the appointment of not more than one member of any commercial concern to the Executive Council. Most gratifying of all was Glenelg's acceptance of the assembly's right to control and appropriate all the public revenues. Later in the year the *Acadian Recorder* would also treat the dispatches as "*no mean Charters of the Rights and Privileges of Nova Scotia,*"[72] but not so the editors and letter-writers of the *Times*, who were appalled that the home government had paid no attention to the council's "Observations" and had acted upon the rescinded resolutions. "Candidus" drew a parallel between Howe and William Lyon Mackenzie. While Howe was not yet contemplating Mackenzie's path, neither had the latter when he began his career; yet "in Downing Street Mr. Howe is now Lord of the ascendant, and the Council must vanish at his bidding."[73]

As on numerous subsequent occasions, Howe was exulting too much in the triumph of the moment and attaching to it a significance not warranted by the circumstances. Some of Glenelg's concessions were in matters that even a Tory was hard put to justify; in others, like the full control of the public revenues, the concession was in the abstract and to secure agreement on specifics was the nub of the controversy. Within days Howe was shocked back into reality, for, when a Reformer requested information from J.B. Uniacke, one of the four assemblymen sitting in the Executive Council, he replied that "he did not consider himself sitting in the house in any ministerial capacity, nor was he bound to support the measures of Government."[74] Determined not to let the matter rest, Howe asked the executive councillors if they would "answer questions put to them relative to the policy and intentions of Government." A second executive councillor sitting in the assembly, E.M. Dodd, admitted to "some degree of responsibility" and saw "no objection to his being a mere organ of communication between [the] House and Government." But all four executive councillors insisted they were as "free and unshackled in the Representative capacity as before,"[75] and Howe had no choice but to leave the relationship between the House and the executive councillors in this ill-defined state.

Meanwhile he was having difficulty in getting the reforming assemblymen to present a united front in a variety of matters. Seeking to bring back the practice of opening the House's sittings with prayer, the Tories again proposed that a minister of the established church be appointed chaplain of the assembly. At that point the differences between the Reformers' left and right wings came sharply into play. Catholic Doyle declared that the appointment of any clergyman would create an invidious distinction, while Methodist Hugh Bell thought it "expedient and prudent"[76] to accept a minister of the established church in order to save useless controversy. In the end Howe got most of the Reformers to agree to have clergymen of the five leading denominations serve as chaplains in weekly succession, and carried his proposal in a division largely along party lines.[77] This settled the chaplaincy question, except for the *Times* which as usual deplored the creeping in of republican usages in place of "the law of the Mother Country, the example of our ancestors."[78]

On the incorporation of Halifax the Reformers were much more seriously divided. A year earlier Howe had attended a meeting of freeholders which had decided to petition the legislature for incorporation.[79] At that time he reflected both his Tory and middle-class attributes in condemning the existing system of local government. Commenting on the conditions in Bridewell, he wondered if "the blessing of God could come down on a town which treats the image of God in such a manner as this."[80] But he also looked forward to a change which would permit "a boy in his office ... [or] who now measured tape and ribbons behind the counter"[81] to rise to the highest civic honours. During the session of 1837 the pressure of other business had prevented the assembly from giving detailed consideration to the petition of 600 Haligonians for incorporation, and when Forrester, who represented Halifax township, introduced a bill to that end in 1838, he met the opposition of 140 merchants and others who contended it was "levelling" and calculated to put the interests of persons of respectability at the mercy of the lower levels of society. While it was only to be expected that the right-wing Reformer Hugh Bell would insist on the elective principle being "properly guarded," much more harmful to the reform cause were William Young's strictures against giving "mere numbers the control of wealth."[82] Doyle asked Young bluntly if "the forty shilling freeholders who sent him [to the assembly, were] unfit to vote for city officers," while J.B. Uniacke made merry of one who "so hesitated between two opinions, that I cannot discover at which side he is."[83]

The debate on incorporation showed Howe that the battle of words had dangers of its own when his old antagonist, W.Q. Sawers, who sat in the gallery as he spoke, demanded satisfaction for something he had said. Only after John Thompson transcribed his notes of the speech did Sawers concede that Howe had not reflected on his character.[84] He was to be only the first of a series of foes who would challenge Howe to a duel. But, as was becoming the case in many matters, the main battle on incorporation was joined between Howe and Uniacke, the de facto Tory leader, who repelled many Reformers by his bombast. Howe had often criticized him for "relying on his imagination when his reasoning powers fail [and] of bringing sarcasm and raillery to bear on every subject, and on every adversary,"[85] but he had never ceased to have a liking and respect for him. In 1837 he often let Uniacke's sorties pass without reply, but early in 1838 he gave warning that if "jest, and anecdote and raillery" were to take the place of argument, he would show he was blest with "a little imagination" too.[86]

Uniacke insisted that he did not oppose incorporation or the elective principle per se; indeed, if Forrester's bill had the protection of the London charter, he would support it, but instead it "put the respectability of the town under the controul of others, who should not possess that power."[87] In reply, Howe expressed confidence that the freeholders of Halifax, like those of London, would choose persons of property, influence, and rank to represent them. While there were "none of the Rothschilds, none of the Bankers of the community" among the original petitoners, still there were "many of honesty and intelligence, and of the best kind of respectability."[88] In contrast, the counter-petitioners included those who generally opposed reform measures. Howe concluded that Uniacke and the

Nova Scotia Tories were more opposed to reform than their namesakes across the water and that there was "a party in the Colonies ... who believe, or affect to believe, that there is a danger in the very sound of British liberty."[89] While almost all the Reformers lined up against Uniacke's attempt to defer the bill, their action came to naught because the luck of the draw had produced a highly conservative grand jury in 1838. In its presentment of March 19 it declared that elective municipal institutions would "not afford the best remedy for existing evils,"[90] and under the circumstances Howe and Forrester had no choice but to put incorporation over to the next session.[91]

The Reformers were also very much at odds with each other on the treatment of the judicial system, even though they all agreed on the need to cut down a bloated establishment. William Young wanted to abolish the Inferior Courts of Common Pleas, except in Cape Breton, and transfer their jurisdiction to the Supreme Court.[92] Because Howe was sceptical of anything favoured by the Halifax lawyers, and not by their rural counterparts, he decided to reverse the usual positions of himself and Young and be "a wise and prudent reformer" rather than "a rash innovator." To Young's obvious annoyance, he moved to retain both courts but to cut down their size.[93] Again it was all for naught, for although Howe's two resolutions were passed by a bare majority, the Legislative Council turned down the bill which sought to enact them.

More than anything else in the session, this debate emphasized those differences of Howe and Uniacke which stemmed from their backgrounds. The previous summer Howe had travelled along sixty miles of coast in eastern Halifax county and found it without a road, bridge, or school. "I often wished that I had the £450 [i.e., the salary of a single Judge] to distribute, that my youthful Countrymen ... might ... at least [be] taught to read the Word of God."[94] Replying with a typical sally, Uniacke wondered if Howe would put the judiciary up for sale to get the cheapest possible administration of justice. "What! £450 a year for a judge to travel the circuit? Why, *Tim O'Shaughnessy! Tim Shea! or Con Lahy!* would do the labour for half that sum."[95] But this time Howe did not let him get away with his witticisms, especially because Uniacke seemed to scorn the idea of an assemblyman entering the unpretentious home of a farmer or fisherman. "... these are the places I love to seek ... to go to the cabins of the poor – to note their wants, and feel my spirit refreshed with their humble virtues. To elevate the industrious classes ... has been my constant aim, and I am not weary of the task. To this work shall be devoted all the powers of mind and body with which heaven has blest me."[96] Uniacke would always be an honoured guest in the homes of the judges and leading officials, where he would be wined at the public expense and win admiration for his brilliant talents, "but give me a seat beneath the poor man's roof – a portion of his humble fare – let me hear ... my name breathed with respect, and feel that I am welcomed as a friend, and I seek no higher distinction."[97] The Reformers who had writhed under Uniacke's scorn and ridicule for two sessions enjoyed every moment of it; Uniacke neither intervened nor replied.

Normally Howe's disagreement was with the Reform right wing; on the civil list question it was with the left wing. When Huntington proposed a "suitable Annual provision" for the attorney general and the solicitor general,[98] Howe moved that it be a permanent one and immediately came under the criticism of the most determined Reformers. Forrester expressed utter bewilderment; Henry Goudge wondered why Howe, of all people, would follow a course that "went to make the House helpless"; Doyle regretted having to oppose someone from whom he seldom differed in principle and reminded Howe that the idea of conferring a permanent salary on the attorney general would "never have entered the mind of Lord Glenelg except through the agency of some at a distance."[99] Again Howe's reply illustrates his general approach to reform. When he entered politics he knew he would have to sustain "the suspicions and hasty opinions of his friends." While Huntington's proposition was right in principle, he knew it would never be accepted in Britain. Accordingly he had proposed the only practicable scheme; yet if his amendment failed he would willingly try Huntington's proposal.[100] Not enough Reformers supported Howe's position, and in the end the House passed a bill conforming to Huntington's views that Howe himself helped to draft. In effect, one executive councillor, Herbert Huntington, had defeated "the propositions which had the sanction of the other eleven."[101]

As late as March 9, Howe expressed satisfaction – at least publicly – that four executive councillors were doing business in the House under some degree of responsibility.[102] But his disillusionment grew steadily during the month, and on March 29 he bluntly told the House that the composition of the councils did not do justice to Glenelg's dispatches, and that the same old influences had been at work behind the scenes in the choice of councillors. The next day Halifax was agog with rumours that the commission issued to the new governor general, Charles Poulett Thomson, differed from the instructions to Campbell, and that it would be necessary to reconstitute the councils with reduced numbers. As a precautionary measure, the Reformers rushed a resolution through the House condemning the earlier appointments for being at variance with the liberal views of Lord Glenelg.[103] Although the Tories were indignant that the assembly had dared to caution the governor, the Reformers were glad they had when the second reconstitution of the councils turned out to be even less satisfactory to them than the first. Howe condemned, in particular, the exclusion of Herbert Huntington, who had been the only genuine Reformer in the first Executive Council.[104] Even the *Times* suggested that the making and unmaking of the council could be only described as "an amusing piece of drollery" when the initial result was the unseating of Enos Collins, the businessman who in the newspaper's opinion had done more to develop Nova Scotia than any other.[105]

Again the assembly resorted to its newfound weapon, an address to the Crown, in which it criticized Glenelg, at least indirectly, for upholding principles of economy on the one hand while proposing an unacceptable scale of salaries on the other. In words that might have come straight from a Howe editorial, and perhaps did, the address pointed to "the natural tendencies of a Colonial Government [to] favor the growth of a pernicious system of official extravagance," and declared that the primary duty of the assembly was to preserve "those 'moderate and simple habits,' which, in a young country, are the best guarantees for public virtue and private happiness."[106] Because it was a matter directly relating to economy, Howe had no difficulty in beating back the Tory challenges to the address, although Uniacke did carry an amendment to have the Queen described as "gracious" rather than "youthful."[107]

Howe was still governed by the naïve belief that, if the Reformers managed to put the true state of affairs in Nova Scotia before the colonial secretary, he would gladly concede their demands. To him the chief obstacle in the Reformers' path was neither Glenelg nor Campbell; it was, as it had always been, the small clique that had entrapped the governor in its clutches on his arrival and sought to "suppress the spirit of searching economy and rational improvement ... [with a] brazen assertion of ulterior views [that] has perhaps rarely been equalled."[108] This was the group, he said exultantly, which had sought to cut down the subscription list of the *Novascotian*, but had succeeded only in raising it by 131; it was also the group that maintained the *Times*, the only newspaper in the province not to accept the Reformers' case as unanswerable;[109] finally it was the group whose little factions around the province outdid themselves in their professions of loyalty and treated as traitors those who did not support their extreme position. This period marks the beginning of the stream of anonymous letters filled with abuse and invective that were to be directed against Howe because of his attacks on the official clique and its supporters. In the columns of the *Times* these letter-writers left no doubt about whom they considered their real enemy to be.

Early in the year Howe exchanged angry words with the official faction of Annapolis county, who because of him had been unable to saddle the county with heavy expenditures for a county courthouse and jail. Twisting a sentence in a letter he wrote to Chapman, they castigated him for suggesting that one-eighth of the province's inhabitants entertained disloyal feelings towards their sovereign.[110] As usual, Howe reacted almost ferociously to any doubts cast upon his loyalty,[111] but he could do nothing to prevent the "pork Loyalists"[112] of Annapolis from continuing to snipe at him. "Ephraim," in "the Wilderness of Port Royal," wondered how his taste could "be so vitiated as to relish the coarse and unsavory garbage thrown to [him] by the rabble,"[113] while a second writer called him "Josephus Verbosus" and derided him for wanting to blow up the Halls of Justice in order to build roads and bridges.[114]

Howe had no less distaste for the ultra-loyalists at a higher level. He showed it particularly when J.B. Uniacke sought the assembly's approval for an address of the Constitutional Association of Montreal. Out-and-out Tories of this ilk, Howe said, were extinct in Britain; not only did they seek to continue a system rife with abuses, but they opposed every concession that the British government offered and wanted to hang every rebel in the Canadas without due process of law. He insisted that a hand be extended neither to the party that had plunged the Canadas into rebellion nor to an official party interested only in misgovernment,[115] and he easily carried the assembly with him. Occasionally he had some counter-ammunition that he threw at the ultras with not a little relish. He was especially delighted to print an editorial from the London *Morning Chronicle* of March 1 which, after quoting from Howe's letter to Chapman, expressed satisfaction that "busy agitators" had been taken to pieces by "a cool, wary, strong-headed, honest-minded lover of his country," who, like John Neilson in Lower Canada, was not to be "played upon by Messrs. Chapman and Roebuck, grievance-fed men, to whom job was not so much a grievance, as grievance was a job."[116]

Of necessity, Howe's primary interest during the session of 1838 was in matters constitutional, but whenever the occasion permitted he showed his usual concern for the material development of the province. Once again he presented himself as the strong exponent of middle-class virtues and extolled the self-reliant independent yeomanry of the province. In resisting direct payments to farmers, he stated that "the best bounty you can give a young Nova Scotian is a good industrious wife – and send him with an axe on his shoulders to chop away at the wilderness lands and make a good farm."[117] But despite Glenelg's objections, he still favoured granting crown lands to bona fide settlers simply for the cost of the survey. If, in eastern Halifax county, the government provided 100-acre lots alternately on each side of the road on the single condition that the grantee build a road fronting his property to a specific width, the through highway would be completed without the expenditure of a sixpence and the alternate lots could be sold at higher prices.[118] But nothing came of Howe's proposal and he remained, as it were, a voice crying in the wilderness.

Although Howe finished the session of 1838 with much less enthusiasm than he had begun it, he was still confident that the Reformers could realize their aims if they could only make the colonial secretary understand the true state of affairs in the province. For a while, however, his pen would be silent on these matters since he was about to fulfil his long-cherished dream of a visit to Britain and the continent.

CHAPTER TWELVE

A Nova Scotian Abroad

Throughout the session of 1838 Howe had struggled with a problem for which there was no easy answer. Should he accompany his friend Haliburton on his projected trip to Britain and the continent? He could not justify it on grounds of business alone, for although he wanted to talk personally to Lord Glenelg, and also make sure that his interests were protected in the publication of the second series of *The Clockmaker*, for which he had contracted with Haliburton, neither reason was compelling in itself. His financial situation and prospects were better than they had been for a long time, but it seemed rash to incur unnecessary expenditures. Worst of all, he would be unable to take Susan Ann with him, as he had been promising for some time to do, since she was expecting another child in June to join Ellen; Mary, born in November 1832; Joseph, Jr, born in July 1834; and, of course, Edward.[1] Howe realized that his place was at her side, but knowing how much he wanted to visit the source of so many things he cherished, she insisted that he go. So, exhausted from a trip to the western counties, he boarded the *Tyrian* in Halifax harbour on April 25 en route to Europe. Because of the lateness of the western stage and a change of wind, he did not get away until the next morning. He was up early to get a last glimpse of home, but Province House stood in the way of his seeing anything but the chimneys of his own house.[2]

Howe began his journey with a childlike excitement that was not to be dissipated in the days which followed. Particularly delightful were his shipboard companions, who, in addition to Haliburton, included Charles Rufus Fairbanks, whom Howe had respected as an assemblyman, although not so much since he had become master of the rolls; a Dr Walker, who would have made a suitable character for one of Scott's novels; and Major Robert Carmichael-Smyth, a bon vivant like Howe, whose acquaintance ripened into a lasting friendship. The *Tyrian* was a ten-gun brig, "deep waisted, with high bulwarks, and of that class of vessels, of which so many had been lost";[3] indeed, her sailors called her – although not affectionately – "the old Tureen." Her very slowness was to have an important consequence, for which Howe and Haliburton could take at least some of the credit. Within a few hundred miles of the English coast, she was overtaken by the steamer *Sirius*, which was returning from a trial run to the United States. After the mails were transferred, the *Tyrian* "rolled about in a dead calm with flapping sails, while the *Sirius* steamed off and was soon out of sight."[4] When the *Tyrian* took a further five days to reach Falmouth, twenty-five days out of Halifax, Howe and Haliburton decided they would intervene.

On landing, Haliburton went to Bristol to confer with the owners, both of the *Sirius* and of the *Great Western*, and later had their assurances that they would put a steamer on the direct line to Halifax if the British government gave them a contract for carrying the mails. Before Howe left for home he joined William Crane of New Brunswick in asking Glenelg for the immediate use of steamers on the packet run to Halifax.[5] One reason they gave was the loss of so many ten-gun brigs with a "fearful destruction of life and property [and] the serious interruption of correspondence." But no less serious was the danger of allowing the British population on both sides of the Atlantic to receive the first intelligence of what occurred in the Mother Country and the colonies through American channels; the result would be to allow erroneous impressions to be circulated for ten days before they could be corrected. Without opposition from Crane, Howe put it to Glenelg that Halifax, 550 miles nearer England than New York, should be the focus of colonial communication from which branch lines would radiate. Glenelg seemed impressed, and even before Howe left for Halifax he was told that a favourable reply might be expected shortly.[6]

For Howe his arrival in Falmouth harbour on May 20 meant that he had come "home." Some time later his readers were to get an account of his trip across the Atlantic and his impressions of southwestern England in seventeen articles entitled "The Novascotian Afloat" and "The Novascotian in England."[7] While these sketches are stylistically superior to the "Rambles," they are still lacking the human qualities of his numerous letters to Susan Ann. In his sketches he kept reminding his readers that, although he had been "fascinated by the splendours and novelties of an old nation," his first love was still "a small countrie that we wot of, far over the billow ... that small spot of earth, between Cape Sable and Cape North."[8] Even when lost in admiration of Exeter Cathedral, he still remembered that "the homage of a contrite heart, offered up where two or three are met together," was no less acceptable to the Deity than "if ... a thousand forms knelt in the attitude of prayer."[9] Statements like these led James A. Roy to suggest that Howe was "never able to rid himself entirely of a certain narrowness of outlook – an almost aggressive provincialism which he mistook for sturdy local patriotism."[10] But in the latter instance Howe was saying little more than that he preferred the small gatherings in his father's Sandemanian meeting-house to the Sunday morning service in St Paul's Church. Perhaps, too, he should not be accused of excessive parochialism for simply maintaining that he had seen "no country more richly endowed with natural resources than our own – none where the ordinary pleasures and luxuries of life may be more easily earned with moderate exertion."[11]

For the readers of the *Novascotian* Howe's account of England ended abruptly when he found it impossible to take notes in London, that "great Babylon," in which the noise in the front room was such that "you can scarcely hear each other," and in the back bedroom "just like what it would be a few yards from the falls of one of our large rivers."[12] Nevertheless, for five weeks Howe positively revelled in the wonders of the great city and its environs: St Paul's, "the most magnificent structure that can be conceived – and it is exercise enough for one day to walk over it"; the Tower and its "collection of every kind of ancient Armour and weapons [that are] wonderful beyond description"; and Hampton Court Palace and its Maze – "a puzzle made up of Green Hedges in which a stranger is certain to be lost."[13] At Ascot he stood in front of the queen's booth for nearly an hour: "she is a pretty little Girl, not beautiful, but with a sweet expression of face, and seemed to take an almost childlike interest in the scene."[14] His "highest honour" was an invitation by the members of the parliamentary press gallery, "a very intelligent set of fellows," to sit with them whenever he pleased. Yet nothing disappointed him as much as Parliament since none of the twenty best speakers he heard was to be compared to Archibald, Uniacke, Stewart, Haliburton, Fairbanks, or William Young, while "such a powerful and graceful Speaker as Old [John] Young is not in the House of Commons."[15]

Howe was also delighted to dine with one whose cause he had warmly espoused in Nova Scotia, Daniel O'Connell, "a fine old fellow, in figure very like my Brother William, but stouter, with a good deal of his springy step and sprightly manner."[16] A dinner for colonial visitors turned out to be a disaster because Sir Francis Bond Head stood for ten minutes without being able to blurt out more than a few sentences, and "then sat down looking like the greatest fool that ever I saw." Howe decided to save his speech, "although, from all the specimens I have yet seen of Parliamentary or dinner oratory, I should not be much afraid to give them a shew upon any general topic."[17] Most of all he was elated that he could be present for the coronation, a spectacle, he prophesied correctly, that would not occur again in his time. While he could have had a ticket to the Abbey, he preferred not to be shut up for twelve hours. Instead he established himself at the foot of Regent Street, where, to his astonishment, he could look in any direction and see more people than there were in Halifax, and sometimes more than lived in the entire province of Nova Scotia. As a newspaperman, he was astonished that the *Sun* would pay 100 guineas for the seats of the seventeen reporters whom it had installed in strategic places along the coronation route. He told Thompson not to use his descriptions of the coronation in the *Novascotian*, but those of the London newspapers which "would take months in small establishments to prepare, and ... without the combined acts of many eyes and minds could not be prepared at all."[18]

Accompanied by Haliburton, Howe moved to the continent in July, and there he almost reached the point of exhaustion trying to see as much as he could of Belgium, Germany, and France in three or four weeks. He spent "one of the most delightful days of his life" in the museum at Antwerp, deeply impressed by masterpieces which in quantity were unrivalled anywhere in Europe. From Antwerp he went to the field of Waterloo, which "lies in my mind's eye like a great picture never to fade away,"[19] then on to Cologne and a steamer trip up the Rhine. Somewhat disappointed, he concluded that the wonders and beauties of that river had been "very much overrated by errant Poets, Novelists and Legend Hunters, and by what is more natural, the affection entertained for it by those who have been born upon its borders." The men of letters had especially exaggerated the so-called delights of baronial halls which in many instances contained no room "as large as our Parlour, and certainly not equal in equipment and comfort to our kitchen."[20]

Howe ended his European tour in Paris where, with a guide, he did nothing but sight-seeing for ten days. The palaces and government establishments he found to be magnificent, but in everything else – "extent, commerce, wealth, cleanliness and comfort" – Paris lagged far behind London. The Parisian women in particular disappointed him: "an uglier race of devils I never saw, and upon this as on many other topics, I never will believe any thing I read." It was the time of the *Fête nationale* in Paris, and Howe got involved with a group of young men who were seeking to carry off the flags from one burial place to another. While Haliburton and the guide beat a hasty retreat, "I felt so much excited and so anxious to see what was going on, that I was soon in the thick of it ... I thought for the moment that a bloody struggle was about to commence, and that a new Revolution was to be added to the list of wonders which it had been my fortune to witness."[21] But it ended almost as suddenly as it had begun, and he never did discover what it was all about.

Next Howe spent a few days with Susan Ann's aunt and uncle, the Westphals, at Carisbrooke on the Isle of Wight, where in order to "justify your good taste in selecting a Husband I put on my best looks and best behaviour."[22] Then he went on to London for two or three weeks to complete his business, before beginning a quick tour of the rest of the British Isles. He concentrated on viewing at first hand Britain's rapidly developing industrial machine as well as the historical sites which prose and verse accounts had made fascinating for him since his boyhood: Windsor Castle; Eton and Oxford, where he saw among "other odd things Guy Faux's Lanthorne"; Blenheim; Woodstock and the site of Scott's novel; Warwick Castle and the cauldron in which the legendary Guy cooked the cow; the watch factories of Coventry; the industrial burgeoning of Birmingham; and the enormous workshop of Manchester.[23]

At Liverpool he delayed his trip to Scotland, hoping desperately to get some news from home. His diary and letters are replete with references to Susan Ann – had she come safely through her pregnancy? – and to his "babes" – every child he saw reminded him of them. Still waiting for information, he made a trip to Wales where at Carnarvon Castle he noted that "one of the Edwards was born in a dim looking chamber about as big as Ned's bed room."[24] He also climbed Snowdon: "harder work I never performed but the reward was great – such scenery I never beheld – and if I live a thousand years [I] shall never forget the half hour spent on the crest of Snowdon – the whole of Wales and the Island of Anglesey lay around me like a map"[25] There was still no news from Susan Ann on his return to Liverpool, but just as the boat was leaving a letter was brought on board in Susan Ann's handwriting. He did not know whether it was a boy or girl until he was well advanced into its contents and read the sentence: "*he* thrives, and I never was better." Immediately he became "the happiest fellow of the hundred persons on the deck, and went off to Scotland with a heart as light as a feather." It was, he told Susan Ann, "another bright link [added] to the chain of the domestic happiness by which we have so long been bound together."[26] He made a rapid tour of Scotland and Ireland before embarking for Halifax in another ten-gun brig, the *Hope*, in mid-October. "Here then," he recorded in his diary, "ends a cruise the most interesting, and instructive, that Providence has permittted me to enjoy, and [one that will] have an important influence on my future life, without a single accident or disappointment. May I use the knowledge acquired for the good of my country."[27]

For the next thirty days there was "nothing for it but salt water," accompanied, however, by a sense of self-satisfaction. For Susan Ann he had the tea set she wanted, "plain white and gold ... of the fashionable pattern"; for the girls, "London dolls that move their eyes, and some trifling toys which cost little, but will amuse them and Josey"; for himself he had picked up invaluable information about type and paper, "out of which, if I dont contrive to save something, it will be devilish odd."[28] But his success in business matters could not be compared to that of Haliburton, who had made an advantageous bargain with Bentley and intended to enter into arrangements for another book. "Slick is a passport to him wherever he goes, and people who never heard of Nova Scotia are reading and talking about the country."[29] Early in his trip Howe had reported that the second series of *The Clockmaker* was rapidly going though the press, and he would be able to land 2,000 copies in Halifax for £70 or £80 less than if he had printed them in his own shop.[30] Later he hoped that the first copies had arrived in Halifax and were helping to ease his financial situation.[31]

Though far removed from Halifax, Howe the political animal had not been that far removed from politics. His friends had told him that Archibald, having suffered two attacks of paralysis, was not likely to continue in the speakership. "I do not set my heart upon it, for it would be almost too high a flight at my age – but would take it if honourably offered, and certainly oppose U. [Uniacke] or any of that party with all my might."[32] Much more significant had been his relations with Lord Glenelg. After a fortnight in London he had called at the Colonial Office, sent up his card, and expected, according to normal practice, to have a day named for an appointment. Instead Glenelg saw him at once, a "very affable, intelligent, gray haired and broad headed looking Scotchman – what passed [between them could not be] put into Note Book which might fall into other hands."[33] Later, just before Howe left for Scotland, he spent a whole morning with the colonial secretary:

[He] pressed me to know *if there was any thing he could do for me at home*, and I had the satisfaction to be able to assure him that I *wanted nothing which the Government there had to give* – that any office under Government would make me less useful and less happy, and that all I asked was *fair play* and kind treatment for the *country of my birth* ... the Tories may now intrigue away, for although I want nothing myself, it is pleasant to know there are few things in the country which would not be within one's reach as long as this man is at the head of affairs.[34]

In Howe's eyes Glenelg had confirmed what he believed, or wanted to believe: that British statesmen had not done the right thing by the colonies largely because their informants, the governors, took their cue from the colonial compacts and they were left in utter ignorance of the true state of affairs on the other side of the water. For Howe the result was unfortunate since he returned to Nova Scotia more sanguine of earlier and easier political successes than he had any right to be.

CHAPTER THIRTEEN

A Convert to Durham

January 18, 1839, was a black-letter day for Howe. On that date Lord Glenelg's reply to the assembly's address of the previous May became public, and to him it was just as crushing as it was unexpected. One year, he said, the colonial secretary had spoken "the language of freedom, ... the next the dictatorial style of a master to his slave."[1] How, he wondered, could a man who, in discussion with him in August, had been so anxious to meet his wishes, write with such different effect in September? For Glenelg now offered the Reformers not even a glimmer of hope for the quick acceptance of their basic position. Not only did he maintain that Governor Campbell had done his best to secure a truly representative Legislative Council, but he withdrew his offer to surrender the casual and territorial revenues, and agreed to put these revenues at the assembly's disposal for a fixed period only if the assembly would make £4,700 available each year for the salaries of the principal officers; he also ordered the judges' fees to be abolished, but at the cost of an increase in their salaries that was to be charged to the casual revenues.[2]

Howe still put no blame on Glenelg or the British government and attributed the Reformers' failure to the fact that most colonials with access to the Colonial Office had a direct interest in maintaining the established system. But more and more he was coming to believe that the fine hand of Campbell was thwarting his efforts. He had good reason, for behind the scenes the governor had dropped all pretence to objectivity and fairness. In Campbell's eyes it was a tragedy that in a province without real grievances, "two or three designing men" were doing their utmost to "excite discontent and make the people believe they are oppressed by their rulers." Had not the time come, he asked, "for arresting their onward course towards Democracy"?[3] The language of Campbell's dispatches could not be known to Howe, but the language of his speech closing the last session still rankled in his mind. What right had the governor to criticize the assembly for not accepting the British government's proposals for the surrender of the casual revenues? What evidence did he have to suggest that much of the dissatisfaction with the composition of the council came from persons who were not named councillors?[4] In scathing terms, many months after the event, Howe denounced the governor's language as "uncourteous, unbecoming, insulting, and such as one branch of the legislature had no right to use to another."[5] Clearly Howe was wondering to what lengths someone who spoke thus in the open might go behind the scene; hence his reference to "a bad system bolstered up by despatches on false grounds."[6]

The publication of Glenelg's reply had the result of uniting every Reformer, lukewarm, moderate and radical, against the colonial secretary. None other than Hugh Bell, whose constituents had begun to doubt his enthusiasm for reform,[7] proposed the appointment of two assemblymen to present the House's case directly to the British government.[8] For five days between January 25 and 30 the debate on the resolution took place in a highly charged atmosphere. Excited throngs crowded the gallery and on one occasion gave Howe such vociferous support that he asked them to subdue their voices, thereby drawing a rebuke from Uniacke for usurping the prerogatives of the Speaker.[9] Even more than before, the real jousting in 1839 took place between Howe and Uniacke, and their exchanges rank high among the oratorical spectaculars of the Nova Scotia House of Assembly. The debate continued to reflect a contest between one who had enjoyed the best in education and knew life lived under the most refined circumstances, and another who was self-taught and had been exposed to the crudities and vulgarities of the less genteel.

To Uniacke, Howe was "like a modern preacher of the name of Irving, ... who tried various moods with his audience, – he first tickled, and then threatened, and then thumped them into his views." He was also like the Babylonian king who set up a golden image, and cast into a fiery furnace everyone who refused to worship it. "He may heat the furnace seven times hotter, and cast me in, and I trust to come out as unscathed as Shadrach, Mesheck, and Abednego."[10] Uniacke was especially critical of Howe's alleged change of stance: "like the frogs in the fable, [he] grew tired of king Log, and cried out for king Stork, *and now* he wants another king ... An old frog might call out for one king, while the pollywogs would cry out for another."[11]

In reply, Howe wished that Uniacke knew as much about British freedom as he did about the names and habits of inferior animals. But had he not forgotten the squid which, when detected "feasting on the property of its neighbour ... squirts out all sorts of black dingy matter; and, amidst the impurity created, baffles its pursuer and covers its retreat"; or the skunk which, "when attacked, emits an odious perfume, and compels its pursuer to resign the chase."[12] Uniacke retorted indignantly that, although he used anecdote and fable, he did not resort to personalities, and he doubted that he merited the appellation of squid and skunk; if Howe continued to rely on personal insults, he would convert the assembly into a bear-garden.[13] But despite the ferocity of their exchanges, Uniacke and Howe continued to have a grudging admiration for each other; would that Uniacke were a Reformer, said Howe, and "I would be proud to follow him."[14] Remarks such as these caused William Young to write disconsolately to his brother George: "Uniacke and I had a set-to & are on terms of open hostility [while] Howe & Doyle cultivate his good graces rather than mine."[15]

Yet Howe and Uniacke were poles apart politically. When Howe labelled all his opponents as anti-reform, Uniacke was moved to scorn: "I also am a reformer, we are all reformers."[16] Howe accused Uniacke and the Tories of trying to cure Nova Scotia by using the new system of medicine known as homeopathic: "they would administer the millionth part of a grain of *reform* every session, and that should satisfy all!"[17] The differences between the two stemmed from thoroughly conflicting views about the very nature of colonial government itself. Howe was coming to the conclusion that "if we are to remain part of the British Empire ... we must be British subjects to the fullest extent of British constitutional freedom,"[18] while Uniacke took the usual Tory position that the Reformers' views, if adopted, would reduce the governor to a cipher and lead to colonial separation. If the governor did not maintain his independence within the colony, he would not be free to carry out the instructions of a colonial secretary whose duty it was to sustain the unity of the empire. Uniacke further maintained that, as an executive councillor, he offered advice to the governor when it was requested, but he neither expected it would be followed nor did he see any need to defend the governor's decision.

Even before Bell moved formally for a delegation to London, Howe had declared the course – admittedly a last resort – the only one left to follow. But to prevent misunderstanding or suspicion, he stated emphatically that he would not be a member of any delegation. For one thing he could hardly leave Susan Ann to assume the burden of a young family for the second year running. But there was also the consideration that, since he had gained nothing by establishing an excellent rapport with Glenelg, he might have greater effect at the Colonial Office through a forceful stance at home.

By January 29 Howe and the Reformers had pushed the principle of a delegation through the assembly; in short order they had adopted instructions for its guidance and appointed Herbert Huntington and William Young to be the delegates. In no sense could the instructions be said to expound abstract rights or levelling democracy. Reflecting the Reformers' middle-class values, they called primarily for greater efficiency and lower expenditures in the administration of provincial affairs.[19] So far the assembly had had things much its own way. But in March, when Howe moved that £1,000 be voted to defray the delegates' expenses, the Tories objected strongly that the expenditure was improper during troubled times. For on February 26 word had come that Governor John Fairfield of Maine intended to settle a long smouldering conflict with New Brunswick, the northeastern boundary question, by force of arms. Within hours the assembly had added Howe and four other Reformers to the Committee on the Military Defence of the Province, and authorized Campbell to call out the entire militia force and spend up to £100,000 for the defence of Nova Scotia and New Brunswick. When the Reform left wing talked of limiting Campbell's powers, Howe persuaded them not to press their views;[20] and in the end the House adopted the resolution unanimously, giving "*three hearty cheers for our Brethren in New Brunswick* [and] *the Queen* ... amidst a scene of the most extraordinary excitement."[21]

To suggest under these circumstances that the Reformers should abandon the delegation was nothing short of monstrous to Howe. He described the £1,000 to be spent on the delegation as a mere drop in the bucket compared with the £80,000 that had been wasted in the previous ten years. As he read the situation, redress of ills was more likely at a time when attention was focused on the colonies and if the assembly awaited more peaceful times, the evils might become altogether entrenched.[22] As usual, he was thinking in pragmatic terms and disregarding abstract principles. When the assembly drew up an address to the Crown, later in March, its basic demand called for the introduction of "the same wholesome grounds and checks, the same control over the public Expenditure, ... which have secured the well-being and happiness of the Mother Country."[23]

Because the session was drawing to a close, and the council's reaction to the assembly's proposals for a delegation had not become publicly known, the assembly conducted a search of the council's *Journals*. It discovered a series of resolutions that both amazed and angered it. The council had devoted its major attention to criticizing

Lord Durham and his *Report*, copies of which had just arrived in Nova Scotia. It denounced especially Durham's proposal for a federal union of the colonies, fearing it would mean the involvement of the "contented, loyal and peaceable" lower colonies in the " political dissentions of Lower Canada."[24] Although it was reluctant in troubled times to bother the British government with matters that, on the whole, were of minor importance, if delegations were to be sent, it would on no account pay the expenses of the assembly's delegates unless its own received similar treatment.

After calling it a red herring to introduce the Durham *Report* at this stage, Howe attacked the constitutional impropriety of the council; imagine, he said, the reaction of the Commons if the Lords sought to coerce it in this manner.[25] Accordingly, he persuaded the assembly not to accept any communication from the council relating to the expenses of the delegates for fear it would acknowledge the right of the upper house either to initiate a money grant or amend one proposed by the lower house. Then, in a last desperate effort before prorogation, he won the assembly's agreement to request £1,000 from the governor for its delegates' expenses, with the assurance that it would vote that amount at the next session.[26] But none knew better than he that Campbell's response would not be favourable.

He was not yet done with either the governor or the council. After calling the council's act the worst of "all the impudent and mad acts ever committed by any Colonial Council,"[27] he sought to show how preposterous it was that a body which had voted £100,000 for the defence of the colony should be denied £1,000, "*which is their own*, to truly exhibit the features of a system that annually robs them of thousands."[28] As for Campbell, if he had wanted to do his duty to his sovereign and the people, he would have replied positively to the assembly's request.[29] Naturally Howe was delighted when Huntington and Young drew on their own resources to go to Britain. He said nothing when the *Times* expressed surprise that they were allowed to leave with such little fanfare, but he had his innings when Alexander Stewart and L.M. Wilkins, the council's delegates, boarded the *Tyrian*; they were, he said, "rowed off as quietly as though they were a brace of young gentlemen in the Dry Good line," and the only sign of emotion was "a man ... waving something that looked very like a dirty shirt out of the back window of the Times Office."[30] Stewart, appointed to the Legislative Council in 1838, was taking the last of a series of steps that was to make him one of the most controversial and detested of all Nova Scotian politicians. Primarily responsible for the council's resolutions and delegation, he was now to become that body's chief spokesman in London. For him there was to be the legacy of bitterness that a convert often incurs at the hand of his former friends; Clim o' the Cleugh was already calling him "the most ambitious, aspiring, time serving, trimming politician in the Province."[31]

By this time Howe had become so identified with the direction of the Reform cause that he was close to being *the* issue in Nova Scotia politics. Noting that he had been the target of about a hundred of the *Times* editorials and letters to the end of June, he wondered, laughingly, how a person who was "already the smallest person in the world, [could be] *a little less.*"[32] While the *Times* denied that it had started "a new policy," and maintained that, no less than before, it was "an independent Conservative Journal" opposed to "that destructive meddling with usage and institutions, which is so prevalent in the present day,"[33] both its editor and its contributors had at least sharpened their weapons. Certainly the attacks on Howe ran the full gamut of the conceivable. "An Old Woman" from Pleasant River laughed at his statement that Uniacke reminded him of an old woman making syllabub – "she beats it all to froth." Surely Howe should be aware that "syllabub is not beat at all ... if he knows no more about politics than he does about making syllabub, he had better give them up."[34]

Throughout June and July the *Times* was reaching the level of the preposterous when it accused Howe of trying to destroy the Mechanics' Institute because it was not "the pliable engine [he] supposed it would be to further [his] political purposes."[35] A little earlier Lucius, the most persistent of his critics, attacked him for his hostility to the Church of England and questioned his qualifications to legislate on religious subjects. "Have you ever commemorated the death of the beloved Son of the Highest ... in the sacrament of the Lord's Supper ... Do you every morning and evening send up your aspirations and thanksgivings unto the throne of grace?"[36] The *Times* and its letter-writers scoffed no less at Howe on "the delegation job." Since he had already strutted his way through the streets of London, he had left it to "Billy" Young to use his talents at the Colonial Office, hoping that if the latter won a seat on the Supreme Court, he himself would have an uninterrupted road to the goal of his ambition, the speakership.[37]

In April Howe notified his critics that the *Novascotian* was entering upon a period of forbearance only to have the *Times* tell him it was too late. "Verily her scarlet ladyship has thrived upon the wages of infamy ... Out upon such hypocrisy. Her ten years iniquities are too thick upon her to permit her to escape so easily."[38] Before long Howe decided he had no choice but to take cognizance of "the manufactory of lies," and he threw two or three hand grenades into its camp in a letter of "Ha-Ha"[39] and a series entitled "The Divan." In one episode of this series Gossip and Coade, the editor and printer of the *Times*, are held in the coal cellar of The Divan until Mick the waiter complains that "the cellar is beginning to have a bad flavor ... a more rotten rascal than that Gossip I never heard of."[40]

For the second year in a row, Howe's treatment of the compact almost led him into a duel. When the Legislative Council appointed John W. Ritchie, the son-in-law of J.W. Johnston and nephew of Dr William B. Almon, as a second law clerk, an office that the Reformers considered unnecessary, Howe thought it best to avoid an unholy row with the council on a comparatively minor matter, but he did point out that, if he had stood in the same relation to Ritchie as did Johnston and Almon, he would have been subjected to scurrilous abuse. That evoked such an intemperate response from Almon that Howe replied in kind; the Doctor, he said, "for his own advantage, had, for half a life, rendered [the Bridewell] which might have been an ornament to the town, a mockery and bye word among his own profession."[41] Taking up the cudgels on his father's behalf, the young Dr W.J. Almon left Howe the choice of an apology or the satisfaction that was appropriate in matters of this kind, but in the end "better sense prevailed ... and the persuasion of friends was used to call the matter off."[42]

Because Howe took a position on almost every matter introduced into the assembly, he was not seldom at odds with non-Tories and even with his own friends. So when Speaker Archibald sought to improve the great roads through an additional issue of provincial paper, Howe – always the defender of a hard currency – turned adamantly against the proposal.[43] He was no less opposed to a bill of the Reformer Zenas Waterman of Queens that sought to reduce the sale of ardent spirits; "while men's passions and feelings were hostile to such a law, it would be impossible to carry it into effect ... All that the Legislature could do, was, to encourage temperance opinions."[44] Howe also ran afoul of the Reformers who belonged to the Church of England because of the position he adopted towards the school lands that were associated with that church. Since most of the province had been settled by non-Anglicans, these lands remained largely unused and Howe insisted that, in changed circumstances, their disposition ought to be altered to promote the education of all Nova Scotians, whatever their religion.[45] Because he spoke his mind on every issue as he saw it, he was, at various times in his career, to annoy, and occasionally alienate, almost every significant interest in the province.

In two matters of special interest to Howe a further incomplete chapter was written in 1839. His sympathies were all with the advocates of the incorporation of Halifax when they asked the assembly why " the opinion of 556 Rate Payers, and others, expressed by Petition, backed by two Town Meetings" had no more weight than "the signature of 153, however respectable, who either did not attend those Meetings, or failed to influence the opinions of the citizens constitutionally elected."[46] But he could do nothing for them, since the assembly turned down all bills relating to the local government of Halifax, including his own bill to incorporate the town, after Hugh Bell and other Reformers made known their opposition.[47]

The university question caused him even more soul-searching. To produce the cultivated minds on which the prosperity of the province depended, he still believed that Nova Scotia needed a first-class, nonsectarian university, and he hoped that Dalhousie, apparently "waked from its death-like sleep,"[48] would be that institution. To that end he introduced a bill to liberalize its trust. His reason became apparent on February 13 when the Rev. Dr Edmund A. Crawley, a Baptist, appeared at the bar of the assembly to explain why he had been turned down for a professorship at Dalhousie. Apparently two of the three trustees, Governor Campbell and Charles Wallace, the provincial treasurer, took the position that it was not open to them to appoint a non-Presbyterian.[49] While the conditions of the trust might have lent themselves to that interpretation, Howe had his suspicions that Crawley was rejected because Campbell and Wallace wanted to retain the exclusivity of educational institutions, or simply because he was a Baptist.

The next day Crawley again appeared before the assembly to support the Baptist Education Society's bill[50] for the incorporation of Queen's (later to be Acadia) College and the provision of financial assistance from the province. These proposals placed Howe in a dilemma which led him to disagree with some of his fellow-Reformers. He took the position that the bills relating to Queen's and Dalhousie should be considered separately, each on its merits. Although a strong supporter of Dalhousie, he preferred that artificers from the barracks he "directed to mine it, and blow the structure into the air"[51] in preference to its becoming a sectarian college. To those who thought there were too many temptations for youth attending a university in Halifax, he replied that "temptations existed in all towns ... At [Windsor, the site of King's College] young men might be seen sitting at the Tavern window, who would not dare to make such displays in the town of Halifax."[52] On Dalhousie he was in agreement with Huntington and William Young, but he could not join them in turning down Crawley and Queen's College. Although, like them, theoretically opposed to sectarian universities, he could not dismiss the fact that the legislature had provided the established church a permanent grant for King's College; also, that the Baptist Education Society had experienced great hardships in making Horton Academy a viable institution and thereby established a claim to something beyond an academy. Hence he was not averse to giving the Society a grant for a stated number of years. But he was not successful on either count. The Legislative Council added an amendment to the Dalhousie bill that the assembly could not accept, and an unnatural combination of Tories and Reformers turned down the Queen's College bill.

While politics was consuming more and more of Howe's time, the *Novascotian* continued to provide him with a livelihood that was, for a short time during these years, a comfortable one. By now its circulation was rivalled by only one or two papers in British North America, and in parts of the eastern provinces, where until recently a newspaper had been something of a curiosity, ten to fifty copies were being circulated every week. The year 1839 presented him with a new challenge as a newspaper publisher. Word had come in April that Samuel Cunard had contracted with the British government to carry the transoceanic mails for £55,000 a year for seven years. To that end he would provide twice-a-month service between Britain and Halifax, using boats of not less than 300 horsepower, as well as services between Halifax and Boston, and Pictou and Quebec, using boats of half that horsepower.[53] Since steamers would be calling at Halifax only ten to twelve days out of English ports, Nova Scotia would not be nearly as dependent as before on the Boston or New York papers for European intelligence. In fact, the *Novascotian* would carry such news to the remote settlements of the eastern provinces before the *Great Western* and other steamers reached New York, and, by way of the Pictou steamer, to Quebec and Montreal as quickly as the New York papers.

Howe's response was a prospectus for a new series of the *Novascotian*, which in mechanical execution would "equal, if it does not excel, any other Periodical of the same kind published on [this] Continent."[54] The enlarged paper would publish a stream of Old World information, as well as a weekly summary of the major news events gleaned from British and colonial papers; there would also be an expanded literary department, no longer dependent on New York for the contents of British magazines and reviews. While correspondence of a local nature would have to be divested of its verbiage, the proceedings of the legislature would continue to be faithfully reported together with original articles by the best writers in the country. But amidst change the *Novascotian* would stand for the same basic principle: "to combine with the preservation of British connexion, a just, enlightened, and responsible system of Colonial Government."[55]

In producing an improved *Novascotian*, Howe wanted at all costs to avoid an increase in the subscription price. In May, confronted with several thousand pounds of unpaid subscriptions on his books, he almost begged the delinquents to pay up so that he would not have to fritter away his time "in the ... tedious process of collecting small accounts, from persons who really ought not to require to be called on a second time."[56] About the same time he was asking his agents two questions: Would the improved *Novascotian* attract more subscribers? What was the better way to prevent the heavy interest payments resulting from subscriptions in arrears: to offer the sale of the paper in each county to the highest bidder or to demand subscriptions in advance?[57] The answer became clear in October when he announced that the rate would remain at 22s. 6d., payable in advance.[58]

Earlier Howe had presented his view of the press at a testimonial dinner to Thomas Chandler Haliburton. Nova Scotians, he said, were inferior to Britons in only one respect: their attitude towards "a free and unrestricted Press." Britons went almost to the point of licentiousness without fear of reprisal; on coronation day he had seen a poor man threading his way through the Strand, displaying an article on "the abomination, absurdity, and blasphemy, of Coronations." No one molested him yet if Howe had similarly "paraded the streets of Halifax ... he would probably have been thrown into the Queen's Dock."[59] On the same occasion Haliburton had referred to Howe's loss in publishing his *History*. " ... it was one," Howe replied, "he never regretted – it was one which [Haliburton] had seized every opportunity to repair."[60] Meanwhile Howe had taken another chance by giving Haliburton "a handsome sum" for the colonial copyright of the third series of *The Clockmaker*. From the start his optimism was dashed. He got little response when he invited bids from publishers in New York and Boston for the American rights, and because Lea & Blanchard of Philadelphia were no more enthusiastic, he had to offer them for what he considered the bargain price of $400.[61]

In anticipation of the new packet service to Britain, Boston, and Quebec, Howe thought in wider terms than simply an improved *Novascotian*. He had much to do with a meeting in Halifax that raised £8,000 towards establishing a hotel. He also offered all sorts of gratuitous advice to anyone who might provide a daily coach service from Halifax to Victoria Beach in Annapolis county. In particular, he suggested a vehicle he had seen in the south of Ireland drawn by two horses and seating eight persons comfortably; though it had no covering, the traveller could get along well with an umbrella and "that admirable contrivance," the Mackintosh. Americans visiting Quebec and Montreal in the summer, he suggested, could take the steamer to Pictou, ramble through the eastern counties to Halifax, and then use the western stage to return home by way of the Saint John.[62] Perhaps Howe should be credited with being the first genuine promoter of tourism in Nova Scotia. Throughout the year he also offered encouragement to the Society for the Encouragement of Trade and Manufactures which he had helped to found late in 1838 as a successor to the Commercial Society following its disintegration in bickerings and quarrels; hopefully, he asked the new organization to keep the legislature informed of the articles that could best bear a revenue duty and the manufactures that were most likely to grow under moderate protection.[63]

Contrary to his usual practice, Howe did not travel far from Halifax in 1839. Regretfully he turned down an invitation to ceremonies in Pictou County marking the opening of the railroad from the coal pits to the landing below New Glasgow, and the operation of locomotive engines for the first time in the province, even though it was an event deserving of "a festival and a frolic, if ever any one ... in Nova Scotia ... did."[64] Instead he was contented with a trip to Margaret's Bay and its "wild and romantic" scenery.[65] For throughout the summer he was engaged in an activity at home that he regarded as of the highest importance.

Late in March the Durham *Report* had arrived in Nova Scotia and Howe was delighted with most of it. Admittedly some of its conclusions were "hastily drawn from slight observations,"[66] especially the one which held that the questions which divided parties in Nova Scotia were "of no great magnitude."[67] Durham, he believed, had been led astray because only one of a Nova Scotia delegation of four to which he talked had been a genuine Reformer.[68] Howe was also dubious about Durham's plan for a confederation of the provinces, the more so because "the seat of government would be nearly as far from us as Downing Street now is."[69] Otherwise, he had nothing but praise for Durham. "We did not believe there was a nobleman in Britain who had the ability and the firmness to grapple with the great questions committed to Lord Durham's care, in a spirit so searching, and yet so frank."[70] As Howe saw it, Durham had two basic proposals to solve the conflict between the people and the colonial executives, both "perfectly *simple* and eminently *British* – it is to let the *majority* and not the *minority* govern, and compel every

Governor to select his advisers from those, *who enjoy the confidence of the People* and can *command a majority of the popular Branch.*"[71]

Week after week Howe published excerpts from the *Report* together with his own commentary. Wherever possible, he singled out passages "*confirming, strengthening* and *justifying* ... *every principle for which the Reformers of this Province have ardently contended.*"[72] Referring to Durham's examples of the absurdities resulting from the dependence of the governor on the official party in Upper Canada, Howe observed: "What a picture of Nova Scotia have we here!" Even had Durham been completely familiar with the last two administrations in Nova Scotia, "he could not have sketched them with more graphic power and faithfulness than he has done in this passage."[73] Howe was especially pleased to have it confirmed that most of the Upper Canadian Reformers wanted nothing more than Durham said they were entitled to, and that only after they despaired of obtaining the privileges of British subjects had they been "driven to seek, even in republicanism, a cure for the petty tyranny, and wretchedness" of the existing system.[74]

Howe's summer work was cut out for him when on June 3 Lord John Russell, the new colonial secretary, introduced his bill for the union of the Canadas. In making it clear that, despite Durham, he stood altogether opposed to the so-called principle of responsible government, Russell used the stock answer of British statesmen of those days: a colonial governor could not be responsible to the Crown and the colonial assembly at the same time.[75] But Howe was not at all critical of the colonial secretary since the latter had obviously considered these matters only from the imperial point of view. Russell had a reputation for open-mindedness, and perhaps Howe could win him over to the colonial point of view. Certainly the attempt was well worth a few weeks of his time. By mid-summer he had finished the four lengthy letters to Russell that Chester Martin says were commonly accepted as "the colonial counterpart of Durham's *Report* and Charles Buller's *Responsible Government for Colonies.*"[76] In an accompanying personal letter Howe sought to counter any charges of disloyalty in advance by describing the unceasing efforts of his father and himself in support of the British connection.[77]

Basically the letters argued that British rule was being reversed on this side of the Atlantic by disregard for a principle that was the cornerstone of the British constitution. Where was the danger in following Durham's advice and commanding the governors to govern with the aid of those who possessed the majority in the assembly? "Of what consequence is it to the people of England whether half-a-dozen persons, in whom the majority have confidence, ... manage our local affairs; or the same number selected from the minority and whose policy the bulk of the population distrust? ... Would England be weaker, less prosperous or less respected, because the people of Nova Scotia were satisfied and happy?"[78] For Russell to suggest that the governor himself was responsible was "mere mockery" to Howe. Every governor whom he had known had been forced to follow the course laid down for him by the major permanent office-holders of the colony. "He may flutter and struggle in the net, as some well-meaning Governors have done, but he must at last resign himself to his fate; and like a snared bird be content with the narrow limits assigned him by his keepers."[79] What had Nova Scotians done to justify the alienation of their birthright? Had not the blood of a Nova Scotian stripling mingled with that of Nelson as they lay dying in the cockpit of the *Victory*? "Am I not then justified, my Lord, in claiming for my countrymen that constitution, which can be withheld from them by no plea but one unworthy of a British statesman – the tyrant's plea of power? ... we seek for nothing more than British subjects are entitled to; but we will be contented with nothing less."[80]

By the second week in October Howe's letters to Russell were available for distribution in pamphlet form, 1,500 of them, and Howe the publicist was ready to take over. While he ruefully admitted that "such an edition costs something," still a pamphlet could be more easily passed from hand to hand than the *Novascotian* and more readily circulated in the other provinces and England. Howe, who had previously demonstrated his talents as a publicist in Nova Scotia, this time spread a much wider net. In addition to Russell, the pamphlet went to Charles Buller, who had materially assisted the assembly's delegates,[81] and other recipients in Britain were the duke of Wellington, Peel, Glenelg, Macaulay, all the members of both Houses of Parliament, the clubs, the reading rooms, and the major newspapers. In British America all the newspapers received the pamphlet, and many of them, especially those in Upper Canada, printed long extracts from it. Men in politics in all provinces, from the governor general down, received it, often accompanied by a personal letter from Howe.[82] If anyone interested in colonial affairs remained ignorant of it, that was clearly not the fault of Howe.

In Nova Scotia the *Pictou Mechanic and Farmer* and the *Yarmouth Herald* published the pamphlet in full. But the Tory press gave it scant attention. The *Times* had known that "the mountain was in labour, and though prepared to behold a mouse, we expected a smart full whiskered chap, not such a weak sickly thing [as this] ... to nibble its way into the Colonial Office"; as it stood, "no mouser ... will think it worthy a stroke of his paw."[83] When no basic criticism of the letters was forthcoming, Howe suggested that "no individual [member of the compact] appears anxious to accept of a pummelling for the good of the whole."[84] Yet, no matter how the pamphlet was regarded in Nova Scotia, Howe's acceptance of the Durham *Report* and its method of ensuring responsibility represented a fundamental change in attitude on his part. Fundamentally pragmatic in his outlook, he had talked and written only generally about introducing some form of responsibility until 1837, when circumstances dictated that he state specifically how it was to be secured. He had then discussed it in terms of an elective Legislative Council or some analogous device, and had rejected the idea of a responsible executive on the British model as altogether too complex to be workable in a small colony like Nova Scotia.

A single reading of the *Report* had made him an instant convert and a powerful expounder of its ideas to a colonial secretary who had rejected them. His own open mind made him receptive to the argument that an executive of the British type was entirely appropriate to the province. But even more surprising than his conversion was the lack of importance he attached to it and the lack of attention it received in the provincial press. Perhaps this said a great deal about the embryonic nature of the movement for responsible government in Nova Scotia and the lack of sophisticated thinking by both the critics and advocates of change.

CHAPTER FOURTEEN

"The Severest Trial"

For Howe the delegation to London was a last resort, and he counted heavily on its success. After talking to Huntington and Young on their return in the fall of 1839, he felt completely let down.[1] Lord Normanby, the colonial secretary for a few months between February and August of that year, had agreed to establish five free ports in Nova Scotia and to combine the Excise and Customs Departments into one. But on more substantive matters he went little beyond his predecessors: some leading assemblymen were to be appointed to the Executive Council, and changes were to be made in the Legislative Council to permit greater cooperation with the assembly, but nothing more. So although Howe put on a bold front in public, he knew the delegates had not secured the break-through he had wanted. But what more could a conservative reformer do?

As he pondered his next move, fate took a hand. Late in the year, by way of Fredericton, he learned that the new colonial secretary, Lord John Russell, in a dispatch dated October 16, had told the new governor general, Charles Poulett Thomson, that the tenure of colonial offices was not to be regarded as one during good behaviour, and that colonial officers might be required to retire "as often as any sufficient motives of public policy may suggest [its] expediency."[2] For Howe in his dilemma the dispatch seemed to herald the death warrant of all the compacts; did it not mean that governors were intended to follow Durham's proposals and surround themselves with popular and able men?[3] As if to confirm Howe's interpretation, the same mail brought a copy of a memorandum from Sir John Harvey, the lieutenant-governor of New Brunswick, suggesting that the dispatch conferred "a new ... and improved constitution upon these Colonies."[4] If further proof were needed, Governor General Thomson published Russell's dispatch in the *Upper Canada Gazette*, and announced he had been instructed to govern "in accordance with the well understood wishes and interests of the people."[5]

Throughout January 1840 Howe awaited action on Campbell's part, but none was forthcoming. Finally, on February 3, he presented a series of resolutions stating that the Executive Council did not possess the confidence of the assembly and ought to be remodelled.[6] Let no one be terrified, he said, because he was simply laying the foundations of a constitution like that of England. "I would feel proud and happy that the commencement of these great changes should be laid here and that they extend into all the British dependencies."[7] It was not much of a contest in the assembly since only twelve out-and-out Tories opposed the resolutions,[8] and there was no one of Howe's mettle to oppose him. Although J.B. Uniacke had in no sense become a Reformer, he had concluded that the effect of Russell's dispatch, coupled with the interpretations of Thomson and Harvey, had been to confer new constitutions upon the colonies, and because "the guide and controlling influence of [his] general conduct" was never to "withdraw [his] humble support from the Parent State,"[9] he could not stand in the way of the colonial secretary's views. No less than before, he feared that the new system would reduce the governor to a cipher and put the province under the control of a few popular leaders; yet he was "willing to try the experiment" because the British government had ordered it.[10]

Even though Campbell refused to recognize any change in the colonial secretary's position and expressed complete satisfaction with his council,[11] Howe accepted, as a fait accompli, "the establishment of the principles for which [the Reformers] had been contending – and of a Constitution, of which no power on earth could now deprive them."[12] For a time he thought of moving an address to the governor general pointing out that Campbell was not acting on the same principles as his superior.[13] But no matter how mildly it was worded it would amount to a vote of censure on Campbell, and he wanted to give the governor another chance to mend his ways. So by himself he drew up an address to Campbell, noting that in his reply to the assembly the governor had made explicit reference only to Normanby's dispatch of August, and directing his attention to Russell's dispatch and the interpretations of Thomas and Harvey, which his advisers had apparently induced him to ignore. Howe made no bones that his tactic was to divide the Executive Council which, by placing the "Old Soldier" in the gap, was sacrificing him for its own aggrandizement.[14]

Bereft of Uniacke, their brightest ornament, the Tories pitted a nonentity, Winthrop Sargent of Shelburne, against Howe. Obviously without thought of repercussions, he suggested that if the

Reformers' demands were met, "a talented Editor of a Newspaper" might control the government because of his ability to influence the return of members who supported his views.[15] No less innocently, Howe replied that he had every right to pursue "any path of ambition within the limits of the constitution," and he "did not want to be made a rebel," as Benjamin Franklin had been, by the system of government. He went further to make comparisons that were altogether odious to the Halifax compact and its sons. Whenever he looked at the boys in his printing shop, "with [their] black faces, but brains above them," he felt like saying: "Some of you are smart fellows, but when you come in contact with the John Hal[l]iburtons, and the Tom Jefferys, and the Master Inglises, and four or five other lads not better than yourselves, what chance of success have you under the government of the country? ... could [his apprentices] enjoy the full privileges of the British Constitution? could they contend, on equal terms, with a few favourite families? and the answer was, they never could under the system."[16] Howe would soon learn that the sons of the compact did not treat these remarks lightly.

In replying to the assembly's address, Campbell stated he could not find in Russell's dispatch "a fundamental change in the Colonial Constitution ... to the extent, supposed by you,"[17] and promised to refer the matter to the colonial secretary. In their strongest language to date the Reformers manifested their utter frustration. The *Recorder* talked of the impeachment of Campbell or stopping the supplies, and Huntington suggested an address for the governor's recall. In the end, on Howe's insistence it was agreed to finish the normal business of the session so as to prevent injury to the country through the cutting off of supply. Seldom was Howe more frustrated than in the six weeks that followed. In turn, the Legislative Council blocked the assembly's bills on the reformation of the judiciary,[18] the civil list, and the registry of deeds, the last two on the thorny question of vested rights.

The registrars bill related to Sir Rupert George, who, in addition to being provincial secretary, was registrar of deeds for the province, through which source alone he received £700 to £800 annually for which he rendered no services. The bill provided that the deputy registrars of deeds in the counties were to become the principals rather than deputies, and that George was to receive £200 annually as compensation. On this bill Howe outlined his position on vested rights as definitively as he was ever to do it. In Nova Scotia, he pointed out, there was not such a dearth of claimants for office that those who accepted one needed to be assured that "all its emoluments should continue for ever."[19] Indeed, whenever he was asked to describe the compact, he told the inquirer to go "down by government house the morning after the death of a public officer, [and there] he would see nearly all the compact trooping that way seeking after the situation." Instead of treating emoluments as personal property on the retirement of office-holders, the right course was to "look to the services, and peculiar circumstances, and claims, of incumbents, and deal kindly and generously with them."[20] But his arguments failed to impress a Legislative Council led by J.W. Johnston, who relied on Normanby's dispatch of August 31 supporting the right of the actual occupants of office to their existing emoluments, and who refused to budge from that position on either the civil list or registry bill.[21]

Meanwhile the *Recorder* had become increasingly frustrated by what it regarded as a charade. "Does the popular party not see, have they not seen for years, that it is this spirit of delay and procrastination which has ruined them? ... Shall the people of these colonies sound a retreat when the battle is won?"[22] Then in the closing days of the session, March 24 and 25, it actually got more than it wanted in a burst of resolutions proposed by Huntington, Goudge, Howe, and Young, and in an address to the Crown drafted by Howe requesting Campbell's recall. At every point Howe and his associates sought to make it clear that they were not acting like the irresponsible Canadians. By making sure that the revenue and appropriation acts were passed, they had seen to it that their constituents were not deprived of the road and bridge moneys upon which they were dependent. But in giving up the leverage they possessed in the voting of supplies, they took pains to say that "they confidently relied upon the justness and firmness of their Sovereign."[23]

The resolutions and address differed from their predecessors in assigning the blame for the Reformers' failures to Campbell himself; more than anyone, he was said to be preventing the government from being conducted as the colonial secretary and the majority of the assembly wanted it to be. Why, for example, was the assembly always wrangling with the councils? Primarily it was because in the governor's nominations to those bodies he had "violated the plain letter and spirit of Lord Glenelg's Despatches in 1837." Even in his recent appointments to the councils he had continued to show a determination to perpetuate the system of which the House complained. He had included not a single assemblyman in his six nominees to the Legislative Council, while in his nominations to the Executive Council he had passed over every man of influence to honour Alexander Stewart, whose appointment, in the words of Howe's resolution, would be "a direct insult to the House"; indeed, "there [were] few men in Nova-Scotia, who enjoy[ed] so little of [its] confidence,"[24] In conclusion, the address accused Campbell of being "determined either not to understand, or not to act on, the [recent] Despatch of Lord John Russell."

When, on March 25, the assembly adopted Howe's address calling for Campbell's removal, it was the strongest action it had yet taken, or would take, during these years.[25] Howe "plead[ed] guilty to the composition of every line of it ... [although] it was ... submitted to a committee of 7 or 8 members ... I take the whole responsibility myself."[26] By his own admission, this was "the severest trial" he had yet experienced in his political career. "I felt pretty much as a soldier would, who should be called out on a firing party, to shoot a man who had been impelled, by circumstances and bad advisers into crime ... if every I performed a task with a heavy heart it was that."[27] For a son of Loyalist John Howe to treat the Queen's representative in this way demonstrated he had come a long way since the 1820s. Yet even a conservative reformer may be forced into extreme action when he has exhausted all the other alternatives.

As usual, Howe intervened in a host of other matters during the session of 1840, but his positions were almost always predictable. He persuaded the assembly to vote £1,800 for the Great Eastern Road through Musquodoboit to St Mary's with his vision of "hundreds of teams ... com[ing] down from the eastern counties laden with Agricultural products."[28] He opposed the spending of large sums of money to encourage agriculture, jocosely telling the assembly it should either advise the farmers to buy a copy of *Poor Richard's Maxims*, or pass an act fining any farmer who had his horse hitched to a tavern for more than three hours between November and April.[29] When Andrew McKim sought to prevent the sale of liquor within six miles of a polling place, Howe scornfully suggested it might be well to prohibit dancing too; at the last election in the county of Halifax one candidate was too staid to dance; another too stout; and he found himself "almost danced to a skeleton."[30] But when the same member proposed to abolish the tax that the established church could levy on anyone who did not profess to belong to a particular church, he was all for it; "let Ministers of every persuasion, take their stand against infidelity, instead of supposing that 5s. would convert infidels to christianity."[31] On the bill to incorporate Queen's College, Howe was again included in a large category of members who spoke against the measure and yet voted for it. "The project," he said, "was like one for making five great roads, where only one should be," but he supported it because Crawley's application for an appointment at Dalhousie had been rejected. "Only for that, nothing could induce him to vote for the Bill."[32]

The session was over, but an incident growing out of it might have cost Howe his life. Although he had disposed of earlier challenges from Sawers and young Dr Almon without harm to himself, he knew that he trifled with the high and mighty of Halifax not without risk, and that he stood a good chance of being challenged and "shot at, by every public officer whose intellect [he] might happen to contrast with his emoluments."[33] The challenge that came from John C. Halliburton, the son of the chief justice, in March 1840 did not quite fall into this category, even though it has often been suggested that Halliburton was demanding satisfaction for Howe's comments on his father during the debate on the civil list bill.[34] But since Howe's most astringent remarks on the chief justice were made after the arrival of the son's letter, John Halliburton was, in fact, reacting to the comparison of himself with the apprentices in the *Novascotian* office. Although Howe had commented on him and the Inglis boys on February 14, the remarks were not printed in the *Novascotian* until March 12, and Halliburton's challenge arrived shortly afterwards. Howe's statement to his half-sister that "there had been only a fair comparison of different classes and no insult in the matter,"[35] confirms the view that John Halliburton was seeking satisfaction for himself, not for his father. In this instance Howe decided he could not ignore the challenge. While Halliburton was younger than he and had no family to support, "still he was in the situation of a gentleman, and had a right to make the demand." Further, the challenger could not now withdraw, and if Howe did, "it would subject [him] to repeated annoyance from others, and perhaps either weaken [his] position as a public man or compel [him] to shoot some fellow at last."[36]

Howe made such preparation as he could for the worst of eventualities. In the hands of his second, Herbert Huntington, he placed four letters, two addressed to his associates in the *Novascotian*, one to the people of Nova Scotia telling them he had no choice but to "hazard [his] life rather than blight all prospects of being useful,"[37] and the last to Susan Ann, explaining that the *Novascotian* would be "a living for you all," that "[John] Thompson and Arthur [Howe's printer?] will not do less than what is right," and that her cousin James McNab "will be a father to you." "You had my boyish heart, and have shared my love and entire confidence up to this hour ... The future for you and my dear Babes, might well unman me, and would, did I not feel that without a protector you could better face the world, than with one whose courage was suspected, and who was liable to continual insults which he could not resist. God in his infinite mercy bless you. There shall be no blood on my hand."[38] At dawn on March

14, near the old tower at Point Pleasant, Howe met the challenge. Halliburton fired first and missed; Howe simply discharged his pistol into the air, and it was all over. "I never intended to fire at him and would not for Ten Thousand Pounds"; yet he had got what he prized highly: "the perfect independence ... to explain or apologize – to fight or refuse, in future."[39]

Within six weeks he had proof of his newly won independence. He had been seeking to show that Sir Rupert George, the provincial secretary, was not being hard done by in having his total income reduced by £300 to £1,300. George, he pointed out, was "a first class red tape man, but nothing more." Inheriting his office as a mere youth, he deigned to "make the pitiable sacrifice of burying himself, for four hours a day, in the South West Wing of our Provincial Building, with the paltry provision ... of some £1,600 a year ... and easy access to the ear of every Governor upon all occasions."[40] Within hours John Spry Morris appeared before Howe with a challenge from George. Had he come before Halliburton, Howe might have found it difficult to decline; now he simply said he had no personal quarrel with Sir Rupert, that he would not fire at him if he met him, and that he would continue to compare public officers' emoluments with their duties. The result, as Howe put it, was that George and Morris "got laughed at and nobody blamed me."[41] Clearly the Halliburton incident had bought insurance for the future.

Howe was done with Halliburton in two or three days; his demand for Campbell's recall left consequences in its wake that were to last for months. The letter-writers in the *Times* became positively apoplectic because of his treatment of "the Lord's annointed." Five hundred of Campbell's friends met in Mason's Hall on March 28 to denounce the authors of the outrage on the governor as "Regular Papineau and MacKenzie men – they ought to be hanged – shot – quartered!"[42] So began what Howe described as "the government agitation," purportedly intended to show that the majority in the assembly spoke for only a minority of Nova Scotians. Because the Reformers had been unable to participate in the earlier assemblage, they convened an open meeting two days later at which, according to Howe, his friends had an overwhelming majority. "Those who call themselves, in Slick's phrase, the 'upper crust' folks, were of course on the side of the Government, but the great mass nobly sustained their Representatives."[43] Probably it was not as one-sided as Howe said it was; certainly confusion and disorder prevented the meeting from expressing its opinion. Later Howe was chaired home and appeared at a window holding his son in his arms. Seeking to make the scene appear ludicrous, "Palinurus" in the *Times* pictured Howe "*devoting*

his young Joseph to the sacred cause of freedom" much as Hannibal made
his son "swear eternal hostility to the Roman nation!"[44]

The meeting was notable in that it saw the first direct entrance into
the political arena of James W. Johnston, a member of both the
Executive and Legislative Councils, and well on his way to becoming
the chief adviser of the governor. Clearly the Tories were sorely in
need of an articulate, respected spokesman. Stewart had lost
credibility; Uniacke had put himself in an ambivalent position and
none could foretell his future course; the other Tory assemblymen
could exercise little influence beyond their immediate constituencies.
Johnston, once an Anglican but now a Baptist, had influence "both in
town and country, among a body of christians who do not usually
think with [the Tories]."[45] Besides, according to Howe, he had only
"the sins of a few years to answer for," since he had not been mixed up
with the controversial measures that were so distasteful to the Reform
assemblymen and their constituents.[46] To answer an opponent whom
he recognized as formidable, Howe addressed two long letters to the
people of the province in the *Novascotian* of April 23 and 30.

The clashes between Johnston and Howe, both at the meeting and
in the press afterwards, were to set the tone of their confrontation
over the next seven years. On specific questions Johnston maintained
that Russell's dispatch, which the Reformers called the Magna Carta of
Nova Scotia, had been distorted beyond all recognition,[47] while Howe
insisted that the Reformers would have been justified in demanding
Campbell's recall "upon the ground of *his violation of Lord Glenelg's
Despatches alone* – to say nothing of his attempt to evade, and final
refusal to act upon, that of Lord John Russell."[48] On the civil list bill
and vested rights, Johnston argued that the council could not permit
an agreement made by the Crown to be altered without violating the
principles of honour and integrity, which were of "more consequence
than a few hundred pounds,"[49] while Howe thought it strange "that so
much solicitude is sometimes manifested to protect the faintest
shadow of claim which wealthy individuals may have upon the
revenues – when wholesale injury is often inflicted upon the poor, for
the public good, without any body ever appealing to the public
honour."[50] Johnston disagreed no less with Howe's contention that
the assembly would continue to be stymied so long as the councils
reflected the interests of only one segment of the society. Had not
three-quarters of the councillors been born in anything but wealthy
circumstances? Had not Cogswell, Sr, Collins, Cunard, Robie, and
others all raised themselves by industry and talent?[51] But, replied
Howe, would any of these men have been so honoured if they had
"rendered themselves conspicuous for the assertion of liberal

principles? ... does [Johnston] not perceive that such a system only holds out a prospect for the poor boys *of one way of thinking?*"[52]

On the more general question of what kind of government was practically best for a colony, Johnston sounded not unlike the pre-1830 Howe. In his view, the radical changes demanded by the Reformers were uncalled for in a colony that was advancing in prosperity and was "as free as air" in the exercise of religious and political opinions. Because Nova Scotians escaped "an hundred burthens which have to be borne in England," they were not opposed to being deprived of a few of the legislative privileges of Britons; further, the checks on the Commons in Nova Scotia were not nearly as extensive as they were in Britain.[53] Howe replied that Johnston preferred "the tranquil reign of irresponsibility" to a government based on public confidence, and that the assembly of Nova Scotia was restrained by all the checks that existed in Britain and an additional one beside: the possible suspension and withdrawal of its constitution by the British authorities.[54] Perhaps Johnston was most vehement of all in his denunciation of party. "Men bound in parties," he said, "cannot at all times follow their own opinions, and may be obliged occasionally to surrender their feelings." Even worse, in the absence of great questions in a colony, the party struggle would simply become a struggle for power. "What would be the objects of contention here?" he asked.[55] Howe, whose conversion to party had required him to rid himself of ideas identical to those of Johnston, denied that there were no questions of importance in a colony that might become the touchstone of party:

... "little things are great to little men," and to little Provinces, – and I could point to a dozen questions of internal policy, upon which the intellectual powers of our public men have been engaged during the past ten years, and to a dozen more which will probably engage them for the ten years to come, that were or will be just of as much importance to the People of Nova-Scotia, as were the questions upon which ministers have come in and gone out in almost every reign since 1688. It cannot be otherwise, in the very nature of things. Such questions arise out of the gradual growth and progress of every country, however small – and are magnified and clothed with importance, real or fictitious, by the ceaseless activity of acute and energetic minds.[56]

Throughout April the *Times* did all it could to create the impression that the "agitation" was steadily increasing in strength,[57] while Howe continued to mock "the sickly imitation of Bond Head's system of Government agitation."[58] By June he felt that the Tories, who had sought to show they were not a minority, had "finished off by proving the fact."[59] Only in Lunenburg, Queens, and Annapolis counties did he think they might have a majority, and even there it was true only in the county towns.[60] Ten days in Annapolis, Hants, and Kings counties had convinced him that the sturdy agriculturists, the men who had "won fine farms from the wilderness, or ... paid for them by the produce of their industry," were staunch Reformers who, unlike the village lawyers and traders, refused to take their cue from the Halifax compact.[61]

Meanwhile Howe had asked the colonial secretary not to be "misled by misrepresentations through other channels."[62] telling him unequivocally that the voters who had signed petitions circulated by the Tories could not, in total, return ten members to the assembly.[63] As he suspected, the not very astute or subtle Campbell had stepped up the denigration of the Reformers in his dispatches. In response to Howe's address for his recall, he told Russell how well he was getting on as governor. Except for the civil list bill, had not the legislature cooperated with him to the full? Had not 400 of the principal inhabitants of Halifax gone out of their way to express their appreciation of his services? Not unnaturally, he took pot-shots at Howe. Was it not evidence of the latter's unscrupulousness that he complained of the composition of the Councils even though he had proposed the appointment of a majority of their members including Stewart? In any case, what had Stewart done to forfeit the good opinion of Howe and his friends?[64]

There was some consternation at the Colonial Office when news of the assembly's address for the recall of Campbell reached Britain towards the end of April. What was the usually well-ordered colony of Nova Scotia up to? Russell and his advisers were agreed that "Sir Colin's despatches were hopelessly prejudiced and unreliable," and Russell appended a personal note that he could not accept "the Lieutenant Governor's reckoning two thirds of the Assembly as 'a few factious demagogues'."[65] Yet his reply to Campbell was "a perfect marvel of cautious confusion,"[66] undoubtedly because it was designed to let Sir Colin down as easily as possible. The queen, he said, would be reluctant to grant concessions to a body that had demanded the governor's recall; he also made it clear that the dispatch of October 16, 1839, was intended in no way to give encouragement to the heresy of responsible government. Beyond that, however, Russell gave Campbell little comfort. He simply could not believe that the majority of the assembly was seeking "any objects dangerous to the connection of Nova Scotia with the United Kingdom," nor could he see how an Executive Council which had been condemned by a thirty to twelve vote of the assembly could carry on the public business successfully until a few leading assemblymen were substituted for some of the incumbent councillors.[67] But to avoid embarrassment to Campbell and to relieve the British ministers of the need to enter into explanations, Russell thought it best to have Governor General Thomson come to Halifax and, in Chester Martin's words, "with his 'wand' and his 'star' and his magic touch,"[68] arrange the details of a solution on the spot. To Campbell the dispatch must have seemed like winning a battle only to lose the war. But he continued to put on a bold front in a letter to Thomson in which, as usual, he painted a picture of a "contented and quiet" colony despite "a few restless individuals who wish a change to forward their own selfish views."[69]

Six weeks before Thomson even set foot in the province, he had formed his own opinion of the Nova Scotian situation, and revealed it with "characteristic certitude" to Russell.[70] With much of it Howe would not have agreed, especially the assertion that Nova Scotia's troubles did not rise from "real grievances" but from "petty and personal ambition on the one hand and ... a not overly prudent management of affairs on the other." Thomson was disturbed, not so much by the assembly's address for Campbell's recall, as by its expression of nonconfidence in the Executive Council. Surely Campbell should have been able to form a council that was acceptable to the assembly, and whose advice he might have sought, and adopted or rejected, without abandoning his responsibility. But he had failed, as would anyone whose previous pursuits left him unacquainted with the working of colonial assemblies. Nonetheless, said Thomson, the colonial secretary should under no conditions concede anything in the way of responsible government or "afford a triumph to a little knot of persons who certainly ought not to receive one."[71] He was to alter these opinions very little after his visit to Nova Scotia.

Howe was at the Queen's wharf when the governor general arrived from Quebec in the steamer *Unicorn* on July 9. Like other Reformers, he looked at Upper Canada "tranquillized" and hoped for the best. Thomson took over the government as soon as he set foot ashore, and from then on it became a favourite pastime to guess in what direction his thinking was tending. The first real opportunity to speculate came on July 11 when he replied formally to a congratulatory address from men of all parties and opinions. Every sentence, every phrase, in fact, every word, was analysed to see if it might be made to convey the meaning that the analyst desired. The Tories were especially pleased that Thomson intended to "put an end to personal and party feuds," and to "lead the people ... from fruitless and idle disputes upon theoretical points of Government, to the consideration of their real and practical interests."[72] Both the Tories and the Reformers expressed satisfaction with Thomson's more basic point that, although he would seek the advice of those who represented "the well understood wishes of the people," he could devolve the responsibility for his acts on no man without endangering the connection with the Mother Country. While the *Times* boasted elatedly that he had given responsible government its quietus,[73] Howe was certain that, when Thomson's ideas were worked out in practice, "there will not be so wide a difference between what was asked, and what he means to do, as [the Tories] imagine."[74]

No sooner had Thomson settled down in Government House than he began to receive a steady stream of visitors. By the time Howe met him on the morning of the second day, he had learned of the dangerous nature, in Tory eyes, of Howe's letters to Russell. When Howe offered to explain them, the governor general readily agreed. Each viewed the outcome differently. Howe was to say that Thomson had raised only occasional objections, and he had met them successfully,[75] while Thomson contended that Howe had "made the amende honorable" and publicly "eschewed his heresies" on responsible government.[76] As evidence, he forwarded to Russell Howe's editorial of July 23, written only two days after Thomson left Halifax. But, as Chester Martin has pointed out, "the article in *The Novascotian* ... will be searched in vain for any recantation, on Howe's part, of responsible government."[77]

Basically Howe contended that any loss resulting from the slight difference between what he had advocated and what Thomson proposed was amply compensated for by other features of the governor general's plan. He himself had suggested an Executive Council which, while distinct from the heads of departments, would control them sufficiently to ensure that the business of the province would be competently conducted, and whose members would resign if they lost the confidence of the House or be dismissed by the governor if they gave him bad advice or got him into scrapes. In contrast, Thomson proposed to make the governor "the leading mind in the Colony," who would "consult [the] wishes and ... feelings [of Nova Scotians and] promote their interest by well-considered reforms." To that end he would not let the heads of department be exempt from responsibility, but make them part of the governor's team; if they could not get parliamentary support to sustain them, they would have to give way to those who could. This, said Howe, was "a very important improvement upon our plan, and ... most completely reverses the old order of things." The essential difference between the two positions, as he saw it, was that Thomson would devolve the responsibility for his acts on no man, while the Reformers felt he should share it with his council. But since under his scheme the council would have to defend his acts or have the privilege of resigning, any governor would be an idiot who did not give due weight to his councillors' views.[78]

Although Howe had not altered his basic position, Chester Martin wonders, nonetheless, if he had not fallen "insensibly ... beneath the spell of that remarkable personality [Thomson]."[79] Clearly the latter had made the most of the argument that Howe, as a good Briton, had a duty to assist the governor general in promoting tranquillity in Nova Scotia and setting an example for the unruly Canadians. Certainly it was not to be the last time that Howe would show an ingenuous faith in the plausible arguments of the great. Obviously he was fascinated by Thomson's picture of a governor leading the way in eliminating abuses and making useful improvements. For the assurance that this would happen, "we have all the guarantees of the Governor General's public character, and of his Canadian policy."

Perhaps one clue to understanding Howe's acceptance of the Thomson or Russellite creed lies in his view of responsible government and the method of implementing it. He had given little thought to the machinery best calculated to give effect to his ideas, and had only recently accepted Durham's idea of a responsible executive. It would have been all the easier, therefore, to persuade him that Thomson's executive differed from Durham's only in form and not in substance. Further, Howe saw responsible government partly in terms of ensuring efficiency in government and eliminating the waste that bore heavily on middle-class entrepreneurs like himself. Possibly he thought that Thomson's proposals, even more than Durham's, would provide the initiative and innovativeness that would ensure the province's development and, with it, the success of his own establishment. Yet surely he should have delved a little more deeply into Thomson's plan and asked himself if it could work in practice. Were men like Thomson likely to be appointed to the governorship of Nova Scotia? Had he insisted enough on adequate representation for the Reformers in the Executive Council at a time when he still possessed strong bargaining power? Could any Reformer work in the same team as Alexander Stewart?

Thomson was nothing if not a fast worker. When he left Halifax on July 28, he knew specifically what needed to be done and had given a detailed prescription to Russell.[80] As W.R. Livingston suggests, his proposals became the core for the reorganization of the administration of Nova Scotia.[81] Even with a first-hand examination he had not changed his view that "no colony in the British dominions ... can be governed more easily than this ... There are no parties here

... in the way we understand them, or as they exist in Canada. At least five-sixths of the Assembly care nothing about politics, and think only of their roads and bridges."[82] What was wrong, he said, was that the half-dozen men of ability on both sides of politics had "all been alienated instead of conciliated to the Government." Even when he had put "a decided negative" upon responsible government as the popular party conceived it, his views had been "received by all parties in the best spirit."

In his opinion, the chief problem lay in the composition of the Executive Council, and he had concluded that its members should either be heads of departments or members of one branch of the legislature. In choosing the latter, he proposed to give "a fair preponderance to those whose general opinions concurred with those of the majority of the assembly without excluding altogether others."[83] But in sketching out the council's actual membership, he departed markedly from this principle, since by inadvertence he left out Susan Ann's cousin James McNab and included none but Howe who might be classed as a genuine Reformer. Yet, with his usual breezy self-confidence, he told Russell that the leaders on both sides were "entirely satisfied with my recomposition of the Council, and I should have proceeded to carry it into effect myself, if I had not found the people perfectly reasonable, and willing to wait."[84] Actually the Reform leaders were not nearly as satisfied as Thomson had made them out to be. While Howe expected the eventual inclusion of McNab, he was decidedly lukewarm about the other rumoured nominees. Away from the charm and blandishments of Thomson, he realized with a start that the majority in the assembly would consider their opinions inadequately represented in council unless it included Huntington or Young, or both. He said as much to Thomson in a note on July 20.[85] By August 12 he had the wind thoroughly up and wrote once again to Thomson, this time in obvious perturbation.

Basically, he was protesting his opponents' tactics. On July 23 he had given up active agitation in order to "calm the public mind and ... prepare all parties for a new state of things"; he had also gone out of his way to shake hands with Campbell and agree to let bygones be bygones. But the other side were doing all they could to frustrate Thomson's intentions and embarrass himself. Above all, they were putting him in a false position by making it appear that he had sacrificed his friends to secure a seat on the council. They were also saying that Huntington and Young, because they had been the assembly's delegates to London, were marked men, without hope of preferment. If, as Howe surmised, neither Huntington nor Young became a councillor, he could only conclude that Campbell was branding them for their past and he would have nothing to do with the government so long as Campbell remained. "It is of no use," he concluded, "for us to smoke the pipe of peace, if he persists in throwing the ashes in our faces."[86]

Howe's understanding of Campbell's conduct was completely on the mark. The same day that Thomson wrote to Russell he had also written to Sir Colin explaining that, although he was recommending additions to both councils from the popular party, there would be no changes which might afford a triumph to that party or cast doubts on Campbell's conduct.[87] Sir Colin reacted indignantly: How could someone who had spent little more than a week in the province know more about its affairs and the merits of its leading men than he had managed to acquire in six years? Why should care be taken to encourage a popular party that was rapidly losing ground at the expense of another party "composed decidedly of the first men in every section of the Country."[88] Why, in view of Howe's "intemperate conduct, and offensive behaviour," might he be expected, as an executive councillor, to give the requisite support to the queen's government?[89]

Through his secretary Thomson told Howe not to let the scuttle-butt circulating in Halifax influence his conduct, knowing as he did its origin,[90] and intimated that nothing more need be said in view of the imminent replacement of Campbell. When, early in September, Howe was finally certain of the change of governors, he expressed satisfaction that the new system would be introduced under happier auspices than if Campbell had remained and been "brought continually into contact with individuals who had been but recently ardent political opponents, if not personal enemies."[91] But still feeling a little concerned about his treatment of Campbell, he again sought to justify it to his readers.

In striking out boldly against him, he said, the Reformers did it only "with the weapons of the Constitution [and] more in sorrow than in anger." Trained in the Wellington school, Campbell might have been expected to oppose "almost instinctively ... every innovation upon the established order of things." That tendency was reinforced when, on his arrival in Nova Scotia, he found himself surrounded by an organized party that was primarily interested in perpetuating its own power. At a time when the spirit of inquiry was abroad in the land, men of talent possessing the confidence of the people were not content to be excluded from the government. For three years the Reformers had taken "the kindest view of the difficulties of Sir Colin's position," and only after exhausting all other means had they adopted the extreme step of demanding his recall.[92] Having thus justified himself, Howe was both moved and gratified by Campbell's taking leave of him; at the new governor's first levee Sir Colin sought him out and said simply: "you did what you thought was right – you did it fairly and honorably, and I have no unkindly feeling toward you."[93]

Howe's relations were now to be with Lucius Bentinck, Viscount Falkland, of whom he knew nothing but that he was "a thorough Whig" and married to one of the Fitzclarences, a daughter of William IV and Mrs Jordan. Over the next four to five years those relations were to reach the heights and plumb the depths. Captivated by Falkland, Howe found it hard to deny anything to one who, temperamentally, especially in his alternating moods of enthusiasm and depression, was not unlike himself. Falkland's initial task looked easy since he had only to follow Thomson's recommendations as confirmed by Russell. He quickly secured the resignation of four councillors whom his instructions said were to be superseded,[94] and he agreed to retain James McNab in his council provided he secured a seat in the assembly.[95] It was now Howe's turn to appear before Falkland and experience his persuasive talents to the full.

The interview is laid bare in a long letter to Huntington in which Howe sought to explain and defend his conduct.[96] Basically Falkland asked Howe's help in setting up a strong administration possessing the confidence of the country and sustained by a majority of the assembly; while he could not meet all the Reformers' demands immediately, he would do all "that was necessary ... hereafter to carry out [their] principles." When Howe asked about Huntington's appointment to the council, Falkland replied that strong objections had been made to him at the Colonial Office because of his "extreme views and violent conduct"; accordingly, Falkland had been instructed to determine on the spot whether Huntington was "an animal that will run in harness, without upsetting the Council and kicking up [his] heels at the rest of the team." Since Howe himself had letters from Huntington vowing not to serve with Stewart, he could not press his claims further. Nevertheless, Huntington would have the chance of the first vacancy, and until it was decided, William Young's claims would remain in abeyance. But the council was open to both of them, and to anyone else whose merits gave them a fair claim to appointment. So, unable to "make any fight about [Huntington], having no hope of Young, and finding McNab shivering in the wind," Howe thought it his duty to "run all hazards, and give the Governor the best assistance in any point, relying upon him to do ample justice to the fair claims of the popular party, when the Elections shall have tested ... its strength throughout the Province."[97]

Howe's entrance into the Executive Council became a little more justifiable when McNab was at length persuaded to retain his seat, but to speak of a genuine coalition at this stage belies the fact. S.G.W. Archibald was best described as a fence-sitter; J.B. Uniacke occupied an ambivalent position; and all the other councillors, except for Howe and McNab, were undisguised Tories. However plausibly Howe might defend his acceptance of Thomson's principles, he was clearly on the defensive in rationalizing the composition of Falkland's council. To suggest, as he did to Huntington, that "all personal feeling had passed away" with Campbell's departure, contradicted his basic contention that Sir Colin was but a pawn in the hands of the Halifax compact. It was no less astonishing that he, who had condemned Alexander Stewart as much as any man, should consent to sit in council with him. Surely Howe ought to have seen that he was surrendering all his bargaining power for very little. At a time when Russell, Thomson, and Falkland were all committed to installing an Executive Council that commanded public confidence, should he not, at the very least, have insisted on more adequate Reform representation in the Executive Council before he agreed to enter it?

Huntington did not criticize Howe for accepting office, but the Youngs did not hesitate to do so. George Young's father-in-law suggested that Howe was "governed by a species of Irish reciprocity, 'all on one side'."[98] The *Times* was quite beside itself that men "in the front rank of the Province for experience, integrity and wealth" – Jeffery, Collins, Cunard, Cogswell, and Tobin – could be superseded because of allegations that they constituted a "detestable" official faction or family compact. It happened because the majority of the assembly were "mere puppets in the hands of an Editor," who wielded his power "not by any intrinsic force, not by native qualities commanding respect and admiration, but through the mere chance of possessing a printing press and enjoying the advantages of the most astonishing family compact on this side of the Atlantic"; truly, said the *Times*, "the leaden types and family compact of our Editor" had made him "the Napoleon of Nova Scotia."[99]

Meanwhile "Fair Play" was using the columns of the *Times* to ask Howe such questions as: Was he not the proprietor of the *Novascotian* and the *Pearl*, as well as printer of the *Christian Messenger*; was his half-brother not the Queen's printer and deputy postmaster general, and in those capacities did he not publish the *Royal Gazette* and appoint his deputies throughout the province?[100] An obviously concerted attempt to attack Howe through his half-brother took many forms. "One of the Injured" even accused John Howe of altering the times of the mail delivery to serve the needs of the

Novascotian.[101] The editor of the *Times* wondered how Joseph Howe, the man who delighted in denouncing the pickings of other officials, could defend the monopoly of the assembly printing enjoyed by his half-brother.[102] How could he demand the abolition of the judges' fees when he permitted John Howe to levy, and put in his own pockets, a "tax" of £500 for the transmission of newspapers.[103] Much of this was unfair, some of it preposterous, but throughout his career Howe was never to feel any need to justify the preferment accorded to his relatives even though he required it of others. In any event, by October he was ignoring all reference to a Howe compact and thinking in terms of a general election.

As a result, he was quite prepared when Falkland dissolved the assembly on October 21. The very next day he called on his constituents to give strong support to the principles enunciated by Thomson and instituted by Falkland. If there were others equally enthusiastic about the changes, they hid their feelings from the public eye. In Yarmouth Herbert Huntington wanted to know more about Falkland's policy before he decided to support it or not,[104] while William Young, smarting because of his exclusion from the council, told his Inverness constituents they would "see in it too many of their old enemies, and too few of their tried friends."[105] Tories like Gossip of the *Times* felt the new system would always be faulty since the governor would have to choose part of the council from "*slippery*" persons who would excite the mob in their favour.[106]

In defending his own position, Howe adopted the stance of the conservative reformer par exellence. Admittedly there were some councillors with whom he would find it difficult to act; admittedly some persons were left out who should have been included; admittedly he had changed his own position somewhat in working out the new principles. But since Falkland had gone as far as he was permitted, "to press organic changes further ... to contend for more than can, or than ought to be yielded, until experience has demonstrated its absolute necessity, would seem to be the duty neither of a good man nor of a good subject." Howe was gratified, most of all, that "by the peaceful agitation of four years, in which, from one end of the country to the other, there has not been a blow struck or a pane of glass broken, great changes have been wrought, and invaluable principles established, for which other countries have for centuries struggled in vain, or have only purhcased by civil conflict, and blood, and tears."[107]

Perhaps he was attaching a greater significance to the changes than others did, or than he genuinely believed, because he had such a large personal stake in their success. But as the election proceeded some difficulties in the new situation that he had not foreseen tempered his enthusiasm and brought him back to earth. More than anyone else, he had set forces in motion to polarize Nova Scotians along party lines. As late as mid-September he was reminding his readers of their duty to return to the assembly only those who had faithfully served the liberal interest. Yet he had gone into an administration which, although it might be only euphemistically described as a coalition, nonetheless required the submergence of party for its successful operation and he had thereby arrested the further polarization of the electorate along party lines. Actually the coalition was one of political leaders, not one of political forces in the constituencies; as a result, few of the candidates presented themselves as coalition candidates. Thus there was the strange spectacle of Tory opposing Reformer, although both professed to support Lord Falkland's government and neither had more than a hazy idea of the principles on which it was based. Under these circumstances Howe and the *Novascotian* made no attempt to assume the leadership role they had adopted in the election of 1836. Consequently genuine party contests of the kind that Howe hoped would convincingly establish the Reformers' superiority were the exception, not the rule.[108]

In the township and county of Halifax the Tories decided to nominate a single candidate for the two township seats and one for the two county seats, hoping to secure their election through a split in the Reform vote.[109] On their part the Reformers nominated three of their former members; the fourth, Hugh Bell, willingly made way for James McNab. Jokingly, Howe suggested how much better it was that "a merchant [McNab] and a dry-good-man [Forrester], and a farmer [Annand] and a mechanic [Howe] should be [their] representatives, than a brewer [Keith], who compounds a substance which makes you drunk, and a lawyer [Murdoch] who manages the broken-head cases which proceed from drunkenness."[110] But although he told the voters to "proceed on this great public duty, as if it were almost one of religion," on the hustings he concerned himself little with major policy questions, and mostly with grass-roots politicking. He told the Tories they had everything they needed to carry on an election except "the hearts of the people."[111] In other words, they did not have a Howe. At Peggy's Cove he took off his coat and enjoyed dancing with the young people. "Towards twelve o'clock, it was pleasant to see how each young fisherman's arm found its way round his sweetheart's neck, – and thus the scene went on, cheerfully and innocently."[112] But there were sad occasions too. In one harbour, where an only child lay dying, he mingled his tears with that of the mother. "These are the ties that bind us to the out-settlements, and I defy all the wealth of the

Tories, – all the influence of Bankers and Merchants of Halifax to destroy and dissipate these bonds of kindliness and sympathy."[113]

There was never much doubt about the results in Halifax. Five days of polling in the town starting on November 3 gave the Reformers a two-to-one lead, and when the first day's voting at Margaret's Bay did not improve the Tories' position, Murdoch and Keith abandoned the contest.[114] But although decisive, it had been a boisterous, even turbulent election. A large number of voters from Musquodoboit, Reformers to the hilt, had swarmed to the capital and, according to the *Times*, had sought to "beat back those opposed to them, [and] frighten others away."[115] Each night as his vociferous supporters accompanied him home, Howe urged on them "the necessity of vigorous but orderly conduct"; yet he also insisted that none "could expect an election to be conducted like a levee."[116] When Murdoch said he retired because "no hearing [could] be obtained for the friends of order," Howe gave him short shrift: 'We have seen as much struggling, screaming and violence, at the door of Drury Lane or the Queen's Opera, on nights when the seats were likely to be occupied early, as there was at the Court House at any time during the five days."[117]

Province-wide the *Times* pictured a pronounced falling off in radical strength, and conjured up a combination of Tory and unpledged new members totalling twenty-six who would see that the country would not again be "agitated by such violent proceedings as characterized the late radical Assembly."[118] But this was only wishful thinking, for the absence of gloating editorials by either Gossip or Howe meant that the changes were, in fact, insignificant. Four years earlier, after the "loose fish" were allocated according to their preponderant voting habits, the result had been twenty-eight Reformers to twenty Tories; this time in an enlarged assembly, it was thirty Reformers to twenty Tories. Although the Tories did not do quite as well as in 1836, they did improve slightly upon their pre-election position.[119] Thus, in its political complexion, the Sixteenth General Assembly was to be very little different from the Fifteenth.

During these years Howe appeared, on the surface, to be having no financial worries with the *Novascotian*, or at least to be sublimating them, but as a publisher he was having troubles with John Thompson and Thomas Chandler Haliburton, albeit of a different kind. After buying the *Pearl*, a "high class" literary, scientific, and religious journal, in mid-1839, primarily to assist John Thompson, he had published it under Thompson's editorship.[120] Imbued with the strong temperance views of an Irish Methodist, Thompson kept pressing Howe to eliminate liquor advertisements from the paper. Since the *Pearl*, which barely made a profit as it was, would be "as dead as Julius Caesar" if it lost that source of income, Howe stoutly resisted. Surely Thompson should see that a policy of open conflict with the world was "not the best way to mend either its manners or its morals," especially if in the process he lost his only means of putting forward his own views through judicious selections and occasional editorials.[121]

As in many matters, Howe took his views on temperance from his father, who had held that to concentrate all one's energies in attacking a single vice was neither in accord with human nature nor "with the example of our Saviour, who associated with publicans and sinners, and who did them good, not by attacking their trade, ... but by teaching them to chasten and dignify every occupation with temperance, mercy and brotherly love."[122] Not satisfied, Thompson went further and offered as much as £40 of his salary to have liquor advertisements banned from the *Novascotian*, suggesting that it would genuinely deserve the title "leading journal" if it helped to save "men from the degradation of intemperance." At that point Howe thought it time to call a halt. Under no conditions would he let the *Novascotian* be destroyed for any such object, especially since "the 2000 persons who take it will drink a great deal more if they had not [it] to read."[123]

Howe's differences with Haliburton were highly painful because they meant the disruption of a long friendship that dated back to the late 1820s when Howe, the young reporter, had delighted in the "alternate salvos of wit and anger" that Haliburton had directed at the Council of Twelve. By facilitating the publication of the *Clockmaker*, first series, Howe had helped Haliburton make an international reputation for himself. But for some time the two had recognized they were separated by what V.L.O. Chittick calls the difference between "an instinctive democrat and a determined aristocrat," and especially by their differing views on "the trustworthiness of public opinion."[124] They had almost broken on the second series of the *Clockmaker*, largely devoted as it was to a condemnation of popular government. "There was," wrote Howe, "enough of what looked very like [a caricature of myself], ... but you denied the applications, and I forgot them."[125]

Haliburton did not return to Halifax with Howe in 1838, but stayed until the following spring in England, where Chittick suggests "the Satan of Politics found abundant mischief for his idle pen to effect." His first effusion was the *Bubbles of Canada*, which sought to defeat the Durham *Report* even before it saw the light of day. Later he produced *A Reply to the Report of the Earl of Durham*, "By a Colonist," which wilfully distorted the meaning of the *Report* and "stooped to contemptible meannessess in the tricks of argument it employed."[126] Finally, aboard ship on his return, he wrote *The Letter Bag of the Great Western, or, Life in a Steamer* which Howe discovered, after publishing it, exhibited such "indecency" as to reduce and diminish its sale abroad.[127] In May and June 1839, when the *Acadian Recorder* was flooded with letters abusive of Haliburton, Howe remained silent.[128]

So matters stood until June 1840. Then, while passing through Windsor on a tour defending the Reformers' address for the recall of Campbell, Howe called on Haliburton only to be grossly insulted by being informed he had "ridden 100 miles to dine with rebels and vagabonds." Haliburton also told him that he had had second thoughts about letting him have the American and colonial rights of the *Clockmaker*, third series, although Howe had already sold the American ones to Lea & Blanchard of Philadelphia; in effect, Howe was to lose $400 simply because Haliburton had changed his mind.[129] Even then the breaking-point had not arrived, for in the early weeks of the coalition Howe recommended Haliburton for appointment to the Supreme Court.[130] But by this time Susan Ann had read the third series of the *Clockmaker* and concluded that her husband had been badly treated; she is "no politician and no great reason[er], but, like most women, can see clearly and feel acutely what deeply concerns the reputation, and touches the feelings of her husband."[131]

It did not take Howe long to decide that Susan Ann had not been severe enough on Haliburton. He did not relish finding himself and his friends mocked for "goin' to the house of representatives without bein' fit for it," nor did he like to be told that they kept "jawin' about public vartue, temperance, education, and what not all day, [but spent] the night in a back room of a market tavern with the key turned, drinkin' hail-storm and bad rum, or playin' six penny loo."[132] He found no less distasteful a description of his alleged recipe for gratifying his ambition. "Call office-holders by the cant tarms of compact cliques and official gang, and they will have to gag you with a seat in the council, or somethin' or another, see if they don't."[133] But what outraged him most of all was to see "patriotism" described as "*the trump card of a scoundrel*," followed by a definition of five classes of colonial patriots, into all of which Howe and the Reformers might fall, except the "real genu*ine*."[134] Nonetheless, Howe bided his time until Haliburton wrote him about the possibility of republishing his *History*. After rejecting the proposal outright, Howe told him that, except for the third series of the *Clockmaker*, "the only other volumes in which my public and private character, my principles and friends, have been treated with the same savage bitterness and disgusting personality are the volumes of the *Times.*" Then, apparently in farewell, Howe concluded: "You and I have been living under a strange delusion. I have recovered my senses."[135]

When Haliburton's reply blamed Howe for "fickleness and want of frankness" in his publishing transactions and for "no profit, and annoyance enough" in their joint ventures, Howe exploded in what James A. Roy calls "a somewhat incoherent and badly worded letter."[136] Even so, the gist of the letter is clear enough. The charge of "want of frankness," Howe said, was strangely directed at one who had always ensured that "the first things to be looked to were [Haliburton's] reputation, feelings, and interests." Indeed, by publishing the first series of the *Clockmaker* at his own risk, Howe had not only made Haliburton's reputation, but "brought [him] ... a handsome sum in subsequent arrangements with Bentley." As for the question of profit, Howe demonstrated that his profits and losses from the three series of the *Clockmaker* and *Letter-Bag* would just about cancel each other out. That left the *History*, to which Howe had devoted the leisure of two of the best years of his life, incurring not only heavy financial loss but also the difficulties "arising from all my little resources being sunk in this vortex for a very long period." So, asked Howe, who had the "no profit, and annoyance enough?"[137]

Aside from finances, Howe was certain that to have one friend the less was far better than to have one who would "rather caricature a friend than want a character" for his books, and who would regard "the utter ruin and destruction of an old and devoted associate, [as] of little consequence, provided those whose newly discovered friendship was regarded as more valuable, were propitiated by the sacrifice." Pressing home the attack, Howe then accused Haliburton of the sin of ingratitude. It had not been easy for him to urge the claims of a high Tory to the preferment of a judgeship of the Supreme Court, and his only reward had been an insult. "Verily," wrote Howe, "I am repaid."[138] A little later, fearing he had wounded Haliburton's feelings unnecessarily, Howe relented a little and told him he would rejoice in his prosperity and be glad to hear that he was "surrounded by troops of friends much more sincere and less troublesome"[139] than himself. Then, at the end of January 1841, he dismissed Haliburton from his mind and concentrated on the problems of coalition government.

CHAPTER FIFTEEN

Testing the Coalition

Falkland and Howe started the coalition experiment with enthusiasm, but they were almost alone in doing so. At best the Tories accepted it as the least distasteful means of carrying on government much as before, while most Reformers were sceptical of the composition of the reconstituted Executive Council and adopted a wait-and-see attitude. Its first test would come with the convening of the General Assembly early in February 1841. But before the lower house could get an inkling of the coalition's legislative proposals, it had a duty to perform in which Howe was highly interested, the election of a Speaker.[1] For two or three months he had let it be known that he would consider it a great honour to be First Commoner, but, despite his opponents' taunts, there is no evidence that he had been canvassing for it "with *horse* power" during his rambles.[2]

By mid-January Howe's foes were doing all they could to dash his hopes. The *Times* declared that the speakership required "more ability of a certain kind" than he possessed, and that, in any case, the office was incompatible with an executive councillorship. What could be more anomalous than "the Speaker ... having to bring forward the measures of Government and advocate them in the Assembly"?[3] The *Morning Post* insisted that, according to the British practice, an executive councillor could not be Speaker: "if we [are] to have the British constitution, we ought to have THE WHOLE of it."[4] To these opinions the assembly paid not the slightest notice since both nominees for the office, Howe and J.B. Uniacke, were executive councillors. By identical votes of twenty-five to twenty-three, Uniacke was rejected and Howe elected.[5] It had been a close thing because, although four or five supposed Reformers voted against Howe,[6] all the Tories supported Uniacke.

In defeat, Uniacke conceded that, since the House had elected

Howe, it apparently recognized that the offices of Speaker and executive councillor could be held by the same person.[7] Howe fared much worse at the hands of out-and-out Reformers. Young insisted that Howe's "election did not affirm that the offices were compatible,"[8] while Huntington wanted the House to "scrutinize the whole framework of the present government ... enquire what alterations had really been obtained," and then decide whether one person could hold the two offices.[9] The debate raised the question, not for the last time, of Howe's willingness to accept a state of affairs advantageous to himself which he might have denied on principle to anyone else. If he wanted the British analogy applied to Nova Scotia, and if he believed that the Executive Council had been converted into something like a cabinet, should he not have taken the position that the Speaker's ability to maintain the independence of the House might be impaired if he also acted as the spokesman of government? Or, because he was Joseph Howe, did he suppose himself to be immune to the weaknesses of other men, and, because of his qualities of leadership and his sacrifices, did he believe he should be exempt from the rules that applied to ordinary men?

Throughout 1841 Howe wrote and spoke upon the new order of things with his usual ebullience. Outwardly at least he contended that everything had turned out much as he wanted it. Yet he had anything but clear sailing. His difficulties first appeared on February 11 when the executive councillors sought to explain the changes that had occurred. In the debate Howe's supporters were his old opponents, Uniacke, Dodd, and DeWolf, while his opponents were tried Reformers, Young, Huntington, Forrester, and Goudge, who, according to the *Acadian Recorder,* assailed him "with all the vengeance and malignity of pretended injured friends."[10] The session saw a complete metamorphosis in his relations with Uniacke as compared with 1838 and 1839; gone in particular were the fierce sallies that had enlivened the debates of the earlier years.[11] No longer regarded in a favourable light by the Tory press, Uniacke was in an ambivalent position, not knowing which direction to take. So, following the course that had got him into his predicament, he kept on saying that his basic "principle of action was, ever to sustain the Home [i.e., the British] Government in its views."[12]

When Howe contended that the popular party had now "the power to determine ... what kind the administration was to be, and by whom carried on,"[13] he drew the fire of both Huntington and Young. Huntington could not understand why most of the councillors should come from the minority in the assembly if the government was to be conducted according to the wishes of the people. How could such an

Executive Council avoid coming into collision with the assembly?[14] Young was even more exasperating, first because he accused Howe of entering the council under circumstances he would not have found acceptable, but even more so because he contended that the new principles would be worked out, not in Nova Scotia but in Canada, which would set the example for the other colonies to follow.[15] Perhaps he was deliberately intending to annoy Howe, who hoped to make Nova Scotia the normal school of the colonies.

Although the administration got out of this debate with scarcely a dent in its armour, its next test was to be much more troublesome. On February 18 the solicitor general, J.W. Johnston, told the Legislative Council that, although the new order of things was beneficial, it had made "no change ... in the constitution, and above all, [Nova Scotians] stood as far from direct responsibility as they did four years ago."[16] That was bad enough, but Alexander Stewart, the bête noire of the assembly, who seemed determined to bring down the council of which he was a member, went further and said that "responsible government, in a Colony, was, responsible nonsense, – it was independence."[17] If the assembly passed a vote of nonconfidence, he maintained it would be "a matter of taste and feeling" for the Executive Council to decide whether it should resign, and for the governor to determine whether it should be dismissed. Bursting with indignation, Howe replied that, if the assembly was true to itself, every administration would henceforth be dependent upon it for its continuance. "It is not a matter of taste or opinion, when the House passed a vote of censure, whether the Council should resign or not. It might be [a] matter of taste with the Governor whether he would dissolve the House or change his Council. The members of that body would have no taste or discretion in the matter, they were bound to tender their resignations, and if they did not do so his Excellency would send for them in half an hour."[18]

Howe's intervention came during a debate which laid bare the impotence of the administration. Thomson (now Lord Sydenham) had been perturbed by the Nova Scotia financial procedures that permitted individual assemblymen a substantial role in proposing money votes. Howe, like Thomson, recognized the inefficiency of those procedures, especially in the allocation of road moneys, where a species of log-rolling permitted thousands of pounds to be frittered away in small amounts. Now that Nova Scotia had a ministry of sorts he suggested the introduction of the British practice which allowed only the executive to initiate money votes. Why, he pleaded, not lay "the key stone on the arch which they had already erected."[19] But when he invited some backbencher, Reformer or Tory, to propose a resolution to that end, he was drawn into a heated exchange with Huntington on the nature of the Executive Council, in which the latter stoutly insisted he had "not sufficient confidence in the administration to concede to them the power of originating supplies."[20] To Howe's discomfiture no one chose to move his proposal, and things stayed as they were.[21]

Though outwardly Howe pretended that all was well, none was more aware than he of the chinks in his position, especially in the composition of the Executive Council. While he could do little to remove those who, like Stewart, were obnoxious to the Reformers, he kept urging the appointment of Huntington. After talking to the latter in January, Falkland concluded that his proposals for strict economy and radical political changes were impracticable; yet, because of overriding political considerations, he decided to offer him a councillorship. He realized that Howe would be unable to retain any influence at all with his party unless its members could be made to feel that they were not shut out from positions of power or that Howe had not made terms for himself alone.[22] But both Falkland and Howe must surely have anticipated Huntington's refusal to join those "who have hitherto been the active and violent opponents of the liberal measures ... that are still unsettled in the Colony."[23]

Nonetheless, Falkland was quick to assure Lord John Russell that the offer to Huntington had served its purpose since Howe might now say: "What more can you in fairness demand?"[24] Yet it was doubtful if the offer strengthened Howe's position as much as the governor suggested. By this time even his friends in the country were forcefully expressing their doubts about the council. A Pictonian wondered that "so much of the old Crew should have been left in the Executive Council and that they should continue to show such a brazen front"; indeed, "if Howe's ears ... [burned] when ... talked about I think for some time past they must have been in a high fever."[25] Howe was therefore all the more gratified when some of "the intelligent Yeomanry" of Queen's county wrote him in highly complimentary terms at a time when old friends "who should have known me better" were withdrawing their support; he hoped the time would come "when to rally round and support a just Government will be considered as sacred an obligation, as to oppose and overturn a bad one."[26]

Set back in some directions, Howe still exulted in the performance of the coalition. In two major articles he presented the picture of a governor who came to a colony rent by party spirit, formed a council of men about whom he knew nothing except that they had been political enemies, and, in effect, achieved wonders. Almost at once these councillors had ascended the hustings and proclaimed that their retention of office depended upon their election. All were returned. "This," said Howe, "was a startling novelty in Colonial Government – one ... that had it been earlier introduced, might have saved torrents of blood, and millions of money."[27] The fact is, however, that few Nova Scotians viewed the election in quite the same light as Howe.

The election over – Howe continued – the council had only two months to "soften mutual prejudices; compare notes, settle the general principles, and perfect the details of measures."[28] Nonetheless, it had got both Houses to accept all its proposals. "Who," he boasted, "ever heard of 7 bills, being submitted to our Assembly, in the name of the Crown, in all the Administrations from Lord Dalhousie downwards? and yet here are seven, proposed and passed in a single session?"[29] Yet, on closer inspection, Howe's right to be exuberant may be questioned. Of the seven bills, four and perhaps five had been drafted by a committee of the Legislative Council, and none of them related to the major issues that had been convulsing the province.[30] The sixth, which dealt with the perennial question of effecting economies in the judiciary, was, by Howe's own admission, not the Executive Council's prodigy at all. Since that body was itself divided on the alternatives, it agreed to sponsor a bill reflecting the assembly's opinion on the matter. So when the House supported Young's resolution for the abolition of the Inferior Court of Common Pleas, the attorney general introduced a measure to that effect. But while his bill was the council's only at second hand, Howe was at least right that, if the "ministry" had not given a lead, Young's resolution would not have reached the statute book.

The seventh bill, which provided for the incorporation of Halifax as a city, became Howe's strongest justification of the coalition. Yet, to get agreement on their chef-d'œuvre, the councillors had had to make all sorts of accommodations among themselves, and the Tory councillors had seen to it that neither the new city's voters nor its elective office-holders would be practitioners of levelling democracy.[31] The effect was to limit the franchise to about 800 persons, and the right to be elected mayor, alderman, or common councillor to a fraction of that total. Forrester, long an advocate of incorporation, was appalled by provisions which, he argued, deprived his constituents of "the full rights of British freemen."[32]

This argument put Howe in a delicate position from which he would not emerge unscathed. Admitting that the bill was not as liberal as he wanted, he warned that any attempt to broaden the franchise would jeopardize incorporation altogether, since the Executive

Council was pledged to support the measure only as it was. Was it not the better part of wisdom to take "what could be obtained rather than [stand] out for full rights"? Had popular measures not progressed that way in the old country? Resorting to his often expressed views of the middling class, and demonstrating, as he would do much more strongly later on, that he was more a liberal than a democrat, Howe argued that if the requirements for voting were low, inordinate power would be given to the poor whom the rich could influence as they willed, but if the franchise was limited to the middle orders, as the council's bill proposed, good government would be assured.[33] Forrester would have none of this. First, he tried to give the vote to anyone assessed for poor rates, but got only eleven members to support him, mostly from the Reform left wing. Next, he sought to reduce the qualifications for mayor and aldermen to an occupancy of £30 and ownership of real estate valued at £500, instead of £50 and £1,000, but with even less support. However, when he proposed to reduce the qualifications for common councillor to the possession of real estate valued at £300, down from £500, he made such good sense that few Reformers could oppose him, and Howe found himself in the invidious position of having to join the Tories and a few loose-fish Reformers to defeat the amendment by a single vote.[34]

While the *Times* kept repeating that the bill satisfied nobody as it stood, neither the owner of property nor the mobocracy – "Tim the scavenger, Crispin the snob, or Nikkel Blok the butcher,"[35] a motion to reject it outright won the approval of only two uncompromising Reformers and six extreme Tories.[36] Clearly Howe was right that incorporation could not have been carried without the full weight of the Executive Council "exerted through the varied channels of official and social life,"[37] but even in success he suffered some of his worst discomfitures. A highly annoyed Forrester attributed his anti-democratic stance to "the company which [he] was now in,"[38] while William Young used the opportunity to vent a grievance he had been nursing against him, even though it was extraneous to incorporation. During Thomson's visit, he said, it had been intimated that Howe, Huntington, and himself were to enter the council, but after Howe called on the governor general, only he was to go in, and Young had been offered no explanation. "That was his ground of complaint against the Speaker."[39] Howe's only reply was that "in going through a somewhat troublesome life," he had found that the best rule was to "do what seemed right for the time, and act fairly towards the public in all public transactions."[40] Inwardly, however, he must have known that his victory on incorporation would be a Pyrrhic one if it led to his losing his party.

Howe found another argument to justify the coalition. Since the council had had time to perfect only a few measures, it decided to let "the active-minded and intelligent men" of the assembly take the initiative in other matters. If they carried their bills, the Executive Council – no matter if it approved them or not – would see that they were effectively administered.[41] But Howe had to admit there were dangers in this mode of proceeding. When the council failed to agree on a bill for the support of agriculture, the assembly produced one which he would have administered with distaste, since it granted a bounty to farmers and farmers' societies, instead of requiring them to "put their own shoulders to the wheel" before they got hand-outs from government.[42] Worse still, when the council could not agree on a bill for the support of education through compulsory assessment, he waited in vain for "the active-minded and intelligent men" of the assembly to take the initiative.

In the end he himself descended from the rostrum to give one of his strongest speeches on education.[43] Nova Scotia, he said, should "emulate the example of that great Country from which it sprung, and if possible go beyond it in the intellectual race"; it should "start with the proposition, that every child shall get the rudiments of Education, – that from Cape North to Cape Sable, there shall not be a family beyond the reach of the Common Schools."[44] When asked if some deference should be paid to public desires, he replied that "by governing according to the well understood wishes of the people, was meant, the well understood wishes of the intelligent; not the wishes of those who might not be informed on the subject." As for himself, he would gladly take whatever action was needed to ensure that education was within the reach of every child and "cheerfully retire from the Assembly, if that should be the penalty, satisfied that he, as one, had done good enough."[45] But his proposal that two-thirds of the money required for education in each county should be raised by assessment went down to overwhelming defeat[46] and the council was left to administer a routine education bill. In this field the coalition had brought no gain.

For Howe the most troublesome problem of all – in fact, a veritable running sore throughout the session – was the civil list question. Although the colonial secretary had withdrawn his offer concerning the surrender of the casual revenues and had instructed Falkland not to assent to any measure on this subject, the persistent Henry Goudge could not be deterred from introducing his own bill. When Attorney General Archibald, acting for the Executive Council, moved that it would be "inexpedient and unavailing" to proceed with Goudge's bill, he lost out by twenty-six to twenty-three.[47] Once again a group consisting largely of Reformers had defeated the Executive Council and most of the Tories. The *Times* made much of the defeat, and in Canada East John Neilson and others contended that the "ministry" should have retired forthwith.[48] In reply, Howe insisted that not even the wildest advocate of responsible government had ever believed that the council should resign on a question in which it was constrained by instructions from Britain. In Nova Scotia, he said, "no man of any shrewdness" had interpreted the division as implying a lack of confidence, while in Britain no ministry would "quit office ... until persuaded, by the state of parties, and by frequent divisions, that they have lost their working majority, and that there is a settled determination in Parliament to turn them out."[49]

Through its patch-up man, E.M. Dodd, the council proposed that, instead of proceeding with Goudge's bill, the assembly should adopt an address to the Crown requesting the withdrawal of the colonial secretary's instruction. Five members, mostly loose-fish Reformers, changed their stance, thus enabling Dodd's motion to be carried.[50] When the council proposed a weak-kneed address,[51] Huntington sought to substitute one so critical and so tough that it led Howe to become indignant, angry, even nasty. Basically it expressed surprise, in view of Thomson's declaration that colonial governments were to be conducted according to the well-understood wishes of the people, that any set of men would become councillors who were not assured that all the casual revenues would be brought under the assembly's control.[52] In Howe's view, this was a challenge to the very basis of the coalition. "To pass [it] would be a direct censure on the Council, and if ... it carried, he would not hold his seat for five minutes."[53]

There followed a series of exchanges between Howe and Huntington that might easily have led to a formal rupture. The latter denied he had any thought of proposing a vote of censure: "if they construed it into censure he could not help it." His object was simply to "do what he could for the people; – farther than that he cared but little."[54] As Howe knew all too well, his reply was as unfair as it was ill-tempered. Who, he asked, was this Huntington who was boasting of consistency? Was he not the man who had voted to commute the quit rents for £2,000? Had he not entered the council in 1837 without stipulating the terms he was now demanding? The forthright Huntington willingly admitted his faults, but to the first charge he made the cutting reply that "he had gained from experience ... that experience taught him not to give up rights for expediency"; to the second, he pointed out that Howe himself had urged him to enter the council in 1837 because "the popular party [had] no representative there, and if he did not go in, the refusal would be construed into a favouring of the Canadian rebellion."[55]

Thoroughly checked in one direction, Howe tried a different set of questions. What, he asked, would replace the existing council if its members resigned? Of what use was the "kind of consistency which would lead to no practical results, which would rather run on a rock, than diverge a little to either right or left."[56] Huntington found this argument more difficult to answer, and only six Reformers supported his version of the address.[57] But when he moved to delete from the council's address a statement of the assembly's willingness to make further concessions, a discomfited Howe had to look on as a majority of the Reformers – sixteen of them – rose to support Huntington. More than a little water had flowed under the bridge since, just over a year earlier, Huntington had stood beside him at Point Pleasant. Clearly the coalition experiment had taken a turn that Howe neither expected nor relished. Outwardly he would keep extolling its successes, but even in its best days it must have caused him anguish and second thoughts.

Dyed-in-the-wool Reformers also took it out on Howe in their letters to the newspapers. In the *Acadian Recorder* Clim o' the Cleugh told him that anyone who had had no confidence in Campbell's council but could support Falkland's was "an ass." What could be more absurd than a council whose members "refuse to exchange the common courtesies of life? ... What province, what country was ever governed thus?"[58] Meanwhile the *Times* and its correspondents, who had never accepted the coalition and were doing their best to undermine it, heaped scorn upon "the queer animals who play the secondary characters in Manager Joseph's company," describing them as "helpless and contemptible" and without his cunning.[59] Undoubtedly relieved to get away from this rough handling for a while, Howe left the province late in May to observe the opening of the first session of the Parliament of United Canada. He wanted to make it all the more memorable by having Susan Ann accompany him on a trip for the first time. Their second son, James, born during Howe's absence in England,[60] had died at fifteen months, but Frederick was only eight months old, and it was with the greatest reluctance that she let herself be persuaded to leave him to the care of others.

Both Howes enjoyed the trip by steamer from Pictou to Quebec City, particularly the "glorious feast of the Montmorency falls." In Quebec City Joseph thrust himself almost at once "into [the] thick of Canadian politics," and was altogether appalled that "such a magnificent Province [was] cursed by an absurd and mischievous hostility between the races."[61] He found the opening of the session in Kingston "great fun" and full of drama too, as he looked on excitedly while assemblymen, previously from two different provinces and strangers to each other, were thrown together for the first time. Naturally he exuded sympathy for Sydenham during the two days when it was touch-and-go if the new system would survive.

Circumstances like these were made to order for his agile, fertile brain, and between June 19 and July 10 he found time to produce a memo entitled "Canadian Suggestions for Governor General,"[62] which, whether or not it was meant to be taken seriously, is highly revealing of Howe the man. From it emerges the picture of one who, almost overnight, seemed willing to abandon Nova Scotia and plunge into the turmoil of Canadian politics, if Sydenham but gave the word. For him to be useful in Canada West Howe suggested that it would have to be as a newspaperman. Had not Mackenzie used a newspaper in Upper Canada to create a rebellion? Had not Sir Colin's government been overturned and responsible government established in Nova Scotia through a newspaper? Uninhibited by modesty, Howe pointed out that "the same paper now defends the Govt. and explains its principles, and they are understood and respected at home and abroad."[63] As he perceived it, the government in Canada was receiving pitiful support from the press. In Quebec City Neilson snarled at the administration every third day, while the only government organ, the *Mercury*, was too dull to have influence. In Montreal the Tory press gave only captious support to the new system, perhaps because it barely understood it. In Canada West the situation was no better. The Kingston papers had "no character – no force – no circulation, beyond a small circle," and in Toronto Hincks was playing Mackenzie all over again.[64]

As a remedy, Howe suggested the establishment of a new paper in Kingston, independent of the government, with a few sound pens to give it character, and later the setting up of similar papers in Quebec, Montreal, Toronto, and perhaps London. The result would be to give "independent men, disposed to do their duty, ... the Aegis of a powerful Press," and finish what Sydenham had begun, perfect his policy, and do justice to his character.[65] With characteristic self-assurance, Howe suggested that he was perhaps more suited to initiate the project than anyone:

I am familiar with the whole business of printing, publishing, reporting, and Colonial agitation – understand the principles – can write and speak as well as most Colonists – have a colonial reputation already. The French would rely upon me, because I went with them as far as I could go, the English because they have approved of my course in Nova Scotia. The people would have what they manifestly want – a leader – and the Govt. would have a publisher who they could rely upon for the exercise of a sound discretion.[66]

Pipe-dream or not, the proposal aptly reflects the thinking of one who always wanted to be in the midst of action, who enjoyed doing things for people of high estate whom he admired, and who thought that almost anything was possible utilizing the arts of the publicist as he knew them.

As it turned out, Howe returned to Halifax to enjoy the most pleasant of summers. He found especially to his liking his position as "Falkland's right hand man" during the period in which "the old Coalition was in the full tide of successful experiment."[67] In Howe's view few men presided over the dinner table "more hospitably, with an air of more frank cordiality" than Lord Falkland,[68] and he enjoyed to the full his exposure to a social world that had previously been denied him. Foremost among the social activities were those connected with the visit of the prince de Joinville, son of King Louis Philippe of France, who arrived in September in command of the frigate *La belle Poule.* Howe described the dinner aboard the frigate "as recherché and perfect as any that I ever ate."[69] After dinner the prince gave the members of the council an opportunity to use the jewelled Turkish pipes the Sultan had presented to him, but only Howe and Uniacke "smoked away lustily for the honor of our Country." As Howe put it, "a great many valuable things have no doubt come out of my mouth, but I do not remember to have put anything more valuable into it than the Prince de Joinville's pipe."[70]

Even the prince's visit became embroiled in partisan controversy. The first mayor of Halifax, Stephen Binney, was keen to enhance the dignity of his office, whether "by an exhibition of gold chains or parading to Church with Constables in silver livery at his heels."[71] Outraged when Falkland did not invite him to the two dinner parties in the prince's honour or present him formally at an evening party, Binney, in Howe's words, "considered the city insulted, wrote impertinent notes, and kicked up a deuce of a row, [into] which I was dragged of course, having to defend Falkland who did not know how to defend himself."[72] Acting, in effect as Falkland's protocol officer, Howe showed that the Colonial Office's table of precedence listed twenty-six categories of officials, none of which included mayors. "I proved, conclusively, that being only Mayor of one town, he had no right to take rank among Provincial officers, and that there were hundreds of persons who in England would be asked to meet a foreign prince before the Mayor of London or Bristol."[73]

The aftermath of these incidents was that Binney became, in Falkland's estimation, "the tool of a party in this Town opposed to my administration."[74] Some Halifax Tories sought to play off a mayor outspokenly hostile to the political changes that had taken place against the governor who had made the changes.[75] The birth of Queen Victoria's son, the duke of Cornwall, precipitated open conflict. Binney, going to England on other business, wanted all the societies of Halifax to transmit their congratulatory messages through him rather than through the governor. The object of those backing him was to induce "a belief in England that [Falkland's] Government [was] unsatisfactory to the majority of the residents in Halifax" and to cast reproach on Falkland himself.[76] The St George's Society, full of the old Toryism of Halifax, immediately fell into line and entrusted its message to Binney. At this juncture Howe took a hand by getting a public meeting to agree to transmit the city's congratulatory message through the governor, not through the mayor.[77] But both Howe and Falkland were worried that the coterie surrounding Binney might convince Lord Stanley, colonial secretary in the new Tory administration of Sir Robert Peel, that it warranted greater recognition than was its due. So, at the first opportunity, Falkland explained to Stanley that although the group was "respectable from position and character," it was "insignificant in point of number, and almost entirely devoid of political influence."[78] Had he known he might have spared himself the trouble, for his difficulties with the ultras were to be in Nova Scotia, not in Britain.

The closing months of the year brought a succession of events that were of significance to Howe. The deaths of two left-wing Reformers, Goudge in October and Forrester in November, meant that he would have a little easier going in the legislature, but the death of Sydenham in Canada and the accession of a Tory government in Britain had no compensating advantages. Yet most important by far was the announcement, on December 30, of his retirement from the editorship of the *Novascotian* and the sale of his entire establishment. Not only was he finding it difficult, even with Thompson's help, to combine the editorship with the obligations of his two offices, but, above all, he wanted the *Novascotian* to remain "untrammelled, even by the suspicion of legislative or official connexions."[79]

As he closed his "connexion, perhaps forever, with the Press of Nova-Scotia," he rejoiced that he had been "a good Mechanic" and had reaped rich rewards from the many Sunday evenings he had devoted to the education of his apprentices. Four of them had risen to the top positions in Maritime newspapers, and a fifth, Richard Nugent, would be the new proprietor of the *Novascotian*. "A Printer's son, himself having passed through every grade of the profession, has won them – and his example will not be lost upon those who are to follow in the same paths." With Nugent as proprietor and Thompson as editor, Howe was sure, as he said somewhat floridly, that the beacon he had "trimmed so long" would shed "far down in futurity its steady and inspiring light."[80] The most striking aspect of his decision to give up the *Novascotian* and to devote himself to politics full time was that he was left with an unpaid executive councillorship and a speakership which brought only a nominal return. Undoubtedly his friend Falkland had assured him of the first suitable remunerative office in his power to bestow.

For Howe it could not come too quickly. Although he had insisted that he could not afford to let his participation in politics interfere with his business, it had become almost a full-time vocation after his appointment as councillor and Speaker. He had openly admitted it, at the beginning of 1841, by formally recognizing Thompson as assistant editor, and Nugent as printer and publisher, of the *Novascotian*, while retaining the editorship and proprietorship somewhat nominally. Even then he had not abandoned the role of promoter of a colonial literature, for on January 14 he published the prospectus of "A Nova Scotia Library," which, in imitation of cheap and highly popular works in Britain, was to show "how much may be done, by a few active minds, from merely Colonial resources."

The intention was to publish, over four years, eight handsomely bound and beautifully printed volumes for five shillings each, including "a clear and succinct History of the Province," choice selections of provincial poetry, "Lights and Shadows of Colonial Life," and a novel having its setting in Nova Scotia. James A. Roy suggests that Howe, in his customary style, had overlooked "certain commonplace but necessary practical details," especially the question of "who would finance the whole undertaking in order either to make it a success, or to guarantee its projectors against financial loss."[81] To be fair, Howe's prospectus did state that the work would go on only if Nova Scotians encouraged it; "if they do not, it will be deferred to some more advanced period, or perhaps be altogether abandoned." Little encouragement being received, it quickly passed into the limbo of forgotten things. Meanwhile Howe's other literary project, the *Pearl*, from which he had expected a net return of £850 to the end of 1842 if he could secure 700 subscribers, was collapsing from lack of support despite its continued acceptance of liquor advertising.[82]

For other reasons as well Howe's financial position steadily deteriorated during 1841. Valuable as it may have been in extending his store of knowledge, his trip to Canada had cost him £153 he could ill afford. It is true that his obligations to banks and individuals of £3,580 were easily counterbalanced by debts owing to him and unpaid subscriptions, even allowing for uncollectibles. But the latter, already amounting to some thousands of pounds, continued to grow because Howe's preoccupation with politics prevented him from making the rambles which had normally been fruitful in the collection of subscriptions. Late in the year his acute financial difficulties led him to insist that Beamish Murdoch pay his longstanding debt within six months, and to use a note of his brother-in-law, James B.D. McNab, to borrow £250 from an estate he was administering.[83] Clearly he had a compelling reason for the continuance of the coalition and the good offices of Falkland.

The euphoria of the summer and autumn of 1841 had made neither Howe nor Falkland forget their difficulties with the Reform left wing in the previous session. There were approaches to Huntington in both July and December, but he was no less opposed than before to sitting in a council that included Stewart.[84] Then, in January 1842, just before the session opened, Falkland gave up on Huntington and appointed Young to the council.[85] For Howe the appointment served two ends: it demonstrated to the Reformers that the governor was taking their interests into account, and it meant that Young's criticism of the administration would end. The opening of the assembly coincided with one of those events that always delighted Howe, the arrival in Halifax by Cunard steamer of Charles Dickens, "the lion of the English speaking world."[86] Howe took him in charge, wined and dined him, and placed him beside himself in the assembly. From that vantage point Dickens observed that the forms at the opening of a new session so closely resembled those in England that "it was like looking at Westminster through the wrong end of a telescope ... in short, everything went on, and promised to go on, just as it does at home upon the like occasions."[87]

Howe and John Thompson were enthusiastic about the early days of the session, Thompson even boasting that "the Government appears to have secured the respect of all parties" and that "more has already been transacted, than in double the time of former Sessions."[88] One of the administration's bills resulted from Howe's discussion with "two very intelligent Indians,"[89] and although Uniacke introduced it because Howe was in the chair, it was essentially Howe's bill.[90] It empowered the Executive Council to appoint an Indian commissioner who, among other things, would protect Indian lands from encroachment and alienation, communicate to the chiefs the government's plans for the permanent settlement and improvement of the Indians, and arrange with the trustees of schools and county academies for the admission of Indian children.[91] While Huntington expected little good from it, Howe's enthusiasm got the better of him and he prophesied great things because of the change being effected in the Indians by the temperance movement. One Indian known far and wide for his drunkenness had taken the pledge and now "*would not partake of [alcohol], if a pistol were placed to his head to force him to do so.*"[92]

In other matters, too, Howe was soon to learn that he had been living in a fool's paradise. The administration had proposed a bankruptcy law based on the English model, but carefully modified to meet the Nova Scotia situation. Howe told the assembly that the lack of such legislation had led to the depopulation of Halifax during the last recession, whereas "a bankrupt law might have enabled [many] to continue and to retrieve their prospects."[93] But he failed to reckon with the alarms of the country members, who were certain the bill would lead to the evasion of just demands and the swindling that occurred under similar laws in the United States. Reflecting their fears, Huntington stated he would incur much fault "in the westward, if the Bill ... did evil, and he had not taken time to reflect on ... it";[94] accordingly he had it deferred over the opposition of five executive councillors.[95] John Thompson told the administration not to be perturbed since the bill had not been given the three months' hoist but simply deferred for further investigation.[96] Yet the council did not take its defeat lightly. The day after the vote it postponed the opening of the House for three hours while it pondered its position. Later, when Huntington asked if the administration intended to resign, Uniacke replied that it would await the further action of the House. Huntington's response was to give notice of a motion disapproving of coalition government.[97]

A single division had demonstrated the flimsiness of the foundations on which the coalition rested. On the one hand, the *Recorder*'s reporter lamented "the miserable intrigues" of the Tories[98] and Howe complained to Falkland about the "folly or treachery around us";[99] on the other, the *Times* reported that Huntington and the "responsibles" had met at Mrs McDonald's boardinghouse and canvassed the possibility of a government based on radical principles with Howe as premier and Young as attorney general.[100] Fearful that Falkland might think that he and Huntington had connived to destroy the coalition, Howe denied it, even though he admitted that it "behooved him to prepare" in case Huntington's resolution passed. He had thought in terms either of conducting a war to the knife against the coalition's enemies or of putting himself at the head of the Liberals and thus ensuring the return of enough members to safeguard the principles of Falkland and himself. In the end he contented himself with sketching out "a party administration" in case "circumstances compell[ed] us to act upon it," and showing it only to

Falkland.[101] But circumstances.did not compel, since Huntington withdrew a resolution he knew could not pass.

The following week two further blows struck the coalition on successive days. A year earlier the Executive Council had been granted £6,000 to spend on the great roads, and to supervise the work it had engaged the experienced George Wightman, a native Nova Scotian and largely self-taught engineer. Howe hoped it was the beginning of a new system in which the administration would be held responsible for road expenditures and he moved that the vote be continued for another year. But he was making an inroad into the prerogative that rural members most cherished, especially the practice of putting all the great road moneys "into the hand of two or three favourites who came from a particular part of the country."[102] So when Huntington moved to reduce the vote to £4,000, particularism won out and rural members, Tory and Reform alike, carried the amendment by twenty-eight to seventeen.[103] Although not a formal defeat of the government, it amounted to much the same thing.

The next day, February 12, Howe and Huntington were at it again, this time over the Legislative Council's demand for additional sums for its clerks. While Howe thought it unwise to force a confrontation with the council on a matter unrelated to its character or constitution,[104] Huntington refused to let himself be blackmailed into giving the council any sum it chose to demand for itself.[105] Knowing he would be beaten, Howe gave way and the credibility of the administration suffered for a third time.[106] To regain some of the ground he had lost, he sought to meet Huntington's charge that he had sacrificed his party for little or nothing. Pointing out that three of the councillors were Reformers, that others were no less liberal on many matters, and that seventy or eighty Reformers had been made magistrates, he argued that if his party had not got all it wanted, it had at least made a good start.[107]

But determined to vindicate the council in a more positive way, he strongly backed, perhaps even originated, a motion by Gaius Lewis, a Reformer from Cumberland, that the principles and policies of the government, as explained by its members, entitled it to the support of the legislature and the people.[108] Huntington contended it was the function of the House, when satisfied with a government, to move such a resolution, not for a government to request a decree of indulgence that would excuse its future acts.[109] Even Howe admitted that the mode of proceeding was not strictly in accord with parliamentary usage, although tolerable because of the circumstances.[110] Only five Tories and three Reformers opposed Lewis's motion.[111]

For the moment the administration remained secure, and the

Reform press mocked the Tory "Obstructives." It also wondered whether Huntington, in attempting to break up the coalition and form a party government, should let himself be put in the position where his only allies were the old Halifax faction. John Thompson gave him full marks for "consistency, manliness, and unswerving fidelity to reform principles," but sometimes doubted "the wisdom, the expediency ... of his conduct."[112] Meanwhile the Tory press was saying that the vote of confidence had changed nothing. The *Times* called the Executive Council "a contemptible body," powerless to do anything without the use of executive patronage;[113] while the *Pictou Observer* was certain that "if some very energetic measures were not speedily adopted, the leaky ship of the Constitution, with its unhappy crew, would go to the bottom."[114] Both papers had their highest hopes confirmed on March 3 when Alexander Stewart, whose propensity for causing mischief seemed unbounded, told the Legislative Council that "the true principle of Colonial Government [was] that the Governor is responsible for the acts of his government, to his Sovereign, and the Executive Councillors are responsible to the Governor ... Any other responsibility is inconsistent with the relations of a colony to the Mother Country."[115] The coalition would never be quite the same again. Howe was nothing if not horrified, and wondered if it was worth preserving at all. But he was in much too deeply to withdraw without the most cogent of reasons, and he stood helplessly by as Thompson and the *Novascotian* demanded that the council rid itself of "the chameleon character it is made to assume,"[116] and the *Acadian Recorder* wondered why Stewart had been retained as councillor in the first place.[117]

Again the assembly delayed its opening on March 14, while the council thrashed out its differences in private. When the session resumed, E.M. Dodd, once again the fence-mender of the council, explained that Stewart had not pretended to deal with the whole question of responsibility in his statement, and that all the councillors were agreed on what would come to be known as the Doddean Confession of Faith. If the assembly, after mature deliberation on a question that ought to involve responsibility, declared it had no confidence in the Executive Council, either a dissolution of the House or a change of government would follow; if an election took place and members having the same opinions were returned, the governor would have to secure other advisers who could conduct the government with satisfaction to the country and the assembly.[118]

Again Howe said little or nothing in public while his friends debated the merits of the Doddean formula.[119] His unease had been developing over a much broader question than the behaviour of

"Sandy" Stewart. Early in February he had told Falkland that, although he had ended all attacks on his new colleagues when he entered the council, "almost every public officer, and almost all the personal friends and relatives of the [Tory] members of the Council," not only opposed him openly, but also opposed the government, at the St George's and other societies, in the City Council, or at public meetings. While for fifteen months neither he nor his friends had published a line criticizing their Tory colleagues, the latter's papers had teemed with "every description of personal abuse." The result was to demand greater sacrifice on his part than he ought to bear; indeed, he had long felt that "unless the coalition [could] secure the aid of an extensive personal influence among the friends of both parties, it ought not to exist."[120]

What was the remedy? Howe told Falkland he had hoped to have the new system introduced without displacing a single office-holder because he expected that the paid heads of departments would act fairly towards those carrying on the public business without pay; instead they had done their best to weaken and embarrass the administration. Hence, if the government failed to carry its measures and the governor called an election, he might request that the heads of departments qualify themselves for office by getting elected to the assembly. If they succeeded, Falkland would be certain of their cooperation; if they failed, men of talent and influence would take their place, and "the administration will no longer resemble a House divided against itself, in a ship in which all parties are doing their duty but the pursers and doctors, who having little work and no perils to encounter, spent their time in starving and poisoning the Crew."[121]

Howe ought not to have been surprised by the conduct of the Obstructives. Clearly the Nova Scotia officials and their relatives and hangers-on were reacting much like similar élites when the perpetuation of their established position is threatened. Falkland's attempt to give the Reformers a reasonable share of the appointments challenged that position and especially the hereditary transmission of offices. The Reformers suggested, apparently correctly, that the *Times* and the *Pictou Observer* became even more violent after the Tory government took office in Britain. Why, asked the *Observer*, did Sir Robert Peel permit a Whig governor to persecute and hold in bondage the members of his own party in Nova Scotia? By year's end it was facetiously suggesting Lord Falkland as governor general in succession to Sir Charles Bagot or perhaps "that little mischievous skunk, Lord John Russell, could be sent out in person to finish the work of alienating the Colonies from the Mother Country."[122] Early in the year Falkland had asked that the *Observer* no longer be sent to him, but once at least his secretary requested Howe to let him have "the last two numbers of that blackguard paper."[123]

Even in public the impulsive Falkland could hardly restrain himself; in the secrecy of council he apparently pleaded more than once that one of its members teach the Obstructives a lesson.[124] The session over, and unburdened by the cares of a newspaper, Howe pondered what to do. His own make-up would let him stand only so much of this sort of thing before he sought an outlet for pent-up exasperation and indignation. Could be respond to Falkland's pleas and satisfy his own compulsive urge at the same time? He was well into writing the *Letters of a Constitutionalist* when he consulted faithful John Thompson about the propriety of publishing them.[125] Cautious as he was, Thompson advised "a more moderate course" because of Howe's position as "a person of family, Colonial rank, and of fixed official expectations." Since the authorship of the letters would be known instantly, Howe should remember that, although "a mistaken step might gratify the momentary feelings, ... it cannot be recalled when cause of regret may appear." He should also think of the community where, although a few were bent on keeping up the old bitterness, abuse was becoming "disgusting and flat." Finally, he should recognize that "atrocity at one side cannot excuse atrocity at the other ... To punish the innocent among one party, because the innocent among another were ill-used, involves the worst possible principles."[126]

Nonetheless, Howe convinced himself that he owed a duty to the friends of the new order to "give a dressing" to the worthies who had for months "over-loaded two profligate Presses with abuse of my principles and my friends," attempted to turn the Charitable Societies of the town into "hot-beds of political discord," and sought to destroy the Corporation of Halifax, and make it "a curse instead of a blessing to the community."[127] From June 22 to August 10 all of Halifax watched, almost with bated breath, as the *Novascotian* published anonymously Howe's indictment of the Obstructives, or the Rump of the old Conservatives, in eight successive "Letters of a Constitutionalist," using his unrivalled knowledge of the specifics of Halifax society and its families. At the head of the Obstructives Howe put "Jeffery, Collins and Co.," who had been forced out of the council in 1840, and others who wanted to transmit their offices to their sons, whatever their abilities. From these materials, he said, a faction had developed whose choice troops were "lawyerlings" like Andrew Uniacke,"who has neither the gait, manners, features, nor brains of the family"; Henry Pryor, "a sly little fellow, with spectacles on," whose Insurance Office would "*insure him for half a per cent from ever setting the world* on fire"; and Charles Hill Wallace, "whose grandfather [had] left him a Nova Scotia fortune, i.e., enough to live on and keep a horse," who spent "his time in various genteel amusements too tedious to mention," and who did "a good deal of the hissing and booing at public meetings." In this group Howe also included Beamish Murdoch who, by his association with the younger lawyers, encouraged the manufacture of lies against the government and wrote some of the scurrilous articles in the *Times.* Forgetting Thompson's warning that savagery on one side did not justify savagery on the other, Howe stooped to saying that Murdoch had "lived so much among old women that he has become very much like an old woman himself."[128]

Howe also directed his fire at the second organ of the Obstructives, the *Pictou Observer,* and Martin Wilkins, whom he charged with editing it behind the scenes. Because of a relationship by marriage, he pictured a Wilkins–Binney compact,[129] and on that basis explained the tirades of the *Observer* when Mayor Stephen Binney was dismissed as the governor's aide. Howe was especially scornful of the pressure being put upon Falkland to keep the collectorship of excise in the Binney family at a time when H.N. Binney, the incumbent, was not likely to live long. "Fortunately, Lord Falkland is a cool sort of person, not easily frightened when he knows he is right."[130] In effect, Howe was deliberately taunting and goading his opponents, since he knew, and they had guessed, that Falkland had earmarked the collectorship for Howe himself.

In his concluding articles Howe dealt with the Rump's charge that the constitutionalists were guilty of "*selfishness, corruption, and an inordinate desire to fill their own pockets at the expense of the people.*"[131] Compare, he said, the forty assemblymen who supported the coalition and who as office-holders received in toto a sum not exceeding £500, with the fifty men of the Rump who, with their families and friends, received £16,040, "more money than, on an average, can be spared for the entire *Cross Road and Bridge service of the Country.*"[132] Howe made the same point in another way by comparing in turn the positions of Henry Hezekiah Cogswell and Hugh Bell, Charles Wallace and Samuel Chipman, and T.N. Jeffery and Joseph Howe, to determine who was really guilty of "selfishness, cupidity, and corruption." Not unexpectedly, Howe came off well in the comparison with Jeffery. While he had received only £400 from the public treasury after fifteen years' service,[133] Jeffery had pocketed £77,500 in his thirty-one years as collector of customs, so much that he could use "the overplus of an enormous official salary" to purchase printing materials to "expose the nefarious designs of a man [Howe] who swallows up so much of the public revenue and leaves [Jeffery] so paltry a share."[134]

For the moment Howe was done, resolved not to write again if the Rump had learned its lesson. His friends justified the writings of "A Constitutionalist" to the hilt. The *Acadian Recorder* wondered why "retaliation [had] not come long before ... even the subjects of Mehemet Ali would eventually resist [such provocation]."[135] Nugent, editing the *Novascotian* in place of Thompson, agreed that the letters were essential to ensure "security for public and private life, its courtesies and best affections," and prophesied that the warfare would soon end when the Obstructives saw they were getting the worst of it.[136] For the moment the Rump was nothing if not violent. Some of its outrage was directed against Nugent for letting the letters be published. Twice he had to defend himself in the streets, and the second time James Cogswell, son of Hezekiah, was convicted of assault.[137]

But their main fury descended upon Howe, since Thompson was right that the writer's identity would be known at once.[138] The *Times* described him as "this mongrel compound – this issue of a cock's egg – who has so long imposed himself upon the people of Nova Scotia as a *patriot* ... [and who] is now employed in endeavouring to restore the suspended animation of the vile print that has done so much mischief in the Province."[139] The *Pictou Observer* singled out tell-tale signs of "the *Honorable* Joseph" in the letters: "a certain poetical disregard of facts, vulgarly called *mendacity*"; "swaggering insolence [and] over-weening vanity"; and indelicate phrases like *"rumpling ladies' petti-coats"* and *"women in a family way."*[140] Beamish Murdoch, writing in the *Times*, attempted to demonstrate that Howe was the kind of person whom decent people chose to avoid.[141] What could be said of someone who, in public letters, "violates the sanctuary of the tomb, vilifies the honored head of one family who died respected in the land in which he had so long lived ... and ... tears open the wounds that half a century ago had lacerated the hearts of another most respected family."[142] Murdoch went on to tell the "poor sans culotte – deluded loafers and self-deceived locofocos" who regarded Howe as a hero that he had acquired a taste for "dining with Lords and Governors General, living in great houses, and walking arm in arm with Counts and Princes"; hence they might no longer find him a Robin Hood when he took over the collectorship of excise at £700 a year.[143] But would he really dare to accept an office he had denounced for many years as "a political sinecure and public excrescence."[144] Following the same line was the *Pictou Observer*, which told him he would "sell the independence of a dozen Provinces ... to feather [his own] nest."[145]

This was barbarous warfare and, as Thompson had predicted, it did Howe's reputation no good. But even if Falkland had not requested it, he would have done it anyway, for, as subsequent events were to demonstrate, Howe the publicist and propagandist could not remain silent in such circumstances even if he had to speak out anonymously. Because he had leisure on his hands he was all the more likely to burst into print. More significant than his outburst was his concern to preserve the coalition, even though he did not like the discomfiture administered to him in small doses by the more advanced Reformers in the assembly, once his strongest supporters, and even though he had given up hope of building a new party from the moderates of the existing parties. Some of his anxiety to maintain the existing arrangements was related to his own credibility. He had argued so strongly about the possibilities and essential goodness of the coalition experiment that he feared a serious loss of face if he left it without a compelling reason. Even now, despite the misgivings and reservations he expressed in his private correspondence, he still believed it had a chance to achieve its end. As a conservative reformer, he counted it no small gain that Nova Scotia for the first time had a ministry of sorts though admittedly it operated under an ill-defined responsibility, and he was content to make further advances step by step. Finally, but not least in this mixture of motives, there was his loyalty and attachment to Lord Falkland, whose duty it was to make the coalition work, and who, if it survived, would shortly be in a position to provide him with the office he needed to help him out of his acute financial distress.

CHAPTER SIXTEEN

Breakdown of the Coalition

By mid-1842 any idealism once existing in the movement for responsible government seemed to have vanished. To the Tories it was nothing more than a struggle for offices of power and emolument. "A Liberal," they said, "could be distinguished only by his desire to have the existing office-holders supplanted by his own friends."[1] The *Times* went further and suggested that the Tory bureaucracy, through its talents and experience, came close to constituting an ideal ruling class, which could transmit offices to its sons with real benefit to the province; at the same time it tended to regard the Reformers as inferior, talentless, and unsuited to the holding of major public office. For his part Howe frankly admitted the importance of patronage in the political struggle, pointing out that unless the Reformers obtained a substantial share of the appointments they would find it difficult to keep their rank-and-file supporters contented and hence be unable to press towards their ultimate objective. Throughout 1842 Falkland was entirely sympathetic to this position, and Howe got a legislative councillorship for Stayley Brown of Yarmouth, who had been useful in moderating the comments and actions of Huntington;[2] an appointment under the new Probate Act for Jonathan McCully of Cumberland;[3] and a legislative councillorship for an excited Alexander McDougall of Antigonish, who told Howe that his appointment would give great pleasure to the Catholics of the county and their bishop, in fact to everyone but "a few partisans of the [Presbyterian] Revd Thomas Trotter."[4]

Wanting to do still more for the Reformers, Falkland complained to Stanley that the lords commissioners of the Treasury were not honouring his nominations for office. Because the new system required him to "lead the Government of the Country in all its details," he needed the support of a majority in the assembly, and it would be all the more readily maintained if he had the power, "incident to all government,"[5] of influencing the appointment of a wider range of inferior officers. As it was, he was surrounded by heads of departments, who were not only hostile to him but in a position to reward those who opposed him. Probably thinking of Howe, he also lamented that he had few means to reward non-lawyers.

Since Howe's ability to participate full-time in politics was itself in jeopardy because of his financial troubles, Falkland knew that he had to do something for him quickly, and Howe was not averse to reminding the governor of his need. In the summer of 1842 he wrote Falkland a long letter equating the good of the province with a major appointment for himself.[6] A like circumstance, repeated at a later stage of his career, has been altogether disillusioning to some students of Howe, and admittedly, no matter how plausible his proposals, they would have sat better had they not been tied directly to his personal fortunes. Howe contended that, as a principal immediate objective, the Reformers needed to "obtain a footing in some of the Departments" so as to "break up or materially neutralize that combined official and monied influence arising out of the expenditure of the Govt. which they believe has been and will ever be exerted against them and against your Lordship." If the Liberals could get their hands on half the departments, the governor, instead of being "surrounded by men only watching an opportunity to trip him up, ... would have a body watching [the] other, true to their own interest to him."[7]

Knowing that Falkland would not mind his introducing "a matter half public and half personal," Howe suggested that in a refurbished administrative machine he could contribute most usefully as provincial secretary, "through whose hands every detail of administration passes," and who was therefore "the best fitted to give views of ... general 'policy'."

With the knowledge I have of the temper of our House, with the friends I have there, and the facility which long practice has given me in speaking and writing I have the confidence to believe that ... in that capacity I could do more good than in any other ... the Secretary's business would be to master the general business and policy of the Administration, and to give luminous views of it and minute details, whenever required ... the study of my life would be the country, the government, its legislation, and relations with the Mother Country and the surrounding Colonies, and having every facility for acquiring information and winning friends, I will be enabled to make up in some degree for the absence of other Heads of Department from the House.[8]

But while the secretaryship would be a far better use of his services "than to set [him] diving into Mail Bags or collecting Provincial duties," he confessed that it would be "criminal for [him], from any feelings of false delicacy, to conceal" that he was in no position to refuse the first offer received.[9]

Howe's desire to be provincial secretary rather than collector of excise is understandable, but his sycophantic approach to Falkland did him no credit and availed him nothing. In the end, Sir Rupert George reconsidered his earlier thoughts of retirement, and Howe's only hope of office was the collectorship, of which Falkland had promised him the first refusal. But the incumbent, Hibbert Newton Binney, now bed-ridden, lay an unconscionably long time dying, and no less a personage than Henry Hezekiah Cogswell had intervened on behalf of Binney's second son and might prevail with a Tory colonial secretary. Adopting a machiavellian approach, Howe advised Falkland not to deal specifically with the collectorship in his dispatches to Stanley, but merely discuss the hereditary transmission of offices in general terms, meanwhile keeping Cogswell quiet by promising to give weight to his representations in the event of Binney's death.[10]

The tactics worked. Binney died late in August and Falkland immediately appointed Howe to succeed him, thus presenting Stanley with a fait accompli. In justification, Falkland again stressed the need to have as heads of departments men who could strengthen the administration in the legislature. Edward Binney, although an amiable young man, could never "be of any material service to the Government in a political capacity," while Howe, the majority leader in the last assembly, had been of incalculable help to him. Although the Excise Office did not suit Howe's "peculiar talents and energies," he had no choice but to give him the only office that was available since he had already rewarded J.B. Uniacke, the leader of the opposing party in the last assembly, with the solicitor-generalship.[11]

While Stanley did not dispute the appointment, Howe's opponents in Nova Scotia vented their righteous indignation as never before. The *Times* denounced "the insatiable greed of a family bred and nurtured on the public money." Calling the appointment "a republican innovation," it suggested that political influence, not proper qualifications, would in future "supersede every other requisite in filling official station."[12] Going still further, the *Pictou Observer* concluded that a "system ... BEGOTTEN IN SIN ... MUST ... END IN CORRUPTION."[13] Could there be a greater folly than to appoint the "slanderer" of the Halifax merchants to an office in which they would be his chief clients?[14] Howe's only regret was that he would have to give up the speakership which he valued "above all earthly prizes." Agreeing that he ought not to "hold the highest office in the gift of the people while receiving pay from the Government," he was consoled for its loss because he had shown he could win it and discharge its duties; besides, it was "not the person who sits in [the Chair] who is 'the head of the House,' but *he who has the best head.*"[15]

Earlier, on Falkland's urging, Howe had taken the unpaid job of Indian commissioner,[16] not without gibes from his usual opponents. In the *Times*, "QUIZ" laughed at the First Commoner being made "whipper-in of the Mic-macs – general blanket distributer – Prince of all the Papooses and defender of their Faith, no doubt!!,"[17] while the *Observer*, which had "always thought Joe an original, ... did not expect ever to find him dubbed an aboriginal."[18] After his appointment Howe found his house besieged at all hours by Indians who had been led to believe that "unbounded wealth was at my disposal, and that they were to be fed and clothed hereafter at the expense of the Government." As a result, he spent hours explaining the objects of the act to them, trying to convince them of "the evil consequences, even to themselves, of indiscriminate eleemosynary relief."[19] In October he roughed it as never before, penetrating deeply into the interior of all the western counties to meet the Indians in their habitat. It was a fact-finding mission, and he got all sorts of facts: no Indians lived on the Clyde but a few had land and small plantations up the Tusket; James Meuse had a cow and pig, and Francis Glode needed an axe, spade, hoe, and hatchet.[20]

Howe's report to the legislature emphasized the need to spend the Indians' legislative grant on objects that would be of more than temporary benefit; seed potatoes, for example, should not be provided, since they would be eaten, not planted. More positively, he noted that all the Indian lands were sterile, worth in toto less than £2,000 in the whole of western Nova Scotia; hence he asked the local surveyors to lay off another 1,000 to 1,500 acres which, if the governor agreed, would be exchanged for the lands they were holding. Finding also that the Indians were opposed to learning to read or write any language other than their own, he had sought to overcome their prejudice and convince them of their capacity to receive instruction. Howe apologized to the legislature for giving the commissionership "only the leisure hours which could be borrowed from other and various duties," and, despite the greatest economy, for incurring expenses of £59 11s. 3d.[21] Yet possibly the legislature had never received so large a return for so small an expenditure.

Meanwhile Howe's relations with the Baptists were developing on two different levels in a direction that would markedly affect his own career, the life of the coalition, and the subsequent course of Nova Scotia politics. In the election of 1836 the Baptists, largely devoid of official influence, had been an important element in the forces that Howe welded together to produce the Reform successes. At that time many of them would, like himself, have supported the idea of a single, nondenominational provincial university, based on liberal principles. The failure of Baptist Edmund Crawley to be appointed to the faculty of Dalhousie altered the situation since it led Howe, however reluctantly, to support the grant of a charter to Queen's (later Acadia) College in 1838.[22] By 1841, when he finally got the kind of board of governors he wanted for Dalhousie, the Baptist leaders were determined to develop and expand Acadia,[23] and they had an articulate and influential spokesman in Tory and Baptist-convert J.W. Johnston.

Rightly or wrongly, Howe felt that his continued advocacy of a single nonsectarian college had implanted in the Baptist leaders a suspicion of him which they acted upon at the first opportunity. He committed his original sin in 1841, when the Catholics petitioned for the incorporation of St Mary's College and the assembly approved their request almost without opposition. Later a Baptist writer was to attribute their success to the "adroit generalship" of Howe and William Young.[24] Howe compounded his sin in the same year when, in response to the Baptist Education Society's request for £500 a year for five years, he proposed that it be reduced to £300 on the ground that 40,000 Baptists ought not to receive more than 70,000 Catholics, if for no other reason than that the Catholics would demand an increase in their own grant. Immediately the Baptist weekly, the *Christian Messenger*, charged him, although not directly by name, with conjuring up the prospect of an additional vote to St Mary's as a "mere bugbear to frighten the Baptists from their just demands."[25] Howe later replied that he knew "no distinctions among religionists in this country – such as have existed, I have endeavoured to trample under my feet," but even if he were wrong in this instance, should he be "held up to the world as hating, betraying, and trampling on the Baptists," simply because he opposed granting them an extra £200.[26]

The session of 1842, in which college grants became the most hotly debated issue, added further to Howe's difficulties with the Baptists. When Samuel Chipman of Kings moved to put Acadia[27] in the same position as King's College, which received a permanent annual grant of £444 8s. 10d., Howe embarrassed the friends of Acadia by asking them if they would vote like sums for the other colleges, especially for Dalhousie. His own proposal was to give Acadia, Dalhousie, and St

Mary's the same grant as King's for a period of three years. After a bewildering series of divisions in which the House reversed itself more than once, it finally voted £444 to Acadia and St Mary's, and £400 to Dalhousie, for three years, provided they were educating "twelve boys of exemplary conduct and poor parentage."[28] Even though Acadia had not come off badly, Howe's participation in these proceedings led to his being labelled an enemy of the Baptists in a series of five letters which "an Observer" contributed to the *Christian Messenger* in April and May.[29]

Basically this was an issue in which there were not so much rights and wrongs as differing conclusions flowing from different premises. "An Observer" took the view of scores of Baptists of moderate means who had made heavy personal sacrifices to establish Acadia, whose efforts had been so successful that an immediate expansion of its facilities was necessary, but whose hopes of a capital grant had been squelched by Howe's insistence that no favouritism be shown to the Baptists. In their opinion, neither St Mary's nor Dalhousie needed the sums they had been voted; in fact, Dalhousie had been given £5,000 before it even had a student, and now an additional £400 a year before it went into operation. Yet, because of the intervention of Howe and William Young, the supporters of Acadia College and associated Horton Academy, with twenty-eight and fifty students respectively, were browbeaten into not requesting a contribution towards the capital costs of a college building and into accepting a moderate grant to meet the college's operating expenses.[30]

Howe, who stood for equal treatment of the denominations and still hoped for a nonsectarian college, was highly indignant at the conduct of the Baptist advocates who were "perfectly willing to *take*, but not to give," and who "haunt[ed] the lobby, to canvass or over awe members who happen[ed] to have any Baptist Constituents."[31] He did not appreciate the reminder of "an Observer" that he and Young owed their elevation to the Baptist population of western Nova Scotia or his implied threat that the Baptists would not "tamely submit to this tyranny of influence and of office, so disrespectful to them as a body, and so injurious to their interests."[32] Mincing no words, he replied that, while he would regret to lose his old allies, he would not sacrifice his political independence to retain them. By this time he was wondering if his Tory opponents were using Acadia College to achieve their political objectives, and if they would have minded if it burned to the ground provided that he and a few others were in it.[33]

Howe's relations with the Baptists need also to be explored at a second level. Between 1832 and 1836 he had printed the Nova Scotia and New Brunswick *Baptist Missionary Magazine* with nothing but amicable relations between him and its editors. When in 1837 the magazine became a newspaper, the *Christian Messenger*, he printed it until January 1841, after which the Baptist Missionary Board did it on its own. At the time Howe contended he was owed about £800, but arbitrators reduced his claim to £600, with a few small items still to be resolved. Assured that the back subscriptions were being collected, Howe arranged his financial affairs in the expectation that most of the debt would be paid by the end of 1841. Disappointed in that hope, he circularized some members of the board late in February 1842, expressing surprise that "a Body of Men, individually so pious and respectable," would withhold the payment of a just debt so long, especially "when they knew that from the peculiar character and constitution of the Board he can resort to none of the ordinary means of redress."[34]

So far the question of the debt had not been connected with the general political debate. That it became connected was due primarily to Richard Nugent, whose very considerable abilities were coupled with an intemperateness that would prove his undoing. Nugent got his first chance to cause mischief when Beamish Murdoch saw fit to discuss Howe's finances in the *Times*. "*To break down* [Howe's] *personal credit*," replied Nugent, "*was the only mode of getting rid of him left to his political enemies*"; hence the "credit crusade" against him.[35] After reviewing the state of Howe's finances in detail, Nugent concluded that although he was often hard up, it was only because he failed to dun his debtors energetically or put any of them in jail.[36]

There matters stood until August, when the *Christian Messenger* published an account of the Baptist Association's meeting at Wilmot which dealt with Howe's claim against the board. Although the statement appeared to be a purely factual one, it did present the board's position in the most favourable light,[37] and Nugent would have none of it. Indignantly he told the editors of the *Messenger* that the Baptists were seeking to evade responsibility for a just debt and put the responsibility on a body that could not be sued. But Nugent saw even deeper motives than merely depriving Howe of his money since some persons who owed it were making "the most disingenuous and foul attacks ever made upon Mr. Howe," and "attempting to embroil him with the Baptists" for political reasons.[38]

The fat was in the fire, for the editors of the *Messenger* replied so vigorously that Howe himself felt impelled to enter the debate, and to the end of the year his long letters in the *Acadian Recorder*[39] alternated with equally long articles in the *Messenger* until the material would have filled a volume.[40] The further the debate proceeded the more irrelevant and nastier it got. The editors of the *Messenger*, John

Ferguson, cocoa and chocolate merchant and manufacturer, and J.W. Nutting, clerk of the Crown and prothonotary of Nova Scotia – both pillars of the Baptist Church – sought over and over again to demonstrate that from the beginning they had insisted they had no personal responsibility for the debts of the *Messenger* and that their subsequent conduct was entirely in consonance with this position. Howe disagreed; how could the only two persons on the *Messenger* with whom he had ever dealt suddenly throw responsibility for payment upon persons with whom he had never contracted and from whom he had never received a payment? " ... my belief is, that *if I could get these men before a Jury*, there are not twelve honest men in the country who would not ... *make them pay the debt.*"[41] Meanwhile the antagonists were introducing anything that suited their fancy into the debate. Howe found himself accused of printing the *Messenger* "on the most worthless paper and in type scarcely legible";[42] in turn, he called Ferguson and Nutting barefaced liars for stating that they had had no communication with him except on matters relating to the *Messenger*. Had not Ferguson sought his aid when a cocoa bill that threatened his interests was before the House? Had not Nutting written to him for help when his emoluments were threatened by the civil list bill?[43] Howe might have done better to rest his case on a simple proposition that he knew was unanswerable: "*that so large an amount, confessedly due to an individual, by somebody, ought, by somebody, to have been paid nine months ago, and six months before this unholy war commenced.*"[44]

As the controversy increased in intensity, Howe gave more and more credence to Nugent's view that he was being made the victim of a conspiracy. Finding that on this question the correspondents of the *Times* and the *Pictou Observer* treated him just as harshly as those of the *Messenger*, he wonderd if less creditable motives than to protect the good names of Ferguson, Nutting, and the Baptist Missionary Board, or even to serve Acadia College, were at the bottom of all the vituperation.[45] Was he being made the victim of an informal Baptist – Tory alliance? Did Nutting fear that Howe and the Reformers would take the same action against him in his capacity as prothonotary as they were attempting against Sir Rupert George in his capacity as registrar? Were the Crawleys similarly fearful of an attack on the emoluments of Henry Crawley, brother of Edmund and commissioner of crown lands for Cape Breton? Were Ferguson, Nutting, and their allies withholding the payment of his account as part of a crusade to ruin their chief opponent? It was good, he said, that these Tartuffes had not got hold of a printer of scanty resources; otherwise "they would have ridden rough shod over him, and, after rioting on the fragments of his shattered reputation, would have strutted off, like a pair of pharisees, to prayer."[46]

As if to confirm his worst fears, Attorney General J.W. Johnston,[47] leader of the Tories and pride of the Baptists, chose to inject himself into the debate in October in a letter to the *Acadian Recorder*.[48] Writing with the voice of authority itself, he declared that from his own knowledge of the initial arrangements Ferguson and Nutting had in no way incurred personal responsibility for the debts of the *Messenger* nor were they dishonestly shirking a just liability. In an obvious attack on Howe, he went on to say that "it was but at a comparatively recent date, that ... the personal liability of Messrs. Nutting & Ferguson [has been] asserted."[49] Although Johnston wrote not as an executive councillor but in a private capacity on a private matter, he must have appreciated that the political consequences might be far-reaching.

Silent at the time, Howe later told Falkland that from then onward the coalition was doomed. How could it be otherwise when Johnston, utterly unconcerned about "the character of the Government, its strength, its harmony, or the comments of the Press," deliberately went out of his way to "lend the weight of his name" to the attacks on one of its members?[50] As Nugent saw it, "the walls of the Executive Council Chamber opened, and a dark figure glided forth, and, while his colleague was ... engaged ... drew his sword athwart his thigh ... and darted back again into the Executive Council."[51] Almost inevitably Alexander Stewart was drawn into the melee, and in November rumours circulated throughout Halifax that he had urged Uniacke to "embark in the same boat as himself and Mr. Johnston, form a junction between the Tories and Baptists, ... and throw Howe overboard."[52] Since Stewart made no public denial until much later, the story circulated for months, doing a little more to shatter confidence in an increasingly rickety administration. Discouraged and disheartened, Howe played a much smaller part than usual in the session of 1843, attempting to use "any little influence [he] had to allay irritation." When he again failed to bring Huntington into the coalition, he became altogether despondent, especially as he saw about him persons "who were deliberately acting in the spirit of Mr. Stewart's proposition to Mr. Uniacke."[53]

Because he had no alternative, Falkland pretended that all was well as 1843 began. With some exuberance, he had outlined to Stanley the government's legislative program, including bills relating to absentee debtors, bankruptcy, waste lands, and the resignation of assemblymen.[54] But he set greater store by the qualification bill, which permitted a candidate to contest any seat in the province, no matter where his freehold was located. Howe himself introduced the bill and used all his persuasive talents to have it accepted. Why, he argued, should Nova Scotians not have the advantages of a wholesome British practice? "To be free of Great Britain a man need ... hold only one property qualification, – to be free of Nova Scotia, with its 300 miles of length, and its 250,000 inhabitants, a man should hold three and twenty freeholds."[55] The existing law, he continued, put an inane restriction on the rights of electors. "Men in search of a horse, or a wife or a farm, have the whole Province to choose from. You would not say to a man in search of a horse, you shall be confined to Lunenburg; where, perhaps, they set as much value on an ox as on a horse."[56] The change would add to the independence of the individual assemblyman by putting him in a position to escape the judgment of "some insignificant fraction," actuated by narrow parochialism.[57] It would also improve the character of the assembly by preventing the loss of "some of the noblest flights of eloquence, some of the wisest laws, some of the most valuable expositions," since men of excellence, deprived of a seat for assertion of principle, might seek one elsewhere.[58]

Despite Howe's best effort, he could not convince seven Reformers that the bill would not add to the influence of the Halifax interest. He had even less success with the backbench Tories, who agreed with the *Times* that the bill was "redolent of rotten boroughs, non-residency and executive influence ... the most dangerous measure ... yet proposed by the Executive ... in its striving for absolute power."[59] Howe scorned the idea that a proposal which strengthened the executive necessarily took liberty from the people: "the stronger you make your Executive under the present system, the more power you give the People"; indeed, the bill was directly connected with "the good old cause of Responsibile Government."[60] Eventually it carried by the narrow margin of twenty-seven to twenty-three, largely through the votes of the Reformers. But for Howe the government's only substantial success of the session was hollow, since once again many Tories who contentedly shared the influence and patronage of government had shown that "they disliked its principles, and never lost an opportunity to weaken and undermine it."[61]

Other things about the session were equally displeasing to him. Before choosing William Young to succeed him as Speaker, the House declared the holding of that office and an executive councillorship to be incompatible.[62] In effect, it was admitting that it had previously taken a wrong step in failing to recognize a correct principle simply because it was injurious to Howe. Although he made no comment, the assembly's action unmistakably spelled out for him the undesirability of letting himself be made the beneficiary of questionable favours simply because he was Joseph Howe. But worse by far was the change in his relationship with Falkland. In the previous year, when Lady Falkland suffered a "melancholy and afflicting calamity" in the form of a family bereavement, Howe had asked solicitously if he and Susan Ann might be of any service.[63] Early in 1843 it was Falkland's turn to reciprocate. On January 12 Howe's half-brother William, "not being of sound mind and memory," shot himself; barely a week later his only surviving half-brother, John, though ailing for some time, died unexpectedly.[64] The concern of Falkland and his wife touched Howe; "while my Brothers are falling around me," he wrote, "there is much comfort ... in the reflection that your Lordship has ever been to me even more than a Brother."[65]

The relations between Howe and Falkland remained no less cordial until March 28, the day prior to prorogation, when J.J. Marshall, a Tory from Guysborough, gave notice that at the next session he would move for the exclusion of customs and excise officers from the legislature.[66] Howe countered it with notice of an amendment that the time had arrived for "the formation of a Provincial Cabinet, united in sentiment, acting in harmony in both branches of the Legislature, and in a [manner] calculated to obtain and secure the confidence of the people."[67] Although Howe was merely reacting on the spur of the moment to what he considered an attack both on himself and his principles, his motion annoyed Falkland exceedingly. Why, he asked, had Howe acted so injudiciously and discourteously in not acquainting the governor and his colleagues beforehand of his amendment, and what exactly had he meant by "cabinet"?[68] Howe insisted that his amendment was "but a fair parliamentary answer to the challenge thrown out by Mr. Marshall," and in no way at variance with the system he understood Falkland was to introduce as soon as circumstances permitted. Since Howe considered his own appointment as collector of excise to be a step towards the establishment of government by heads of departments, he thought he had no choice but to treat Marshall's motion as an attack on the administration's basic principles.[69]

For his part, Falkland was worried that Howe's call for a cabinet would be regarded as an attack on his colleagues and thereby weaken the administration.[70] In reply, Howe traced the steady loss of public confidence in the coalition, contrasting the course followed by himself and his friends with that of many Tories, who sought from the beginning to ensure the coalition's failure. After recounting the recent conduct of Johnston and Stewart, he concluded that

There is something more required to make a Strong Administration than nine men, treating each other courteously at a round table – there is the assurance of good faith – towards each other – of common sentiments, and kindly feelings, propagated through the friends of each, in society, in the

Legislature and in the Press, until a great party is formed acting in the spirit of which Members of Government set the example, and which secures a steady working majority to sustain their policy and carry their measures.[71]

Apparently Howe's fault was not in commenting on the disunity in the council, but in doing it publicly, for Falkland freely admitted to Stanley that the council had been lowered in public opinion to a dangerous degree.[72] But the dispatch is most notable for its striking change in stance. Hitherto Falkland had blamed the difficulties of the administration on the Tory Obstructives; now he attributed them to the differences in the private feelings of members of the council, particularly in those of its leading members. The Reformers were put in a particularly bad light because they did not appear to accept Falkland's view that party government was undesirable in "this comparatively petty province." He had warned both parties that he would consider "as deserting me" anyone who originated a movement towards party government, and told them that for the moment he would carry on as best he could, even though he might be forced into dissolution at any time. Then came the most revealing part of his dispatch: because J.W. Johnston agreed with him fully on the unwisdom of party government, he was forwarding his memorandum on the subject.[73] Clearly a new star had risen in Falkland's political firmament.

The pessimism of Falkland and Howe about the administration was not unfounded, for its deterioration continued unabated after the session of 1843. Richard Nugent, who more than is commonly supposed affected the course of politics in these years and who had precipitated Howe's quarrel with the Baptists in 1842, did as much as anyone to deepen and exacerbate that conflict in 1843.[74] Fiercely independent, unwilling to give or take quarter, he lost no opportunity to assail Tories and Baptists legitimately, and even illegitimately. Injudicious and foolhardy, he published without reflection the submissions of his correspondents whatever their content. Almost inviting the Tories to sue him for libel, by the end of 1843 he had been mulcted in heavy damages and costs, imprisoned, and forced to dispose of his interest in the *Novascotian* to William Annand.[75] Although Nugent was utterly loyal to the Reform cause, Howe was powerless to restrain him. Howe's jottings, after examining the file of the *Novascotian* at a later date, indicate his reaction to Nugent's performance: "Dick at it again"; "Nugent pitching into government"; "Seeds of mischief. Nugent doing more mischief."[76]

Even before the end of 1842 Nugent was assailing the coalition almost as vigorously as were the *Times* and the *Pictou Observer*. In 1843 he went all out on the Baptist question. On January 18 a special Baptist Association meeting at Nictaux passed resolutions which condemned Howe for attempting to make Nutting and Ferguson responsible for the debts of the *Messenger* and asked Nugent to print a 43-page letter containing the resolutions. In an apparent effort to show its hands were clean, it also had the *Messenger* publish Howe's receipted bill for the full amount due him.[77] Under the heading "Nictaux Sanhedrim [*sic*]" Nugent refused the association's request because a "gross injustice has been done the Hon. Mr. Howe," and because in a recent tour Dr Crawley had allegedly sought to prejudice his listeners against Nugent himself because he was a Catholic.[78]

By itself this editorial would have been enough to keep the controversy going even if a second factor had not raised it to higher pitch. In mid-February the Baptists presented to the assembly two memorials and a host of petitions requesting substantial assistance for the college building they were to start in the spring.[79] Nugent immediately warned the House not to let the expenditures on colleges swallow up the entire revenue, and published a letter signed "Fair Play" which accused the Baptists of seeking enough power to "hamper, if not control the Government."[80] Actually Nugent had little need to worry, since by this time half the assemblymen had developed doubts about the wisdom of supporting denominational schools through public funds. They had plenty of opportunity to express those doubts in the session of 1843, for in one form or another the problem seemed to be continually before the House.

Between February 22 and 24, largely in committee, the House debated a string of resolutions proposed by Annand and Huntington, the two most determined foes of public grants to sectarian colleges, which deplored the skimping of aid to common schools in order to maintain a superfluity of colleges, and favoured one good college free from sectarian control. The Tory S.P. Fairbanks of Queens countered with an amendment pointing out the impracticability of getting the denominations to agree on a single college and favouring the continuance of the existing grants to the extent that the needs of the common schools permitted it. Fairbanks's resolutions being defeated by twenty-eight to twenty-one,[81] the House confirmed Annand's proposals and chose a committee to draft a bill for their implementation.

Although Howe had kept a low profile in the debate, he was named to the committee and in short order became the chief villain in Baptist eyes. In two letters to the *Messenger*, Dr Crawley stated that the assembly had acted to "fulfil some wild freak of some two or three individuals, who happen for *the present* to possess a little power!"[82]

and that foremost among them was Howe who, appreciating the convenience of a college at his own door, within the circle of his own political influence, and in conformity with his own cherished notions, was blind to the truths that he, Crawley, had presented.[83] For these statements Howe described Crawley as "full of the gall and bitterness of a malignant and unchristian disposition."[84] He was soon to compound his fault in the eyes of his Baptist critics. When the granting of capital funds to Acadia came up for consideration on March 10, he moved that, since the assembly had always refused money for the building of schoolhouses even in the poorest settlements, it could not possibly provide funds to erect new buildings at Acadia. Despite all sorts of aspersions on his conduct, he kept his temper and promised he would continue to do so.[85] Apparently feeling that their cause could not succeed, the Baptists withdrew their petition for funds but asked to make their case at the bar of the House. Again Howe annoyed them by opposing their request on the ground that it was couched "in insulting language."[86]

But Howe's worst sin of all was committed a little later when, in debating McLelan's bill to withdraw the permanent grant to King's College,[87] he stated that some Baptists "exhibited as much ambition and persecution as Catholics, – and if [we] were to have a Pope, he would as soon have one in Rome as at Horton, – if a time of persecution was to arrive, it might as well be under solemn pontificals, as under a black coat and tights."[88] Thinking back on the simple faith of his father, he deplored the existence of sectarianism in general and sectarian colleges in particular. "When he looked abroad on the work of Providence, he saw no sectarianism in the forest, or in the broad river that sparkled through the meadows, – and should we be driven to the conclusion that men could not live together without being divided by that which ought to be a bond of Christian union?"[89] Although McLelan's bill passed the Committee of the Whole by a single vote, it got no further in the closing days of the session. A little earlier the *Messenger* had gloated that the committee to draft the one-university bill could not even agree on a site. So while the Baptists did not get their capital grants, neither did their opponents have their principles practically recognized.

Clearly Howe had decided that, instead of continuing to accommodate the Baptists, he would return to the principles from which he had deviated a few years earlier in order to recognize their sacrifices. Perhaps he believed that Acadia should now stand on its own feet; more likely he thought himself wronged by those whose interests he had tried to meet. Though writers in the *Messenger* scattered his name about liberally and to his disadvantage throughout the summer, not until late September did he engage them in a nasty disputation which had more than one strand. Earlier the *Messenger* had warned that those who sought to wrest the education of their offspring from 40,000 Baptists might expect "consequences which they may hereafter sorely deprecate, but will be little able to avert,"[90] and subsequently it repeated that scarcely veiled threat more than once. Huntington's reply was to warn his constituents that if a combination of religious bodies could force money from the legislature in this way, it would have lost its independence. "Political power must then fall into the hands of the Clergy ... religious fanaticism should again be suffered to usurp the place of Representative Government. The thumbscrew – the scourge – and the rack – have been too recently in operation for mankind to desire such a consummation."[91] Nonetheless, Johnston appeared before the Baptist Education Society at Yarmouth in June to denounce bitterly some assemblymen from strongly Baptist constituencies, especially the two Chipmans, for being "on that side which was led by the bitter and avowed enemies of Acadia College."[92]

A second threat, closely related to the first, was the obvious attempt to identify the Tories and their leaders with the Baptist interest. Apparently with that end in mind, Johnston had given the meeting in Yarmouth a veritable profession of faith, including the detailed story of his conversion. When the Baptist Education Society met at Bridgetown in September, its president, Edward Manning, contended that the advocacy of a single college was "an artful and malignant device ... the real object [of which] was to destroy Acadia College, and put the Baptists in the ditch." He was certain that "God had given [Acadia] to the Baptists, and they were bound to sustain it. It was an Institution that breathed benevolence, and looked benignly even on those who have 'a dagger under their coats ready to thrust into it' ... It was God's Institution ... do not let us desert it."[93] Undoubtedly Manning was sincere, but the obvious inference was that the Tories, who generally opposed the one-college idea, were doing God's work.

But by far the most potent promoter of the increasing polarization along politico-religious lines – a development that gave Howe cause to shudder – was the open and continuous confrontation between Crawley and the editors of the *Messenger* on the one hand and Nugent on the other. When Crawley stuck to his last, he was highly credible. Thus, when Howe stated that Acadia was "perfectly willing to *take* but not to give," Crawley could legitimately reply that Acadia had a right to insist on the bona fides of the other institutions before they received equal treatment.[94] But when Crawley denounced the qualification and registrars of deeds bills, he identified himself completely with the Tory position and played right into the hands of Nugent, who delighted in writing editorials headed "Professor Crawley Turned Politician" and "Parson Crawley's Politics."[95] When Crawley wrote that the Qualification Act would permit a person with a salary of £600 or £700 – in the context he obviously meant Howe – to light on any seat he pleased, Nugent wondered why he had not looked around his own coterie and singled out for the same treatment his brother Henry Crawley,[96] Attorney General Johnston, or J.W. Nutting, whose incomes were £500, £750, and £900 respectively.[97] When Crawley denounced the registrars bill, Nugent told him that his real intention was to protect Nutting, against whom the same action might be taken in his capacity as prothonotary as was being attempted against Sir Rupert George as registrar.[98] "Brother Nutting's Fees and our civil and religious rights are fearfully menaced!" wrote Nugent laughingly.[99] Clearly he revelled in poking fun at the Baptist members of the Tory compact.

When Howe hesitated to participate for fear of further escalating the religio-political conflict, his silence and that of his friends displeased Nugent. "A few Baptists and Tories," he wrote, "are vigorously agitating the Country and getting up 'demonstrations' in support of those Sectarian hot-beds of intollerance and narrow politics, Denominational Colleges ... Where [are] Annand, Young, Huntington, Howe, McLellan [sic], Dickey, etc? Why are they not calling their constituents together, and getting up 'demonstrations' in favour of one General Institution – open to all parties and creeds?"[100] Finally succumbing to pressure, Howe addressed a public meeting in Halifax on September 27, in which he was harsher than ever before in denouncing denominational schools and colleges: "in a short time they would banish [religion] from the province. One of them [Pictou Academy] kept the eastern counties in hot water for sixteen years; and another [King's] has produced more strife, division and bad feeling than any other bone of contention, religious, social or political." Now it was the turn of some arrogant professors of philosophy and religion, especially Edmund Crawley, who in six years had created more strife and descended to meaner arts of representation than previous Baptist preachers had done over long, laborious lives. "Let them not suppose that their being stuck up in professors' chairs gives them the right to fire their pop-guns at people without retaliation."[101] Completely beside itself, the *Messenger* described Howe's speech as the natural reaction of one who could no longer use the Baptists to serve his ambition.[102]

To counter his opponents' demonstrations, Howe got out into the country in October. Late in the month he was at Londonderry, Maitland, and Noel; earlier he had been at Musquodoboit and

Stewiacke. But most dramatic of all was his confrontation with Professor Crawley at Onslow on October 9. The Baptists, responding to "the call of the Great Gun of Acadia College," arrived early; the Presbyterians, supporters of Howe, came later; and from 10:30 a.m. to 8 p.m. they were subjected to an orgy of speech-making filled with countless interruptions. "An Eye-Witness" reported in the *Christian Messenger* that "possibly for the first time the great political lion [Howe] felt himself held at bay,"[103] whereas a correspondent of the *Novascotian* was of the opinion that Howe had administered a "merciless castigation" to those who had been "travelling over the country, circulating wholesale slanders at his expense."[104]

On returning to Halifax from the interior on October 27, Howe discovered that Falkland had dissolved the assembly on the previous day.[105] With the governor's permission, he stated it was done "without my sanction, and contrary to my expressed opinion"; indeed, the only councillors who supported it were the Tories Robie, Johnston, Stewart, and George, none of them in the assembly.[106] Charitably, Howe told Jane that Falkland had made his first mistake in more than three years,[107] but that he would stay in the council despite "jealousies and intrigues among the members themselves," because of the "avowed principles of the Administration," and the "large proportion of Liberal appointments made."[108] Howe would have been much less kindly disposed to Falkland had he seen his long justification of the dissolution to Stanley.[109] Basically it was an expanded version of his dispatch of March 31,[110] although this time Johnston emerges in an even more favourable light, and Howe even less so.

In essence, Falkland told Stanley that dissolution was "the only means by which [he] could hope to escape the necessity of immediately forming [the] Party Government"[111] that Howe and his friends were trying to force upon him. In council, he said, Howe had told him that no bill was likely to be carried as a government measure next session. Hence, other than dissolution, he had only two courses open to him, neither of them agreeable: either to meet the assembly with a council that could not carry out measures of importance, or to remodel it so as to strengthen its position. But in the existing House that could only have meant the installation of a Reform council and party government, and the exclusion of Johnston, "a Gentleman endowed with first rate talents, and of the highest personal character, possessing great weight, in the community."[112] Howe, on the other hand, had unwisely allowed his personal feelings to involve him in a bitter feud with the Baptists in which he had adopted a tone that understandably offended Johnston. Accordingly Falkland had let Johnston defend himself at Baptist meetings, not only because his religious feelings were deeply wounded, but also because, not having a seat in the assembly, he had no other appropriate forum from which to reply. Obviously Falkland was viewing Nova Scotian politics and politicians through spectacles of a different tint from those he had earlier used. While the motives for his change of stance can only be the subject of speculation, the suggestion that he was currying the favour of a Tory government in Britain cannot altogether be dismissed.

Meanwhile the enfant terrible of the Reformers had put Howe and the Reformers of Halifax in immense difficulties. Howe had arrived back in Halifax to find its Catholic population in an excitable state, and for it Richard Nugent was largely responsible. Fiercely independent of all authority, Nugent – himself a Catholic – had got himself involved in a matter of internal church discipline involving Dr. Walsh, the Roman Catholic bishop of Halifax, and a popular priest, Father Loughnan, the rector of St Mary's Parish. When the bishop took under his care the Total Abstinence Society of the parish, of which Father Loughnan was president, Nugent found the circumstances "as novel as they are reprehensible," and published two letters of "A Catholic Teetotaller" which charged the bishop with seeking to degrade Father Loughnan in the eyes of the community.[113] The fat was in the fire. On October 26, 1,700 Catholics met to proclaim their abhorrence of the "calumnies" against their bishop in the columns of the *Novascotian*.[114] Nugent nonetheless held his ground, saying that he would "disregard the threats of any faction" and publish what he pleased on any public matter.[115]

Howe was soon to discover that the Tories were describing the *Novascotian* as his paper, and associating him with the attacks on Dr Walsh in order to estrange him from the Irish Catholics, always a very large portion of the Liberal vote in Halifax. Because rumours were rife of Tory overtures to the Catholics, Howe and some leading Liberals decided to demonstrate that "our party relations were not those of creed, or descent from any particular portion of the Empire."[116] While it is difficult to penetrate deeply into a murky situation, it appears that one, perhaps two, of the sitting members for Halifax, expressed a willingness to retire in order to ensure Catholic representation. Gratified to be accorded something they had not requested, the Catholics accepted with pleasure. But the offer to them was more easily made than fulfilled.

Some rank-and-file Liberals strongly opposed the retirement of an incumbent member; if an Irish candidate, they said, why not a Scotchman? According to Howe, a committee of thirty meeting at his home would have ironed out the difficulties if some Irish leaders had not tortured the proceedngs into an insult.[117] Or perhaps, as the

Messenger suggested, he was displaying his well-known "ingenuity ... in the explanation of nice political intricacies."[118] Whatever the case, the Catholics felt they had been offered no more than a reversion of some of the "crumbs," a nomination sometime in the future when a sitting member chose not to run. In the end the incumbent members, McNab and William Stairs,[119] were nominated as the Reform candidates for the township on November 6. At the meeting Howe thanked the Catholics for not exhibiting jealousy, and pleaded for their support on the basis of "old services and feelings,"[120] but the reason the meeting was quiet was that the Catholics had stayed away and the hall was barely half full.

The next day the Catholics held their own meeting to lambaste the Liberals. "How obliged ought we to be," asked Michael Tobin, Jr, "for the kindness which permits us to pick up the crumbs which fall from their table? ... And what have [the Reformers] done for us?"[121] Lawrence O'Connor Doyle could have understood it if he, as an active worker for Irish repeal, had shut himself out from a place of preferment, but it was "illiberal and unjust, that the whole Catholic population of the Town should be disfranchised because he sympathised with his countrymen in Ireland."[122] Those in attendance pledged themselves, "one to the other, and each to all," not to participate in the approaching elections. Paraphrasing Sam Slick, the *Times* suggested that "the Great Liberal Party" had been shaved to "the little end of nothing."[123]

For the most part, the Catholics kept their pledge to maintain a strict neutrality in the election for the township of Halifax, which included the city and the western part of Halifax county.[124] Since McNab's election was assured, the contest was between Stairs and Andrew Uniacke, the only Tory candidate. Because of the absence of Catholic support, Stairs was forty-six votes behind Uniacke in the city. Normally the Reformers would have made it up at Margaret's Bay, but scenting victory the Tories had hired one of James Whitney's steamboats to pick up voters along the bay and, allegedly, to dispense liquor and provender in unprecedented quantities.[125] When Howe upbraided Whitney, the latter blamed his agent Binney, who, he said, "did it merely to make the Steamer earn something."[126] While Howe accepted Whitney's assurances that he would never have let his property be used to injure an old friend, he saw the fine hand of a Binney at work in behalf of the Tories. In any case Uniacke beat out Stairs by seventeen votes and gave the Tories a seat that was to prove crucial.[127] The *Messenger* was elated at the breaking up of the compact which, it said, had controlled the capital of the province and was fast making it "a *close Borough*."[128]

Meanwhile rumours had spread that a Catholic and a Tory

merchant would run against Howe and Annand in the county of Halifax.[129] Feeling their strength, but insisting that they acted on their own, the Catholics met on November 23 to nominate Doyle and appoint a committee of 100 to promote his election, though they quickly accepted an offer from the Liberals to have Annand retire in favour of Doyle. As the *Register* put it, "it became the 'Liberals' to make the amende as much as it became the Catholics to require it. They are now all united."[130] The Tories saw it as a device to ensure Howe's election, but Annand insisted that he had withdrawn only to "prevent a permanent breach among the Liberals – to bring parties together who had been temporarily estranged."[131] Naturally the *Times* chuckled at the "curious" combination of Howe, "Her Majesty's Premier Executive Councillor," and Doyle, "the President of the Repeal of the Union Society,"[132] but the Tories decided not to oppose them.

Beyond Halifax the most significant happening was the decision of J.W. Johnston to abandon the Legislative Council and contest the seat for the county of Annapolis. The outcome was to be that for the next fifteen years or more the political battle in Nova Scotia would be directly joined between him and Howe. In the election of 1843, however, neither leader appears to have ventured beyond his own constituency, and it is difficult to determine how the generality of Nova Scotia voters perceived the election. At Annapolis Johnston "unequivocally denounced the system of a Party Government,"[133] while the *Times* spoke no less strongly against it, especially against a party government of the "Great Liberals," a term it now used derisively to describe the Reformers. Although Howe did not condemn the coalition government per se, he made it clear he had no desire to remain a member "except pressed to it by the action of the people at the election." If the Reformers secured a large majority, he supposed that some Tory executive councillors would resign; if those who advised the dissolution won decisively, he would give up his seat.[134]

But it is doubtful if many voters perceived the election, as Johnston and Howe did, in terms of coalition versus party government, or of acceptance or rejection of the principles of Sydenham and Falkland. In the non-Baptist counties the voters appeared simply to have followed their previous partisan attachments; there the college question played no part, and the changes were few and accrued to the Reformers' advantage: one seat in Richmond, and two in Pictou, where the lessened conflict between Kirkmen and Secessionists assisted them.[135] But wherever the college question dominated the election, the Reformers usually fared badly, hurt by the kind of arguments used by the *Messenger*, which bluntly told its readers that, if

Howe and his party won, all the Baptists would get was "an occasional crumb bestowed on some renegade ... who has betrayed the interests of the Denomination."[136] This type of logic did not bring about the defeat of Huntington because, according to Annand, the people of Yarmouth were "much too intelligent to be priest-ridden";[137] much more inexplicably the Reformer P.M. Benjamin beat out William Johnson, a member of the executive of the Baptist Education Society, in the township of Horton, the locus of Acadia College. But elsewhere in the Baptist belt, Annapolis, Kings, and Hants counties and stretching over into Colchester, the Reformers had nothing but reverses. In addition to their former seats, the Tories took the Kings county seat; two seats in Annapolis, where Johnston defeated S.B. Chipman; three in Hants; and two in Colchester. Overall, the Tories gained nine seats to the Reformers' four and converted a minority of nine seats in the last House to a majority of one. The Reformers' loss to Andrew Uniacke in the township of Halifax had turned out to be crucial.

Howe was more optimistic about the results than he had any right to be. To Jane he expressed confidence that Huntington, Young, and himself would control "a clear half of the House"; Johnston something more than a quarter; and J.B. Uniacke the remainder. Hence, if Uniacke and his friends joined him, "Stewart or Johnston or both may be thrown out."[138] Although Uniacke would finally throw in his lot with the Reformers, Howe was wrong that he commanded any support other than himself. Sizing up the situation much more accurately, the *Eastern Chronicle* saw "a decided increase of the Conservative party both in numbers and influence," but prophesied that Howe, Huntington, William Young, Doyle, and J.B. Uniacke would provide a strong opposition.[139]

The election over, Falkland invited Howe to remain in the council, indicating at the same time his belief that the new House would be opposed to party government. Howe disagreed, and replied that "nothing but the most imperative necessity" would induce him to remain a councillor.[140] On consulting his political friends, he changed his mind, but not for long. Falkland, allegedly wanting to demonstrate the principles on which the administration would henceforth be conducted, decided to appoint a new councillor hostile to party government. By some incomprehensible exercise of logic, he contended that neither Howe nor his friends had any right to complain, since "a few days previously, and after mature deliberation," they had "given in their renewed adhesion to the Government."[141] Accordingly he named M.B. Almon, brother-in-law of J.W. Johnston, to the council.

The reaction, immediate and definite, was the retirement of Howe,

McNab, and Uniacke as councillors. Taking the position that he had been stabbed in the back, Falkland demanded written explanations for their resignations. Both Howe and Uniacke replied that since Almon's appointment indicated "a change of policy,"[142] of which they could not approve, they had no choice but to get out. An indignant Falkland wondered how persons who had conceded his right to make appointments were justified in seceding from the council whenever he made an appointment they did not like. Were they not seeking to strip him of the prerogative and place it in their own hands? Falkland was certain if Howe had been in a position to insist on Johnston's dismissal, he would have done it; all that Johnston had asked was to have a vacancy in council filled by someone agreeing with him on a major issue, and he, as governor, had made the appointment as evidence of his confidence in Johnston, "the leader of my government."[143] That Falkland could give such recognition to Johnston in a letter to the councillors who had resigned, and then have it published in the *Royal Gazette*, is nothing less than astounding. Clearly it rested on a belief, implicit throughout the letter, that the voters had utterly rejected the idea of party government and given a majority to its foes. Howe could only wonder about the fickleness of Falkland's friendship; had it depended largely upon Howe's own political strength at a particular time?

In a reply he was permitted to publish, Howe denied that he had ever demanded a party government consisting of only one interest. But would it not be better, he asked, to form a strong government consisting of persons agreeing upon common principles and common measures than to "attempt by any exercise of the prerogative, to bind men together who have but few private or public ties, and who cannot fail to weaken any Government by the absence of that united personal influence upon society and public opinion which the Members of Council should steadily exert"?[144] In defending his conduct to Stanley, Falkland rejected the view that there were two well-defined parties and two only; he himself saw a "third and moderate party distinct from either, the weight of which is beginning to be felt, and which will I trust be powerful in the Assembly."[145] But if he was thinking in terms of some new force headed by Johnston, he was doomed to disappointment, for Johnston at no time indicated any intention to divorce himself from the extreme Tories, whom both Howe and Falkland had been fighting since 1841.

Falkland criticized Howe most of all because he appeared to want the parties represented in the Executive Council "in the Exact proportion they bear to each other in the Assembly." To meet this demand, he said, would make it impossible to construct a working government and, worse still, require a governor to hand over the prerogative to five or six councillors and produce such evils as would "involve the early separation of these colonies from England."[146] Seemingly he sought the good opinion of Stanley by putting Howe in the worst possible light. Yet, for the moment, Howe was still well disposed towards him. He told Jane that the governor had "acted foolishly" for the second time in three years, and that he would "soon get sick of the mess in which he has been involved." With some pleasure he also told Jane that, because he was giving up the excise position, his constituents had tendered him a year's salary, but that he had declined it. "Have no fears – all will be right, and our position stronger than ever. We parted with the Governor on good terms."[147] But he could not have been more wrong in assuming that he would continue to have good relations with Falkland.

CHAPTER SEVENTEEN

"War to the Knife"

Even more quickly than he expected, Howe's prophecy that Falkland would soon be sick of the mess into which he had got himself came to fruition. In an effort to avoid party government he had ended up with an Executive Council of Tories; now he could find no one but Tories to replace them. By February 1, 1844, he was desperate enough to ask if Irish repealers on "this side of the Atlantic" could sit in the council;[1] the next day he wondered if he could balance some extremists with some moderates and thereby confirm the very important principle that "the Council should be a mixed body."[2] Meanwhile Howe was winding up his connection with the Excise Department and handing over the accounts to the commissioners appointed to arrange the transfer.[3] But he also looked on interestedly as the *Novascotian* and the Tory press debated whether he had tried to force party government on the governor and had withdrawn from the council when he failed.

Falkland gave his answer to the question on February 8 when, in the Speech from the Throne, he insinuated that the Reformers were seeking to strip him of the prerogative and thereby make him "an instrument of oppression to some portions of the community for the aggrandizement of others."[4] This was to be the first of a series of acts by the governor which would shortly produce a complete rupture between him and Howe. In the debate that followed Howe argued that the Tories had been the first to make the move towards party government by allying themselves with the Baptists, and that Falkland himself had caused his resignation by breaking an agreement to bring the Reformers into better balance with the Tories on the council. While Howe insisted that he would protect the prerogative at all costs, the union between it and the local parliament had to be intimate and unbroken; "strike away either and you establish a depotism – let them act and re-act upon each other and you have a British Constitutional Government."[5]

Nothing could have demonstrated better the state of the parties in the House than the division on the address. With all the assemblymen present and the Reformer William Young in the chair, it was barely carried by twenty-six to twenty-four. In effect, the Reformers' difficulties with the Catholics in Halifax and the election there of the Tory Andrew Uniacke had prevented a constitutional crisis. Still faced with an incomplete council and thinking the time to be propitious, Falkland offered Howe, Uniacke, and McNab their old places, using Dodd as an intermediary. But believing that even the barest of victories in the assembly had strengthened his position, he put strict conditions on their reappointment: they were to disavow the doctrines that the governor stood in the same relation to the assembly as the queen did to the Commons, and that any party had a right to representation in the council proportionate to its membership in the assembly; they were also to agree that Falkland could select his council from the various interests "in the proportions which expediency, the efficient conduct of public affairs and the exigencies of the times seem to him to demand."[6] Even the *Times* criticized Falkland for seeking to fill up the council with the "Great Liberals," but it had no need to fear since the three ex-councillors declined the offer within hours.[7]

Howe should have had enough of coalitions and if he needed further evidence against them it was accumulating around him from day to day. Late in January he had noted that a "loyal meeting" in the Halifax Hotel presided over by ex-Councillor Samuel Cunard had concluded, at least by inference, that a party had grown up espousing principles which might lead to severing the colony from Britain; he noted with even greater interest that the governor gave tacit agreement by replying that he was "determined to preserve his independence" at all cost whatever the demands upon him.[8] Nevertheless, through a mutual friend of Falkland and himself, whom he met by chance in Dutch Town, Howe offered the governor a way out of his dilemma: he would give up his own claim to a council seat to a Liberal less objectionable to the Tories, provided that Falkland was "disposed to consult the feelings of the Opposition by a corresponding removal of an individual on the other side."[9]

Although Howe kept insisting that he had meant his offer as a serious overture towards peace, the governor reportedly reacted by saying that henceforth there would be "war to the knife" between him and Howe.[10] Almost as if to confirm Annand's opinion that he had "not done one wise thing" since the dissolution and that he had "lost all self control and judgment,"[11] Falkland placed in the *Royal Gazette* of February 29 an extract from a dispatch in which Stanley praised him for "resisting the PRETENSIONS" of the retired councillors.[12] Altogether shocked, Howe could only conclude that the governor had been sending highly biased reports to Britain, and he had his suspicions confirmed when Falkland refused to table the correspondence. "Down to this moment," Howe said, "I would have burnt my house over my children's head to have served or to have saved Lord Falkland,"[13] and to the end of his days he called this incident the clinching blow that turned him irrevocably against Falkland. With it any possibility of reconstructing the old coalition government was gone.[14]

In desperation Falkland turned to Stanley for assistance, making Howe the chief author of all his troubles. Self-pityingly, he pointed out that, despite his kindness to Howe and his friends, they were according him a treatment that would "render a renewal of official connexion with them extremely painful." Howe, he said, had recently "compared the office of Governor to that of a King at a Tournament who had nothing to do but to remain neuter during the Contest and then distribute the prizes among the Victors." Unless there was "a decided interference on the part of the British government," a governor might soon have to appoint his councillors from among those who temporarily commanded a majority in the Assembly without regard to "the feelings of the people ... and to the general welfare."[15]

Howe was in no mood to give Falkland and Johnston a respite. Never in his life would he take kindly to any suggestion that he had designs on the prerogative and thereby permit his loyalty to be called into question. Accordingly he presented a resolution which set forth his views of the principles of colonial administration in terms of three well-known and accepted declarations that the Tories would find difficult to challenge: the Harrison Resolutions embodying the theory of the Sydenham régime as adopted by the Parliament of Canada in September 1841; the Doddean statement approved by the Nova Scotian Assembly in March 1842;[16] and part of the recent reply of the governor general, Sir Charles Metcalfe, to an address from the district council of Gore, in which he conceded that a governor should administer a colony according to the well-understood wishes and interests of the people.[17] In an amendment, Johnston included another portion of that reply in which Metcalfe declined to express an opinion on responsible government until it was more carefully defined, and forcefully asserted that a governor was responsible only to the Crown for his acts.[18] Eventually Johnston carried his amendment by a majority of two and Falkland boasted to Stanley about the victory of his first minister.[19] If success there was, it was that the Tories had somehow been able to lure John Ryder of Argyle from the Reform ranks, a defection that was to be permanent.[20]

In effect, this meant that the administration would have no trouble fending off attacks in the form of nonconfidence motions. On theoretical questions relating to the status of the governor and the protection of the prerogative, the Tories could be counted upon to coalesce to a man. Thus, late in the session, when Doyle responded to Dodd's challenge and moved that, in retiring, the ex-councillors had done no more than exercise a constitutional right and had advanced no pretensions of which the House disapproved, he was turned down by a straight party vote of twenty-six to twenty-three.[21] Exactly the same fate befell a second amendment of Doyle that the governor should at all times be surrounded by a council that possessed the confidence of the assembly and brought vigour and efficiency to government.[22] In fact, it was the line-up of members on these divisions that the *Novascotian* and *Morning Chronicle* kept publishing daily after April 22 to let the public know exactly how the assembly was divided along party lines.[23]

But questions of confidence aside, the administration was powerless to carry a single bill of importance through the assembly. On specific matters, particularly those designed to effect economy and retrenchment, a few Tories, mostly from the rural districts, invariably supported the Reformers' proposals. In contrast with the late 1830s, this time the particularism of the assembly favoured the Reformers; this time the loose fish were Tories. For Howe it was 1837 to 1840 all over again. Once again he was providing leadership for members with whom he was in complete rapport; almost invariably he and Huntington got the specific provisions they wanted incorporated in bills, even though they were slightly outnumbered by the Tories.

Howe lost no opportunity to scoff at "a mockery of a Government," reserving his strongest ridicule for its civil list bill, "the finishing act of Administrative absurdity."[24] For Johnston and the compact that supported him the bill was of no little urgency since a diminution in the returns from the casual and territorial revenues had led to large arrearages in the salaries of the office-holders whom these revenues supported. While Falkland and Johnston knew it was "inexpedient" to ask the assembly to meet the arrearages,[25] they hoped it might be persuaded to provide these salaries in the future. But because they lacked confidence in their ability to carry such a measure, their bill was little more than a skeleton, the assembly being permitted to fill in the salaries as it pleased. "Have we an Administration or no?" asked Howe. Was Johnston really trying to "overthrow the new system altogether" by refusing to assume the leadership that it required?[26] To the delight of the *Morning Chronicle*, Howe and Huntington did very much what they wanted with the civil list bill, and it was in effect their bill, not the administration's, that eventually went to Britain.[27]

In other matters Johnston fared no better, whether it was to amend Huntington's road scale,[28] permit the Church of England to subdivide its parishes,[29] or prevent "manifest injustice" to Sir Rupert George in the registrars bill,[30] but despite his obvious frustration the general tone of Nova Scotia politics remained much the same during the session. There was one event, however, which proved to be a major factor in the escalation of bitterness after the session was over. Again it was February 29 when the *Royal Gazette*, to Howe's amazement, announced that John H. Crosskill, the publisher and editor of the *Morning Post*, would succeed John Thompson as Queen's printer. After Howe, Uniacke, and McNab resigned, Thompson had decided on strict neutrality as the duty he owed to himself, the ex-councillors, the government, and the public.[31] That was not good enough for Falkland, for although the unobtrusive Thompson refused to let himself be made the centre of public controversy, Howe knew he had been forced out because of his unwillingness to do the governor's bidding. He also knew that Gossip of the *Times* had not been chosen to succeed Thompson because he was critical of Falkland's efforts to entice the "Great Liberals" back into the administration. So he concluded that Crosskill was prepared to surrender himself completely to the governor.

Crosskill, he knew, had kept the *Morning Post* editorially neutral. But of late he had opened his columns to Tory letter-writers, and while straddling the fence himself had, in Annand's words, "allowed every ... dirty scribbler who chose to besmear gentlemen of the Liberal party, with their filth, [to use] his columns."[32] Howe was particularly indignant over an imaginary letter in which "Papineau" warned him to subdue his besetting sin, personal vanity and ambition, or he too might "slowly and insensibly become a traitor and rebel, *Facilis descensus Averni*."[33] Although Howe's friends wanted him to institute an action for libel, he let the matter drop, only to have "Punch" in like manner deride him and his friends in the *Post* between February 15 and April 20. Legitimate enough by the standards of that day, these letters left Howe seething with indignation in that they were being published by a man to whom Falkland had given preferment at the expense of his friend Thompson.[34]

No less annoying to Howe was the change that Crosskill wrought in the *Gazette* at Falkland's bidding. Thus, on March 7, it heaped encomiums on the Tory Sir Robert Peel and ranked him inferior to none of the leading luminaries in the annals of the British Empire. Had it really reached the point, asked Annand (or was it Howe?), that "the pupil of Holland, the associate of Melbourne, the protégé of Russell, can so cooly turn his back on his old friends, and trumpet forth the triumphs of their great opponent over them?" Perhaps, continued the editorial, the rumours were correct that Falkland's quarrel with the Liberals and his surrender to the Tories were "deliberately designed to propitiate the favour of Sir Robert Peel's Government, and ensure for himself some other employment when his term expires here."[35]

Thus the stage had been set for a violent clash between Howe and Falkland, and it became all but inevitable when Howe, now without employment, concluded an arrangement with Annand by which, early in May, he took over the major responsibility for the editorial direction of the *Novascotian*, and its accompanying tri-weekly, the *Morning Chronicle*, which Annand had established in January to give the Reformers of Halifax the advantages of a penny press.[36] Howe left no doubt about his eagerness to be back. For three and a half years, he said, he had lost his identity; how could it be otherwise when he was "part of a nine stringed instrument, which sometimes produced harmony and sometimes discord, but in which there was no clear ringing tone, neither modified nor subdued." Now, "like the lark, we can rise on our own wing, and pour forth our own strains, rejoicing in a sense of freedom that we have not felt for years." Howe hoped and expected that his readers would say: "why, here is Howe amongst us again, – not Mr. Speaker Howe, not the Hon. Mr. Howe, – but Joe Howe, as he used to be, sitting in his Editorial chair, and talking to us about politics, and trade, and agriculture – about our own country, and other countries, making us laugh a good deal, but think a good deal more, even while we were laughing."[37]

What, basically, would he try to do as editor? Reflecting his earlier fears of political parties, he did not want – like Nugent – to reduce "the liberal party to a solid compact body of fighting men, armed and disciplined after the most approved fashion, and driving all the loose fish into the opposite ranks." To do that would be to forget that the qualities which made a Liberal forbade too rigid an adherence to party discipline or that "the Battle of Bannockburn was half won by the camp followers." But Howe did want to "rouse, to inform, to organize, the 200,000 People who compose the Liberal party; ... to make their voices heard, not only in the Legislative Halls, but also in the Councils of their Country, with a weight and authority that cannot be misunderstood."[38]

However high-intentioned Howe's opening editorial appeared to be, he had clearly concluded that not only the Tory clique but Falkland himself would pay for the campaign of "executive defamation" between December and April. Not only had writers in the *Post* made all sorts of insinuations about his loyalty, but an army surgeon "who had long been a sort of upper servant about Government House [had] commenced the war" in the New York *Albion* under the signature of "Scrutator."[39] Both Howe and Annand took the position that Falkland must accept the responsibility for what his close associates wrote and for what Crosskill printed in the *Post* as well as in the *Royal Gazette*. "The Government had the command and the direction of both. If a person kept a Brothel, and a Boarding House, under the same roof, and if the former was a nuisance to the neighbourhood, could those who frequented, and patronized, and encouraged the Proprietor, plead that they were only accountable for what was done in a single suite of apartments? I think not – and, acting on this principle, I have claimed my right to hold the Lieut. Governor personally responsible for all the defamation published ... by his paid official servant."[40] Chester Martin has suggested that in the process Howe "coarsened his nature,"[41] but if that occurred at all, it took place earlier, since Howe went to no greater extremes after May 1844 than in the letters of "a Constitutionalist" two years earlier. In 1842 he had hearkened to Falkland's pleas that someone save him from the ultras; in 1844 the excesses of the ultras, apparently committed with the governor's approval, induced him to make Falkland the recipient of similar attacks.

The governor's friends objected most to the "torrent of pasquinades and lampoons" directed against him. The first of these effusions, "The Lord of the Bed-chamber," appeared in the *Novascotian* on May 20 as part of a deliberate plan to show Falkland's friends that there were "some wit and humour on the opposite side" and that "they were not to have a monopoly of the elegant manufacture of political pasquinade."[42] Basically the poem outlined the perplexities and conflicting feelings experienced by Falkland and his advisers during the two-week debate on the address in February, and in most respects it was unexceptionable. But the somewhat humourless J.W. Johnston, who sought to turn every lampoon into a state paper,[43] could hardly restrain himself because of the opening line: "The Lord of the Bed-chamber sat in his shirt." Later Howe kept the House in stitches while maintaining that it was not "a grave offence ... to hint that Noblemen wore shirts, ... [certainly not one] to be prosecuted, in the high Court of Parliament, by an Attorney General. Had the Author said that the Lord of the Bedchamber had no shirt, or that it stuck through his pantaloons, there might have been good ground of complaint."[44]

Howe intimated at the time that the papers under his direction would continue to reply in the same kind to the outpourings of the *Post*. Yet there might have been a deescalation of the conflict had it not been for the intrusion of two other incidents. In Crosskill's first months as Queen's printer, the editorial comments on Nova Scotia politics in the *Post* were moderate and deserved none of the criticism that Howe levelled at the correspondents of the same paper. Then in June, as one Ellen Murphy lay dying from the effects of poison, she told her confessor, Father Loughnan, it had been administered by no less a person than John H. Crosskill. By gentlemen's agreement, the newspaper publishers decided not to print the evidence of the coroner's inquest until it was completed, but when Crosskill made an ex parte justification of his conduct in the *Royal Gazette*, Howe published an account of the proceedings to date on the ground that it was a "duty to the public – a duty paramount to all feelings of delicacy."[45] Crosskill cried foul, although a little later he boasted that a jury had vindicated him.[46] When Howe still expressed doubts because it was an all-Protestant, non-Irish jury that gave Crosskill a clean bill of health, the latter lost all inhibitions in dealing with the Reformers, especially after "Veritas" hinted further in the *Acadian Recorder* that he had had disreputable relations with half-a-dozen females.[47] Crosskill promised in his turn to lacerate his assailants until their heart's blood flowed, especially one "who was kicked out of his father's house for seducing one of its inmates" and another "who at this moment keeps a seraglio beneath his mother's own roof."[48]

A second circumstance which kept politics in a highly embittered state occurred in January when Annand printed correspondence which intimated that Andrew McCoubrey, the proprietor of the *Pictou Observer*, had submitted voluntarily to the cutting of his ear in order to present the appearance of a horrible outrage and thus "get up the blood of the Kirk party" against the Reformers.[49] Not unexpectedly, Annand was accused of libel and mulcted in damages. But the trial made a farce of the normal judicial process. It was not so much that the legal counsel in the case were leading members of the political parties, but that, for some devious reason, it was held in Amherst, where the local court officials appear to have rigged the selection of the jury against Annand. Of 312 possible jurors, 226 lived in rural Cumberland and 86 in Amherst, but, as drawn, only two of the jury panel of 48 came from Amherst where the Reformers were strongest. For weeks Howe kept a box containing 226 black beans and 86 white ones in his office, but none who tried the draw came close to a proportion of 46 to 2 and Howe said he put "*more faith in his own box of beans than in the Amherst Jury Box.*"[50]

In these circumstances there could be no let-up in the newspaper war. Thus, in November, when the *Post* published two letters that were highly objectionable to Howe, he replied with a pasquinade in which Falkland complained to Stanley of the straits into which he had got himself:

> I'm sorry to own, yet the fact must be stated,
> The game is all up, and I'm fairly check-mated.
> The Poacher in Chaucer, with goose in his breeches,
> Was betrayed by the neck peeping through the loose stitches;
> And I must acknowledge, unfortunate sinner,
> As my griefs are enlarging, my breeches get thinner;
> And I feel, if I do not soon make a clean breast,
> That, from what you observe, you will guess at the rest.[51]

Howe was amused that "this allusion to his Excellency's breeches, [was] regarded by the Government with as much alarm, as the former reference to the startling fact of his wearing a shirt."[52] But surely, he continued, passages of this kind were not nearly as objectionable as dozens in Shakespeare, Sterne, or Pindar that were to be found in Johnston's own library.

Allegedly the *Post* followed with a "violent and scurrilous attack" on Howe and the Speaker,[53] although on this occasion, as on some others, Howe exaggerated beyond reason the gravity of the offence against him. But whether the *Post* deserved it or not, Howe quickly applied two doses of retaliative medicine, the first of which prescribed "a few grains of 'truth'" for the "administrative scribes" of that paper,[54] and the second, the poem "Pharaoh," made Falkland and Johnston the prime targets:

> King Pharaoh stood within his Hall, and Sycophants were round him,
> Whose oily tongues had render'd him, just twice the fool they found him ...
> The Leader of his host stood by, a Satrap fierce and wily,
> Who hoped on Pharaoh's mad resolve to build his power slyly,

He fanned his rage, and drew him forth, with all
his hosts behind him,
And now, engulphed, o'erwhelmed and lost, the
Chroniclers may find him.[55]

This "barbarous style of warfare" undoubtedly did Howe no good, and Chester Martin may be on strong ground in suggesting that it lost him "the first premiership under responsible government overseas in 1848" and "contributed not a little to fasten upon him the cardinal sin of indiscretion that barred him from the career he coveted beyond his native province."[56] But Howe reacted as he always did to someone like Johnston, whom he regarded as a hypocrite for professing to be horror-stricken at Howe's "coarse ribaldry" and "breaches of decency" after May 6, while conveniently passing over the previous four months of defamation. " .. he can chuckle over lampoons and pasquinades, when they appear in the Government Press – indecency is a virtue, when it raises a laugh at an enemy's expense, and a falsehood is no longer a falsehood, when it makes in favor of his own side."[57] To assess Howe's share of responsibility for this unedifying style of politics, it would be necessary to determine whose was the primary fault for the continuing escalation of the conflict after May 1844, and at what point, if any, Falkland's conduct had passed such bounds that he deserved to be treated simply as another participant in the political struggle. Yet, however improper or unwise his own behaviour may have been, Howe could not have acted differently. Thompson had warned him in 1842 that he had attained such a stature that he owed it to himself to behave with moderation and circumspection in order to preserve his reputation. But in 1844, no less than in 1842, it was simply not in him to resist replying in kind to the provocations of lesser men.

Seeking to get out of an impossible situation, Falkland took steps in July to fill the vacancies in the council. Instead of using an intermediary as in February, he had Provincial Secretary George offer appointments to a moderate Tory, Benjamin Smith, and five Reformers, McNab, Huntington, Uniacke, Brenan, and Tobin, the latter two Catholics.[58] Each letter contained the provisio that Howe was not to be included, apparently because he had committed "the high offence of attacking and laughing at His Excellency and his advisers in the newspapers."[59] While the House would in time debate violently the precise nature of the Reformers' response, Howe maintained that the Liberal caucus would not agree to an increase in the membership of the council, and insisted on a fair share of the council seats, including the reappointment of all the retired councillors.[60] For his part Falkland told Stanley that although he had "reason to know that a great proportion of the opposition look on the demand that I should receive Mr. Howe as unreasonable," they were "unwilling to separate themselves from those with whom they have lately acted."[61] Either he was badly misinformed or he was deliberately seeking to mislead the colonial secretary.

No less brazenly Falkland told Stanley that, because of his rejection of Howe, not only was the latter's influence greatly diminished, but the council had "acquired firmness and stability in the Assembly," and the opposition was exhibiting "a want of concert and determinate action."[62] Obviously Falkland was resorting to deceitfulness in seeking a favourable answer to the crucial question of whether Howe should be offered a councillorship. While he conceded to Stanley that his quarrel with Howe was preventing a juncture of parties that was highly desirable, yet to admit him into the council would make him "de facto Governor of Nova Scotia," and if Stanley thought that course desirable, he would have to name a new governor.[63] Even if Falkland really believed he had strengthened his government, he must have been sorely disillusioned when he toured the province later in the year. Although the Tory county of Queens welcomed him without reservation, the people of Hants, like those of Pictou and Kings, told him unequivocally that "this country can never be peaceful, contented or happy, while those who have been the subtle and intriguing enemies of responsible government and popular rights exclusively surround your Excellency."[64] A little later 1,500 freeholders of Colchester sent him an address stating that "the policy of the administration for many months has been ... injurious to the best interests of Nova Scotia."[65]

With this background, 1845 could not but be a year of Falkland versus Howe, and no matter at what point the debate started it invariably got round to the contentions between the two. Even before the session opened, Falkland told Stanley that the government would introduce no bill on any matter in which an accidental difference of opinion even on some immaterial point might lead to a "most embarrassing" defeat in the assembly and provide ammunition for the "ultra party" throughout the province.[66] At the same time, almost as if to make the session the "stormy and troublous one" he prophesied it would be, he made public the confidential negotiations through which he had hoped to complete the council and his explanation of their failure to the colonial secretary. A most unusual course, it illustrated, as Howe suggested, how blind intemperateness had displaced cool judgment.

It was, in fact, the publication of Falkland's dispatch to Stanley of August 2, 1844,[67] and its comments on the attitude of other

Reformers towards Howe, that produced the unholy row which determined the tenor of the entire session. Chester Martin suggests that the governor's weapon was "aimed at close quarters and with deadly precision at the morale of the Reformers," and that in the end the dispatch "did more perhaps than any other [incident in Nova Scotia] to discredit the whole Russellite theory of governance from Downing Street."[68] Hardly had it been presented to the House when Doyle, Uniacke, Huntington, and G.R. Young were on their feet to deny that the Liberal party had agreed to Howe's exclusion on any conditions. Uniacke stated unequivocally that Howe had "voluntarily offered to waive his claims to a place in the Executive, [but] *the Party would not consent to his being left out, declaring that from his position he ought to be in the Government.*"[69] Howe himself resented the attempt to demean him both in England and Nova Scotia. "An honest fame is as dear to me as Lord Falkland's title is to him – his name may be written in Burke's Peerage, mine has no record, but on the hills and vallies of the country which God has given us for an inheritance, and must live, if it lives at all, in the hearts of those who tread them."[70] The Tories had no ready answer, and the *Novascotian* summed up the situation by asking: "What will the people now say of an Administration that has not only the moral turpitude to deliberately misstate the fact, but the eggregious folly and effrontery to publish to the world what every Member of the Liberal Party in the House knows to be untrue."[71]

Making the dispatches public had the effect of bringing J.B. Uniacke fully and wholeheartedly into the Reform camp. For when the administration moved what amounted to a vote of confidence in Falkland's conduct as it was manifested in the dispatches, Uniacke, who had never before spoken with anything but veneration of the Crown and its representative, proceeded to heap scorn on a governor who could "so far forget his high position as the Representative of Royalty," as to proscribe a single individual and thereby violate the constitution. If Falkland could "with impunity proscribe one man, because he dislikes his politics, he may exclude another because he is not pleased with the contour of his features, or [because] he has not mixed in fashionable circles."[72] In his dispatch Falkland had sought to denigrate the Reformers further by pointing out they had "no acknowledged leader." Hardly had it been made public when Howe rose in the assembly to say: "let there be no mistake about that point hereafter, for the Opposition 'acknowledge' the Honble. and learned member for Cape Breton [i.e., Uniacke] as their leader."[73] He did not divulge how the choice had been made, but he was, in effect, acknowledging that he had forfeited his own chances by his treatment of Falkland.

Howe made his announcement during the thirteen-day debate on a motion of confidence relating to the dispatches that was perhaps the most bitter in the entire history of responsible government in Nova Scotia. Highly excited spectators filled the gallery and the lobby to capacity, and some legislative councillors and military men had to sit behind the members on the floor of the House. In the country there was no less excitement. The residents of Middle Musquodoboit hastened to the post office to pick up the *Novascotian*, elated to discover that Howe had "escaped unscathed from the Goliaths of Government House." The Rev. John Sprott philosophized that, "if a man wishes to get rid of an anthill he can crush it by putting a flat stone on top of it but it is a more difficult business for a Tory Lord to get rid of a band of Patriots."[74]

To the debate Howe made two major and several minor contributions; "it was hard work, but rare fun," he told Jane.[75] Basically he held that the lieutenant-governor should be held "so far above the strife and conflict of party, as to seek only the general good, regardless of likes and dislikes, of personal enmities or predilections." He would not have complained if the calumnies had been showered upon him by an independent party press; indeed, Falkland would have been "untouched by a single pasquinade" if they had not been "conveyed in speeches from the throne, in despatches to the Secretary of State, and by Lord Falkland's physician and official printer." Howe gladly conceded that the governor had "many high qualities of head and heart," but he also had "a host of passions" which the men surrounding him had encouraged and abused. Perhaps his "sage Councillors" had thought "more of revenge than of his honor or the peace of the country."[76]

When the administration carried the day by a vote of twenty-seven to twenty-three, the same majority it had enjoyed in a full House after the defection of Ryder,[77] the *Novascotian* expressed delight that despite all the Tory "lures and wiles, and influence, social and Administrative, [they had] been unable to entice one man from the sturdy band who compose the Constitutional Opposition."[78] Howe was no less pleased that the Reformers had repudiated Falkland's "canard" that they were agreeable to his exclusion, and had done it by "unanimity and ability rarely surpassed by any Colonial opposition."[79] But the *Post* was decidedly unhappy about the hostile reaction of the spectators to the results of the division. As part of the campaign of Howe's foes from the governor down to destroy his credibility in the public eye, it pictured the adherents of Howe and Company accosting the country members "with insulting language – hooting, hissing, and even personal violence. One member was collared, and others rudely cuffed, jostled and taunted, while the Halls of the building resounded with the wild yelpings of the multitude."[80] Throughout the year the same paper kept telling its readers that no future governor would dare admit Howe into his council since he was wont to proscribe all those "who would not become servile tools of the advancement of his public ambition."[81]

The effort to besmirch him proceeded in other directions as well. Tory John Ross of Colchester followed where the *Pictou Observer* left off by condemning his conduct as excise officer, alleging that he had taken more in the way of salary, and kept larger amounts of public funds in his hands than the law permitted.[82] Every now and then the *Post* would depict the indelicate Howe whom decent people ought to shun, using some of Howe's illustrative material that it thought would shock the sensitive ear. In the debate on the dispatches, he had pointed out that some persons extolled a weak government because from it a man might get what he wanted. "The same may be said of a weak woman," he argued, "but surely the strength of virtue and of principle is to be preferred."[83] A little earlier, at a meeting called to protest the Tories' rigging of juries, someone yelled "it was all chance," and drew Howe's rejoinder: "Yes, so the woman said when she lay in of a black child, but her husband was not satisfied, and neither ought we to be, when these black lists, out of all resemblance to justice and fair play were concocted."[84] On each occasion the *Post* was suitably horrified: "for a sage Politician – a dignified Legislator – to employ language from which even the male portion of his audience turned with disgust – throws, indeed, a dark shade over the picture of the proceedings of the current session ... Heaven forbid that these dark spots in the constellations of genius should become the standard for imitation among the Sons, or the choice reading of the Daughters, of Nova Scotia."[85]

The *Post* also reminded its readers of Howe's boon companions, warning them that, if he came to power, "the affairs of Nova Scotia will be gravely debated and disposed of in Joe Jenning's Grocery, or Sam Carten's shoe shop."[86] At another level Howe was attacked for his insistence on violating the honour of the Crown. He had been highly indignant when Sir Rupert George persuaded Stanley to disallow the act which reduced his emoluments as registrar. While Howe did not deny George or any Nova Scotian the right to petition the sovereign, "if any one did so and induced the Crown ... to set his interests above those of the whole people, the representatives of the people under responsible Government ought to withdraw their confidence from that man and from his colleagues in office if they sustained him."[87] Falkland told Stanley that such statements were utterly reprehensible, but in this instance at least Howe had no need to fear the bad opinion of the ordinary Nova Scotian. "Sir, I am compelled to smile when grave Attorneys stand up here and declaim about the vested rights of an individual, as though the whole people had no vested right in economy and justice."[88]

Fearful that Falkland was using the same tactics as his other detractors to destroy his credibility with Stanley, Howe addressed a letter to Charles Buller only a few days after the conclusion of the debate on the dispatches. After explaining that his only offence was "laughing at the Governor, and defending myself and my friends in the newspapers," he asked Buller to find out, if he went to England in the spring, whether Stanley would let him defend himself against the charges that undoubtedly had been laid against him at the Colonial Office.[89] But Buller told him that with the best will in the world he could not be "the medium of any very friendly communication with Ld. Stanley,"[90] because of his recent collision with him on matters relating to New Zealand.

Howe made one serious attempt to show that his Nova Scotian denigrators were at best hypocrites. Perhaps taking undue advantage of Falkland's permission to reveal whatever was necessary to defend himself,[91] he pointed out that after Falkland, his family, and his council had been coarsely assailed in 1842, the governor had called upon someone in council to put an end to it by a little wholesome retaliation, and that, as the letters of "a Constitutionalist" were published, the governor and all the councillors appeared to give them their approbation.[92] Why then should they pretend horror when he performed the same function in 1844 that "a Constitutionalist" had done in 1842? The outcome of Howe's revelations was a series of angry confrontations in the assembly. Dodd threatened Howe menacingly with a large stick, while Johnston deplored the disclosure of the secrets of council and stated that his recollections differed from those of Howe. This induced Howe to go further and say that Falkland had "thanked the author, wherever he was, in the warmest manner, for his services."[93] Despite all their bluster the Tory councillors made no serious attempt to refute him: "Uniacke, McNab and Young declared their readiness to state what they know [if] 'my statement was contradicted,' but [I] thought it unnecessary to make disclosures till it was. [Our foes] did not venture to contradict, and the disclosures were not made."[94] In this instance at least Falkland and Johnston had been hoist with their own petard.

It had been largely a wasted session, and Howe could not resist poking fun at the administration, and especially at Johnston. For over three years, he said, the attorney general had felt "he was too near the tail – he would play 'afterparts' no longer." So for a year "he has thrust himself into the foreparts, and got his brother-in-law in behind, but unfortunately ... there is very little animation in the Elephant, and sometimes it will scarcely move at all."[95] Since Johnston brought down no proposals relating to education and simply referred the subject to a committee, Howe accused him of abrogating the new responsible system: "two whole sessions had passed away, and a third had commenced, but [the administration] had not submitted a single measure by which the House could try them. How were they to be tested if not by their acts?"[96] When Johnston replied that he was dealing with education no differently than the administration of which Howe was a member, the latter retorted that Johnston now headed a government of his own and could therefore bring in legislation based on his own views.[97] But Howe was simply making political points, for none knew better than he that the particularism of the assembly would likewise have prevented him from getting the educational bill he wanted even under a Reform administration.[98]

Violent interchange was at a minimum after prorogation, but hardly had the session of 1846 begun when Howe's foes turned again to attacking his credibility. C.B. Owen, a Tory assemblyman from Lunenburg, initiated the new round by condemning Howe's performance as collector of excise even more strongly than John Ross and the *Pictou Observer* had done earlier. Howe replied that the two commissioners who had taken over his accounts had found no fault with them, nor had the assembly's Committee of Public Accounts, even though it was chaired by a political opponent. To Owen's charge that he kept larger quarterly balances than was permitted, he showed that the law entitled him to hold even larger ones; to the charge that he had received payments for some months at £3 3s. per day instead of the 31s. 8d. a day to which he was entitled, he demonstrated that Owen had not taken into account his payments to clerks and other expenses. Why, he asked, should he be forced to "defend every act of [his] sixteen months tenure of office,"[99] even though he had followed exactly the same procedures as Binney? The answer, as he very well knew, was that he was the protagonist on one side of a barbarous war.

Howe himself was to provide even more powerful ammunition for the Tories' attempt to damage him in the public eye. On February 20 Johnston tabled Falkland's dispatch relating to the two companies that were proposing to build railways from Halifax to Quebec and Windsor, Nova Scotia. It suggested that William and George Young, as colonial solicitors of the two companies, had associated themselves with English speculators of dubious reputation, and had been guilty of "reckless conduct" in publishing prospectuses of these companies which used the names of "some of the most respectable Gentlemen in Nova Scotia" without their authorization.[100] For a governor to have tabled material of this kind was so extraordinary that Gladstone, the colonial secretary in the last months of the Peel administration, suggested to him it must have been an "inadvertence."[101] But Falkland insisted he had done it with deliberate intent as a public duty, since the legislature was pressing for details about the railways. If the mere recital of facts damaged the characters of the Youngs, "the fault is theirs not mine, and such injurious consequences must be attributed solely to the acts recorded." To suggestions that he was simply continuing his vendetta with William Young – he had refused to accord him the civilities normally given the Speaker and declined to recognize him on the street – Falkland simply replied that he was not called upon to account for his distaste for the society of the Messrs Young.[102] Thus personal considerations had come to dominate the gubernatorial conduct of Lord Falkland.

Although the Youngs were not Howe's favourite Reformers, he simply could not contain himself following the tabling of the dispatches. A governor who had previously used the *Royal Gazette* to accuse his ex-councillors of trying to wrest the prerogative from him and of putting forward other unjustified pretensions was now seeking to "damage [the] characters [of those he deemed refractory] by misrepresentation and inuendo under the sign manual."[103] Bursting with indignation, Howe blurted out that "the system pursued [in the dispatch] with respect to individuals, having no means of redress, was infamous, and if persevered in, would leave no course but for some Colonist to hire a black man, to horsewhip a Lieutenant Governor in the Streets."[104] Almost immediately the House adjourned in an uproar.

The next day, behind closed doors, Uniacke proposed that, while the House should record its unqualified disapprobation of language reflecting on the governor, it should also accept Howe's explanation that he was simply denouncing a system, not the governor. But by a straight party vote, with Howe abstaining, it chose to express its "strong censure and disapprobation" of Howe's disrespect for Falkland.[105] The *Post*, delighted with this new evidence of Howe's unworthiness, suggested that his "gross, and yet deliberate outrage" was the culmination of his "riotous revelling in unprincipled demagoguism."[106] In its view "Joseph and His Brethren" were making Nova Scotia more like the United States, where the president had even been threatened with assassination. Because of them, the epithets "liar, traitor, apostate, swindler, villain, scoundrel, the slang of the brothel" were becoming commonplace.[107] Howe's associates, "a worthless set, haunters of the fishmarket purlieus, and commonly designated by the title of 'fish-market sharks'," were continuing to intimidate the representatives of the people.[108] But perhaps, said the *Post* hopefully, Howe had gone a step too far this time since the officers of the garrison had ostracized him and refused to play racquets with him.[109]

Howe did not let his enemies have the field to themselves, the more so because he thought he owed an explanation to his constituents, who had been excluded from the assembly for a day, and whose elected member had been severely rapped over the knuckles. In a lengthy letter to them,[110] he made it clear that above all he wanted to "put an end to a system, unknown in this Colony until 1844 – practiced in no other on this Continent – abhorrent to an Englishman's nature – dangerous to every Colonist." Hitherto, no Nova Scotia governor had included "the names of respectable men, without their knowledge or consent, in Executive communications, of a disparaging and injurious character," and then laid "his own libellous attacks and innuendoes, by the hands of his Executive advisers, upon the tables of both branches of the Legislature." To find an analogy, Howe had to go back to barbarous times in England; indeed, the wealth of English and colonial precedent he used indicated that he had been gathering material for some time to compare Falkland's conduct with that of English monarchs and colonial governors over the years. To those who might accuse him of over-reacting, he said he "wanted to startle – to rouse – to flash the light of truth over every hideous feature of the system," so that hereafter, "whenever ... our rulers desire to grille a political opponent in an Official Despatch, they will recall my homely picture, and borrow wisdom from the past."

Falkland and the *Times* to the contrary,[111] it was an unproductive session, and the governor's woes did not end with prorogation. It was hardly over before he got into controversy because of his appointment of Alexander Stewart as master of the rolls. "Why the idea of it is perfectly ridiculous," complained the *Novascotian*. Unscrupulous as the administration was, surely it would not appoint to that office someone whom the assembly said "enjoys so little of [the] confidence" of the People.[112] But Falkland had to swallow an even more bitter dose of medicine administered by Howe who, while he had no desire to resume warfare with the governor on a personal basis, was no less determined than before to hold him responsible for all the writings of the Queen's printer, whether in his official capacity or otherwise. The renewal of trouble had its origin on March 3, when Crosskill described Howe as "a mendicant place-hunter" in an editorial in the *Post*. Since giving up the Excise Office, Howe was undoubtedly hard up. Although he had simplified and reduced his style of living, he always "required all and more than [he] could scrape together ... [and he] rarely had £10 at his command." Annand gave him what he could towards the purchase price of the *Novascotian*, but bills unpaid for several years and some other "obligations afloat ... take every shilling I get from [him] faster than he can collect it." When faithful John Thompson asked Howe to back a note, he agreed, but told him regretfully to "get some friend whose credit is good to put his name under mine. *Without that, it will be useless to try.*"[113]

Finding Crosskill's epithet particularly provocative in these circumstances, Howe turned again on Falkland,[114] whom he felt needed yet another lesson. Who truly was the place-hunter, he asked. While Falkland had held the governorship for six years at a cost to Nova Scotians of £20,000, he himself had been an office-holder for sixteen months in eighteen years and had received about one-thirtieth of that sum. "Yet your minion reproaches me with place-hunting! forgetting another curious contrast, that I retired with my party, while you held on when your's threw up the reins, and changed your policy that you might hold your 'place'. Pray instruct your minion to think before he writes."[115]

Next Howe asked himself if he was a "mendicant." About the time he was giving up the Excise Office and his opponents were trying to involve him in Nugent's ruin, some Liberal friends in Halifax had offered him an annual allowance equal to the salary of the office he had abandoned. He declined it, but to prove "there was no poor pride at the bottom of the business on my part – to show to those who might perhaps tread my path in future, that the unpurchaseable faith, and open purses of the people, could sustain Colonists against injustice and oppression, I consented to accept a sum, not near so large as I had lost while attending to your Lordship's business instead of my own – and less than some friends of yours have received, for doing almost nothing, year by year, out of the resources of this people, as far back as my memory extends."[116] Had not Nelson, Wellington, and Grattan accepted similar gifts, and could anyone but "a narrow minded sceptic ... imagine that the recipients, in these cases, were 'mendicants'?"[117] If Falkland was looking for a mendicant, why not turn to the Lord Falkland who in 1693 had begged and received £2,000 from His Majesty "*contrary to the ordinary method of issuing and bestowing the King's money*," and was committed to the Tower for the offence. Indeed, "my Lord," concluded Howe, "it strikes me that if you were stripped of what you never earned, we should still have bread, with some to spare to the mendicants over the way."[118]

Possibly Howe protested too much; certainly there is something sanctimonious and self-righteous about the letter. Worse still for him, his opponents could not help noting that he had kept his acceptance of the gift secret for months. Why, asked Crosskill, if the money was honourably given and honourably received, "did he not proclaim a year ago the fact – and not have it extorted from him?" Once again Crosskill suggested that Howe's wages came from a clique in Halifax, whose "ruffian hirelings" assailed the assemblymen within the legislative walls, and who expected to "procure a lucrative place" for Howe and "batten on the spoils" themselves in the event of a Liberal victory.[119] For the next two years the *Post* continued to gibe at the man who "subsisted on the charitable offerings filched from the pockets of the people."[120]

Howe had one last fling at Falkland after Crosskill attributed to him a letter he had never seen and made it the basis of a charge of treason. This time he told Falkland that "a Governor who keeps a reckless creature in pay to defame those whom he happens to hate, will be very apt to create more disaffection than he subdues."[121] After the publication of this letter on April 9 Howe retired from the editorship of the *Chronicle* and the *Novascotian* to "turn up the soil of Musquodoboit," but it was not in him to resist a parting shot at Falkland: "be comforted, I shall not be so far away but that we can 'take sweet counsel' together. I shall be a peaceful agriculturist, no doubt; but, hark ye, my Lord, in order that we may be good friends you had better keep your pigs out of my garden and not attempt to plant tares among my wheat."[122]

Falkland, however, had had enough of it. In May he told the Colonial Office that, although his term would not expire until October, he would like to be relieved earlier since the principal members of his family were in delicate health, and since his successor should have a chance to acquaint himself with the affairs of the province well in advance of the new session.[123] But his undisclosed reasons for wanting to leave early may have been even stronger. Even he would have had to concede that his governorship of Nova Scotia had been a disaster, and month by month his position was becoming more uncomfortable. Further, although a Whig, he had, in his last years as governor, seemed bent on currying the favour of a Tory colonial secretary, and he may have felt he would be in an equivocal position when the tottering government of Sir Robert Peel finally gave way to a Liberal administration. In any case, before mid-August he was gone with few open lamentations on anyone's part. Howe did not note his departure publicly, but Annand, speaking for him, said he was tending his crops, and finding that a little red insect, the weevil, which did not threaten but destroyed, had much greater "powers of mischief ... [than] ... the Nobleman who threatened a great deal, but could not destroy."[124] Privately Howe told the Newfoundland Reformer John Kent that, because of Falkland, he recognized "at their true value, some sneaking dogs that I should have been caressing for years to come."[125]

This was a small return for more than two years of nastiness that was quite uncongenial to Howe's nature. Of it he grew no less tired than Falkland. But in his case he also attempted constructive work along several lines which he hoped would contribute towards an eventual Reform victory. While the squibs, pasquinades, lampoons, and other writings which he directed towards the governor between 1844 and 1846 drew the most attention and evoked the strongest reaction, he mingled these works with articles containing "trenchant arguments of another sort"[126] which showed he had lost none of his old art. Typical of these productions in 1844 were the series "Provincial Politics" and "The Government Scribes," where, in one article, he wrote that the prerogative was "not like an Irishman's shilellah at a fair, shaking every five minutes in every body's face, but like the electric fluid in the cloud, reserved for great occasions and blasting where it fell."[127]

More significant than either his pasquinades or his other literary endeavours during the "war to the knife" were the speeches aimed at preventing Falkland from turning the clock back and nullifying the gains he had earlier helped the Reformers to make. The longstanding question of the tenure under which departmental heads held office was the predominant theme of these speeches. In May 1845 Charles Wallace, the provincial treasurer, defaulted to the extent of thousands of pounds. Although Wallace had been the beneficiary of the hereditary transmission of offices – he had succeeded his father Michael Wallace as treasurer – Falkland took the position that the province would suffer if the treasurer held a seat in the assembly and if his tenure depended on his belonging to a party having a majority in the House. In his opinion, if government was to be carried on through heads of departments, new offices would have to be created, all of which was contingent on the dubious proposition that the assembly would be willing to pay the holders of these offices adequately.[128] Almost as if to show his contempt for the Reformers' demands that the heads of departments should sit in and be responsible to the assembly, he required S.P. Fairbanks to resign his seat before he appointed him treasurer. While the letter of appointment described Fairbanks's tenure as one during pleasure, it also assured him that in practice his tenure would be that of a judge, and not dependent upon political fluctuations and the change of parties.[129]

To Howe this was a challenge to everything for which the

Reformers had contended. In granting tenure for life to the provincial treasurer, Falkland was perpetrating an act that would have been fatal to responsible government as known in Britain and as practically introduced into Canada. Howe saw it as another instance of Falkland's change of position. Had he not requested the treasurer and surveyor general in 1841 to get seats in the assembly? Had he not appointed Howe collector of excise in 1842 on the same conditions? "The last blow at the Responsible system, will doubtless be followed by others ... This time the work must not be done by halves. The Liberals must neither faint nor wax weary."[130]

No sooner had the session of 1846 begun than the Tory J.J. Marshall of Guysborough sought to expand the practice which Falkland had introduced with the appointment of Fairbanks. His so-called disqualification bill, which required the exclusion from the legislature of any officer connected with the Customs, Excise, and Post Office Departments, produced the most acrimonious debate of the session for a two-week period between February 4 and 18. In it Howe assumed the role of Nova Scotia nationalist rather than loyal Briton. Indignant because L.M. Wilkins had pictured the provincial constitution as the work of a colonial secretary, he insisted that "our Constitution was worked out on the floor of this House – by the conflict of Colonial opinion – by the energy and sagacity of Nova-Scotians themselves, aided by a combination of circumstances in the other Colonies."[131] He was equally annoyed at Wilkins's assertion that he would be unable to stand five minutes under the lash of the "chief gladiator of the Imperial lists," Lord Stanley. "Sir, I respect Colonial Secretaries and Members of Parliament, but I abhor the spirit of tuft hunting toadyism, which leads some persons to seek for infallible wisdom under a Coronet, and to undervalue every thing in our own Country, and to worship what comes from abroad."[132]

On the bill itself Howe argued, as usual, that it struck a blow against the operation of the new system as conceded by Russell, Sydenham, and Falkland himself, and especially against responsible government by heads of departments. But he did admit to Johnston that he had nothing to show in writing that he had accepted the collectorship of excise as a head of department responsible to the legislature,[133] and he knew all too well that the Reformers were fighting a rearguard action without any chance of success, since this was the type of measure in which all the Tories could coalesce. This time at least Falkland could boast about the defeat, by twenty-seven to twenty, of those who wished to "place all the offices in the Colony at the disposal of a temporary majority in the elective branch of the legislature and to supersede all efficient supervision or control on the part of either the local or imperial authorities."[134]

But in a second confrontation relating to the public officers Howe, not Falkland, had the last laugh. Fortified by a dispatch from Stanley stating that he would consider no proposals for the surrender of the casual and territorial revenues unless they dealt satisfactorily with the question of arrears,[135] Johnston proposed that the assembly provide the £7,800 owing to the public officers. Unlike the disqualification bill, however, this was not a question of some abstract principle of government, but one which involved the expenditure of funds that were normally spent on roads. Further, if Cape Breton reverted to independent status as it was trying to do, the peninsula of Nova Scotia would have had to assume the full burden of arrears, while giving up half of the casual revenues that came from Cape Breton. Accordingly some Tories would have none of Johnston's proposal, and when a moderate Tory, Benjamin Smith of Hants, moved, and Howe seconded, a resolution to let the matter remain in abeyance while the status of Cape Breton remained unsettled,[136] Johnston had no choice but to acquiesce. Naturally the *Times* lamented that some of the "loose gentlemen" who supported the government could have been deluded so easily,[137] but Howe put it simply: "Why did Lord Falkland not carry his arrears the other day? Because three or four plain country gentlemen refused to sustain his Government."[138] All that Falkland could do was to ask the colonial secretary to honour the commitment respecting his own salary and see that he was paid the £1,900 owing to him.[139] Meanwhile Howe was rubbing salt into the governor's wounds by getting the House to agree that in appointing new officers Falkland should stipulate that their salaries were to be those provided by the Civil List Act of 1844 which the Reformers had approved, but which was rejected in Britain. Undoubtedly it was useful for Howe to keep the Reformers' position on these matters before the assembly and the public with a view to implementing them in more favourable times. But incontestably his most important work in the years of "war to the knife" was his almost single-handed effort to marshal the Liberals into a force that could win the next election.

CHAPTER EIGHTEEN

"There Will Be Corn in Egypt Yet"

Late in 1844, with an election still three to four years away, Howe did some testing of public opinion of his own. In visits to more than a dozen places from Wilmot to Amherst, his normal routine was to "ride forty to fifty miles on horseback, address three meetings in a day, and attend a public dinner, or a country ball or party in the evening."[1] As usual, he found it exhilarating to joust with Johnston in Annapolis, Wilkins in Hants, Ross in Colchester, and Stewart in Cumberland; as usual, he boasted that the Liberal party "as elsewhere, embraces the sturdy independence and agricultural wealth of the country ... The traders and attorneys and officials, or a majority of them, may be against us, but the sturdy yeomanry, the real aristocracy are with us."[2] Everywhere he emphasized that, if the ethos of the political system was to be changed, the middle-class men who composed the backbone of the party would have to be permitted to exercise their talents in government. "Make public offices heirlooms, and the intellect which should be found in the service of the Government is at once arrayed against it; give them life tenures, and one generation must pass away before the ambitious have anything to aspire to, or a nation anything to bestow."[3]

Delighted with his reception, Howe told Jane that after four months of doubts about which way the struggle was going to go, the shadows, clouds, and darkness had dissipated. "My countrymen are with me, and for aught else I care not – with me as unanimously and affectionately as in 1836 or 1840, and are conducting themselves with a spirit and intelligence which will entitle them still to take rank in advance of all British America." Having spent "the flower of [his] days in teaching them" and thrown away his living to set them an example, he confessed it would have broken his heart to "find them giving [him] up for any Lord in Christendom." Even though the government might stagger on for a session or two, "the first appeal to the People will set all to rights ... *The waters have risen and there will be corn in Egypt yet.*"[4]

Occasionally, over the next three years, Howe's exuberance would change to disgruntlement, especially if he believed he was being allowed to carry on the party battle single-handedly. When he withdrew from the council, the administration had a majority of only two with Young in the chair, and he thought in terms of defeating it on a vote of nonconfidence. Even the defection of John Ryder of Argyle left him not without hopes. But they were completely dashed in April 1845 when, because of the Reformers' failure to contest a Pictou seat they had won in 1843, they were confronted with an adverse majority of six.[5] What ruffled Howe was not so much the loss of the seat as the manner of losing it. The administration had sent "Sammy" Cunard to Pictou as its emissary, and somehow or other he had persuaded the Liberals to abandon the contest for a few magistrates and road commissioners. Howe told a leading Pictou Liberal that it was "a poor truckling compromise with the enemy," which would "damage the ... Party more than half a dozen defeats ... Suppose your Boy [was] bullied and patted and struck in the street, what would you think if he agreed to lay down in the gutter, and for three sticks of molasses candy let his adversary kick him without resistance?"[6]

Soon recovering his equanimity, Howe began to plan his overall strategy for winning the next general election. Since nineteen of the twenty-six Tory members had been returned in Queens, Lunenburg, and the four counties of the Baptist belt, all in reasonably close proximity to Halifax, he decided to concentrate his effort there. His activities to that end began innocently enough in July 1845, when the residents of Lawrencetown, Annapolis county, paid him a "special compliment," which turned out to be a love feast: a two-hour speech by Howe, a series of laudatory resolutions, and a dinner at Hall's Inn with "fine salmon from the neighbouring streams, and strawberries from the neighbouring mountains."[7] Later there were similar festivities at Digby and Lower Granville, and on his way homeward at Cornwallis and Falmouth.

At Cornwallis he spoke to 1,500 persons for four hours, and after partaking of "viands ... of most generous proportions," he was at his felicitous best in proposing a toast to the ladies. Germany, he said, might have its Drachenfels, Scotland its mountains, France its vineyards, and England its busy marts, but "he could place the girls of his own wild Country beside those of any portion of the globe ... He would not undertake to decide the question whether King's County was, or was not, the garden of Nova Scotia, but he had never seen a garden graced with so many exquisite flowers."[8] At Falmouth he "roasted" the absent Tory members, L.M. Wilkins and Elkanah Young, who, if Falkland had requested it, would have met him "up to their necks on a mudflat ... on their hands and knees, with the most abject servility; but they could not meet a body of plain farmers, their neighbours and constituents, when courteously invited."[9]

On October 1 Howe returned to Hants County for a public confrontation with Wilkins at the courthouse in Windsor.[10] After Wilkins had talked more than three hours, the crowd would hear him no further and he departed in high dudgeon; in his reply Howe exulted that Falkland's proscription, instead of crushing him, had given him "additional strength," while the man who proscribed him could hardly "find a corner of the Province in which the act could be justified, or the policy of his Government could be sustained."[11] By this time the *Post* had got the wind up about the success of Howe's meetings and it kept assuring its readers that they were a "*dead failure*," that Howe had got a "meagre reception" and "disgusted what few good friends he had."[12] Laughingly Howe replied that he did not fear to go single-handedly into the country to agitate, while Johnston "never stirs without being attended by a bevy of [Baptist] clergymen."[13]

By then he was off to the South Shore counties of Shelburne, Queens, and Lunenburg. In the first two there was the usual flurry of meetings and dinners, but they were not of special interest to him since the former was Liberal, the latter Tory, and both were likely to remain so. Primarily he was concerned with Lunenburg, even though he had been advised not to go there because its people "venerated Tories as some of the heathen nations reverence the Ape." But a leading Liberal of the county, Dr Slocumb, had told him the Tory grip was weakening, and Howe put it up to the Lunenburgers: "Does the old German blood lose its generous and ennobling qualities when it circulates through a Nova-Scotian's veins? Have you the industry, the frugality, the honesty of fatherland, yet lack its love of light – its patriotic ardour – its aspirations after knowledge – its devotion to rational liberty? Forbid it heaven! The German an enemy to free discussion! That would be strange indeed."[14] So favourable was the reaction that Howe told Jane there was "no county in which my popularity is higher or more universal than in Lunenburg,"[15] and he made it a key county in his planning for the election to come.

Late in November Howe closed "the agitation" with a meeting in Mason's Hall in Halifax. In all, he had attended twenty-three public gatherings and eleven dinners in eight counties, and except for

Annapolis he would not write off any of them. But while it was exciting and he would "fight the battle through till after the elections," he was tired and had "an intense desire to shake himself clear of the melee."[16] He felt much the same way when, in the spring of 1846, he departed for Musquodoboit. He had spent two years, with little relaxation, in what often seemed to him a one-man fight against the government. Irritated in all sorts of ways by members of his own party, he released in one fell swoop his pent-up feelings to his friend, John Leishman, a Liberal organizer in Halifax.[17]

What, he asked, had happened in the twenty-seven-month period since he retired from the council? While he had written quires in support of the Reformers' views, not a Liberal assemblyman, other than Doyle and Young, had written a line. When Crosskill came under attack, Johnston led the defence; but when he himself was assailed for his editorials, not one Liberal defended him, and "several timidly declared they never wrote in Newspapers." When Falkland insulted the Speaker and himself, the Liberal assemblymen showed their sympathy by going to dine with him. Although the Reformers were honest, well-meaning people, they were seeking to "capture [the] Sepulchre, with good intentions," not realizing they had to "deal with pagans, who while they trust in the Prophet, know the value of close ranks, discipline and chain mail." Why should he exert himself almost beyond endurance when everyone else did what seemed right in his own eyes, or did nothing, or did worse. "You know what Nelson felt, when serving under Parker in the North – you know what a Spaniard feels when abandoning an ill-regulated Army in the plain, and taking to the hills, he becomes a guerilla. I obey the signals, *when they are hoisted* – I still stick in the Army in the plain, but I must confess I am heartily sick of the service."

At Musquodoboit he soon recovered his equanimity. In taking over the vacant William Annand farm he hoped not only to obtain more time for rest and thought but also to cut down his living costs until the next election determined his future course of action. But his new vocation had other benefits too. "Hard work was devilish hard at first, but I stuck to it till the body hardened and fatigue was overcome, and since the commencement of haying and harvest, I have worked like a laborer." Susan Ann and the children – Edward had apparently left home to make his own way, but there were still six of them: Ellen, sixteen; Mary, fourteen; Joseph, twelve; Frederick, six; Sydenham, three; and John, two – were no less happy in the new environment. "We have all learnt more in two months than we would have picked up in the hurry of town life in two years, and the blessed long quiet winter evenings are still before us." Events in Halifax seemed to become remote and inconsequential; "the squabbling politicians in town afford us a laugh once in a while – their hopes, and fears, and expectations, just now are very amusing."[18]

Howe emerged from his country seat with reluctance and only on special occasions. Keeping his promise to give "Charlie" Owen his come-uppance for his accusations relating to the Excise Office, he boarded the packet *Sylph* for Lunenburg in mid-June 1846, in company with Nugent who was now editing the *Sun*. The reader's view of the confrontation would have depended upon whether he subscribed to the *Sun* or the *Post*. Nugent boasted that Howe had demolished Owen with the approval of the crowd;[19] Crosskill called "the whole affair ... a piece of arrant humbug and political trickery."[20] Late in September, in response to repeated requests from the eastern counties, Howe left Musquodoboit by horse, again accompanied by Nugent, for speaking engagements at Sherbrooke, Guysborough, Antigonish, Barney's River, Merigomish, and the East River of Pictou. At the last place Kirkmen who had been taught to "believe that Joe Howe was only another name for the Devil [listened] with deep interest."[21] Everywhere Howe used the old familiar topics, but adapted them with Scottish variations and illustrations; in all, it was 300 miles, six speeches and, according to Nugent, "spirit and confidence infused into the Liberals in each district visited."[22]

From Musquodoboit, early in the summer of 1846, Howe had noted with interest the appointment, as successor to Falkland, of the soldier Sir John Harvey, who had previously shown tact and good sense as governor of Prince Edward Island, New Brunswick, and Newfoundland. Chosen by Gladstone, the colonial secretary, in the closing days of the Peel administration, Harvey was not highly regarded by Buller, who conceded to Howe, nonetheless, that the new governor was "prudent ... *civil* ... [and] not likely to commit himself to any party or individuals in opposition to public opinion."[23] Perhaps, as Chester Martin suggests, Harvey might have gone the way of Campbell and Falkland if the Tories had stayed in office in Britain, but in July Lord John Russell finally replaced Peel as prime minister.[24] Russell had, of course, personally opposed party government in the colonies and favoured the kind of coalition that Sydenham and Falkland had instituted. Harvey had followed a similar course in New Brunswick and Newfoundland, and even before he came to Nova Scotia he had met Dodd and discussed the best way of reinstituting coalition government.[25] Could he, like Sydenham, turn Howe from the business of polarizing the political forces of the province which had been the main focus of his political activity since 1844?

The debate between Howe and the Tory press on men and events in Canada during the previous two years left the distinct impression that Howe might still be open to the persuasive talents of a Sydenham. Late in November 1843 Baldwin and La Fontaine had demanded that the governor general, Sir Charles Metcalfe, make no appointment without seeking the advice of his council or offer one that was prejudicial to their influence. Metcalfe refused to be "prostrated ... at their feet" or reduced to a "nullity," as he put it, and was left without an Executive Council. Again playing the part of the conservative reformer, Howe blurted out that the Canadian Reformers had "bungled the business," and although he may have appeared to make "amends handsomely"[26] in a letter to Hincks printed in the Montreal *Pilot*, he still felt that the Canadians were "acting unwisely" in pressing "the theory [relating to appointment] to an inconveniently strict definition."[27]

The *Post* immediately took up the cry that Falkland's troubles began because he refused a similar "stipulation" by the Nova Scotia Reformers about the manner in which patronage was to be distributed.[28] "*No such demand was ever made here*," replied Howe, "*none was ever dreamt of ...* We left [the government] ... because the *Attorney General* had 'demanded' the appointment of his brother-in-law to both Councils, as a public and unequivocal declaration of '*confidence in himself*,' involving our complete 'nullification' as politicians, if we submitted to it."[29] Howe continued to insist that, unlike the Canadians, the Nova Scotia Reformers were prepared to engage in give-and-take dealings with the governor: "Responsible government is ... as simple as matrimony, but those husbands and wives get on the best, who respect each others rights and say as little as possible about them."[30] Would he be willing to agree to that kind of accommodation in his dealings with Harvey in 1846?

A similar question emerged from the debate between Howe and the *Post* on the relative merits of Falkland and Metcalfe. In mid-1844 Howe pictured Falkland as "not a very wise, but a choleric man," who had "got things into a mess," and contrasted him unfavourably with Metcalfe who, if he were the man Howe took him for, could bring all the politicians of Canada into line with "a little tact – and good temper" on their part.[31] Later the Canadian Reformer Adam Fergusson sought to make Howe see Metcalfe in a different light, as "a benevolent kind man with *certain* views of *liberality to boot*," but who was also "selfwilled and quite ignorant of what is due to a Govt, founded upon a representation of the People," and who was shamelessly sacrificing the business of Canada to "keep together one of the most imbecile and heterogeneous cabinets, that ever a country was cursed with."[32] Nonetheless, Howe continued to compare Metcalfe and Falkland to the latter's disadvantage. Whereas Metcalfe had governed a large province with dignity and success, Falkland had failed completely after violating Sydenham's policy and substituting one of his own; although both had quarrelled with their ministers, Metcalfe had explained his policy to the country, and got a clear working majority and a complete cabinet, whereas Falkland's council remained incomplete; finally, unlike Falkland, Metcalfe had not forced out the Queen's printer that he might hire a creature to defame his opponents.[33]

The *Post* was partly right in labelling Howe's presentation as a minimum of facts "with a very nicely laid covering of sophistry."[34] It was particularly amused when Hincks accused him of aiding and abetting Metcalfe's supporters by contending that Falkland resembled Metcalfe no more than an elephant did a giraffe.[35] Yet Howe still refused to give ground; possibly Metcalfe and Falkland might be "'rowing' in the same boat, but we must confess we doubt that fact. We fancy the boats are going in different directions."[36] Most of Howe's vehemence may be attributed to his animus against Falkland, as great perhaps as he exhibited towards any man. Nonetheless, his general position still seemed to suggest that he might be open to persuasion by a governor possessing tact and good will.

Yet the situation had altered substantially in 1846 when, in Chester Martin's words, Harvey explored "for the last time the barren subtleties of a coalition."[37] With the return of the Whigs to office in Britain, the Nova Scotia Reformers, using Charles Buller as liaison officer, were "perfecting their historic alliance with the British Durhamites, now in the Colonial Office," where Lord Grey, Durham's son-in-law, served as colonial secretary. Already Buller and Howe were exchanging letters which would predetermine "not only the general principles but the tactics in detail for the impending change."[38] Some of Howe's friends urged him not to turn down a coalition lightly. John Kent, who had become enamoured of Harvey during his stay in Newfoundland, told Howe that "coalitions even in Britain are becoming less objectionable; and in my humble opinion for the successful working of the principle of responsibility, they are absolutely necessary in the Colonies."[39] But Howe, thinking only in terms of an early election, wrote to Leishman from Musquodoboit, wondering if Harvey might dissolve the legislature and urging the Liberal Executive Committee to put the party organization in order.[40]

Having ascertained that Johnston would not oppose a coalition, Harvey turned to Howe, Doyle, and George Young, suggesting that the "distracted" state of political affairs in Nova Scotia was due "far more to Personal than to Political Causes," and expressing the hope that he might "make [himself] both a mediator & a moderator between the influential of all Parties & by inducing them to meet occasionally at [his] Table gradually to soften down asperities."⁴¹ An immediate dissolution, he argued, would not only be fatal to his eventual objective of a coalition, but would also force him to depart from one of his basic principles of not letting himself be identified with any one party. Doyle and Young disagreed that the differences in the parties rested on personalities rather than principle. Nova Scotian parties, they told him, were divided basically by "a struggle for the establishment of certain constitutional rights," and to establish a coalition would "create a disbelief in the principles and virtues of public men."⁴²

Next it was Howe's turn. On the day he was to see Harvey, September 14, he received an advance memorandum from the governor accompanied by a note addressing him as "my excellent and talented friend." This, his "first communication ... from Government House after [his] 'proscription' and banishment therefrom," so elated him that he noted the fact on the document itself.⁴³ But the interview, though friendly enough, changed none of Howe's thinking; indeed, most of his reply may have been written beforehand since it was ready the next day. While he agreed that the governor's benevolent example might reduce the evils resulting from social and political proscription, it would not touch the basic difficulties. "Political principles, and the rights of vast bodies of people, are involved in the present struggle. For any man to abandon, or sacrifice these, after a ten year's contest is to declare himself infamous, and to earn the character of an apostate and a deserter."⁴⁴

Howe also made it clear that the Reformers could not tolerate the state of affairs as it existed. If the Tories reconstructed and completed the council, there would be no complaint; if they could not, "they ought to retire, and get out of your Excellency's way," or at least there should be an election. But if the council carried on as it was, there would be "a stormy session, fruitless of good measures"; the governor would be supported by every Tory and opposed by every Liberal; and "many warm hearts, ready to aid you at the present moment, may be chilled or estranged."⁴⁵ Clearly Howe had become so impatient for a dissolution that he was making demands that could not be justified by the practices of the British constitution. Harvey was right that he ought not to dissolve until his council requested it, but because Howe argued the point so strongly, he left the decision to the colonial secretary.⁴⁶

Not content to seek a dissolution only through Harvey, Howe also sought one indirectly through Buller. "If you have, as I suppose, influence with Earl Grey, request him to dissolve our House, and you will have no more of troubles in Nova Scotia for the next four years."[47] Chester Martin noted, perhaps with some surprise, that Howe's "casual suggestion" was taken "very seriously" in England,[48] but the fact is that Howe was deadly serious, and both Grey and Buller knew it. Grey told Harvey that, while he ought not to identify himself with any party, he should give his council his full support and make sure that any transfer of power was "the result not of any act of yours but the wishes of the people themselves."[49] For his part Buller read Howe a lecture on constitutional practice. Harvey, he said, could dissolve Parliament against the advice of his ministers only in the most extreme circumstances, and had no choice but to let them carry on unless they were defeated in the assembly. "And to you it is of paramount importance that the ordinary practice of Responsible Govt. should be rigidly respected." Even if the Reformers had to await the result of an election, that in itself would be "a recognition of the Principle of Responsible Govt."[50]

Just as Howe had seen fit to enlighten Lord John Russell concerning the mysteries of colonial government when the latter was colonial secretary, so he now thought it best, as a form of insurance, to expand his earlier work for the benefit of Russell the prime minister. Accordingly, after the harvest was in, he took time off to compose two further letters – "a little work"[51] he called it. The first paid tribute to Russell's dispatches of 1839 for providing the theory for a "new and improved constitution." Since then the colonies had moved steadily towards self-government through precedent based on British conventions and customs; so should it continue. "You have no Act of Parliament to define the duty of the Sovereign when ministers are in a minority; we want none to enable us to suggest to a Governor when his advisers have lost the confidence of our colonial Assemblies. But what we do want, my Lord, is a rigid enforcement of British practice, by the imperial authorities, on every Governor; the intelligence and public spirit of the people will supply the rest."[52]

In the second letter Howe gave free rein to his imagination. Now that the internal constitutions of the colonies would soon be regulated satisfactorily, British statesmen should see to it that the colonies were "indissolubly incorporated as integral portions of the glorious British Empire"[53] lest their citizens be deprived of the opportunities that were open to the citizens of Britain and the United States. "The Boston boy may become President; ... The young native of Halifax or Quebec can never by anything but a member of an Executive Council, with some paltry office, paid by a moderate salary."[54] The remedy was to permit colonials to be elected to the British Parliament and to be employed in the Colonial Office. "My father left the old colonies at the

Revolution, that he might live and die under the British flag. I wish to live and die under it too; but I desire to see its ample folds waving above a race worthy of the old banner and of the spirit which has ever upheld it ... We must be Britons in every inspiring sense of the word."[55]

The letters finished, Howe became their publicist and propagandist. For the moment he concentrated on Britain, sending them to the *Times* because of "its immense circulation and influence," and asking Buller to offer them to the *Morning Chronicle* if "the thunderer" failed to publish them.[56] He told Grey that his principal object was to "vindicate the system originally propounded by your lamented and distinguished relative [Durham]," and do justice to Russell's earlier policy which had paved the way for further improvements.[57] To Buller he was very frank. "The men who drove the old Colonies to separation, thought Jefferson, and Franklin and Washington, very inferior to the merest drivellers by which they were surrounded, and now we suppose the prevailing idea, at home is, though 'there were giants in those days,' the race is extinct. God send them all more wisdom – if this Whig Government disappoints us, you will have the questions I have touched discussed in a different spirit, ten years hence, by the Enemies of England, not by her friends."[58]

But "this Whig government" was not to disappoint him, for his letter to Buller crossed in the mails Grey's dispatch to Harvey of November 3, which "marked a turning point from the old Empire to the new Commonwealth by conceding *self-government* not only to Nova Scotia but to the other North American provinces as well."[59] While Harvey was told to give "all fair and proper support to [his] Council for the time being," he was to remember, above all, that it was "neither possible nor desirable to carry on the Government of any of the British Provinces in North America in opposition to the opinions of the inhabitants."[60] Howe would not know the exact contents of the dispatch until 1848, but Buller assured him that Grey had "impressed on Sir John Harvey the fullest adoption of the principle of Responsible Govt.," and that neither the influence of Falkland nor anyone else in Britain could turn the clock back. "Ld. Grey's good intentions you may rely on. I do not think that even Ld. Stanley in his place could thwart you: but even if he could, depend upon it he has no chance of being in a position to molest you."[61] Perhaps Buller was most elated that Howe and his friends had stood "so firm against the Lt. Govrs. notion of a Composite Ministry. These Military statesmen think such Ministries the strongest, & the most useful instruments for themselves – not knowing that Coalitions always damage all engaged to them, & fail all who lean on them."[62]

Luckily for Howe, J.B. Uniacke was absent in England and learning of events in Nova Scotia only through Howe's letters. In a reply which threw a great deal of light upon the man who had been drawn almost unwillingly into the Reform party, and who was still dubious about the workability of party government in a small colony, Uniacke wondered, since Harvey did not want a council of one party, if he "ought ... to be pressed too closely on [a] point which will require a long time to work so as to be acceptable to the people." Would it not be sufficient to humiliate Johnston by forcing him to sit at the same board with the men he had forced out in 1843? But Uniacke admitted to no strong feelings on this point, promised to "keep these sentiments to himself," and wanted only a triumph over the party "who planned and endeavored to work out the dirty intrigue of 1843."[63] As he knew all too well, he led the Reformers in name only and the decision was not his to make.

By the third week in November everyone in Halifax knew there would not be a dissolution and the government press hailed the news with delight. When the *Novascotian* suggested that "the Harts never panted for the water brooks more ardently than do the Tories, just now, for another Coalition,"[64] the *Times* willingly admitted it, contending that "a coalition to prevent the evils that flow from the indulgence of party spirit, should be the object of all good men."[65] Moaning that "no measure of general utility can be passed ... in the present distracted state," the *Post* also called for a coalition, not "for our own sakes, but for the sake of the country."[66] It was too late, however, for, as Howe told John Kent, "the time for seduction, intrigue, and splitting of parties after the French fashion, has gone by in Nova Scotia." Unless public exigencies created a need for a coalition, and unless there was a likelihood its members could act in good faith towards each other, he wanted none of it. "... a Governor who attempts to compel men who cannot eat together, and who are animated by mutual distrust, to serve in the same Cabinet, and bullies them if they refuse, is mad. A Coalition, like a marriage, may turn out well, if there is mutual forbearance, respect, and singleness of view, but if the woman be 'taken in adultery,' surely the person who performs the ceremony, has no right to horse-whip the man for refusing to live with her again."[67]

With that, Howe was off to Musquodoboit, hoping to remain there until the General Assembly opened in January. But he reckoned without Harvey, who justified his further intervention by that section of Grey's letter which stated he could appropriately call on the Executive Council to fill its vacancies. Nothing suited the council more, since it was anything but sanguine about the results of the next election. It told Harvey that it had deliberately left the vacancies unfilled to "evince the principle" of non-party government, and that it was quite willing to "unite at the Council Board with gentlemen who bear a different Party name" than was attributed to the present councillors. Furthermore, to promote that union, Almon would resign from the Executive Council and Dodd give up the solicitor-generalship.[68]

Meanwhile Harvey was seeking a closer rapport with Howe. On December 3 he told him that he had received "a Communication from England which I should have been glad to shew you."[69] Six days later he complimented Howe for his letters to Russell, saying he had made similar proposals about the year 1830, and agreeing that Howe's views on colonial representation in Parliament were "perfectly reasonable & deserving of the favorable consideration of the Home Government."[70] The next day, December 10, he informed Howe he was finally in a position to "make a distinct proposition to the Leaders of your Party," and hoped to see him at his convenience.[71] Howe had been playing coy about returning to Halifax, but he now had no choice, and on December 15 and 16 he was busy consulting his political friends about their attitude to coalition and the governor's proposals. When he and William Young approached Harvey for clarification on the second day, he learned that the Reformers could have four councillorships and Howe the new office of inspector of accounts. Stating unequivocally that he would accept no office created for his own advantage, Howe asked to have it confirmed that the Tory councillors were agreeable to his readmittance to council. Later in the day a shocked Harvey told him that, after three months of assurance to the contrary, he had found there were personal objections to him, but that he hoped to remove them quickly. Whatever his form of persuasion, he succeeded almost at once,[72] and on December 17 he was awaiting Howe's answer. The Reformers, who had at no time taken his proposals seriously and were simply seeking a way to let him down easily, declined his offer the same day.

Yet Harvey should have known there could be no other outcome. The Reformers' answer, described by Chester Martin as "a master-piece of advocacy,"[73] contended that to let them share the responsibility of office while they held only one position of subordinate importance was far from meeting their ideas of equal justice. "In every proposition made to us [the Tories] sought, as they do now, 'a party triumph,' and not the peace of the country ... Our opponents preferred a monopoly of official income, and the undivided possession of power."[74] But actually the Reformers rested their main case on Howe's contentions that coalitions rarely worked well and should be avoided except as a last resort; and that before the Reformers allied themselves with the Tory executive, "the people of Nova-Scotia [should] decide between them and upon various matters drawn into controversy during the last three years."[75]

That ended Harvey's attempts to get a coalition. Henceforth all he expected from Howe was that he would "obstruct no measure of public utility," avoid "fractious opposition, to measures calculated to promote the Public interests," and "abide the result of the election for 1847."[76] Howe was pleased that Harvey could be satisfied so easily, but the Tory Executive Council faced the inescapable dilemma of being forced to continue the party government that it opposed. It could do no more than present two memoranda,[77] largely the work of Johnston, and the most "formidable briefs ... ever drawn for the old order in Nova Scotia."[78] After denouncing the Reformers' "extravagant comparisons" with British usage and their "unrestrained and unsound analogies" which gave "an air of burlesque and caricature" to the political struggle, the council requested an "authoritative declaration" from the Colonial Office. It came in Grey's dispatch of March 3, 1847, which confirmed the principles of the previous November. The people themselves would have to decide the issues raised by Howe and Johnston. Howe would have had it no other way.

Since ordinary Nova Scotians would be making the crucial decision within a few months, Howe thought it high time that they be made acquainted with his recent letters to Russell, and on January 4 and 11, 1847, he had them published in the *Novascotian*. Not unexpectedly, the *Times* derided him for considering himself "worthy of a place at the Premier's right hand, or perhaps as an Under Secretary in the Colonial Office." Surely, it concluded, Nova Scotians ought to be suspicious of their being "made the tools to help a few aspiring characters onward in the path of ambition."[79] In the other colonies the response, at least on the part of Reformers, was highly favourable. The Newfoundlander John Kent informed Howe he had opened a new vista for colonists,[80] while Adam Fergusson was certain he had regained the confidence of those Canadians who had developed doubts about him because of his favourable opinion of Metcalfe.[81]

To avoid incidents that might damage the Reformers in the election to come, Howe sought to have the legislative session of 1847 completed as quickly as possible. While resisting the council's attempts to use the governor to serve its own ends, he fully honoured his commitment not to oppose any useful act for purely partisan purposes.[82] The most significant measure of the session was Johnston's simultaneous voting bill, which required all voting throughout the province to take place during prescribed hours on a specified day, and to that end divided the constituencies into polling districts. Howe wanted a much more comprehensive measure, including provisions for the secret ballot and against bribery and intimidation. He also thought that Johnston was too optimistic in expecting the bill to prevent large assemblages of voters and hence disturbances; might there not be "a Grog Shop and Fiddler for every place in which the Poll would be opened"? But he could find no "fault with the principle of the Bill – it was English,"[83] and the Reformers let it become law without serious objection.

In contrast, Johnston's second measure relating to elections, the fraudulent conveyances bill, produced angry confrontation. Doyle had warned Howe there would be an attempt to terrify the electors or limit the franchise, and this bill appeared to bear him out. While its ostensible object was to attach severe penalties to anyone who transferred or accepted freeholds merely to manufacture votes for the elections, it exacted the same penalties against anyone who voted, but could not demonstrate a clear title to his land. In no mood to tolerate any "trickery" that might set at naught his heavy investment in the next election, and bitterly recalling the composition of the juries in the Nugent and Annand cases, as well as Johnston's relentless prosecution, or persecution, of Nugent, Howe castigated the administration of justice in the strongest terms he would ever use against it. The Tory voters, "sure of immunity, will rush exulting to the Polls," knowing they had on their side "a Tory Counsel, a Tory Judge, and a Tory Jury," while "the other [party] will be thinking of misdemeanours, fines, and the luxuries of the Penitentiary."[84] Had not a venerable judge, "trailing his ermine in the mire of party politics," descended from the bench to give political addresses to Falkland and Stewart? "I blushed for the Country," and "a very large portion of the people have [now] no confidence in the Supreme Court."[85] Worse still was J. W. Nutting who, while editing a newspaper which heaped slander on the leading Reformers, was also drawing juries in his capacity as prothonotary. When Johnston suggested that the legal and judicial system had treated Howe's excise accounts with great "delicacy," he got an angry response from Howe. "What delicacy? ... I have asked no indulgence – no delicacy." No matter what Johnston said, Howe still called his bill the last refuge of the desperate.[86]

The session over, Howe spent about two weeks at Musquodoboit, "kissing the children, chopping wood, and preparing for seed time – writing a long letter to the People and reading Beaumont and Fletcher's old Plays and Howitt's Priestcraft in all ages as variations."[87] By the time he returned to Halifax in late April, the Tories had organized themselves for the most determined election campaign they had ever fought in Halifax. It was to be an unedifying election with no holds barred, mostly because the stakes were so high, and the nastiest ingredient was a religious controversy. The previous October, when Howe's friend, John Leishman, a Presbyterian and a Reformer, was elected as an alderman in Ward 3 largely through Catholic support, the Tory press began to talk of Catholic ascendancy, even though only two of the eighteen aldermen were Catholics.[88] In February 1847 the Catholic *Cross* warned that anyone who appeared as a monk or nun at a fancy dress ball would insult the Catholics, and in its turn the Presbyterian *Guardian* published a letter describing the demoralizing tendency of monastic institutions.[89] The *Cross* kept the controversy going with its denunciation of Protestant Reformers, particularly "the traitorous and bloody Knox." Suitably horrified, the *Times* told Nova Scotians to watch carefully "the proceedings of a Denomination which is striving for undue power, spiritual and temporal, in every part of the Christian world,"[90] and warned that, since the Catholics constituted the strongest part of the Liberal party, its victory in an election would lead to Catholic dominance in Nova Scotia. *The Standard and Conservative Advocate*, established in February to further the Tory cause in the election, wondered at the failure of the Liberal organs in Halifax to answer the attacks on the Protestant faith, and concluded it was because all but one were edited by Catholics.[91]

Inevitably Howe was drawn into the controversy, especially since he was serving a second time as president of the Charitable Irish Society and attended Mass with that body in St Mary's Cathedral on St Patrick's Day. Subsequently he was charged with everything from subservience to his Catholic supporters to outright conversion. One opponent even alleged that "in his great zeal to shew the intensity of his conversion ... he actually drank a whole bucket of holy water."[92] Howe laughed it off: "Well, they used to call me an Infidel, and I am glad that they have given me a religion at last." In going to St Mary's on March 17, he had acted just as Attorney General Uniacke, father of Andrew, and most Protestant members of the society had done for half a century. Dismissing the charge that he was helping to establish a Catholic ascendancy as "a wicked cry, got up for electioneering purposes," he asked why Nova Scotians should be "taught to fear, and then to hate, [our] fellow creatures, merely because they are Catholic."[93]

Howe also had to defend himself against what he called "the old thread-bare story" of his alleged misconduct as collector of excise. The younger Tories canvassing the County of Halifax, especially

"Johnny" McGregor, circulated "slips" on this matter, and McGregor later repeated his accusations in the *Standard and Conservative Advocate*.[94] The charges that Howe had taken higher emoluments than the law intended and retained larger sums than were permissible in his own hands were clearly thread-bare; he had, in any case, simply followed the practice of his predecessors.[95] But his opponents had dug more deeply and come up with two other charges which were not nearly as easy to defend. While Howe contended he had delayed paying the £650 still owing the province until the assembly's Committee of Public Accounts had verified his statement, McGregor had some evidence to show that, in order to avoid being labelled a defaulter, Howe had asked the committee again and again to delay its report until he could settle the balance.[96] Even though the facts were a little cloudy on this point, they were all too clear on another. When Howe finally paid the balance on March 13, 1844, it was only partly in cash, and partly in orders on the Treasury, including one of Nugent for doing the assembly's printing that had not yet been approved by the Committee of Public Accounts. Sternly, Johnston upbraided Howe, observing that the money ought not to have been out of the chest, but either there, or in the Treasury, and nowhere else.[97]

When McGregor wondered where Howe kept the balance, he replied that he "could easily enlighten him, but [begged] to say that it is none of his business."[98] Although admitting it was irregular for the treasurer to accept Nugent's order, he simply introduced a red herring into the discussion by suggesting that any fault of his was insignificant compared with Crosskill's acceptance of £150 he had never earned.[99] Apparently a hard-up Howe had taken funds for his own use from the Excise chest at least to the amount of Nugent's order and probably more. While not a few office-holders of the day failed to keep their private and public business separate, it was hardly a defence that Howe cared to use. Yet in the end the irregularity or worse hurt him very little since, in a climate of vituperation, the public passed it off as another instance of vindictive politics.

In other ways the contest in Halifax was no less unedifying. When Howe returned from Musquodoboit, he found that Tory workers from the city had spread all over the rural areas taking sheaves of *Standards* and *Posts* with them for free distribution, and using a boat along the shore to distribute all sorts of goods to secure votes. Later, at Bridgetown, Howe delighted in reminding an angry Johnston that his son was "found on the shores, acting with those who had charge of the vessel."[100] Howe scheduled his first meeting at Preston, knowing that the Tories were making an all-out effort to win the black vote there and at Hammonds Plains. Already they had sent to Preston "a lying young scamp ... with bread and cheese, and liquor," and hay for the cattle,[101] and the worst was still to come.

The day of the Reform meeting at Preston, the Tories called one of their own three hours earlier, took possession of the school house, and locked the Reformers out of the meetinghouse. After the deacons pried open the door, Howe had a chance to laugh at the Tories' sudden interest in the blacks. "When did you ever see them before? ... How often have your cattle perished, and no hay came? ... to see a Tory crying over a half starved horse in Preston, holding a whisp of hay to his mouth with one hand while he steals the owner's vote with the other, is a picture that would make a horse laugh, even if he had been on a short allowance for a month." The blacks had been "stuck down here, in the good old Tory times, on little 10 acre lots of land ... much of it ... swamp and barren"; if they had been given suitable land, they would now be independent farmers "above the reach of want, and but little liable to corruption."[102]

Not one black attended Howe's meeting at Hammonds Plains, because the Conservatives had arrived earlier and distributed "a glorious feed of sandwiches and a lot of Indian Meal besides."[103] But Howe was not at all pessimistic; "we shall steal a lot of them by and bye, although from present appearances, they will not be wanted. We have more than half the whites in the Plains with us, nearly all of whom voted last time for [Andrew] Uniacke."[104] He was especially pleased that Doyle, running this time for the township seat, had made himself acceptable to the Protestants around Margaret's Bay: "Larry ... behaved very well, and made the fellows laugh abundantly."[105] Other than to travel night and day to attend a meeting which Johnston had scheduled for Musquodoboit,[106] Howe spent the rest of the campaign largely outside of Halifax in those counties where the outcome would be decided.

In the initial stages he told Susan Ann he had "no bad news ... from the country ... but not much of any sort that is decisive."[107] He turned first to the county of Lunenburg, which he considered crucial to the Reformers' success, and between June 10 and 15 he addressed meetings at Chester, Mahone Bay, Lunenburg, and Bridgewater. Then it was over the South Mountain for meetings in the enemy territory of Annapolis country between June 17 and 21. The first, at Bridgetown, saw a classic confrontation between him and Johnston, in which the Conservative leader devoted himself largely to denouncing the Liberals' approach to politicking. Why were Howe and William Young in Bridgetown? Did the people of Annapolis need to be instructed in politics? "Agitation was said to be good, – yes if you have anything to agitate about? What is this agitation for, but to provide an office for Mr. Howe?"[108] He hoped that the time would come when Howe and others would be stripped of the power to call men together, and when the people would refuse to assemble, merely to serve politicians' personal ambitions.

Howe's reply demonstrated the differences between him and Johnston on the nature and meaning of the electoral process. If "agitation" caused disturbances and disorder, as Johnston alleged, who had been the culprits in the past? Was it not a Tory mob which pelted the assemblymen in the "brandy dispute" and was it not Tory Kirkmen who agitated the mobs in Pictou elections? Perhaps Johnston was mortified because of "the good order preserved by the Liberal party. The constitutional struggle has been conducted without a pane of glass being broken."[109] Most of all, Howe stressed the importance of the vote, "for the right use of which [a man] is responsible to heaven and to his country. You come to such meetings as this, that you may form your judgments, and exercise the elective franchise with spirit and independence."[110]

Then, for Howe, it was on to Cornwallis in Kings; Maitland in Hants; New Glasgow, Barney's River, and Pictou Town in Pictou; by boat to Arichat; and so on. "So strong did he feel in his own county," he told the voters of Cornwallis, "that he could afford to be weeks away from [home] – addressing freeholders in other portions of the Province, on public affairs."[111] But he was back in Halifax by July 29 to witness the near-riot following the nomination day proceedings. The Tories had brought many blacks into Halifax by boat, and on their way back to the Market Wharf they had several skirmishes with whites. The Tories blamed it on the insults that the Liberals hurled at the blacks; the Liberals suggested that, if the Tories had left the blacks at home, and not plied them with liquor or paraded them through the streets, there would have been no disturbance.[112]

This incident indicates, once again, that because of the stakes involved the parties were going to inordinate lengths. The *Sun* charged the Tories with intimidating voters by threats of discharge from employment. Supposedly Dr Almon dispensed with a milkman who did not heed his threats, and some businessmen allegedly threatened to dismiss their truckdrivers if they did not vote Conservative.[113] To prevent similar intimidation being practised on workers employed at Citadel Hill, Howe forwarded to Harvey the names of engineering officers tampering with the voting rights of civilian employees.[114] The governor responded by ordering their commanding officers to tell the labourers that their future employment would not suffer as a result of the way they exercised their franchise.[115]

The Reformers had warts of their own. Howe must have blushed when, on the eve of the election, a letter written in the *Acadian Recorder* declared the Tories to be the same party that was responsible for "the blood, groans, and suffering of the early Acadians."[116] Three days before the election the *Post* told its readers that the Liberals of Onslow had been given a puncheon of rum to ensure the election of their candidate Isaac Logan, while Major A.L. Archibald, the Reform candidate in Truro, had been consigned twenty-five gallons.[117] But it all seemed a little picayune at a time when Tory wealth was being showered in profusion to prevent the destruction of the old order.

The Liberals won all four seats in Halifax, although by a smaller margin than usual because of the unprecedented efforts of the Tories.[118] Seeking a scapegoat, the Tory press blamed their loss on the Irish ("Walshite") vote. After examining the city returns, the *Times* concluded that 395 freeholders, almost all Protestant, had voted Tory; in contrast, only 199 Protestants had supported the Liberals, but they got the votes of all but half-a-dozen Catholics.[119] For Howe personal success left one sour note. On Declaration Day he waxed indignant at Dr Henry of the Garrison medical staff, who still wrote for the New York *Albion* under the pseudonym "Scrutator,"[120] and who had recently described the Liberals as a party "with no hold on any large class of the community above the most needy, most ignorant, and most violent – distrusted and disliked by seven eighths of the gentry, clergy, and mercantile body, and under the ban of Downing Street." Why, asked Howe, should an outsider paid by Her Majesty to defend Nova Scotians, be permitted to insult the great majority of them? Who was this Dr Henry anyway? "... the grandfather of his wife was a decent Halifax mechanic, and used to mend my father's shoe buckles many years ago."[121]

Yet, despite this and other discomfitures, Howe felt elated by the overall returns. Although the *Post* might contend that some members elected with Radical support could not be counted upon to "act Great Liberally,"[122] it was clearly wishful thinking on its part. This time the voters in each constituency were presented with a choice between candidates whom they could clearly identify as Liberal or Conservative, Reformer or Tory, and it could be said with certainty that twenty-nine Liberals, twenty-two Conservatives, and no loose fish had been returned. It would not be true to say that the election was an out-and-out referendum on a single issue, a choice between the political ideas of Howe and Johnston. But although irrelevancies seemed to dominate the campaign, and the great issues which had agitated the province for so long were less in evidence, the latter were so well known as not to require further discussion and were likely the crucial factor in most constituencies.

As in Halifax itself, the Tory press attributed the province-wide Liberal success to the Catholic vote. But when the *Times* complained that the Liberals, "reckless of principle," had allied themselves with a religious body which sought ascendancy over every party and denomination in the province,[123] Nugent willingly admitted the union of Catholics and Liberals, arguing it was "well based, ... natural, and reasonable," since both wanted greater extension of political rights and civil liberty.[124] The Liberals, in their turn, might have made something of the Baptist–Tory alliance, which generally held firm except in Hants county.

Howe regretted the outcome of a few contests, especially the defeat of his tried and trusted friend Peter Spearwater in Shelburne township and the election of the defector Ryder in Argyle "in consequence of the deception practiced by the Tory Party on the credulous Frenchmen at Eel Brook."[125] Although he was aware that "the Baptist Hierarchy – the worthy Deacons and Elders, ... [had kept] the Tory mill grinding"[126] in Annapolis and Kings, he believed nonetheless that the Liberals should have done better in these counties and also in Queens. As he saw it, they had lost one or two seats "by overweening confidence on the part of ... Liberals, who trusted in Providence, without putting their shoulders to the wheel – one by bungling – and one by flat perjury on the part of our opponents."[127]

Collectively the results seemed to bear out Howe's contention that the sturdy yeomanry of the country were the backbone of Liberal strength, while the Tories were dependent on the "compacts" in the built-up areas, for although the Liberals won only ten of the twenty-four townships, they took twelve of the seventeen counties.[128] They were delighted by the defeat in Guysborough of J.J. Marshall, to them the most objectionable of all the Tories. But their real victory was forged in Hants and Lunenburg, in each of which they gained three seats. Seemingly a little immodestly, Howe attributed these victories to "my own unaided exertions," but actually he did not exaggerate. Almost alone, he had wooed both counties assiduously for three years, and "into [Lunenburg] none of our Leaders would venture but myself."[129] Having prepared the way, I took a stranger from Halifax, combined him with two resident Farmers and in the face of a remonstrance signed by nearly all the Tory merchants of Halifax, in five days, cleared the way for complete success, for which no member, even of our own party ventured to hope."[130]

The election was not the decisive victory that Howe made it out to be, since the Liberals had a majority of only seven, and had won some seats marginally. If Lunenburg had gone the other way, the parties would have been tied with a Liberal Speaker in the chair. But because he knew there were no loose fish, he could exult that the election "closes up, honorably, the labour of my past life." Almost gloatingly, he boasted that the victory meant the introduction of the "system for which I have been contending and with the advancement and illustration of which my name has been identified."[31] His aim now was to put the system into practical operation at the earliest possible moment.

CHAPTER NINETEEN

Provincial Secretary at Last

Decisive though the election was, Howe knew that Johnston would not resign, but would hang on until "kicked out by a vote of Want of Confidence." So for the moment he consoled himself with the thought that "reading, kissing the children and shooting moose" would amuse him till the House met.[1] But as the autumn advanced, he and his friends viewed the prospect of waiting till spring with less equanimity. For what reason, asked the *Novascotian*, should they be patient: until "some ambiguous despatch can be elicited [from Britain], on which to hang a doubt or a claim for further procrastination" or until a third governor was "dragged downwards by the dead weight of Tory hatred and incapacity"?[2]

Howe told Buller that normally he would have no complaint, but he thought it absurd that a ministry which had kept "the Country in hot water since 1843, – proposing impracticable Coalitions, and governing with half a Council" should stay in office four or five months after being formally condemned.[3] At least the assembly should be convened without delay. Otherwise the change in government would occur in midwinter, and the new Reform ministers would have to run by-elections "amidst the snows of February"; worse still, the province would not be represented by an effective government at a colonial conference that the governor general was calling at Montreal to "arrange a Zollverein – a North American Post Office, Railroads and Colonization."[4] But however reasonable his arguments, he knew all too well that, constitutionally, Johnston was fully entitled to remain in office until the normal spring session of the assembly decided his fate.

Meanwhile the *Times* was continuing to call for a coalition and almost inviting J.B. Uniacke, never an enthusiastic supporter of party government, to turn traitor and dismember the party he led.[5]

Though Uniacke was leader in name only,[6] Howe took the matter seriously enough to have his old friend and political associate, Dr William Grigor, sound him out. He reported that Uniacke was "right," and quite insistent that "the first stroke of liberal policy" must be to "get hold of the government and then dictate terms – that the whole executive council must go out."[7] Later Grigor confirmed even more strongly that Uniacke would "stop at nothing but to clean out all," including Sir Rupert George.[8] For Johnston and the Tories the die was irrevocably cast.

With the approach of January 22, 1848 – the day fixed for the beginning of the first session of the Eighteenth General Assembly – the *Novascotian* prophesied that "the first week, aye! the first day may do much to cheer the heart of every Reformer from Cape Sable to Cape North."[9] As befitted the occasion, the General Assembly opened with an unusually showy spectacle.[10] Sir John Harvey and his suite proceeded to Province House on horseback, there to be greeted on the outside by a guard of honour from the 23rd Fusiliers, and inside by one from the 46th. But Johnston and the Tories made it clear that they would be fighting a last-ditch battle. The assembly having been asked to choose a Speaker, Howe proposed that William Young be reelected. To his surprise, Johnston objected, alleging that Young had pursued a course of "heated partizanship" in four previous sessions.[11] Indignant because the governor was being kept waiting at the other end of the building, Howe told Johnston that the House must "select a Speaker from the 51 gentlemen who are here, and I ask you to look with me around these benches and tell me who is not [politically oriented] ... Where shall we find such a *black swan?*"[12]

In their turn the Reformers refused to accept the former sergeant-at-arms and assistant sergeant-at-arms, who had identified themselves as Tories, and installed Reformers in their place. Bewailing the use of "the odious Republican practice" that to the victor belongs the spoils, the *Times* wondered if the Reformers would be as plucky on important questions as on small ones.[13] It had not long to wait. At the first opportunity, on the address in reply to the governor's speech, Uniacke moved nonconfidence in the administration. When Johnston complained that the House was being asked to condemn the government before any charges were preferred against it, Howe intervened, even though he was suffering from a cold. Could Johnston really think that Uniacke's topics of debate, the post office, railroads, commerce, and colonization, had nothing to do with the government of Nova Scotia? Were not "the honor, the prosperity, and elevation, of our country" involved in all these subjects, and might not "a sound principle, propounded here, be adopted and acted upon by North America"? Surely, then, it was of "the utmost importance, while such questions are to be dealt with, that His Excellency should be surrounded by a complete and vigorous Administration."[14]

Johnston could delay the execution only so long, and after nightfall on Wednesday, January 26, the end came. Not a Reformer broke ranks; there were no loose fish; and nonconfidence was carried by the straight party vote of twenty-eight to twenty-one.[15] In contrast with earlier sessions, the multitude in the galleries and lobbies showed becoming moderation and dispersed quietly.[16] The next day the whole assembly waited on Harvey with its address, and received his assurance that he would "take such measures to restore confidence as he should deem expedient." At long last, on Friday, January 28, Johnston laid Grey's history-making dispatches on the table,[17] and announced that, as a result of Wednesday's vote, the members of the Executive Council were resigning, and that he and Dodd were relinquishing the offices of attorney general and solicitor general. While Sir Rupert George resigned as executive councillor, he made it known that he intended to remain as provincial secretary. But when the Reformers formed the first responsible ministry in the colonies on February 2, with Uniacke as leader of the government, they did it only on condition that the secretaryship was to be at their disposal.

Nugent expressed elation that he had lived to see a Liberal cabinet,[18] not realizing, as Howe did, that there would be a struggle to get the kind of cabinet the Reformers wanted. While it was easy enough to fill the Executive Council with nine Liberals,[19] it was much more difficult to confer on them the offices that Howe deemed essential to implement his concept of responsible government. He and the other leading Reformers had insisted, as a condition of assuming office, that they control not only the home, i.e., the provincial secretary's department, but the legal and financial departments as well. Since Johnston and Dodd had tendered their resignations, they would have no trouble with the legal departments; they were quite prepared to reorganize the financial offices by legislation; but they were still adamant on the immediate surrender of the provincial secretary's office, which was at the very centre of the provincial government.

Because Sir Rupert George refused to make way, Harvey had the choice of removing him either by his unaided use of the prerogative or on the advice of his ministers. To relieve him from embarrassment, the new councillors agreed to the second course even before they were sworn in. As a preliminary they sought the assembly's approval of a resolution which vacated the office of provincial secretary and provided an annual retiring allowance of £400 stg. for Sir Rupert, which was to be charged to the casual and territorial revenues.[20] Battling to the end, Johnston countered with legalistic though at least partly valid arguments: that Grey's dispatches did not permit a public officer appointed, as George had been, by Crown patent, to be supplanted unless specific conditions were met; that his removal could be effected only by an act, not simply by a resolution of the assembly;[21] that the assembly had no right to put additional burdens on the casual and territorial revenues; and that until these revenues were brought under the assembly's control, it was in no position to regulate the office of provincial secretary.[22]

While Howe was in no mood to take such legalisms seriously, he found his own position decidedly uncomfortable, since his opponents would make much of the fact that the secretaryship was destined for him. Accordingly he told Harvey that he was prepared to place the salary proposed for himself at the governor's disposal.[23] Actually he was in no position to make a sacrifice of this kind, and he could not have meant his offer to be taken seriously; probably he was seeking to demonstrate to Harvey the importance which the Reformers attached to their demands. Howe closed the debate by contending, as his fellow Reformers had done, that Russell's dispatch of October 1839 and the more recent ones of Lord Grey, when properly interpreted, meant that George's resignation from the Executive Council vacated the provincial secretaryship as well. Further, even though the Tories believed that one office was sufficient to ensure responsibility, he contended that the Reformers had the right to say how many offices they required, and the governor was free to follow their advice.[24] After the resolution was adopted by the usual party vote on February 7, it did not take Harvey long to act. Within two days Doyle reported to the House that Uniacke had become attorney general, DesBarres solicitor general, and Howe provincial secretary.

At about the same time Howe warned Buller that the Tories would burden the British government with all sorts of memorials and remonstrances. Already they were almost threatening to rebel, but "we are strong enough to hang them without John Bull's assistance." The Reformers, he continued, would give Nova Scotia something it never had before, "a working Government, properly checked, and responsible in every Department"; they would, like Harvey, seek to cultivate a kindlier tone of feeling throughout the society; and above all, they would "keep within the ropes" and follow the best examples of the Mother Country. "Earl Grey's Despatches, clear as a sun beam, breathe a spirit of generous confidence in our discretion and right feeling. He shall not be disappointed. It will be our pride to make Nova Scotia a 'Normal School' for the rest of the Colonies, showing them how representative Institutions may be worked, so as to insure internal tranquility, and advancement, in subordination to the paramount interests and authority of the Empire."[25]

The Tories did not give up easily and put up candidates in the by-elections against the three executive councillors who had vacated their seats on accepting offices of emolument. Confirming Howe's prophecy, none had any difficulty,[26] and Howe was back in the assembly by March 9. As was usual at such moments, he became very humble, expressing his gratitude to Providence, "by whose wise ordinations the things, which seem to have been the work of our hands, have come to pass." Most gratifying to him was that his province had, without violence, completely overthrown an ancient system more quickly than any country he knew. "The part which Nova Scotia has played in all this matter – elevated, intelligent, steady, peaceful, makes me proud of her. She shed no blood, like Canada – she did not wait to have the new system forced upon her by the Secretary of State, after the fashion of New Brunswick."[27]

It was a little too patronizing. At the very least Howe might have acknowledged that the violence in Canada had contributed not a little to accelerating the concession of the new system. It was true, nonetheless, that his approach to change generally accorded with the only way in which it could be effected in the colonial system of the day. He had started out with the belief that, barring a few minor defects, the government of Nova Scotia performed its functions admirably. A closer look caused him to magnify those defects, but he still believed they could be remedied by a piecemeal approach. It took him an extraordinarily long period of five or six years to appreciate that no public officer, municipal or provincial, could be kept accountable except through some comprehensive system of responsibility, and another three years to accept Durham's proposals and the principle of executive responsibility based on the British model. Even then he was willing to try out the Russellite–Sydenham creed as a substitute for Durham and an appropriate way of meeting the Reformers' demands, or at worst as an important step in that direction. Compelling circumstances led him to abandon the Russellite–Sydenham system, and he spent another three years in persuading its Whig sponsors in Britain to give up on it too because it was impracticable and unworkable. Thus, step by step, he was led towards the inevitable outcome in colonial evolution even as he helped prepare the way for it.

In the process – as he would boast throughout the rest of his career – he had done nothing to weaken the British connection or break faith with his father. Perhaps his one regret was that the struggle had immersed him in nasty, bitter infighting which was neither congenial or natural to him. Although his original contributions to the Reformers' basic stock of ideas were distinctly minimal, none could dress up those ideas with more fitting illustrations than he, and none could practise the art of persuasion upon successive colonial secretaries more eloquently and skilfully. In Nova Scotia, through his newspaper, he had almost single-handedly created the Reform party that emerged from the election of 1836, and he had been the publicist and tactician who, just as single-handedly, made possible the Reform victory of August 5, 1847. Now, in February 1848, by accepting the provincial secretaryship he had committed himself to helping to devise the administrative machinery that was needed to implement the Reformers' concept of responsible government, but to nothing more.

Immediately after the election he had asked Providence to show him "new fields of usefulness to be cultivated." Perhaps he would "go over and help the Liberals to put things to rights in New Brunswick. They are on the track but have much lee way to bring up."[28] Howe's uncertainty thoroughly disturbed his friend Grigor. "Nova Scotia has been and must be your field – it is all your own – to desert it and break ground anew at your time of life, without unmistakable reasons and pecuniary certainties would be dangerous."[29] Later, becoming more philosophical, Grigor argued that Howe was completely attuned to the Nova Scotian psychology. Nova Scotians, he suggested, were "too worldly to be fond of things as they are [or] to be carried up on the wings of ideality and fancy." As a result, the province's politics had "a substantiality which, though it may not refine or embellish," yet afforded hope and confidence to "those who lead and expound the greater principles of political movement." Because the provincial mood and outlook coincided so closely with Howe's own psychological preferences, Grigor described them as not only the "sheet anchor" of his past success, but also the portent of greater things to come.[30]

Howe would have been the last to deny his complete rapport with Nova Scotia and Nova Scotians. But for the moment he was in the grip of the restless, agitating uncertainty that would always seize him after he had exhausted himself in one activity. As usual, it was causing him to look ahead, and no one, certainly not Howe himself, could tell where it might lead him.

The Howes

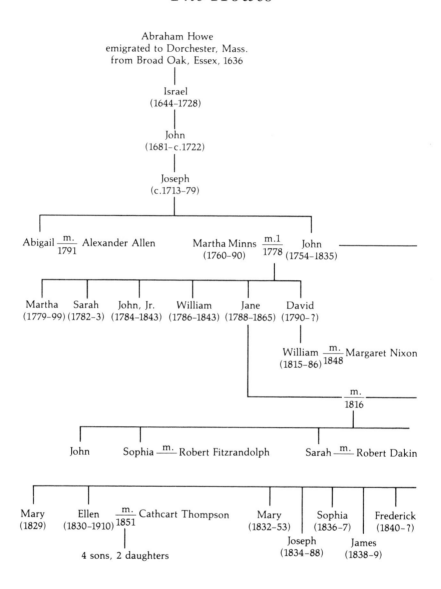

Abraham Howe
emigrated to Dorchester, Mass.
from Broad Oak, Essex, 1636

Israel
(1644–1728)

John
(1681–c.1722)

Joseph
(c.1713–79)

Abigail —m.— Alexander Allen   Martha Minns —m.1— John
        1791   1778 (1754–1835)
                                 (1760–90)

Martha   Sarah   John, Jr.   William   Jane   David
(1779–99) (1782–3) (1784–1843) (1786–1843) (1788–1865) (1790–?)

William —m.— Margaret Nixon
(1815–86) 1848

m.
1816

John   Sophia —m.— Robert Fitzrandolph   Sarah —m.— Robert Dakin

Mary   Ellen —m.— Cathcart Thompson   Mary   Sophia   Frederick
(1829) (1830–1910) 1851   (1832–53) (1836–7)   (1840–?)

                                            Joseph   James
4 sons, 2 daughters   (1834–88) (1838–9)

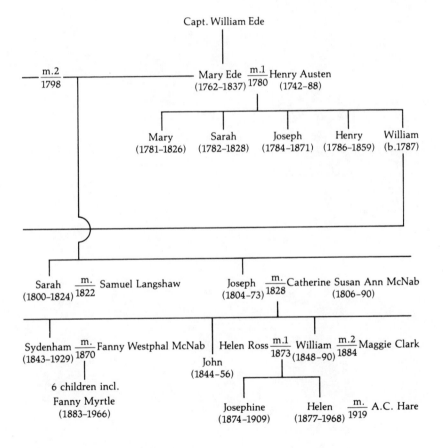

Capt. William Ede

m.2
1798

Mary Ede $\frac{m.1}{1780}$ Henry Austen
(1762–1837) (1742–88)

Mary   Sarah   Joseph   Henry   William
(1781–1826)   (1782–1828)   (1784–1871)   (1786–1859)   (b.1787)

Sarah $\frac{m.}{1822}$ Samuel Langshaw
(1800–1824)

Joseph $\frac{m.}{1828}$ Catherine Susan Ann McNab
(1804–73) (1806–90)

Sydenham $\frac{m.}{1870}$ Fanny Westphal McNab
(1843–1929)

6 children incl.
Fanny Myrtle
(1883–1966)

Helen Ross $\frac{m.1}{1873}$ William $\frac{m.2}{1884}$ Maggie Clark
(1848–90)

John
(1844–56)

Josephine   Helen $\frac{m.}{1919}$ A.C. Hare
(1874–1909)   (1877–1968)

The McNabs

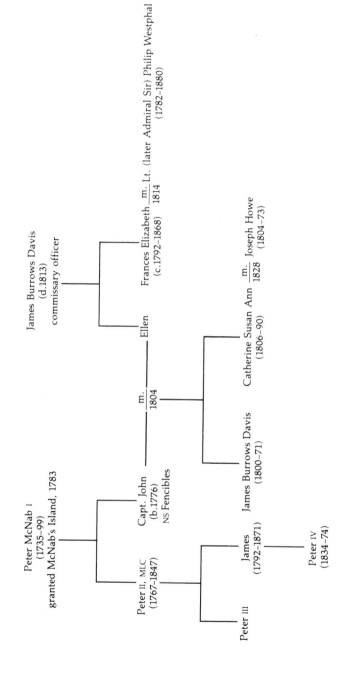

Peter McNab I
(1735–99)
granted McNab's Island, 1783

James Burrows Davis
(d.1813)
commissary officer

Peter II, MLC
(1767–1847)

Capt. John
(b.1776)
NS Fencibles

Ellen

m.
1804

Frances Elizabeth   m. Lt. (later Admiral Sir) Philip Westphal
(c.1792–1868)   1814   (1782–1880)

James
(1792–1871)

James Burrows Davis
(1800–71)

Catherine Susan Ann   m.   Joseph Howe
(1806–90)   1828   (1804–73)

Peter III

Peter IV
(1834–74)

Edward Howe and the Illegitimate Line

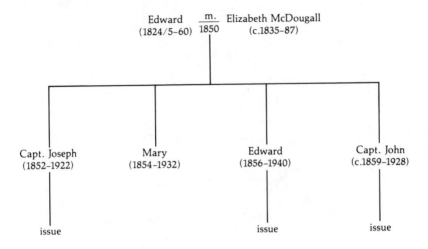

Edward   m.   Elizabeth McDougall
(1824/5–60)   1850   (c.1835–87)

Capt. Joseph	Mary	Edward	Capt. John
(1852–1922)	(1854–1932)	(1856–1940)	(c.1859–1928)

issue   issue   issue

Notes

ABBREVIATIONS

Chisholm	Joseph A. Chisholm, ed., *The Speeches and Public Letters of Joseph Howe*, 2 vols. (Halifax: Chronicle Publishing Company, 1909)
"Howe Letters"	Joseph A. Chisholm collection of typewritten transcripts, Public Archives of Nova Scotia.
JHA	*Journals of the Nova Scotia House of Assembly*
JHP	Joseph Howe Papers, Public Archives of Nova Scotia (microfilm)
JLC	*Journals of the Legislative Council of Nova Scotia*
PAC	Public Archives of Canada
PANS	Public Archives of Nova Scotia

CHAPTER ONE

1 Howe to half-sister Jane, Mar. 26, 1826, PANS, "Howe Letters," p. 4.
2 It was said he could play a good game with "an ordinary walking stick," a substitute never used by any other person. See "Historicus," "Random Recollections of Joseph Howe and His Times," no. 1, *Progress*, Nov. 7, 1891, JHP, reel 22. (Reels 21–24 lack page numbers.)
3 "Nova Scotia's Old Families," *Morning Herald*, Dec. 28, 1885.
4 The several variations of the spelling of Ede include Edes, Ead, Eade.
5 JHP, vol. 30, p. 58.
6 See excerpts from letter of John Howe to his wife, Aug. 5, 1808, PAC, George Johnson Papers.
7 Joseph Howe, *Poems and Essays* (Montreal, 1874), p. 97.
8 Sydenham Howe to George Johnson, Dec. 9, 1902, PAC, George Johnson Papers. The cottage in which John Howe lived was on the North-West Arm just north of the penitentiary; Bible in hand, he frequently visited the inmates.
9 Ibid.
10 See George Johnson biography of Joseph Howe, p. 7, PAC, George Johnson Papers, and Sydenham Howe's account of his father, JHP, reel 22.
11 George Monro Grant, *Joseph Howe* (Halifax: A.&W. MacKinlay, 1904), p. 23.

12 Ibid., p. 19. See Chisholm, 2: 624.
13 George Johnson biography of Joseph Howe, p. 7, PAC, George Johnson Papers.
14 Memoir of Joseph Howe, JHP, reel 22; see also George Johnson Papers.
15 Ibid.
16 Thomas Dunbabin, "John Howe – Secret Agent Extraordinary," Halifax *Chronicle-Herald*, Sept. 5, 1960; *A Journal kept by Mr. John Howe while he was employed as a British Spy during the Revolutionary War* (Concord, NH, 1827). One of the few stories of his father's early life that Joseph Howe remembered related to the events following the engagement at Bunker Hill on June 17, 1775. A young British officer rebuked the doctor who wanted to cover his eyes while he amputated his leg: "Damn ye, did I fight with my eyes shut?" John Howe reported that he nursed the young man throughout the night, and left him cool and comfortable in the morning. Memoir of Joseph Howe, JHP, reel 22.
17 Chisholm, 2: 350. In the context of his other writings, Howe is using "Sovereign" loosely here.
18 Its founder, Robert Sandeman, had come to Boston from Glasgow in 1764.
19 Charles St. C. Stayner, "The Sandemanian Loyalists," *Collections of the Nova Scotia Historical Society* 29 (1951): 66. For its account of Sandemanianism and the Sandemanians, this chapter relies largely on Stayner's work.
20 Ibid., pp. 79–80.
21 Ibid., p. 100.
22 Ibid.
23 His sister Abigail, who also came to Halifax, married Alexander Allen of Halifax, the son of Ebenezer Allen, another Sandemanian Loyalist. Ibid., pp. 94, 100.
24 See statement of Walter Barrell in Stayner, "Sandemanian Loyalists," pp. 108–9.
25 See Joseph Howe's "Memo. about my Father," August 1859, JHP, reel 22.
26 C. Bruce Fergusson, "The Halifax Post Office," *Dalhousie Review* 38 (Spring 1958): 44.
27 See Joseph Howe's "Memo. about my Father," August 1859, JHP, reel 22.

CHAPTER TWO

1 The property on which the cottage stood later came to be known as Emscot or Emscote.
2 See "To My Sister Jane" in Howe, *Poems and Essays* (Montreal, 1874), p. 98.
3 Howe to Henry ("Harry") Austen, Dec. 28, 1855, JHP, vol. 31, p. 32.
4 Ibid., pp. 32–3. Howe was replying to a letter of Harry Austen who, by reason of his own folly, was in impecunious circumstances and was basing his claim for assistance on some allegedly unrequited service he had rendered to old John Howe and John, Jr. Joseph gave him short shrift: "All I can say is that I know of no debt which my Father and John left unpaid to you at their deaths, and that as regards kindness and hospitality they certainly owed the world at large very little on that score." Ibid., p. 34.
5 George Stupka (pseud.), "A Coach to Take the Air: On Joe Howe and

Alternatives to Schooling: II. The Education of Joseph Howe," *Journal of Education* (Nova Scotia) 22 (Spring 1973): 43.

6 George Johnson biography of Howe, p. 11, PAC, George Johnson Papers; also extracts supplied by Sydenham Howe to George Johnson, p. 28, George Johnson Papers. Jane Howe married William Austen, her stepmother's son by a first marriage, and moved to Saint John. Because her husband was ill for many years, she supported her family by teaching school, assisted in some measure by John Howe until 1843 when, on the death of her brother William Howe, she became the chief beneficiary of his estate.

7 Extracts by Sydenham Howe, p. 28, PAC, George Johnson Papers.

8 Sydenham Howe's account, JHP, reel 22.

9 George Monro Grant, *Joseph Howe* (Halifax: A.&W. MacKinlay, 1904), p. 21.

10 William Smith, "The Early Post Office in Nova Scotia, 1755–1867," *Collections of the Nova Scotia Historical Society* 19 (1918): 60. Howe, of course, had it easier in Nova Scotia where, in contrast with Canada, the post office did not produce a surplus and controversy did not constantly arise because thousands of pounds of its net proceeds were sent annually to Britain.

11 William Smith, *The History of the Post Office in British North America: 1639–1870* (Cambridge: Cambridge University Press, 1920), pp. 100–1. Under John Howe the post office spread gradually over the province, and for his services he received, when he retired in favour of his son John in 1818, the warm commendation of the secretary of the General Post Office and of two lieutenant-governors, Sir John Sherbrooke and the Earl of Dalhousie. Smith, "Early Post Office," p. 61.

12 See David W. Parker, "Secret Reports of John Howe, 1808, I," *American Historical Review* 17 (October 1911): 72.

13 Ibid., p. 73.

14 See letters of Howe to Prevost, May 5, May 31, June 7, June 22, August 15, 1808, ibid., pp. 77–102. Howe also reported that "Bonaparte is promoting with great zeal the study of French in New England," and that the American government was winking at the supply of French privateers in Washington, Philadelphia, and Charleston.

15 Howe to Prevost, Nov. 27, 1808, PANS, RG 1, vol. 385, doc. 3.

16 See Joseph Howe's "Memo. about my Father," August 1859, JHP, reel 22.

17 Joseph Howe to half-sister Jane, January 1832, extracts by Sydenham Howe, p. 30, PAC, George Johnson Papers. Joseph added: "Perhaps it is better as it is. I think we all love him the more."

18 *Morning Herald*, Dec. 28, 1885.

19 Wentworth described Tonge as a sower of "discord and hatred both in and out of the House, more especially directed against those who are in the Kings service & longest established." Wentworth to Scrope Bernard, Feb. 24, 1800, PANS, RG 1, vol. 53, p. 20.

20 See J.M. Beck, *The Government of Nova Scotia* (Toronto: University of Toronto Press, 1957), p. 49.

21 Ibid., p. 18.

22 A.G. Archibald, "Sir Alexander Croke," *Collections of the Nova Scotia Historical Society* 2 (1881): 123–4.

23 For details, see Beck, *Government of Nova Scotia*, pp. 59–61.

24 See Memoir of Joseph Howe, JHP, reel 22.

25 Ibid.
26 Ibid.
27 J.D. Logan, "Old John Howe's 'Three R's'," *Sunday Leader*, Jan. 27, 1924.
28 See "The Birth-Day," in Howe, *Poems and Essays*, p. 133.
29 See "To My Sister Jane," ibid., pp. 98–9.
30 George Johnson biography of Howe, p. 3, PAC, George Johnson Papers.
31 Sydenham Howe's account, JHP, reel 22.
32 Logan, "Old John Howe's 'Three R's'."
33 Sydenham Howe's account, JHP, reel 22.
34 Although Bromley opened his school in mid-1813, apparently Howe did not attend until 1816 when it was located in the stone building known as the Acadian School.
35 Logan, "Old John Howe's 'Three R's'."
36 Sydenham Howe's account, JHP, reel 22.
37 Logan, "Old John Howe's 'Three R's'."
38 Grant, *Howe*, p. 14.
39 Ibid.
40 Although sixty-four in 1818, John Howe continued to do useful work in the office for another dozen years or more.
41 Beamish Murdoch, *A History of Nova Scotia or Acadia* (Halifax, 1865–7), 3: 351–2.
42 See J.S. Martell, "Halifax during and after the War of 1812," *Dalhousie Review* 23 (October 1943): 291.
43 D.C. Harvey, "Pre-Agricola John Young," *Collections of the Nova Scotia Historical Society* 32 (1959): 158.
44 Ibid., pp. 125–42.
45 Stayner, "Sandemanian Loyalists," p. 116.
46 See "Historicus," "Random Recollections of Joseph Howe and His Times," no. 1, *Progress*, Nov. 7, 1891, JHP, reel 22.
47 T.B. Akins, "History of Halifax City," *Collections of the Nova Scotia Historical Society* 8 (1895): 158.
48 Stayner, "Sandemanian Loyalists," p. 116.
49 Memoir of Joseph Howe, JHP, reel 22.
50 Lieutenant-governor from 1811 to 1816.
51 Memoir of Joseph Howe, JHP, reel 22. Howe noted that "no two Governors think alike or patronize the same things." Thus Dalhousie posed as the patron of agriculture, and his example "set all the Councillors, and officials, and fashionable mad about farming and political economy ... Every fellow who wanted an office or wished to get an invitation to Government House, read Sir John Sinclair, talked of Adam Smith, bought a South Down or hired an acre of land and planted mangel wurtzels." In contrast Kempt had "a passion for road making and pretty women ... the agricultural mania passed away ... and the Heifers about Government House attracted more attention than the Durham Cows." Ibid. Also see Joseph Howe, "Notes on Several Governors and Their Influence," *Collections of the Nova Scotia Historical Society* 17 (1913): 197–8.
52 Lieutenant-governor from 1816 to 1820.
53 Memoir of Joseph Howe, JHP, reel 22.
54 Ibid.
55 Ibid.
56 Ibid.
57 Ibid.

58 Stupka, "Education of Joseph Howe," p. 44.
59 The story usually cited to demonstrate Howe's vulgarity was told by George Johnson to G.M. Grant: An old Dutchwoman of Lunenburg was asked if Mr Howe was companionable and pleasant in his intercourse with her family. "Oh! yes. Mr. Howe's just the nicest man I ever knew. No nonsense about him. He's just one of ourselves. He stands up with his back to the fire, puts his hands under his coat-tails and breaks wind (that's not the word she used) like one of the family." Johnson to Grant, Aug. 1, 1900, PAC, George Johnson Papers. Edward's mother is unlikely to have been Agnes Wallace, with whom Howe consorted and corresponded in 1826 and before (see chapter 4). More probably she was Mrs Charles Wallace, to whom Howe would write years later: "'Beauty' is 'truly a joy forever,' and yours was as conspicuous from early girlhood, when I saw you first with my Brother's daughter in the Printing Office down to those conferences not unmixed with pain and anxiety which preceded your departure for California" (Dec. 14, 1871, JHP, vol. 41, pp. 130–1).
60 A former employee of the *Royal Gazette* and *Halifax Journal*, then in New York.
61 *Acadian Recorder*, Dec. 18, 1824.
62 Sydenham Howe's account, JHP, reel 22.
63 For accounts of the trial, see *Acadian Recorder*, Dec. 18, 1824, and *Halifax Free Press*, Dec. 14, 1824. By a bare majority, the Court of Sessions decided that, although no formal indenture had passed between the Howes and Sentell, he was committed to serving out his apprenticeship with them. At the trial Howe met for the first time his major political opponent of the future, James W. Johnston, who acted as counsel for his family.
64 Howe to half-sister Jane, Jan. 1824, extracts by Sydenham Howe, p. 1, PAC, George Johnson Papers.
65 Grant, *Howe*, p. 24.
66 Stupka, "Education of Joseph Howe," p. 48.
67 Ibid., p. 47. For a full account of the nature and extent of Howe's reading, see ibid., pp. 47–51.
68 Ibid., pp. 47–8. Stupka erred in suggesting that there were no allusions to Coleridge.
69 Ibid., p. 49.
70 Grant, *Howe*, p. 24.
71 *Weekly Chronicle*, Jan. 12, 1821.
72 Ibid., May 2, 1823; see also *Poems and Essays*, p. 158.
73 Stupka, "Education of Joseph Howe," p. 48.
74 See p. 3.
75 Howe to half-sister Jane, Nov. 7, 1824, PANS, "Howe Letters," p. 2.
76 In the capacity of King's printer they did the printing for the legislature.
77 Memoir of Joseph Howe, JHP, reel 22.
78 Howe to half-sister Jane, May 2, 1824, PANS, "Howe Letters," p. 1.
79 Before Sarah left Saint John she asked Joseph to visit her: "As you don't mind fatique you could ride with the courier, the expense would not be very great, and I flatter myself you would like to see me again, before I cross the Atlantic." See extracts by Sydenham Howe, p. 25, PAC, George Johnson Papers. There is no evidence that Joseph made the trip to Saint John.
80 Howe to half-sister Jane, Nov. 7, 1824, PANS, "Howe Letters," p. 2.

81 Ibid., p. 3.
82 This was Sydenham Howe's belief; see notes accompanying his letter to George Johnson, Dec. 9, 1909, JHP, reel 22.
83 Howe to half-sister Jane, Mar. 26, 1826, PANS, "Howe Letters," p. 5.
84 Ibid.
85 *Weekly Chronicle*, Jan. 6, 1826. In the poem Howe recalls vividly that French and American prisoners were kept on Melville Island in the North-West Arm during the War of 1812.
86 *Acadian Magazine or Literary Mirror* 1, no. XI (1827): 434. But James A. Roy suggests that although Howe displayed "the urge towards poetry and poetic expression ... his ear was defective; he was imitative and trite, and ignorant of the most elementary prosodic principles." See *Joseph Howe: A Study in Achievement and Frustration* (Toronto: Macmillan, 1935), p. 66. Professor M.G. Parks, editor of *Joseph Howe: Poems and Essays* (Toronto: University of Toronto Press, 1973), calls Roy's position "extreme" even though he agrees that Howe's poetry exhibits tendencies of conventionality, triteness, tedious moralizing, and "poeticality." These faults, he suggests, stem from Howe's view that serious poetry was "morally edifying and emotionally affective," and did not concern itself with the specific but presented "universal themes and feelings in an elevated manner by means of elevated or 'poetic' diction" (Introduction, xvi–xx).
87 Memoir of Joseph Howe, JHP, reel 22.
88 Howe to half-sister Jane, Mar. 26, 1826, PANS, "Howe Letters," pp. 4–5.
89 Ibid., p. 5.

CHAPTER THREE

1 The *Halifax* (later *Royal*) *Gazette* dated back to 1752 and the *Halifax Journal* to 1780; the *Weekly Chronicle* was first published in 1786.
2 Minns gave up none too soon, for within two weeks (Jan. 19, 1827) his former newspaper came out with its columns bordered in black to announce his death.
3 The description of Archibald MacMechan.
4 Howe to Harry Austen, Dec. 28, 1855, JHP, vol. 31, p. 24.
5 Later in the year they moved to a location near the southwest corner of Province House. See *Acadian*, Oct. 12, 1827.
6 Charles Stayner reached this conclusion after his research failed to reveal the public notice that was required to give legal status to the partnership.
7 *Acadian*, Jan. 5, 1827.
8 Howe to half-sister Jane, May 19, 1827, PANS, "Howe Letters," pp. 6–7. When Howe left the *Acadian* at the end of 1827, Spike admitted openly to his deficiencies by announcing that he had "committed the Editorial part to a Gentleman fully competent to the task." *Acadian*, Dec. 28, 1827.
9 *Acadian*, Feb. 2, 1827.
10 Ibid., Mar. 16, 1827.
11 Ibid., under date of Mar. 30, 1827, but actually Apr. 6, 1827.
12 Howe to half-sister Jane, May 19, 1827, PANS, "Howe Letters," p. 6.
13 *Novascotian*, Jan. 3, 1828. He was referring to the post office.
14 Howe to half-sister Jane, May 19, 1827, PANS, "Howe Letters," p. 6.
15 "The Micmac," *Acadian*, Jan. 5, 1827; "La Tribune," Jan. 12, 1827;

"Home," Jan. 19, 1827; "What is a Friend?," Feb. 9, 1827; "Song," Nov. 9, 1827; and "Woman," Nov. 16, 1827.
16 Ibid., Apr. 6, 1827.
17 Ibid., Jan 12, 1827.
18 Ibid., Feb. 9, 16, and 23, 1827.
19 Ibid., July 20, 1827.
20 George Johnson biography of Howe, p. 19½, PAC, George Johnson Papers.
21 *Acadian*, Apr. 13, 1827.
22 *Free Press*, Apr. 17, 1827.
23 *Acadian*, Apr. 20, 1827.
24 *Free Press*, Apr. 24, 1827.
25 *Acadian*, Apr. 27, 1827.
26 Ibid., Jan. 12, 1827.
27 Ibid., Apr. 13, 1827.
28 Ibid., Mar. 16, 1827.
29 Ibid., Aug. 3, 1827.
30 James A. Roy (*Joseph Howe* [Toronto: Macmillan, 1935], p. 21), assumes that Howe is the author without even raising the question. While Howe later attributed them to an authority on colonial matters (*Novascotian*, May 8, 1828), they are unmistakably his in style and viewpoint.
31 *Acadian*, May 4, 1827.
32 *Canadian Spectator*, Mar. 31, 1827.
33 *Acadian*, May 18, 1827.
34 Ibid.
35 *Acadian Recorder*, May 19, 1827.
36 Ibid.
37 *Acadian*, May 25, 1827.
38 *Acadian Recorder*, May 19, 1827.
39 *Acadian*, May 25, 1827.
40 Pictou *Colonial Patriot*, May 28, 1828.
41 Ibid.
42 Ibid.
43 J. M. Beck, *The Government of Nova Scotia* (Toronto: University of Toronto Press, 1957), pp. 33–4n.
44 See above, p. 14.
45 *Acadian*, Apr. 20, 1827.
46 Ibid., Mar. 23, 1827.
47 Ibid., Feb. 9, 1827.
48 Ibid., June 8, 1827.
49 Ibid., Nov. 9, 1827.
50 Ibid., June 8, 1827.
51 Ibid.
52 James A. Roy suggests (*Howe*, p. 20) that the editorial, marked as it was by "language of great dignity and restraint," revealed a definite advance. But it is dubious if Howe's style had improved that much in less than three months; certainly the editorial still had a strained artificiality about it.
53 "Nova Scotia-ness" was the term of Archibald MacMechan; Dr D.C. Harvey told the author that he regarded Howe as its greatest exponent and exemplification.

54 *Acadian*, Mar. 16, 1827.
55 Ibid.
56 Ibid., July 20, 1827.
57 Ibid., Feb. 16, 1827.
58 Ibid., Aug. 3, 1827.
59 Ibid.
60 D.C. Harvey, "The Intellectual Awakening of Nova Scotia," *Dalhousie Review* 13 (April 1933): 1–22.
61 Ibid., p. 2.
62 See above, p. 14.
63 Harvey, "Intellectual Awakening," p. 1.
64 Roy, *Howe*, p. 22.
65 *Acadian*, Dec. 26, 1827.
66 Howe to half-sister Jane, May 19, 1827, PANS, "Howe Letters," p. 6.

CHAPTER FOUR

1 John Howe, Sr, to Capt. John McNab, Dec. 15, 1827, JHP, reel 24.
2 In one of his letters Capt. John McNab expressed the hope that "his brother and him [i.e., Joseph] will soon be reconciled." Capt. John McNab to John Howe, Sr, Dec. 17, 1827, ibid.
3 Howe's letters to Agnes are in the Burgess Collection, PANS, MG 1, vol. 162A, April 1826 (06 w); Aug. 20, 1826 (02 w); and n.d. (04 w).
4 George Stupka (pseud.), "A Coach to Take the Air ... The Education of Joseph Howe," *Journal of Education* (Nova Scotia) 22 (Spring 1973): 45.
5 Howe to McNab, Dec. 15, 1827, JHP, reel 24; McNab to Howe, Dec. 17, 1827, ibid.
6 McNab to Howe, Dec. 17, 1827, ibid.
7 As quoted by Professor Currie of Pine Hill in the George Johnson Papers. Susan Ann's statement is not to be taken literally.
8 *Novascotian*, Feb. 1, 1827.
9 Ibid., July 13, 1826.
10 Ibid., Jan. 31, 1828.
11 Ibid., Jan. 17, 1828.
12 Ibid.
13 Ibid., Jan. 3, 1828.
14 Ibid., Feb. 7, 1828.
15 Ibid., Mar. 20, 1828.
16 Ibid.
17 Ibid., supplement, Mar. 29, 1827.
18 *JHA*, Apr. 4, 1827, p. 139.
19 *Observations – Upon ... His Majesty's Council ... with a few remarks upon ... Pictou Academy*, p. 17. See also V.L.O. Chittick, *Thomas Chandler Haliburton: A Study in Provincial Toryism* (New York: Columbia University Press, 1924), p. 99n.
20 See Chapter 9. Brenton was in no way related to Thomas Chandler; in fact, as the wits said, there was an l of a difference between them.
21 *Novascotian*, May 15, 1828.
22 Ibid.
23 Ibid.
24 Ibid.
25 *Colonial Patriot*, Dec. 7, 1827.

26 For McCulloch's complete lack of connection with the paper, see ibid., Jan. 5, 1833.
27 *Colonial Patriot*, Dec. 7, 1827.
28 Ibid., Jan. 11, 1828.
29 Quoted in the *Novascotian*, Apr. 17, 1828.
30 *Colonial Patriot*, Jan. 5, 1833.
31 *Novascotian*, Apr. 17, 1828.
32 See *Colonial Patriot*, Apr. 30, 1828. The original letter had been published in 1827, when Howe was still with the *Acadian*.
33 *Novascotian*, May 8, 1828.
34 Ibid.
35 *Colonial Patriot*, May 7, 1828.
36 *Novascotian*, Jan. 17, 1828.
37 *Colonial Patriot*, May 7, 1828.
38 Howe's major attack was contained in two editorials entitled "Pictou Patriot" and "Pictou Scribblers," dated May 29 and June 12. The *Patriot* replied on June 4 and June 18. Actually Howe guessed correctly that "The writer of the Canadian Letter" and the editor of the *Patriot* were one and the same (*Novascotian*, May 29 and June 12, 1828), but the *Patriot* could deny it because Blanchard had moved to Halifax and was not editing the paper at the time (*Colonial Patriot*, June 4, 1828). However, Blanchard did write the editorial replies to Howe's editorials of May 29 and June 12 (*Colonial Patriot*, Jan. 5, 1833).
39 *Colonial Patriot*, June 4, 1828.
40 Ibid.
41 *Novascotian*, June 12, 1828.
42 Ibid., May 29, 1828. By 1817 the Presbyterians of Pictou county appeared to have settled their differences, but subsequently the relations between the adherents of the Church of Scotland or Kirk and those of the anti-burgher branch of the Secessionist (Free) Church steadily worsened, especially after the arrival of the Kirk minister, the Rev. Kenneth John McKenzie in 1824. He allied himself with the extreme Tories on the council in an attempt to weaken Pictou Academy which was headed by the Rev. Thomas McCulloch of the Free Church. The great majority of the Highlanders were Kirkmen; most Lowlanders were Secessionists.
43 Ibid.
44 Ibid., June 12, 1828.
45 Ibid., June 26, 1828.
46 Ibid., Sept. 11, 1828; *Colonial Patriot*, Sept. 17, 1828.
47 See George Patterson, *A History of the County of Pictou* (Montreal, 1877), p. 377n.
48 *Colonial Patriot*, June 4, 1828.
49 For a more detailed discussion of the significance of the rambles see chap. 6.
50 R.D. Evans, "Stage Coaches in Nova Scotia, 1815 to 1867," *Collections of the Nova Scotia Historical Society* 24 (1938): 110.
51 *Novascotian*, July 23, 1828.
52 Ibid., Aug. 7, 1828.
53 Ibid., July 30, 1828.
54 Ibid., Aug. 14, 1828.
55 Ibid., Aug. 20, 1828.
56 Ibid.

57 Ibid.
58 Ibid., Sept. 24, 1828.
59 Ibid., Oct 9, 1828.
60 James A. Roy, *Joseph Howe* (Toronto: Macmillan, 1935), p. 38.
61 Ibid., pp. 39–40; M.G. Parks, ed., *Western and Eastern Rambles: Travel Sketches of Nova Scotia*, by Joseph Howe (Toronto: University of Toronto Press, 1973). Introduction, pp. 42–3.
62 Roy, *Howe*, p. 39.
63 Griselda E. Tonge, one of the province's earliest women poets, had died at Demerara in May 1825.
64 *Novascotian*, Aug. 14, 1828.
65 Ibid., Sept. 18, 1828.
66 Ibid., Aug. 28, 1828.
67 Ibid.
68 Chittick, *Haliburton*, p. 121.
69 Roy, *Howe*, p. 27.
70 Ibid.
71 Chisholm, 1: 4.
72 *Novascotian*, June 5, 1828.
73 Ibid., June 12, 1828.
74 Ibid., May 15, 1828.
75 Roy, *Howe*, p. 27.
76 *Novascotian*, Jan. 1, 1829.

CHAPTER FIVE

1 *Novascotian*, Jan. 1, 1829.
2 Ibid., Feb. 5, 1829.
3 Ibid.
4 See George Cox, "John Alexander Barry and his Times," *Collections of the Nova Scotia Historical Society* 28 (1949): 136–7.
5 Halifax *Free Press*, Apr. 7, 1829.
6 *Novascotian*, supplement, Apr. 9, 1829.
7 See Cox, "Barry and his Times," p. 139.
8 *Novascotian*, Apr. 15, 1829.
9 *Colonial Patriot*, May 6, 1829.
10 *Novascotian*, Apr. 15, 1829.
11 See letter of Barry, *Acadian Recorder*, Apr. 25, 1829.
12 *Novascotian*, Apr. 16, 1829.
13 Letter of Barry, *Acadian Recorder*, Apr. 25, 1829.
14 *Free Press*, Apr. 21, 1829.
15 *Novascotian*, Apr. 23, 1829.
16 Letter of Barry, *Acadian Recorder*, Apr. 25, 1829.
17 *Free Press*, Apr. 28, 1829.
18 Letter of Barry, *Acadian Recorder*, Apr. 25, 1829.
19 *Novascotian*, Apr. 30, 1829.
20 Ibid., Feb. 3, 1830.
21 See *Colonial Patriot*, Dec. 7, 1827.
22 Ibid., May 6, 1829.
23 Ibid., May 20, 1829.
24 Ibid., May 6, 1829.
25 Ibid., May 13, 1829.
26 *Novascotian*, July 9, 1829.

27 Ibid., Sept. 9, 1829.
28 Ibid., July 16, 1829.
29 Ibid.
30 Ibid., Aug. 5, 1829.
31 *Free Press*, Aug. 11, 1829.
32 *Novascotian*, Aug. 5, 1829.
33 Ibid.
34 *Free Press*, Aug. 11, 1829.
35 *Novascotian*, Aug. 13, 1829.
36 Ibid., Jan. 27, 1830.
37 Ibid., Jan. 20, 1830.
38 Ibid.
39 *Colonial Patriot*, Feb. 20, 1830.
40 Ibid.
41 Ibid. Blanchard was referring here to a grievance that he found highly distasteful. For a dissenter to marry, he had either to publish his intention by banns in his own church, or purchase a licence and be married according to the forms of the Church of England.
42 For the details see M. Gene Morison, "The Brandy Election of 1830," *Collections of the Nova Scotia Historical Society* 30 (1954): 151–83.
43 Apparently some councillors had intimated to a committee of the assembly, in a conference on the revenue bill, that the council intended to reduce the provincial expenditures from £60,000 to £45,000, and that roads and bridges would bear the brunt of the decrease. See extract from speech of John Young, *Acadian Recorder*, Oct. 30, 1830.
44 *Novascotian*, Apr. 7, 1830.
45 Ibid., Apr. 22, 1830.
46 *JLC*, Apr. 7, 1830, PANS, RG 1, vol. 218 (xx), pp. 181–2.
47 The assembly ignored this demand.
48 *Novascotian*, Apr. 7, 1830.
49 Ibid., Apr. 29, 1830.
50 *Acadian Recorder*, Apr. 24, 1830.
51 *Novascotian*, Apr. 29, 1830.
52 *Acadian Recorder*, Apr. 24, 1830.
53 *Novascotian*, Apr. 29, 1830.
54 *Free Press*, May 11, 1830.
55 *Novascotian*, May 14, 1830.
56 Ibid., May 20, 1830.
57 See above, p. 47.
58 *Novascotian*, May 20, 1830.
59 Ibid.
60 Ibid.
61 Ibid., May 27, 1830.
62 Ibid., June 2, 1830.
63 Ibid., May 20, 1830.
64 *Colonial Patriot*, Apr. 10, 1830.
65 Those of May 20, May 27, and June 3 contained his articles on the revenue dispute.
66 Howe to John Howe, Sr, June 9, 1830, JHP, vol. 10, p. 256.
67 *Novascotian*, June 16, 1830.
68 Howe to John Howe, Sr, June 9, 1830, JHP, vol. 10, p. 256.
69 Howe to Susan Ann, June 9, 1830, JHP, reel 23, item 1.

70 Howe to John Howe, Sr, June 9, 1830, JHP, vol. 10, p. 256.
71 *Novascotian*, May 20, 1830.
72 See speech of William Young, ibid., May 10, 1838.
73 Ibid., Sept. 1, 1830.
74 Ibid., Aug. 18, 1830.
75 Ibid., Sept. 9, 1830.
76 Ibid., Sept. 1, 1830.
77 Ibid.
78 Ibid., Sept. 23, 1830. See also Morison, "Brandy Election of 1830," p. 179.
79 See above, p. 73.
80 *Novascotian*, Sept. 23, 1830.
81 Ibid., Sept. 30, 1830.
82 See extract from a letter dated Pictou, Tuesday evening, *Acadian Recorder*, Oct. 2, 1830. For some time the Kirkmen had been using the council to prevent a permanent grant to Pictou Academy, whose principal was Free Churchman Thomas McCulloch. This also brought them into conflict with McCulloch's friend and supporter, Jotham Blanchard.
83 *Novascotian*, Oct. 20, 1830.
84 Howe to Susan Ann, n.d., JHP, reel 23, item 117.
85 *Novascotian*, Oct. 7, 1830.
86 Ibid.
87 See, for example, *Acadian Recorder*, Oct. 23, 1830.
88 *Novascotian*, Nov. 11, 1830.
89 Ibid., Nov. 18, 1830.
90 Ibid.
91 Howe to Susan Ann, n.d., JHP, reel 23, item 116.
92 *Novascotian*, Oct. 28, 1830.
93 Howe to unknown, Nov. 3, 1830, PANS, "Howe Letters," p. 9.
94 *Novascotian*, Oct. 28, 1830.

CHAPTER SIX

1 Howe's letters to Susan Ann during this period, for the most part undated, are to be found in JHP, reel 23.
2 See below, pp. 98–9.
3 Howe to Susan Ann, n.d., JHP, reel 23, item 4.
4 Ibid.
5 Ibid., n.d., item 100.
6 Ibid., n.d., item 4.
7 Ibid., n.d., item 92.
8 Ibid., n.d., item 147.
9 Ibid., n.d., item 144.
10 Ibid., n.d., item 98.
11 Ibid., n.d., item 142.
12 Ibid., n.d., item 4.
13 Ibid., n.d., item 92.
14 Ibid., n.d., item 142.
15 Ibid.
16 Ibid., n.d., item 144.
17 Ibid., n.d., item 4. Apparently David drowned shortly afterwards while duck-shooting.

18 Ibid., n.d., item 142.
19 Ibid.
20 Ibid., n.d., item 105.
21 Ibid., Aug. 26, 1829, item 5.
22 See "Eastern Rambles," no. 2, *Novascotian*, Dec. 31, 1829.
23 Ibid.
24 Howe to Susan Ann, n.d., item 142.
25 Ibid., n.d., item 2.
26 Ibid.
27 Ibid.
28 Ibid.
29 Ibid.
30 Ibid., June 9, 1830, item 1.
31 Ibid., n.d., item 99.
32 Ibid.
33 Ibid., n.d., item 2.
34 Ibid., n.d., item 18.
35 Ibid., n.d., item 99.
36 Ibid., item 6.
37 Ibid., item 17.
38 Ibid., June 9, 1830, item 1.
39 Ibid., n.d., item 18.
40 Howe to Susan Ann, June 9, 1830, item 1; ibid., n.d., item 18.
41 See above, pp. 71–2.
42 See "Eastern Rambles," no. 11, *Novascotian*, Aug. 18, 1830.
43 Ibid., no. 15, Aug. 3, 1831. Miller's name had been Müller.
44 Howe to Susan Ann, n.d., item 121.
45 Ibid., n.d., item 127.
46 Ibid.; *Poems*, pp. 102–3. Earlier, bad weather at Bridgetown had permitted him to complete fifteen verses on the Talbots in French history. Howe to Susan Ann, n.d., item 124; *Poems*, pp. 151–4.
47 Howe to Susan Ann, n.d., item 133.
48 Ibid., n.d., item 112.
49 Ibid., n.d., item 127.
50 Ibid., n.d., item 122.
51 Ibid., Aug. 1, 1832, item 13.
52 Ibid., July 11, 1832, item 10.
53 Ibid., July 16, 1832, item 11.
54 Ibid., item 112. He was later relieved to hear that Susan Ann had got something out of Bowes at Halifax; "the rascal had made a sad hole in my Windsor monies." Ibid., n.d., item 121.
55 Ibid., item 122.
56 Ibid., n.d., item 127.
57 Ibid., July 25, 1832, item 12.
58 Ibid.
59 *Novascotian*, July 11, 1832.
60 Ibid., July 18, 1832.
61 Howe to Susan Ann, September 1833, item 14.
62 Ibid.
63 Ibid.
64 Ibid.
65 Ibid., n.d., item 109.
66 Ibid.

67 Ibid., Sept. 27, 1833, item 15.
68 See below, pp. 100–1.
69 Howe to Susan Ann, May 27, 1834, item 26.
70 Ibid., n.d., item 91.
71 Ibid., May 11, 1834, item 24.
72 Ibid., June 5, 1834, item 28.
73 Ibid., Apr. 30, 1834, item 19. See also ibid., May 11, 1834, item 24.
74 Ibid., June 3, 1834, item 27.
75 Ibid., May 11, 1834, item 24.
76 Ibid., May 12, 1834, item 24.
77 Ibid., May 11, 1834, item 24. For outcome of Thomson and Fulton transaction, see below, p. 100.
78 Ibid.
79 The tree produced "thousands of little green hard sour apples which could not be cooked tender." Waterman Papers, PANS, MG 1, vol. 933.

CHAPTER SEVEN

1 Howe to half-sister Jane [?], July 5, 1829, PANS, "Howe Letters," p. 8.
2 Ibid.
3 *Novascotian*, Apr. 1, 1829.
4 Howe to unknown, Jan. 15, 1831, JHP, vol. 32. (Vols 32–35 lack page numbers.)
5 *Novascotian*, Apr. 1, 1829.
6 His receipts during the ramble amounted to £132, a not insignificant portion of the total return from the *History*.
7 JHP, vol. 33.
8 Howe to unknown, Sept. 28, 1831, ibid., vol. 32.
9 Ibid., vol. 33.
10 Ibid., vol. 32. For a somewhat different accounting, see Howe to Haliburton, Jan. 2, 1841, ibid., vol. 33.
11 Ibid. The full title was: *A Compendious History of the Northern Part of the Province of New Brunswick, and of the District of Gaspé, in Lower Canada.*
12 For authors and titles of the pamphlets as well as other imprints issued from the *Novascotian* office, see George L. Parker, "Joseph Howe as Publisher," *Dalhousie Review* 53 (Autumn 1973): 476–8.
13 JHP, vol. 33.
14 Howe to Harry Austen, Dec. 28, 1855, JHP, vol. 31, p. 29.
15 See above, p. 96.
16 JHP, vol. 33.
17 Ibid.
18 Peter Lynch, "Early Reminiscences of Halifax – Men who have Passed from us," *Collections of the Nova Scotia Historical Society* 16 (1912): 202–3.
19 Ibid., p. 203.
20 See J. M. Beck, "Joseph Howe: Mild Tory to Reforming Assemblyman," *Dalhousie Review* 44 (Spring 1964): 49–50.
21 Roy Palmer Baker, *A History of English-Canadian Literature to the Confederation* (Cambridge, Mass.: Harvard University Press, 1920), p. 60.
22 *Novascotian*, May 13, 1830.
23 J.S. Martell, "Early Parliamentary Reporting in Nova Scotia," *Canadian Historical Review* 21 (December 1940): 392.
24 *Novascotian*, May 2, 1833.

25 Ibid., Nov. 25, 1830.
26 Ibid., Apr. 23, 1834.
27 Ibid., Nov. 25, 1830.
28 Ibid., Mar. 31, 1830.
29 Ibid., Apr. 23, 1834.
30 Ibid.
31 Ibid., Jan. 1, 1829.
32 Ibid., July 6, 1831.
33 Ibid., Sept. 28, 1831.
34 Ibid., Nov. 11, 1830.
35 Howe to Susan Ann, July 11, 1832, JHP, reel 23, item 10.
36 *Novascotian*, Aug. 28, 1834.
37 Ibid., Apr. 10, 1834.
38 Ibid.
39 Ibid.
40 Ibid.
41 Ibid., Sept. 10, 1834.
42 Ibid., June 12, 1833.
43 D.C. Harvey, "The Intellectual Awakening of Nova Scotia," *Dalhousie Review* 13 (April 1933): 18.
44 Parker, "Joseph Howe as Publisher," p. 472.
45 See above, pp. 99–100; *Novascotian*, July 23, 1829.
46 Ibid., June 4, 1829.
47 Ibid., Mar. 1, 1832.
48 Ibid., Nov. 10, 1831.
49 Ibid., Mar. 1, 1832.
50 Ibid., Dec. 31, 1829.
51 Ibid., Dec. 28, 1831.
52 Ibid., Feb. 17, 1832.
53 Harvey, "Intellectual Awakening," p. 19.
54 *Novascotian*, Jan. 22, 1829.
55 Ibid., Oct. 13, 1831.
56 Ibid., Apr. 7, 1831
57 Ibid., Jan. 12, 1831
58 Ibid., Mar. 1, 1832.
59 Ibid., Aug. 11, 1831.
60 Ibid., Jan. 12, 1831.
61 Ibid., Mar. 1, 1832.
62 Harvey, "Intellectual Awakening," p. 19.

CHAPTER EIGHT

1 *Novascotian*, June 2, 1831. Among those with whom Howe played racquets at one time or other were a regular companion, Lieutenant Nortcott of the Rifle Brigade, and Capt. William Pitt Canning, RN, son of the late prime minister of Britain.
2 *Novascotian*, July 6, 1831.
3 Ibid., July 21, 1831.
4 Ibid., July 28 and Aug. 4, 1831.
5 Ibid., July 28, 1831.
6 See, e.g., ibid., Jan. 18, 1832.
7 Ibid., Apr. 26, 1832.
8 Ibid., Apr. 19, 1832.

9 *Colonial Patriot*, Apr. 14, 1832.
10 *Novascotian*, Apr. 26, 1832.
11 Ibid., Sept. 26, 1832.
12 Ibid., Apr. 19, 1832.
13 Ibid., Aug. 22 and Sept. 20, 1832.
14 Ibid., May 17, 1832.
15 Ibid., Aug. 22, 1832.
16. J.S. Martell, "A Documentary Study of Provincial Finance and Currency 1812–36," *Bulletin of the Public Archives of Nova Scotia* 2, no. 4 (1941): 20–21.
17 Samuel Cunard in 1830; H.H. Cogswell in 1831; Joseph Allison in 1832; and James Tobin in 1832.
18 *Novascotian*, Mar. 8, 1832.
19 Martell, "Provincial Finance and Currency," p. 22.
20 *Novascotian*, Mar. 29, 1832.
21 Ibid., Feb. 7, 1833.
22 Ibid.
23 Martell, "Provincial Finance and Currency," p. 24.
24 Ibid., 23.
25 *Novascotian*, Feb. 7, 1833.
26 Ibid., Apr. 4, 1833.
27 3 Wm. IV, c. 38.
28 Martell, "Provincial Finance and Currency," p. 27.
29 *Novascotian*, Apr. 18, 1833.
30 Ibid., May 2, 1833.
31 Ibid.
32 Ibid., Sept. 4, 1833. Also, ibid., May 29, 1833. Neilson, journalist, politician, and publisher of the *Quebec Gazette*, broke with Papineau in 1834.
33 Ibid., Feb. 7, 1833.
34 So called because it was designed to reduce the costs of litigants, usually at the expense of the lawyers.
35 *Novascotian*, Aug. 7, 1833.
36 Ibid., Oct. 30, 1833.
37 Ibid., Nov. 27, 1833.
38 Ibid., Dec. 14, 1833. According to his estimates, there were in circulation £80,000 in Treasury notes; between £125,000 and £150,000 in Halifax Banking Company notes; and £68,000 in Bank of Nova Scotia notes.
39 Ibid., Dec. 11, 1833.
40 Ibid.
41 Ibid.
42 Ibid.
43 See *JHA*, 1833, App. 59, pp. 42–3.
44 By a vote of eighteen to sixteen. See *JHA*, 1833, p. 503.
45 *Novascotian*, Dec. 11, 1833.
46 Ibid.
47 Ibid., Jan. 22, 1834.
48 Ibid.
49 Ibid.
50 Ibid.
51 For the moment the doubloon at £4, and later the coins of Great Britain at their sterling par value.

52 *Novascotian*, Feb. 12 and 19, 1834.
53 Ibid., June 19, 1834.
54 Howe to Susan Ann, June 3, 1834, JHP, reel 23, item 27.
55 *Acadian Recorder*, July 12, 1834.
56 *Novascotian*, July 16, 1834.
57 See editorial under heading "State of a Town," ibid., July 23, 1834.
58 Ibid., July 3, 1834.
59 Ibid., July 30, 1834.
60 Ibid., Aug. 20, 1834.
61 Ibid., Jan. 8, 1835.
62 For the details see Martell, "Provincial Finance and Currency," p. 31.
63 Ibid., p. 30.
64 *Novascotian*, Oct. 23, 1834.
65 Ibid.
66 Ibid., Jan. 1, 1834.
67 Ibid., Jan. 15, 1834.
68 Blanchard wanted to go even further and deprive the Crown of its right to appoint councillors. Ibid., Feb. 27, 1834.
69 Goderich to Jeffery, Dec. 8, 1832, PANS, RG 1, vol. 69, item 38.
70 Jeffery to Goderich, Mar. 20, 1833, PANS, RG 1, vol. 114, pp. 101–2.
71 *Novascotian*, July 3, 1834.
72 See D.C. Harvey, "The Civil List and Responsible Government in Nova Scotia," *Canadian Historical Review* 28 (December 1947): 366.
73 Ibid., pp. 376–8.
74 Ibid., p. 377.
75 *JHA*, Mar. 1, 1833, p. 361.
76 E.G. Stanley to Jeffery, Sept. 30, 1833, ibid., 1834, App. 1, p. 3.
77 *Novascotian*, Mar. 20, 1834.
78 £2,500 stg for the lieutenant-governor; £1,000 for the incumbent provincial secretary and £700 for his successors; and £500 for the attorney general.
79 *Novascotian*, Apr. 3, 1834.
80 Ibid., Mar. 27, 1834.
81 *JHA*, Apr. 3, 1834, p. 653.
82 *Novascotian*, Apr. 24, 1834. Later Stewart admitted that he had responded to strong feelings in his own constituency and throughout the province against the level of the assembly's proposals. Ibid., Dec. 18, 1834.
83 Ibid., Apr. 24, 1834.
84 Ibid., Apr. 9, 1834.
85 Harvey, "Civil List and Responsible Government," p. 379.
86 *Acadian Recorder*, Apr. 5, 1834.
87 *Colonial Patriot*, Apr. 1, 8, 15, 1834.
88 *Novascotian*, Nov. 12, 1834.
89 Ibid.
90 Ibid., Nov. 19, 1834.
91 Ibid., Nov. 27 and Dec. 3, 1834.
92 Jeffery to Stanley, Apr. 15, 1834, PANS, RG 1, vol. 114, p. 132.
93 Stanley to Campbell, May 27, 1834, PANS, RG 1, vol. 72, pp. 55–60.
94 Campbell to T. Spring Rice, July 16 and Dec. 29, 1834, PANS, RG 1, vol. 114, pp. 139–40, 157–9.

95 *Novascotian*, Dec. 3, 1834.
96 Ibid.
97 *Acadian Recorder*, Nov. 29, 1834.
98 *Novascotian*, Dec. 3, 1834.
99 Ibid., supplement, Dec. 15, 1834.
100 The vote was twenty-seven to ten. See *JHA*, Dec. 13, 1834, pp. 729–30.
101 *Novascotian*, supplement, Dec. 15, 1834.
102 Ibid., Dec. 18, 1834.
103 Ibid.
104 Ibid., Nov. 27, 1834. See letter of "R," ibid.
105 Ibid., Dec. 3, 1834.
106 Ibid., Dec. 18, 1834.
107 Ibid., supplement, Dec. 29, 1834.
108 Ibid.
109 Ibid.
110 Ibid.

CHAPTER NINE

1 J.M. Beck, *The Government of Nova Scotia* (Toronto: University of Toronto Press, 1957), p. 40.
2 Ibid., p. 136.
3 D.C. Harvey, "The Struggle for the New England Form of Township Government in Nova Scotia," *Report of the Canadian Historical Association*, 1933, p. 22.
4 David Sutherland, "Gentlemen vs. Shopkeepers: Urban Reform in Early 19th Century Halifax," paper read at the annual meeting of the Canadian Historical Association, 1972, p. 2.
5 Ibid., p. 3.
6 Ibid., pp. 2–3.
7 3 Wm IV., c. 51.
8 In this period he served actively on two committees which presented memorials on matters he was pressing in the *Novascotian*. One declared that the shortage of coinage was causing harm to all classes of the community; the other that the slaughtering of cattle in the heart of the town was producing a "range of nuisances" that would put the residents at "the hazard of their lives during the heat of Summer," and might facilitate the appearance and spread of cholera morbus. See proceedings of Jan. 17 and 20, and Mar. 9 and 10, 1832, "Grand Jury Minute Book," 1828–34, PANS, RG 34-312 (P 13).
9 See above, p. 45.
10 Proceedings of Mar. 19, 1832, "Grand Jury Minute Book," 1828–34, PANS, RG 34-312 (P 13).
11 See proceedings of Mar. 22, 1832, "Minutes of Sessions," PANS, RG 34-312 (P 10).
12 See proceedings of June 11, 1832, "Grand Jury Minute Book," 1828–34, PANS, RG 34-312 (P 13).
13 Grocers' Petition, Jan. 4, 1832. Assembly Petitions, Trade and Commerce, 1825–32, PANS, RG 5, series "P", vol. 121.
14 Petition of Grocers' Society to Maitland, July 6, 1832, PANS, RG 1, vol. 412, doc. 90.

15 Ibid., doc. 95.
16 See extracts by Sydenham Howe, p. 30, PAC, George Johnson Papers.
17 Proceedings of Dec. 17 and 18, 1832, "Grand Jury Minute Book," 1828–34, PANS, RG 34-312 (P 13).
18 Chisholm, 1: 45.
19 *Acadian Recorder*, Sept. 13, 1834.
20 Ibid.
21 *Novascotian*, Nov. 6, 1834.
22 Ibid., Nov. 20, 1834.
23 Proceedings of Nov. 14, 1834, "Grand Jury Minute Book," 1828–34, PANS, RG 34-312 (P 13).
24 Ibid., Dec. 13, 1834.
25 Ibid., Dec. 12, 1834.
26 Ibid., Dec. 11, 1834.
27 *Novascotian*, Dec. 18, 1834.
28 Magistrates to Campbell, Jan. 8, 1835, PANS, RG 1, vol. 237, doc. 141. John Howe, Sr, was not among the twelve magistrates who made the request, but John Howe, Jr, was. While his motives are not entirely clear, he probably acted as he did because of an entire lack of sympathy with his half-brother's methods of bringing about municipal reform.
29 *Novascotian*, Feb. 5, 1835.
30 *Acadian Recorder*, Feb. 14, 1835.
31 Howe's speech to the jury, cited in Chisholm, 1: 57.
32 See *Acadian Recorder*, Feb. 28, 1835.
33 Howe's speech to the jury, cited in Chisholm, 1: 35.
34 Comments of Howe to his friends, cited in ibid., p. 23.
35 Attorney General Archibald's speech to the jury, cited in ibid., p. 75.
36 Ibid., p. 78.
37 Howe to half-sister Jane, Mar. 17, 1835, PANS, "Howe Letters," p. 10.
38 Comments of Howe to his friends, cited in Chisholm, 1: 24.
39 Howe to half-sister Jane, Mar. 17, 1835, PANS "Howe Letters," p. 10.
40 Joseph A. Chisholm, "*The King v. Joseph Howe*: Prosecution for Libel," *Canadian Bar Review* 7 (October 1935): 587. All cases in the Supreme Court of Nova Scotia had been tried by two or more judges up to 1834, when, because the practice had been found "difficult and inconvenient," the legislature made it lawful for one judge to sit by himself (4 Wm. IV, c. 4). While the old practice was continued in the Howe trial, there are no records to indicate how many judges actually sat with the chief justice.
41 See above, p. 115.
42 Report of Committee of Council to Campbell, Jan. 14, 1835, PANS, RG 1, vol. 312, doc. 108.
43 David Hall, Robert Lawson, Samuel Mitchell, Edward Pryor, Jr, and Robert Story.
44 See record of the trial in Chisholm, 1: 24–30.
45 See speech of James F. Gray, cited in ibid., p. 26.
46 Comments of Howe to his friends, cited in ibid., p. 24.

47 Howe's speech to the jury, cited in ibid., p. 37.
48 See above, p. 104.
49 Howe's speech to the jury, cited in Chisholm, 1:40.
50 It was Howe's contention, nonetheless, that W.H. Roach and possibly Richard Tremain might have requested damages for themselves in a civil suit. Ibid., pp. 32–3.
51 See speech of Archibald, cited in ibid., p. 74.
52 Howe's speech to the jury, ibid., p. 36.
53 Ibid., pp. 44–5. Howe based his calculations on "an actual and very low" property valuation of £1,200,950.
54 Ibid., p. 45.
55 See proceedings of Dec. 11, 13, and 16, 1834, "Grand Jury Minute Book," 1828–34, PANS, RG 34-312 (P 13).
56 Howe's speech to the jury, cited in Chisholm, 1: 50–1.
57 Ibid., p. 53. Howe did not mention Tremain by name.
58 Ibid., p. 56. The magistrate appears to have been Matthew Richardson.
59 Ibid., p. 52.
60 Ibid., p. 70.
61 Ibid., p. 71.
62 Comments of Howe to his friends, ibid., p. 24.
63 This was the argument used by Beamish Murdoch when he intervened on Howe's behalf. Ibid., pp. 72–3.
64 Ibid., p. 74.
65 The newspaper reports are clear on this point. See, e.g., that of the *Temperance Recorder* in the *Halifax Journal*, Mar. 9, 1835.
66 Ibid.
67 Chisholm, 1: 82.
68 *Acadian Recorder*, Mar. 7, 1835. The *Recorder* suggested that the sessions could "no longer sit in judgment on misdemeanors or offences, till it has clean hands and has set its house in order."
69 Quoted from the *Temperance Recorder* in the *Halifax Journal*, Mar. 9, 1835.
70 The *Novascotian's* reporter at the trial was Howe's friend, John Sparrow Thompson, whose son would be prime minister of Canada. A year later, on the anniversary of the trial, Howe offered Thompson a gift of money for his services, only to be told by Thompson that he was already too much in Howe's debt. See Thompson to Howe, Mar. 2, 1836, JHP, vol. 1, pp. 9–10.
71 Chisholm, "*The King* v. *Joseph Howe*," p. 592.
72 See below, p. 256.
73 Chisholm, "*The King* v. *Joseph Howe*," p. 589. Nova Scotia continued to rely on the British example and did not enact a libel law of its own.
74 Tidmarsh to Provincial Secretary George, Mar. 4, 1835, PANS, RG 1, vol. 252, doc. 7.
75 Starr to George, Mar. 4, 1835, ibid., doc. 8.
76 Hartshorne to George, Mar. 11, 1835, doc. 12. For the other refusals see ibid., docs. 13 to 20.
77 Minutes of Council, Mar. 11, 1835, PANS, RG 3, vol. 214½C, p. 121.
78 *Novascotian*, Mar. 26, 1835.
79 *Times*, Mar. 31, 1835.

80 *Novascotian*, Apr. 23, 1835.
81 See, e.g., ibid., Dec. 22, 1836.
82 Chisholm, 1: 51–2. Attorney General Archibald concurred: "I readily assent to all that has been said by a son of a father who is an honour to him." Ibid., p. 78.
83 Reference to John Howe by Joseph Howe in January 1832, extracts by Sydenham Howe, p. 30, PAC, George Johnson Papers.
84 John Howe, Jr, to George Hutton of Dundee, May 23, 1838, JHP, reel 22.
85 See proceedings of Mar. 6, 1832, "Minutes of the Court of Sessions," PANS, RG 34-312 (P 10).
86 *Novascotian*, Mar. 26, 1835.
87 Ibid., Apr. 2, 1835.
88 During the trial Attorney General Archibald had said that John Howe's "unsullied reputation would never have left him obnoxious to any such charge" as was brought against the other magistrates. Chisholm, 1: 78.
89 *Novascotian*, Apr. 2, 1835.
90 *Acadian Recorder*, Apr. 18, 1835.
91 *Times*, Apr. 14, 1835.
92 Ibid., Apr. 21, 1835.
93 See letter of "Inquirer," ibid.
94 See memoir of Joseph Howe, JHP, reel 22.
95 *Novascotian*, Apr. 30, 1835. This editorial is headed, "Mr. Sawers and His Friends."
96 See *Acadian Recorder*, May 9 to June 6, 1835.
97 Actually the sessions had voted down a motion to this effect by four to three, Dr Head, Fairbanks, Albro, and Joseph Starr opposing J.L. Starr, Russell, and John Howe, Jr; see proceedings of Mar. 5, 1835, "Minutes of Court of Quarter Sessions," PANS, RG 34-312 (P 11).
98 *Novascotian*, Apr. 16, 1835.
99 See letters of Tremain to Campbell, Mar. 9 and 21, 1835, PANS, RG 1, vol. 412, docs. 137 and 138.
100 *Halifax Journal*, Apr. 20 and 27, 1835.
101 *Novascotian*, May 7, 1835.
102 A silver pitcher, above twelve inches in height, and holding nearly three quarts, with a handsome gilt stand four inches high. See *Times*, June 2, 1835.
103 Howe to Susan Ann, July 7, 1835 (second letter), JHP, reel 23, item 32.
104 Howe to Susan Ann, July 3, 1835, reel 23, item 31. Surprisingly he did considerably better in Liverpool and Lunenburg, and he later reported: "shall be able to bring about £20 with me – very little for all our wants, but better than nothing." Howe to Susan Ann, July 13, 1835, JHP, reel 23, item 94.
105 Howe to Susan Ann, July 1835, JHP, reel 23, item 30.
106 A bill of the Nova Scotia Legislature separating the district of Pictou and the district of Colchester from the county of Halifax was awaiting approval in England.
107 Howe to Susan Ann, July 3, 1835, JHP, reel 23, item 31.
108 Ibid.

CHAPTER TEN

1 See the four articles on "Halifax and its Prospects" in the *Novascotian*, Aug. 27 to Sept. 17, 1835.
2 Ibid., Sept. 3, 1835.
3 Ibid., Oct. 1, 8, and 15, 1835.
4 Ibid., Oct. 1, 1835.
5 Ibid., Nov. 19, 1835.
6 Ibid., July 23, 1835.
7 Ibid., May 7, 1835.
8 Ibid., Aug. 13, 1835.
9 Chapman to Howe, May 30 and July 18, 1835, ibid., Dec. 21, 1837.
10 For Howe's reply of Oct. 2, 1835, see ibid.
11 See below, p. 170.
12 *Novascotian*, Aug. 27, 1835.
13 Ibid.
14 Howe to Blanchard, Oct. 26, 1835, JHP, vol. 6, pp. 2–7.
15 Howe wrote none too soon, for Blanchard's health had deteriorated to the point that he would never again sit in the assembly.
16 *Times*, Oct. 20, 1835.
17 T.C. Haliburton to Howe, Nov. 15, 1835, in material sent by Sydenham Howe to George Johnson, Dec. 1, 1902, pp. 12a–12b, PAC, George Johnson Papers.
18 Ibid.
19 Ibid.
20 *Novascotian*, Nov. 26, 1835.
21 The seat had been vacated by Charles Rufus Fairbanks on his appointment as master of the rolls.
22 *Novascotian*, Nov. 26, 1835.
23 Ibid.
24 Howe to Susan Ann, July 13, 1835, JHP, reel 23, item 94.
25 See *Novascotian*, Feb. 3, 1836. In the end, both houses were "content to slip back into the acceptance of the doubloon as a practical measuring stick." J.S. Martell, "A Documentary Study of Provincial Finance and Currency 1812–36," *Bulletin of the Public Archives of Nova Scotia* 2, no. 4 (1941): 20.
26 *Novascotian*, Apr. 6, 1836.
27 Ibid.
28 Ibid., Apr. 20, 1836.
29 Ibid., May 18, 1836.
30 Ibid.
31 Ibid., May 5, 1836.
32 Ibid., Feb. 3, 1836.
33 Ibid., Feb. 10, 1836.
34 Ibid., June 1, 1836. He had first proposed it almost three years earlier. Ibid., Aug. 21, 1833.
35 Ibid., Aug. 10, 1836.
36 Ibid., Mar. 30, 1836.
37 Ibid., June 1, 1836.
38 Ibid., Jan. 27, 1836.
39 Howe to Gladwin, May 31, 1836, JHP, vol. 32.
40 Ibid.

41 *Novascotian,* June 22, 1836.
42 Howe to Gladwin, June 21, 1836, JHP, vol. 32.
43 *Novascotian,* Oct. 19, 1836.
44 Ibid., Oct. 27, 1836.
45 Ibid.
46 Ibid., Nov. 10, 1836.
47 Ibid.
48 Ibid., Nov. 17, 1836.
49 Ibid., Dec. 1, 1836.
50 Ibid., Aug. 4, 1836.
51 Ibid., July 13 and Aug. 4, 1836.
52 His speech is reported in the *Novascotian,* Nov. 17, 1836.
53 Howe to half-sister Jane, n.d., 1837, PANS, "Howe Letters," pp. 14–5.
54 Ibid.
55 *Novascotian,* Dec. 21, 1836.
56 Ibid.
57 Ibid.
58 Gladwin, a candidate in the county election, polled so few votes that he did not affect Annand's chances. William Lawson, the long-time member for the county of Halifax, now president of the Bank of Nova Scotia and county treasurer, had once earned Howe's approval for his sympathy to popular causes. But in 1836 Howe hoped he would be replaced by someone "more alive to the spirit of the times." Howe to Gladwin, May 31, 1835, JHP, vol. 32.
59 *Novascotian,* Nov. 17, 1836.
60 *Acadian Recorder,* Dec. 3, 1836.
61 *Novascotian,* Jan. 19, 1837.

CHAPTER ELEVEN

1 *Acadian Recorder,* Feb. 4, 1837.
2 Letter to half-sister Jane, n.d., 1837, PANS, "Howe Letters," p. 14.
3 See *JHA,* Jan. 31, 1837, pp. 9–10.
4 Speech of Jan. 31, *Novascotian,* Feb. 2, 1837.
5 Speech of Feb. 4, ibid., Feb. 9, 1837.
6 Ibid.
7 Ibid.
8 Ibid.
9 Speech of Apr. 7, ibid., Apr. 13, 1837.
10 Speech of Feb. 10, ibid., Feb. 23, 1837.
11 Ibid. Because of the council's failure to proceed with the bill, it did not finally become law until 1840.
12 *JHA,* Feb. 2, 1837, p. 17.
13 Ibid., Feb. 4, 1837, pp. 24–5.
14 See for example, William Young to George, Nov. 11, 1837, PANS, William Young Papers, MG 2, box 732, item 184.
15 Speech of Feb. 11, *Novascotian,* Feb. 23, 1837.
16 For the original resolutions as presented by Howe, see Chisholm, 1: 112–15.
17 *Times,* Mar. 7, 1837.
18 Speech of Feb. 11, *Novascotian,* Feb. 23, 1837.
19 Ibid.

20 Ibid.
21 Ibid.
22 *JHA*, Feb. 25, 1837, p. 79.
23 Ibid., Feb. 27, 1837, p. 81.
24 Ibid., Mar. 1, 1837, p. 85.
25 Ibid.
26 Speech of Mar. 3, *Novascotian*, Mar. 16, 1837.
27 *Acadian Recorder*, Mar. 11, 1837.
28 Speech of Mar. 8, *Novascotian*, Mar. 23, 1837.
29 Ibid.
30 Ibid.
31 Ibid.
32 Ibid.
33 For the address that actually went to England, see Chisholm, 1: 152–5.
34 *JHA*, Apr. 13, 1837, p. 200.
35 *Novascotian*, Apr. 20, 1837.
36 Ibid., May 4, 1837.
37 See above, p. 147.
38 Speech of Feb. 1, *Novascotian*, Feb. 9, 1837.
39 Speech of Mar. 22, ibid., Mar. 30, 1837.
40 Speech of Feb. 20, ibid., Mar. 2, 1837.
41 Ibid., May 25, 1837.
42 Ibid.
43 Ibid.
44 Ibid.
45 Howe to half-sister Jane, n.d., 1837, PANS, "Howe Letters," p. 14.
46 *Novascotian*, July 20, 1837.
47 Ibid.
48 Ibid., Oct. 12, 1837.
49 Ibid., Oct. 19, 1837.
50 Ibid.
51 *Novascotian*, Jan. 5, 1837.
52 Howe to Bentley, Oct. 16, 1837, JHP, vol. 32.
53 *Times*, Apr. 4, 1837.
54 The *Recorder* (Apr. 8, 1837) noted that the *Novascotian* "never deigns to notice the creature [i.e. the *Times*], – Mr. Howe will not break a *grub* on the wheel."
55 *Novascotian*, Nov. 2, 1837.
56 Ibid.
57 Campbell to Glenelg, Mar. 9, 1837, PANS, RG 1, vol. 115, doc. 65, pp. 32–3.
58 Ibid., May 1, 1837, doc. 71, pp. 36–7.
59 Ibid., June 5, 1837, doc. 78, pp. 42–3.
60 Note of Howe to Campbell, Oct. 21, 1837, JHP, vol. 6, p. 10.
61 This is Howe's recollection of the events twenty years later. See Chisholm, 1: 157.
62 *Times*, Aug. 8, 1837.
63 *Novascotian*, July 13, 1837.
64 Ibid., Dec. 21, 1837.
65 Ibid.
66 Ibid.

67 Ibid.
68 Ibid., Feb. 1, 1838.
69 See speech of Feb. 3, ibid., Feb. 8, 1838.
70 Ibid., Feb. 1, 1838.
71 See, esp., ibid.
72 *Acadian Recorder*, Nov. 24, 1838.
73 *Times*, Feb. 6, 1838.
74 *Novascotian*, Feb. 8, 1838.
75 Ibid.
76 Ibid., Feb. 1, 1838.
77 *JHA*, Jan. 27, 1838, pp. 237–8.
78 *Times*, Jan. 30, 1838. Hugh Bell still opposed the proposal.
79 The meeting was held at the Exchange Coffee House on Jan. 28, 1837.
80 *Times*, Jan. 31, 1837.
81 Ibid.
82 Speeches of Feb. 23 and 24, *Novascotian*, Mar. 15, 1838.
83 Ibid.
84 In this case matters had proceeded to such a length that Sawers had asked J.B. Uniacke to represent his interests, while Howe had named E.M. Dodd. Because Howe thought it "likely, that in the strife of politics and the bitterness of personal hostility, some attempt may be made to revive [the incident], for the purpose of personal annoyance," he preserved all the papers even though they "may never be made public." Howe's note, dated Apr. 10, 1838, JHP, reel 24.
85 Speech of Feb. 10, *Novascotian*, Mar. 1, 1838.
86 Ibid.
87 Speech of Feb. 24, ibid., Mar. 15, 1838.
88 Ibid.
89 Speech of Feb. 23, ibid., Mar. 8, 1838.
90 See *JHA*, 1838, App. 70, pp. 158–60.
91 Ibid., Mar. 20, 1838, p. 360.
92 Ibid., Mar. 3, 1838, p. 317.
93 Ibid., pp. 317–8.
94 Speech of Feb. 9, *Novascotian*, Feb. 22, 1838.
95 *Acadian Recorder*, Feb. 17, 1838.
96 Speech of Feb. 10, *Novascotian*, Mar. 1, 1838.
97 Ibid.
98 *JHA*, Mar. 9, 1838, pp. 332–3.
99 See speech of Mar. 9, *Novascotian*, Apr. 12, 1838.
100 Ibid.
101 Chisholm, 1: 161.
102 Speech of Mar. 9, *Novascotian*, Apr. 5, 1838.
103 *JHA*, Mar. 30, 1838, p. 396.
104 *Novascotian*, Apr. 5, 1838. It is doubtful, however, if Huntington would have accepted reappointment since he was having second thoughts about his initial acceptance. Later, when Campbell was authorized to confirm his original appointments, Huntington resisted all the governor's overtures on the ground that his acceptance of an executive councillorship would do nothing to further the Reform cause. See Campbell to Glenelg, Nov. 2, 1838, PANS, RG 1, vol. 115, doc. 49, pp. 114–5.

105 *Times*, May 22, 1838. Apparently Collins's name had been omitted in error.
106 *JHA*, Apr. 12, 1838, p. 427.
107 Ibid., p. 429.
108 *Novascotian*, Apr. 26, 1838.
109 Ibid.
110 Howe told Chapman that "at least seven-eighths of the population ... would be opposed ... [to] a sudden and forcible breach of the connection with Great Britain."
111 *Novascotian*, Jan. 11, 1838.
112 Howe suggested that their professions of loyalty and the benefits they secured by way of patronage were closely linked.
113 *Times*, Feb. 20, 1838. "Ephraim" also accused him of writing dozens of letters which the *Novascotian* published as having come from its correspondents.
114 Ibid.
115 See Howe's speech on Canadian affairs, Chisholm, 1: 180–7.
116 *Novascotian*, Apr. 26, 1838.
117 Speech of Jan. 29, ibid., Feb. 8, 1838.
118 Speech of Feb. 3, ibid. Howe also condemned Glenelg's policy on Crown lands in the first of his major references to the black population of Preston. They had been settled on ten-acre plots, half barren or half swamp, but although he had tried in the last session to have them moved to better land, he failed, largely because of the need to adhere to the principle of sale on which the colonial secretary insisted.

CHAPTER TWELVE

1 Sophia, born in August 1836, had lived only thirteen months.
2 Howe to Susan Ann, Apr. 26, 1838, JHP, reel 23, item 33. Susan Ann was to tell the children that "their Father would like to be sitting among them around the porridge this morning."
3 See Howe's description much later, JHP, reel 24.
4 Howe's words in Chisholm, 1: 188.
5 See letter to Glenelg, Aug. 24, 1838, *Novascotian*, Nov. 15, 1838.
6 See George Grey to Howe and Crane, Sept. 14, 1838, ibid. Howe was even more impressed with steamers after seeing the *British Queen* being built on the Clyde at Glasgow: "She is a noble vessel, and the magnitude of her boilers and machinery strikes one with astonishment." Ibid.
7 See ibid., July 5, 1838 to Aug. 15, 1839.
8 Ibid., Aug. 16, 1838.
9 Ibid., Dec. 20, 1838.
10 James A. Roy, *Joseph Howe* (Toronto: Macmillan, 1935), p. 70.
11 *Novascotian*, Nov. 15, 1838.
12 Howe to Susan Ann, June 26, 1838, JHP, reel 23, item 38.
13 Ibid.
14 Ibid.
15 Ibid.
16 Ibid.
17 Ibid.
18 Ibid., July 3, 1838, item 39.
19 Ibid., July 25, 1838, item 41.
20 Ibid., Aug. 12, 1838, item 42.

21 Ibid.
22 Ibid. Susan Ann's maternal aunt, Frances Davis, had married Philip Westphal, a captain in 1838, and later an admiral.
23 Ibid., Sept. 4, 1838, item 43.
24 Ibid., Sept. 11, 1838, item 44. The reference is to Edward Howe.
25 Ibid.
26 Ibid., n.d. ("wonder what he looks like – whether Saxon or Norman – black eyes or blue – can't think of a name for him"). JHP, diary, vol. 45, p. 51. The boy, named James, died in the following year.
27 JHP, diary, vol. 45, p. 60.
28 Howe to Susan Ann, Aug. 22, 1838, JHP, reel 23.
29 Ibid.
30 Ibid., June 26, 1838, item 38.
31 Ibid., Aug. 14, 1838.
32 Ibid.
33 JHP, diary, vol. 45, p. 25.
34 Howe to Susan Ann, Sept. 4, 1838, JHP, reel 23, item 43.

CHAPTER THIRTEEN

1 Speech of Jan. 25, *Novascotian*, Jan. 31, 1839.
2 Glenelg to Campbell, Sept. 27, 1838, *JHA*, 1839, App. 1, pp. 1–2.
3 Campbell to Glenelg, Apr. 8, 1839, PANS, RG 1, vol. 115, doc. 16, p. 134.
4 For Campbell's speech, see *JHA*, Apr. 17, 1838, p. 451.
5 *Acadian Recorder*, Jan. 26, 1839.
6 Speech of Jan. 25, *Novascotian*, Jan. 31, 1839.
7 See *Acadian Recorder*, Jan. 26, 1839.
8 For the resolution see *JHA*, Jan. 29, 1839, p. 475. Apparently William Young drafted it.
9 "If one member may address the gallery for the purpose of keeping order, another may to excite cheers or hisses." See speech of Jan. 28, *Novascotian*, Feb. 21, 1839.
10 Ibid.
11 Speech of Jan. 25, ibid., Feb. 7, 1839.
12 Speech of Jan. 26, ibid., Feb. 14, 1839.
13 Speech of Jan. 28, ibid., Feb. 21, 1839.
14 Speech of Jan. 29, ibid.
15 William Young to George, Mar. 26, 1838, PANS, William Young Papers, MG 2, box 732, item 193. A little later George's father-in-law in Britain told him to have as little as possible to do with that windy demagogue Howe, a conclusion he could have reached only on information provided by Young himself. See T.H. Brooking to George Young, May 7, 1840, PANS, George Young Papers, MG 2, box 720, item 228.
16 Speech of Jan. 28, *Novascotian*, Feb. 21, 1829.
17 Speech of Jan. 26, ibid., Feb. 14, 1839.
18 Speech of Jan. 25, ibid., Jan. 31, 1839.
19 For the instructions see *JHA*, Feb. 6, 1839, pp. 503–5.
20 *Novascotian*, Feb. 28, 1839.
21 Ibid.
22 Speech of Mar. 1, ibid., Mar. 14, 1839.
23 *JHA*, Mar. 21, 1839, p. 590.
24 See *JLC*, Mar. 30, 1839, p. 102.
25 Speech of Apr. 2, *Novascotian*, Apr. 25, 1839.

26 *JHA*, Apr. 3, 1839, p. 632.
27 *Novascotian*, Apr. 11, 1839.
28 Ibid., Apr. 4, 1839.
29 Ibid., Apr. 11, 1839.
30 Ibid., May 16, 1839.
31 *Acadian Recorder*, July 13, 1839.
32 *Novascotian*, June 27, 1839.
33 *Times*, Mar. 19, 1839.
34 Ibid., Feb. 26, 1839.
35 Ibid., June 25, 1839.
36 Ibid., Mar. 26, 1839.
37 See letter of "A Nova Scotian," ibid., Mar. 12, 1839.
38 Ibid., Apr. 30, 1839.
39 *Novascotian*, May 9, 1839.
40 Ibid., May 23, 1839. Howe's part in the writing of this material is not clear.
41 See speech of Mar. 30, ibid., Apr. 18, 1839.
42 This is the conjecture of J.A. Chisholm in "More Letters of Joseph Howe," *Dalhousie Review* 12 (January 1933): 490. Later Almon became a friend of Howe and acted as one of his pallbearers.
43 See speech of Feb. 18, *Novascotian*, Mar. 7, 1839.
44 Speech of Feb. 1, ibid.
45 Speech of Feb. 2, ibid., Mar. 14, 1839.
46 See statement in *Novascotian*, Jan. 10, 1839.
47 See *JHA*, Feb. 25, 1839, pp. 541–2.
48 Speech of Jan. 18, *Novascotian*, Jan. 31, 1839.
49 See proceedings of Feb. 13, reported in *Novascotian*, Mar. 21, 1839.
50 The society ran the academy at Horton.
51 Speech of Jan. 18, *Novascotian*, Jan. 31, 1839.
52 Speech of Feb. 19, ibid., Mar. 28, 1839.
53 Ibid., Apr. 11, 1839.
54 Ibid., Oct. 31, 1839.
55 Ibid.
56 Ibid., May 9, 1839.
57 Circular of Howe to agents, May [?] 1839, JHP, vol. 32.
58 *Novascotian*, Oct. 31, 1839.
59 Ibid., June 13, 1839.
60 Ibid.
61 Howe to Messrs Lea & Blanchard, June 18, 1839, JHP, vol. 32.
62 Howe to Gentleman [?], Apr. 18, 1839, ibid.
63 *Novascotian*, Dec. 27, 1838 and Jan. 3, 1839.
64 Ibid., Oct. 31, 1839.
65 Ibid., June 27, 1839.
66 Ibid., May 2, 1839.
67 See Howe to Christopher Dunkin, Oct. 23, 1839, JHP, vol. 33.
68 Ibid. The Reformer was William Young.
69 Ibid.
70 *Novascotian*, Apr. 11, 1839.
71 Ibid.
72 Ibid., Apr. 25, 1839.
73 Ibid., May 2, 1839.
74 Ibid., May 9, 1839.

75 See W.R. Livingston, *Responsible Government in Nova Scotia* (Iowa City: University of Iowa Press, 1930), p. 98.
76 Chester Martin, *Empire and Commonwealth: Studies in Governance and Self-government in Canada* (Oxford: Clarendon Press, 1929).
77 Howe to Russell, Oct. 14, 1839, JHP, vol. 33.
78 Chisholm, 1: 229.
79 Ibid., p. 230.
80 Ibid., pp. 264–5.
81 See Howe to Buller, Oct. 14, 1839, JHP, vol. 33.
82 See, e.g., Howe to R.J. Parsons of Newfoundland, Oct. 22, 1839, JHP, vol. 33, in which Howe stated that the colonies had failed to "put down the Compacts ... by asking *for different things at different times*": to get what they wanted, they would have to unite in "one general demand ... sustained by a joint delegation."
83 *Times*, Oct. 15, 1839.
84 *Novascotian*, Nov. 7, 1839.

CHAPTER FOURTEEN

1 They had been shown a copy of the dispatch that was being sent to Campbell. See Normanby to Campbell, Aug. 31, 1839, *JHA*, 1840, App. 1, pp. 1–4.
2 Russell to Thomson, Oct. 16, 1839, ibid., App. 10, pp. 31–2.
3 *Novascotian*, Jan. 2, 1840.
4 Harvey to Heads of Departments and Executive Council, Dec. 21, 1839; See W.R. Livingston, *Responsible Government in Nova Scotia* (Iowa City: University of Iowa Press, 1930), p. 118, and Chester Martin, *Empire and Commonwealth* (Oxford: Clarendon Press, 1929), p. 189.
5 Livingston, *Responsible Government in Nova Scotia*, p. 110.
6 *JHA*, Feb. 5, 1840, p. 700.
7 Speech of Feb. 3, Chisholm, 1: 292; also *Novascotian*, Feb. 13, 1840.
8 As a result, the *Times* (Feb. 4, 1840) demanded an immediate appeal from an assembly "elected at a time when men's minds were drunk with excitement" to the people of Nova Scotia, now "sobered by reflection, exercising an impartial judgment upon the progress of Republicanism."
9 See Uniacke's statement to the freeholders of Cape Breton county, *Novascotian*, Mar. 5, 1840. Uniacke's position has been pieced out from this letter to his constituents and his several speeches on the resolutions.
10 See speech of Feb. 4, *Novascotian*, Feb. 20, 1840. Uniacke abstained from voting on the resolutions because, in his opinion, they ought to have gone further and stated that the country should be "governed by a ministry." The *sine qua non* was a responsible ministry, and if Howe headed it, the House should be able to hold him responsible for his acts.
11 Chisholm, 1: 294. But Uniacke resigned from the Executive Council on the ground that, because of Russell's dispatch and the assembly's resolutions, it would be "a mere mockery" to remain a councillor without the confidence of the country. *Times*, Feb. 11, 1840.
12 See summary of Howe's speech of Feb. 10, *Novascotian*, Feb. 13, 1840.
13 Speech of Feb. 13, ibid., Mar. 5, 1840.
14 Ibid.
15 Speech of Feb. 14, ibid., Mar. 12, 1840.
16 Ibid.

17 *JHA*, Feb. 15, 1840, p. 721.
18 The assembly proposed to abolish the Inferior Court of Common Pleas and add one of its judges to the Supreme Court.
19 Speech of Feb. 1, *Novascotian*, Feb. 6, 1840.
20 Ibid.
21 See *JLC*, Feb. 25, 1840, pp. 55–60.
22 *Acadian Recorder*, Mar. 7, 1840.
23 See address of the assembly, *JHA*, Mar. 25, 1840, p. 833.
24 See Howe's resolution, ibid., Mar. 24, 1840, p. 824.
25 The vote was twenty-five to sixteen. Two members who normally supported the Reformers, as well as Uniacke, were included in the minority. See ibid., Mar. 25, 1840, p. 835.
26 Speech of Mar. 30 at a meeting in Halifax, *Novascotian*, Apr. 2, 1840. Strangely enough, the *Recorder*, which had been demanding strong action for weeks, told the instigators of the address they were doing "themselves no credit by insulting the first officer of the government." *Acadian Recorder*, Mar. 28, 1840.
27 *Novascotian*, Apr. 2, 1840.
28 Ibid., Feb. 27, 1840.
29 Speech of Feb. 28, ibid., Apr. 2, 1840.
30 Speech of Jan. 25, ibid., Feb. 6, 1840.
31 Ibid.
32 Speech of Feb. 14, ibid., Mar. 19, 1840.
33 Howe to half-sister Jane, May 24, 1840, JHP, vol. 6, p. 17.
34 According to Howe, Brenton Halliburton became chief justice only by accident and none of his talents was so outstanding that anyone would have regretted their loss. Normally he would have gone to his grave like any other judge, neither expecting or getting more than an annual salary of £700 or, perhaps, £800; now he was complaining that the public honour would be violated if his emoluments were reduced to £1,100 a year. See Howe's letter to the people of Nova Scotia, no. 1, *Novascotian*, Apr. 23, 1840.
35 Howe to half-sister Jane, May 24, 1840, JHP, vol. 6, p. 16.
36 Ibid.
37 Howe to the people of Nova Scotia, n.d., ibid., p. 12.
38 Howe to Susan Ann, n.d., ibid., p. 13.
39 Howe to half-sister Jane, May 24, 1840, ibid., pp. 16–17.
40 See Howe's letter, no. 1, *Novascotian*, Apr. 23, 1840.
41 Howe to half-sister Jane, May 24, 1840, JHP, vol. 6, p. 17.
42 *Acadian Recorder*, Apr. 4, 1840.
43 *Novascotian*, Apr. 2, 1840.
44 *Times*, Apr. 7, 1840. Mistakenly, this number of the *Times* is dated Apr. 6.
45 See Howe's letter, no. 1, Apr. 23, 1840.
46 Ibid.
47 See Johnston's speech of Mar. 30, *Novascotian*, Apr. 9, 1840.
48 See Howe's letter, no. 1, ibid., Apr. 23, 1840.
49 Speech of Mar. 30, ibid., Apr. 9, 1840.
50 Howe's letter, no. 1, ibid., Apr. 23, 1840.
51 Speech of Mar. 30, ibid., Apr. 9, 1840.
52 Howe's letter to the people of Nova Scotia, no. 2, ibid., Apr. 30, 1840.
53 Speech of Mar. 30, ibid., Apr. 9, 1840.
54 Howe's letter, no. 2, ibid., Apr. 30, 1840.
55 Speech of March 30, ibid., Apr. 9, 1840.

56 Howe's letter, no. 2, ibid., Apr. 30, 1840.
57 See, for example, *Times*, Apr. 21, 1840.
58 *Novascotian*, Apr. 23, 1840.
59 Ibid., June 4, 1840.
60 Ibid., May 7, 1840.
61 Ibid., June 25, 1840.
62 Howe to Russell, May 8, 1840, JHP, vol. 33.
63 Ibid.
64 See, for example, two letters of Campbell to Russell, Mar. 28, 1840, PANS, RG 1, vol. 115, pp. 184–6, 186–8.
65 See Martin, *Empire and Commonwealth*, p. 192.
66 Livingston, *Responsible Government in Nova Scotia*, p. 125.
67 Russell to Campbell, Apr. 30, 1840, PANS, RG 1, vol. 79, doc. 46, pp. 170–1.
68 Martin, *Empire and Commonwealth*, p. 192.
69 Campbell to Thomson, June 1, 1840, PANS, RG 1, vol. 115, pp. 217–8.
70 Martin, *Empire and Commonwealth*, p. 194.
71 Thomson to Russell, May 27, 1840, PRO, G. series, 387, 209:184; see Martin, *Empire and Commonwealth*, p. 195.
72 See Thomson's reply to address of welcome, *Times*, July 14, 1840.
73 Ibid.
74 *Novascotian*, July 16, 1840. As for Thomson, he told Russell he had "read people, parties, Assembly and all, a good lecture" and placed "a decided negative upon the demand for what is called "Responsible Government" in the sense in which it is supposed to be used by the Popular party." Thomson to Russell, July 27, 1840, PRO, G. series, 184; see Martin, *Empire and Commonwealth*, p. 197.
75 Chisholm, 1: 327–8.
76 Thomson to Russell, July 27, 1840, PRO, G. series, 184; see J.M. Beck, *The Government of Nova Scotia* (Toronto: University of Toronto Press, 1957), p. 79.
77 *Empire and Commonwealth*, p. 197.
78 Howe's viewpoint is to be found in the *Novascotian*, July 23, 1840.
79 *Empire and Commonwealth*, p. 196.
80 Livingston, *Responsible Government in Nova Scotia*, pp. 133–5.
81 Ibid., p. 133.
82 Thomson to Russell, July 27, 1840, PRO, G. series, 184; see G. Poulett Scrope, *Memoir of the Life of Charles Lord Sydenham*, 2nd ed. (London: John Murray, 1844), pp. 179–81.
83 Ibid.; see Livingston, *Responsible Government in Nova Scotia*, p. 133.
84 Ibid., see Scrope, *Memoir of Sydenham*, p. 181.
85 Howe to Thomson, July 20, JHP, vol. 6, p. 18.
86 Ibid., Aug. 12, 1840, p. 24.
87 Thomson to Campbell, July 27, 1840 (confidential), CO 217/175, 411–22.
88 Campbell to Russell (no. 38), Aug. 1, 1840, ibid., p. 396.
89 Ibid., p. 399.
90 Col. R.W. Grey to Howe (Private and confidential), Sept. 21, 1840, JHP, vol. 1, pp. 25–7. Over this period Howe had taken a holiday from controversy, except for the *Novascotian* of Aug. 20, in which he expressed elation that Thomson had mercilessly shown up Bishop Strachan, a leader of the Upper Canada compact. The same issue mourned the death of Durham; the time would come, Howe prophe-

sied, when the pictures of Durham and Thomson would adorn "our Public buildings ... as those of benefactors, who, by a peaceful revolution, so enlarged and extended the British Constitution, as to make it cover the Provinces of the West, without impairing the foundations of the venerable pile."

91 *Novascotian*, Sept. 10, 1840.

92 Ibid., Oct. 1, 1840.

93 Howe to Thomson, n.d., JHP, vol. 10, p. 9.

94 Jeffery, Tobin, Cogswell, and Collins. A fifth, Samuel Cunard, was absent in England. While Falkland said they got out with good grace, Howe maintained that they "died hard; but were in firm hands, and, after a good deal of bickering and struggling, were disposed of." Howe to Huntington, n.d., JHP, vol. 10, p. 39.

95 McNab had been appointed to the council in July 1840, some months after the assembly had voted nonconfidence in its members. Having "a horror of going into the Assembly," he at first demurred and "determined to resign his honors and stick to his fireside." Ibid.

96 Ibid., pp. 39–41.

97 Ibid., pp. 40–1.

98 T.H. Brooking to George Young, Oct. 17, 1840, PANS, George Young Papers, MG 2, box 720, folder 3, item 238.

99 *Times*, Oct. 6 and 13, 1840. Laughingly, Howe wondered why the *Times* did not use its own printing press to counteract him. It "groaned every week under its leaden load, – but, unfortunately, the Press, although it could make white black, could not make black white." *Novascotian*, Oct. 7, 1840.

100 *Times*, Mar. 10, 1840.

101 Ibid., Feb. 4, 1840. Joseph Howe called it a "slanderous" falsehood, and denied he even knew of the change in the mail route, *Novascotian*, Feb. 13, 1840.

102 *Times*, Feb. 11, 1840.

103 Ibid., Mar. 24, 1840.

104 See speech to freeholders of Yarmouth on Nov. 16, Yarmouth *Herald*, Nov. 20, 1840.

105 *Novascotian*, Nov. 19, 1840.

106 *Times*, Oct. 27, 1840.

107 See Howe's letter to the freeholders of the county of Halifax, *Novascotian*, Oct. 22, 1840.

108 In addition to Halifax, the principal exceptions were the contests for the seat in Annapolis township and all the seats in Shelburne, Kings, Hants, and Cumberland counties.

109 They thought this the more likely because their candidates, Alexander Keith and Beamish Murdoch, were not closely identified with Halifax Toryism.

110 *Novascotian*, Nov. 12, 1840.

111 Ibid.

112 Ibid.

113 Ibid.

114 While Howe led Annand by 1,085 to 923, the margin was much less than in 1836, and the Tories gibed that Annand was the strong man on the ticket.

115 *Times*, Nov. 10, 1840.

116 *Novascotian*, Nov. 12, 1840.
117 Ibid., Nov. 19, 1840. For Murdoch's reply see *Times*, Nov. 24, 1840.
118 *Times*, Dec. 15, 1840.
119 At dissolution the Reformers had gained four seats since the election of 1836, one through a defection and three through by-elections. In 1840 the Reformers took one of the two new seats and five former Tory seats, while the Tories also won a new seat and eight seats formerly held by Reformers. In these calculations S.G.W. Archibald is treated as a neutral, while J.B. Uniacke is considered to be a Reformer, both prior to and after the dissolution, an admittedly questionable assumption.
120 Howe had agreed to pay Thompson £45 for the first half year and then £100 a year up to Dec. 31, 1842. Thompson was also to have the right to buy a half-proprietary interest for £22 10s, the same amount it had cost Howe. See memo of agreement between Howe and Thompson, Nov. 8, 1839, PAC, John Sparrow Thompson Papers, MG 24, C4, vol. 1.
121 Howe to Thompson, Jan. 29, 1840, ibid.
122 Ibid.
123 Ibid.
124 V.L.O. Chittick, *Thomas Chandler Haliburton* (New York: Columbia University Press, 1924), pp. 389, 392.
125 Howe to Haliburton, Jan. 2, 1841, JHP, vol. 33.
126 Chittick, *Haliburton*, p. 263.
127 Howe to Haliburton, Jan. 2, 1841, JHP, vol. 33.
128 Eventually the *Recorder* restricted the printing of the letters to prevent its columns from being monopolized by one subject, *Acadian Recorder*, June 1, 1839. To vindicate Haliburton, his friends held a testimonial dinner, at which Howe gave the toast to the press.
129 Howe to Haliburton, Jan. 2, 1841, JHP, vol. 33.
130 Haliburton got the appointment in March 1841, on the abolition of the Inferior Court of Common Pleas.
131 Howe to Haliburton, Jan. 22, 1841, JHP, vol. 33.
132 T.C. Haliburton, *The Clockmaker or The Sayings and Doings of Samuel Slick of Slickville*, 3rd ser. (London: Richard Bentley, 1840), pp. 25–6.
133 Ibid., pp. 104–5.
134 Ibid., pp. 28, 187–8.
135 Howe to Haliburton, Dec. 25, 1840, JHP, vol. 33. Howe also expressed pleasure that the 200 copies he had ordered from Lea & Blanchard for his own subscribers had been shipwrecked. "I would rather beg my bread than sell a copy of it."
136 James A. Roy, *Joseph Howe* (Toronto: Macmillan, 1935), p. 106.
137 Howe to Haliburton, Jan. 2, 1841, JHP, vol. 33.
138 Ibid.
139 Ibid., Jan. 22, 1841.

CHAPTER FIFTEEN

1 Falkland had made Attorney General S.G.W. Archibald's appointment to the Executive Council conditional upon his relinquishing the speakership.
2 *Times*, Jan. 19, 1841.
3 Ibid.
4 *Morning Post*, Jan. 23, 1841.

5 See *JHA*, Feb. 3, 1841, p. 7. The *Acadian Recorder* (Feb. 6, 1841) called it a felicitous choice: "the first Speaker who has risen to such distinction from the 'types and press' in Nova Scotia."

6 Including Turnbull (Inverness), Forrestall (Sydney county), DesBarres (Guysborough), and Martell (Arichat township).

7 See debate of Feb. 3, *Novascotian*, Feb. 11, 1841.

8 Ibid.

9 Ibid.

10 *Acadian Recorder*, Feb. 13, 1841.

11 See "Living Likenesses," *Acadian Recorder*, May 1, 1841.

12 See debate of Feb. 11, *Novascotian*, Feb. 18, 1841.

13 Ibid.

14 Ibid.

15 Ibid.

16 See speech of Feb. 18, ibid., Feb. 25, 1841.

17 Ibid.

18 Speech of Feb. 25, ibid., Mar. 4, 1841.

19 Speech of Feb. 26, ibid., Mar. 11, 1841.

20 "He would not give them a certificate of character. If they had the power to carry the point why not move it?" Speech of Feb. 25, ibid., Mar. 4, 1841.

21 See *JHA*, Feb. 26, 1841, p. 65.

22 Falkland to Russell, Feb. 14, 1841, PANS, RG 1, vol. 116, doc. 39, pp. 33–4.

23 Howe to Falkland, Feb. 15, 1841, JHP, vol. 6, pp. 27–8. Falkland did not follow Huntington's refusal with an offer to Young, perhaps because he and Howe thought it prudent to have a vacant seat in case Huntington might be induced to change his mind later.

24 Falkland to Russell, Feb. 14, 1841, PANS, RG 1, vol. 116, doc. 39, p. 35.

25 A.F. Ross to Howe, Feb. 23, 1841, JHP, vol. 1, pp. 37–40. Ross also remarked on "the curious cutting & carving [Howe's] mangled reputation had been subject to," especially after Blackadar, the Tory member for Pictou, told his friends that Howe had "joined them – not they you."

26 Howe to Richard Telfer et al., July 22, 1841, JHP, vol. 33.

27 *Novascotian*, Apr. 29, 1841.

28 Ibid.

29 Ibid.

30 Four modernized the criminal law and the other improved the working of the Court of Marriage and Divorce.

31 The basic qualifications for voting were occupancy or ownership of a dwelling house having an annual value of £20, while the mayor and aldermen were to be £50 occupiers and possess real estate valued at £1,000. For common councillors the requirements were to be £30 and £500 respectively. See 4 Vic., c. 55.

32 See speech of Mar. 8, *Novascotian*, Mar. 11, 1841.

33 Ibid.

34 See *JHA*, Mar. 15, 1841, pp. 98–9; also *Novascotian*, Mar. 18, 1841.

35 *Times*, Mar. 9, 1841.

36 See *JHA*, Mar. 15, 1841, p. 100.

37 *Novascotian*, Apr. 29, 1841.

38 Speech of Mar. 10, ibid., Mar. 18, 1841.

39 Ibid.

40 Ibid.

41 See "The Late Session, no. 3," ibid., May 5, 1841.
42 See speech of Mar. 17, ibid., Mar. 25, 1841.
43 The speakership did little to inhibit Howe's expression of views since the assembly did much of its work in some form of the Committee of the Whole, especially the Committee on the General State of the Province, and there Howe spoke as frequently as anyone.
44 See speech of Mar. 22, *Novascotian*, Mar. 25 and Apr. 1, 1841.
45 Ibid.
46 Later Howe observed philosophically that any attempt to adopt such a principle until the people were prepared for it might have injured rather than advanced the cause of education. Ibid., May 5, 1841.
47 *JHA*, Feb. 22, 1841, pp. 53–4.
48 See "The Late Session, no. 3," *Novascotian*, May 5, 1841.
49 Ibid.
50 By twenty-eight to twenty-one. See *JHA*, Feb. 22, 1841, p. 54. The members were the Tory Marshall, and the Reformers Martell, Forrestall, Turnbull, and Upham.
51 Falkland told Russell that its sentiments were "more in accordance with the views of Her Majesty's Government than any which have hitherto been expressed by [the assembly]." Falkland to Russell, Apr. 13, 1841, PANS, RG 1, vol. 116, doc. 57, pp. 50–3; for the address see *JHA*, Mar. 3, 1841, pp. 150–1.
52 Ibid., p. 152.
53 See debate of Mar. 30, *Novascotian*, Apr. 8, 1841; also, "The Late Session, no. 3," ibid., May 5, 1841.
54 Ibid., Apr. 8, 1841.
55 Ibid.
56 Ibid.
57 Clements, Lewis, McLelan, Forrester and Ryder, in addition to himself. See *JHA*, Mar. 30, 1841, p. 152.
58 *Acadian Recorder*, Apr. 10, 1841.
59 *Times*, Jan. 12, 1841.
60 See above, p. 183.
61 Howe to John S. Thompson, June 6, 1841, PAC, John Sparrow Thompson Papers, MG 24, C4, vol. 2.
62 See JHP, vol. 29, pp. 86–91. Whether Howe actually sent the memo to Sydenham is uncertain.
63 Ibid., p. 86.
64 Ibid., pp. 87–8. Inferior to Baldwin, "with much less character, but *with the means* [i.e., a newspaper] of misrepresenting him in his hands," Hincks had driven Baldwin out of office. Ibid., p. 88.
65 Ibid., pp. 89–90.
66 Ibid., p. 90.
67 See memoir of Joseph Howe, JHP, reel 22.
68 Ibid. Howe found Lady Falkland as kind as she was pretty. "She had a good deal of the mobility of feature, and variety of expression, for which it was said her mother, Mrs. Jordan, was remarkable." Ibid.
69 The best wine from Louis Philippe's cellars and the music of a fine string band breathing, not banging, into his ears reconciled Howe to "the conversational difficulties, for it must be acknowledged that the whole Coalition Council could muster but little French." Ibid.
70 Ibid.

71 *Novascotian*, Sept. 30, 1841.
72 Memoir of Joseph Howe, JHP, reel 22. Binney's "impertinence" led to his being superseded as governor's aide by a relative of Susan Ann, Capt. John McNab. Howe said jokingly that 99 out of 100 Haligonians could not have cared less "whether Colonel Binney or Capt. McNab cut up the Governor's Turkies, or [led] Dowagers into Dinner." *Novascotian*, Sept. 30, 1841.
73 Because of something that Howe wrote on this occasion, his old adversary Judge Sawers demanded satisfaction. "The matter was easily explained and soon adjusted, but, if my nephew Bill Howe had not soon after married Sawers Niece, we could hardly have helped shooting each other, so determined did he appear to [want] a rencontre." See memoir of Joseph Howe, JHP, reel 22.
74 Falkland to Stanley, Dec. 22, 1841, PANS, RG 1, vol. 116, doc. 21, p. 127.
75 *Novascotian*, Sept. 30, 1841.
76 Falkland to Stanley, Dec. 22, 1841, p.127.
77 Binney and his friends withdrew from the meeting when they could not restrict voting to the £20 householder. *Novascotian*, Dec. 23, 1841.
78 Falkland to Stanley, Dec. 22, 1841, pp. 128–9. He admitted, nonetheless, that it had reduced his ability to cultivate better feelings within the Halifax society.
79 *Novascotian*, Dec. 30, 1841. The *Recorder* (Jan. 1, 1842) called it "unwelcome intelligence," but the *Times* (Jan. 11, 1842) was not sorry to lose one who had spent ten years raking "all the sins of the political calendar ... together in one vast muck heap, baptized as *Toryism*," with the end of creating an opposing party that seized "upon the republican spirit ... of the unsophisticated people."
80 *Novascotian*, Dec. 30, 1841.
81 James A. Roy, *Joseph Howe* (Toronto: Macmillan, 1935), p. 109.
82 Most of the material on the state of Howe's finances in this period may be found in JHP, vol. 33.
83 Howe to Murdoch, Oct. 26, 1841, and Howe to McNab, Nov. 1, 1841, ibid.
84 See Huntington to Howe, July 13, 1841, ibid., vol. 1, p. 33, and Falkland to Howe, Dec. 13, 1841, ibid., vol. 1, pp. 61–3.
85 For details see Falkland to Stanley, Jan. 19, 1842, PANS, RG 1, vol. 116, doc. 26, pp. 132–3.
86 "Historicus," no. 17, *Progress*, Feb. 27, 1892, JHP, reel 22.
87 Charles Dickens, *American Notes* (Collins: London and Glasgow, n.d.), p. 39. Dickens wrote of his reception in Halifax: "Then, sir, comes a breathless man who has been already into the ship and out again, shouting my name as he tears along ... The breathless man introduces himself as The Speaker of the house of assembly; *will* drag me away to his house ... Then he drags me up to the Governor's house ... and then Heaven knows where; concluding with both houses of parliament, which happen to meet for the session that very day, and are opened by a mock speech from the throne." *The Letters of Charles Dickens*, vol. 3, ed. Madeline House et al. (Oxford: Clarendon Press, 1974), pp. 14–15.
88 *Novascotian*, Feb. 3, 1842.
89 See Howe's lengthy letter on Indians to Falkland, n.d., JHP, vol. 33.
90 Uniacke admitted as much in his speech of Jan. 24, *Novascotian*, Feb. 3,

1842. He told of an Indian family which had indicated to Howe that they wanted to send their son to school; Howe had replied: "Send him to me." A few days later the family had appeared with the boy, decently and comfortably clothed, saying: "Here's the boy." In the end Howe persuaded the Superior of St Mary's to take him.

91 5 Vic., c. 16.
92 Speech of Jan. 29, *Novascotian*, Feb. 10, 1842.
93 Speech of Feb. 1, ibid., Feb. 10, 1842.
94 Ibid.
95 See *JHA*, Feb. 2, 1842, p. 227.
96 *Novascotian*, Feb. 10, 1842.
97 Ibid.
98 *Acadian Recorder*, Feb. 5, 1842.
99 Howe to Falkland, n.d., JHP, vol. 10, p. 47. Only two Tory backbenchers had supported the bill.
100 *Times*, Feb. 8, 1842.
101 Howe to Falkland, n.d., JHP, vol. 10, pp. 46–9.
102 Speech of Feb. 11, *Novascotian*, Feb. 17, 1842.
103 Uniacke's attempt to reverse the first vote was defeated by twenty-eight to sixteen. See *JHA*, Feb. 11, 1842, p. 252.
104 Speech of Feb. 12, *Novascotian*, Feb. 24, 1842.
105 Ibid.
106 Ibid.
107 Ibid.
108 See *JHA*, Feb. 16, 1842, p. 264.
109 Speech of Feb. 14, *Novascotian*, Mar. 3, 1842.
110 Ibid.
111 For division see *JHA*, Feb. 16, 1842, p. 264.
112 *Novascotian*, Mar. 31, 1842.
113 *Times*, Feb. 22, 1842.
114 *Pictou Observer*, Mar. 1, 1842.
115 See speech of Mar. 3, *Morning Post*, Mar. 8, 1842.
116 *Novascotian*, Mar. 10, 1842.
117 *Acadian Recorder*, Mar. 12, 1842.
118 See *Novascotian*, Mar. 17, 1842.
119 Thompson (*Novascotian*, Mar. 17, 1842) wanted something more "plain and direct" than an arrangement of words that left the exact meaning questionable, while the *Recorder* (Mar. 19, 1842) strangely enough maintained that the formula "seems to embrace every thing" and hailed Stewart as a convert, no less committed to sound principles than his colleagues.
120 Howe to Falkland, n.d., JHP, vol. 10, pp. 32–3. Apparently the date was Feb. 3, the day after the bankruptcy bill was deferred.
121 Ibid., p. 34.
122 *Pictou Observer*, Dec. 13, 1842.
123 Count de Barruel to Howe, Oct. 19, 1842, JHP, vol. 5, p. 52.
124 See below, p. 282.
125 Since Thompson was just leaving the *Novascotian* to become Queen's printer, he thought he might be "presumed to be influenced by views independent of his personal feelings." Thompson to Howe, June 11, 1842, PAC, John Sparrow Thompson Papers, MG 24, C4, vol. 3.
126 Ibid.

127 See "Letter of a Constitutionalist," no. 1, *Novascotian*, June 22, 1842.
128 Ibid., no. 3, *Novascotian*, July 7, 1842. Murdoch replied that the reference to his grandmother filled him with "inexpressible contempt." Although she was over eighty, her mind was clear, and "perhaps she might read Mr. Howe a lesson yet, old as she is." *Times*, July 12, 1842.
129 The wives of Martin Wilkins's brother Lewis and H.N. Binney, the collector of excise, were sisters.
130 "Letter of a Constitutionalist," no. 4, *Novascotian*, July 13, 1842.
131 Ibid., no. 6, July 27, 1842.
132 Ibid., no. 7, Aug. 3, 1842.
133 The Speaker's allowance for two years.
134 "Letter of a Constitutionalist," no. 8, *Novascotian*, Aug. 10, 1842.
135 *Acadian Recorder*, July 2, 1842.
136 *Novascotian*, July 6, 1842.
137 Ibid. The *Acadian Recorder* (July 2, 1842) charged the Rump with mistaking "fisticuffs for argument, and brawlers for courtiers."
138 But Howe at no time publicly admitted their authorship and the only direct evidence is Thompson's letter.
139 *Times*, July 12, 1842.
140 *Pictou Observer*, Aug. 9, 1842.
141 Annoyed at being called "the pale student with the delicate frame of constitution," Murdoch stated he did not want to become "the physical force" man if he had to spend his summers fishing and his winters on the Racket Court, take lessons from either Fuller or Bellows, or indulge in "midnight orgies over the wassail bowl." *Times*, July 26, 1842.
142 Ibid., Aug. 16, 1842.
143 Ibid., Aug. 9, 1842.
144 Ibid., July 19, 1842.
145 *Pictou Observer*, July 12, 1842. The *Observer* again condemned the "Joseph Howe compact," and wondered how Howe could oppose the hereditary transmission of offices since his half-brother had succeeded to his father's two offices. It also raised the old grievance of the "tax" of 2s. 6d. on newspapers picked up at the post office, alleging that Joseph Howe had received favoured treatment in this exaction.

CHAPTER SIXTEEN

1 J.M. Beck, *The Government of Nova Scotia* (Toronto: University of Toronto Press, 1957), p. 81.
2 See Stayley Brown to Howe, Mar. 12, 1842, JHP, vol. 1, pp. 69–76.
3 McCully to Howe, Oct. 26, 1842, ibid., pp. 80–1.
4 Alexander McDougall to Howe (private), Nov. 17, 1842, ibid., pp. 90–2. Howe was pleased to do this for "an old companion in arms, who stood by me in days of trial, and having served his country deserves to share her honours." Howe to McDougall (private), Nov. 21, 1842, JHP, vol. 6, p. 33.
5 Falkland to Stanley, August [?] 1842, PANS, RG 1, vol. 117, doc. 30, p. 34.
6 Howe to Falkland (private and confidential), n.d., JHP, vol. 10, pp. 12–25.
7 Ibid., pp. 19–20.
8 Ibid., pp. 23–4.
9 Ibid., pp. 22, 24.
10 Howe to Falkland, n.d., ibid., pp. 26–9.

11 Falkland to Stanley, Sept. 13, 1842, PANS, RG 1, vol. 117, doc. 104, pp. 38–41.
12 *Times*, Sept. 13, 1842.
13 *Pictou Observer*, Aug. 30, 1842.
14 Ibid., Sept. 27, 1842. Surely, said the *Observer*, the only influence Howe possessed was of "the vulgar kind which is created by flattering the rabble and defaming the higher orders." Howe's majority was "composed of fishermen and the Negroes of Preston and Hammond's Plains, who were landed in Halifax a few years ago in a state of the lowest degradation, whose freeholds of rocks as naked as themselves, were conferred on them out of charity, and who have eked out a precarious existence by vending blue-berries and frost-fish."
15 Howe to half-sister Jane, Sept. 25, 1842, PANS, "Howe Letters," p. 38.
16 Created by the act he had helped to draft.
17 *Times*, Apr. 12, 1842.
18 *Pictou Observer*, Apr. 19, 1842. When the "Letters of a Constitutionalist" were being published, the *Observer* (June 28, 1842) said that the Indian commissioner had assumed the garb of an Indian chieftain, "staining his cheek with the war paint – sallying forth with the scalping knife and tomahawk."
19 See "Report on Indian Affairs," *JHA*, 1843, App. no. 1, p. 4.
20 Howe left a rough diary of his trip that is very difficult to decipher. See diary for 1841–2, JHP, vol. 45.
21 See "Report on Indian Affairs," *JHA*, 1843, App. no. 1, p. 8. He added that if his expense account was a bar to his going on a similar mission to the eastern counties in 1843, he was prepared to relinquish it in whole or in part.
22 See above, p. 193.
23 "They have abandoned [their opinions] – I have not," said Howe. See his letter in *Novascotian*, Nov. 24, 1842.
24 See letter of "an Observer," *Christian Messenger*, Apr. 8, 1842. Young had married Anne Tobin, a Catholic.
25 *Christian Messenger*, May 14, 1841.
26 See Howe's letter, *Novascotian*, Nov. 24, 1842.
27 Provided that its friends contributed £250 to its support annually, and that it had at least two professors and twelve students. Chipman was a Baptist, a friend of Howe, and the uncle of a professor at Acadia.
28 See debate of Mar. 5, *Novascotian*, Mar. 10, 1842.
29 *Christian Messenger*, Apr. 8, 15, and 29; May 13 and 27, 1842.
30 See letter of "an Observer," ibid., May 13, 1842.
31 See Howe's letter, *Novascotian*, Nov. 24, 1842.
32 Letter of "an Observer," *Christian Messenger*, May 27,1842.
33 See Howe's letter, *Novascotian*, Nov. 24, 1842.
34 The board, as a noncorporate body, could not be sued as such. Circular of Howe to some members of the board, Feb. 24, 1842, JHP, vol. 6, pp. 31–2.
35 *Novascotian*, Aug. 10, 1842.
36 When Howe's critics wondered where Nugent got his information, Howe replied he was in a special position to know it.
37 *Christian Messenger*, Aug. 12, 1842.
38 *Novascotian*, Sept. 7, 1842.
39 These letters were reprinted in the *Novascotian*.

40 The *Messenger* responded to Nugent's editorial on Sept. 16, 23, and 30; when it refused to publish Howe's two letters in reply, he had them inserted in the *Acadian Recorder* of Oct. 8. Subsequently the *Messenger* dealt with the question on Oct. 21, Nov. 25, and Dec. 9 and 23, while Howe replied with letters in the *Acadian Recorder* of Nov. 12, and Dec. 3 and 17.

41 *Acadian Recorder*, Oct. 8, 1842.

42 *Christian Messenger*, Sept. 30, 1842.

43 See Howe's letter, *Acadian Recorder*, Nov. 12, 1842.

44 Ibid., Dec. 3, 1842.

45 Ibid., Oct. 8, 1842.

46 Ibid., Dec. 17, 1842.

47 He had been promoted from the solicitor-generalship in April 1841 when S.G.W. Archibald became master of the rolls.

48 *Acadian Recorder*, Oct. 22, 1842; reprinted in *Christian Messenger*, Oct. 28, 1842. He wrote the letter with Falkland's permission.

49 Ibid.

50 Howe to Falkland, Apr. 3, 1843, JHP, vol. 6, p. 48.

51 *Novascotian*, Apr. 17, 1843.

52 Howe to Falkland, Apr. 3, 1843, JHP, vol. 6, p. 49. See also *Novascotian*, Apr. 17, 1843. While Stewart apparently denied the incident to Falkland at the time, and the latter allegedly communicated the denial to Howe, Stewart made no public statement on the matter until February 1844, allegedly because for twenty years he had not deigned to notice attacks on him in the press. See report of Stewart's speech of Feb. 23, *Times*, Feb. 27, 1844.

53 Howe to Falkland, Apr. 3, 1843, JHP, vol. 6, p. 52.

54 See Falkland to Stanley, Dec. 2, 1842, PANS, RG 1, vol. 117, doc. 124, pp. 61–2.

55 Speech of Feb. 8, *Novascotian*, Feb. 13, 1843.

56 Ibid.

57 Ibid.

58 Ibid.

59 *Times*, Feb. 7, 1843.

60 Speech of Feb. 11, *Novascotian*, Mar. 27, 1843.

61 Ibid.

62 See *JHA*, Jan. 26, 1843, p. 359.

63 Howe to Falkland, n.d., JHP, vol. 10, pp. 2–3.

64 A few days earlier he had been granted six months' leave of absence to get medical aid in Boston.

65 Howe to Falkland, n.d., JHP, vol. 10, p. 4.

66 *Novascotian*, Apr. 3, 1843.

67 Ibid.

68 Falkland to Stanley, Mar. 31, 1843, PANS, RG 1, vol. 117, doc. 151, p. 89.

69 Howe to Falkland, Apr. 3, 1843, JHP, vol. 6, pp. 39–40.

70 Falkland to Stanley, Mar. 31, 1843, PANS, RG 1, vol. 117, doc. 151, pp. 87–9.

71 Howe to Falkland, Apr. 3, 1843, JHP, vol. 6, pp. 53–4.

72 Falkland to Stanley, Mar. 31, 1843, PANS, RG 1, vol. 117, doc. 151, p. 89.

73 Ibid., p. 90.

74 See above, p. 243.

75 In a suit brought by Silas Livingston Morse of Annapolis county the

damages were £110; in one action by Judge Sawers they were £40, with two further actions pending. The costs assessed in the two suits were about £100. In a very real sense the actions were political since acting for Morse and Sawers were J.W. Johnston, his brother James, and Alexander Stewart, while acting for Nugent were William and George Young. See, e.g., *Novascotian*, Apr. 3, July 24, and Dec. 4, 1843.

76 See JHP, reel no. 22.

77 *Christian Messenger*, Feb. 24, 1843.

78 *Novascotian*, Mar. 6, 1843.

79 In supporting letters addressed "To the People of Nova Scotia" Dr Crawley denied Howe's contention that the Baptists had not wanted a college until he was denied a teaching position at Dalhousie. See *Christian Messenger*, Feb. 24, 1843.

80 *Novascotian*, Feb. 20, 1843.

81 *JHA*, Feb. 24, 1843, p. 426. While six Reformers, mostly from Baptist counties (S. Chipman, S.B. Chipman, Palmer, Dimock, McKay, and Lewis), voted with the minority, four Tories (Heckman, Taylor, Creighton, and Dickey) opposed the majority of their own party.

82 See letter of Crawley in *Christian Messenger*, Mar. 3, 1843.

83 Ibid., Mar. 10, 1843. The *Messenger*, at the same time, suggested that Howe was the author and Annand simply the mover of the resolutions. Annand responded indignantly that, in contrast to Howe, he had always opposed grants to sectarian colleges and that the resolutions were in fact his own. See Annand's letter in *Novascotian*, Mar. 13, 1843.

84 Speech of Howe at public meeting in Halifax, Sept. 27, *Novascotian*, Oct. 9, 1843.

85 Speech of Mar. 10, ibid., Mar. 20, 1843.

86 After the request was defeated by twenty-four to seventeen, the *Messenger* (Mar. 24, 1843) stated that the petitioners expressed themselves in "necessarily strong, but entirely respectful terms."

87 G.W. McLelan, a Reformer from Londonderry township, took this action so that the assembly might consider the support of schools and colleges *ab initio* when the existing laws expired.

88 See speech of Mar. 20, *Novascotian*, Apr. 17, 1843.

89 Ibid.

90 *Christian Messenger*, Mar. 3, 1843.

91 See letter of Huntington, *Novascotian*, May 1, 1843.

92 See speech reported in *Christian Messenger*, July 21, 1843.

93 Speech of Sept. 25, ibid., Oct. 6, 1843.

94 See Crawley's letter in ibid., Mar. 24, 1843.

95 *Novascotian*, Apr. 17 and 24, 1843.

96 Commissioner of Crown Lands for Cape Breton. For Edmund Crawley's letter, see *Christian Messenger*, Mar. 31, 1843.

97 *Novascotian*, Apr. 24, 1843.

98 This was the bill which made the deputy registrars of deeds in the counties principals in their own right instead of being deputies of Sir Rupert George, who pocketed half the fees.

99 *Novascotian*, May 22, 1843.

100 Ibid., Aug. 28, 1843.

101 Chisholm, 1: 431–5.

102 *Christian Messenger*, Oct. 6, 1843. Later it said that Howe's speech was marked by "the utter recklessness with which he has always treated the

subject of truth, or the character of his neighbours, when it suited his purpose to sacrifice either." Ibid., Oct. 13, 1843.

103 *Christian Messenger*, Oct. 27, 1843.

104 *Novascotian*, Oct. 16, 1843.

105 Actually he had got an inkling of it at Schultz's on the way back.

106 See Howe's letter "To the Freeholders of the County of Halifax," n.d., JHP, vol. 30, p. 1. The Reformers Howe, Uniacke, and McNab had opposed dissolution. Apparently the letter did not see the light of day, perhaps because its publication might have meant the immediate end of the coalition.

107 Howe to half-sister Jane, Dec. [?], 1843, PANS, "Howe Letters," p. 39.

108 Letter "To the Freeholders of the County of Halifax," n.d., JHP, vol. 30, p. 2. In addition to the executive and legislative councillorships, seventy or eighty Reformers had been made magistrates, seventeen or eighteen appointed registrars of deeds and judges of probate, and many more named to local boards.

109 Falkland to Stanley, Nov. 28, 1843, PANS, RG 1, vol. 117, doc. 195, 122–35.

110 See above, p. 256.

111 Falkland to Stanley, Nov. 28, 1843, PANS, RG 1, vol. 117, doc. 195, p. 134.

112 Ibid., p. 125.

113 See letters of "A Catholic Teetotaller" in supplements to *Novascotian*, Oct. 16 and 23, 1843.

114 *Register* (Halifax), Oct. 31, 1843.

115 *Novascotian*, Oct. 30, 1843.

116 Howe to Edward Kenny, reprinted from *Acadian Recorder* in *Novascotian*, Nov. 13, 1843.

117 Ibid.

118 *Christian Messenger*, Nov. 24, 1843.

119 Stairs had been returned at a by-election after the death of Forrester.

120 See report of Howe's speech, *Novascotian*, Nov. 13, 1843.

121 *Register*, Nov. 7, 1843.

122 Ibid.

123 *Times*, Nov. 14, 1843.

124 *Register*, Nov. 28, 1843.

125 According to Howe, Whitney, a pioneer of steam navigation on the Bay of Fundy and Minas Basin, had a number of small boats, "dirty, badly found, weak in power ... always out of order, and always meeting with accidents, but always going." See Howe's note, JHP, reel 24.

126 Whitney to Howe, Dec. 1, 1843, JHP, reel 24, item 268.

127 While 581 persons voted the "straight" Reform ticket compared to 436 for the Tories, only 11 voted for Uniacke and Stairs compared with 186 for Uniacke and McNab, and that made the difference.

128 *Christian Messenger*, Nov. 24, 1843.

129 On his own initiative, the sheriff had decided to run separate township and county elections at different times.

130 *Register*, Nov. 28, 1843.

131 See Annand's editorial, *Novascotian*, Dec. 18, 1843.

132 *Times*, Nov. 28, 1843.

133 Falkland to Uniacke, McNab, and Howe, Dec. 25, 1843, *Royal Gazette*, Dec. 28, 1843.

134 Speech of Nov. 6, *Novascotian*, Nov. 13, 1843.
135 *Eastern Chronicle*, Dec. 28, 1843. The parties exchanged seats in Cumberland.
136 *Christian Messenger*, Nov. 17, 1843.
137 *Novascotian*, Dec. 4, 1843.
138 Letter to half-sister Jane, Dec. [?], 1843, PANS, "Howe Letters," p. 39.
139 *Eastern Chronicle*, Dec. 28, 1843.
140 At his nomination Howe had said he was often disgusted by the "treachery and rascality which he had to contend against" in his relations with other councillors. *Christian Messenger*, Nov. 10, 1843.
141 Falkland to Uniacke, McNab and Howe, Dec. 25, 1843, *Royal Gazette*, Dec. 28, 1843.
142 Howe to Falkland, Dec. 21, 1843 and Uniacke to Falkland, Dec. 21, 1843, ibid. Falkland admitted that Almon's "affinity to Mr. Johnston" was a basic reason for his appointment.
143 Falkland to Uniacke, McNab, and Howe, Dec. 25, 1843, ibid.
144 Howe to Falkland, Dec. 26, 1843, JHP, vol. 6, p. 64.
145 Falkland to Stanley, Jan. 1, 1844, PANS, RG 1, vol. 117, doc. 201, p. 145.
146 Ibid., pp. 145–6.
147 Howe to half-sister Jane, Dec. 22, 1843, PANS, "Howe Letters," p. 40.

CHAPTER SEVENTEEN

1 Falkland to Stanley, Feb. 1, 1844, PANS, RG 1, vol. 117, doc. 208, p. 152.
2 Ibid., Feb. 2, 1844, doc. 209, p. 152. Stanley refused to let him nominate up to twelve councillors as he wished, but promised to give sympathetic consideration to specific nominations. Stanley to Falkland, Feb. 25, 1844, PANS, RG 1, vol. 83, doc. 158, pp. 33–4.
3 See Howe to Falkland, Feb. 12, 1844, JHP, vol. 6, pp. 69–71. The letter was completely businesslike and exhibited none of the warmth that formerly existed between the two men.
4 See *JHA*, Feb. 8, 1844, p. 11.
5 See speech of Feb. 15, *Novascotian*, Feb. 26, 1844.
6 Falkland to Dodd, Feb. 24, 1844, PANS, RG 1, vol. 117, p. 162.
7 Dodd to Falkland, Feb. 26, 1844, ibid., p. 163.
8 See *Morning Chronicle*, Jan. 29, 1844; also Howe's speech of Mar. 15, *Novascotian*, Apr. 29, 1844.
9 Howe to Falkland, Feb. 29, 1844, JHP, vol. 10, pp. 36–8.
10 Chisholm, 1: 470.
11 *Novascotian*, Feb. 26, 1844.
12 *Royal Gazette*, Feb. 29, 1844.
13 Chisholm, 1: 471.
14 W.R. Livingston, *Responsible Government in Nova Scotia* (Iowa City: University of Iowa Press, 1930), p. 178.
15 Falkland to Stanley, Mar. 2, 1844, PANS, RG 1, vol. 117, doc. 214, pp. 155–60. While Stanley agreed with Falkland in principle, he also told him that a group in a minority of one or two could not be expected to give up its views without a struggle, and he indicated no intention to intervene. Stanley to Falkland, Mar. 22, 1844, PANS, RG 1, vol. 83, doc. 160, pp. 41–2.
16 See above, p. 239.
17 *JHA*, Mar. 5, 1844, p. 67.

18 Ibid., p. 68. Johnston also added the qualification that the Nova Scotia Assembly, in accepting the Harrison Resolutions, did not accept other features of Canadian institutions, such as the initiation of money votes by the executive.
19 See Falkland to Stanley, Apr. 2, 1844, PANS, RG 1, vol. 118, doc. 222, pp. 6–7.
20 See division, *JHA*, Mar. 5, 1844, p. 69.
21 Ibid., Apr. 10, 1844, p. 140.
22 Ibid., Apr. 12, 1844, p. 145. During this debate there were unruly scenes in the precincts of the assembly, and the Tories alleged that their opponents had sought to intimidate the country members in order to prevent them from exercising their independent opinions. *Morning Post*, Apr. 13, 1844.
23 The list did not include the Liberal Speaker, William Young, nor the ailing John Creighton of Lunenburg, a Tory. By this time John Ryder of Argyle had become firmly accepted as a Tory.
24 See editorial in *Morning Chronicle*, Mar. 11, 1844.
25 Falkland to Stanley, Apr. 2, 1844, PANS, RG 1, vol. 118, doc. 221, pp. 1–2. The governor included a letter from Johnston and Dodd, who pointed out that only a Nova Scotian could appreciate the importance attached to road moneys in the rural districts, and the utter impracticability of asking the assembly to reduce them, at a time of "general depression of business of all kinds," to meet arrears in salaries. Ibid., pp. 3–5. During the next few months Falkland was forwarding the pleas of the officers whose salaries were in arrears. But he made the most eloquent plea for himself, saying he would never have accepted the governorship if he had known its emoluments were to depend "upon the success of the speculations of the General Mining Association" and the royalties it might pay into the casual revenue fund.
26 See editorial in *Morning Chronicle*, Mar. 11, 1844.
27 The administration had had to withdraw the amount it had moved for the lieutenant-governor's salary, and had had its proposal for the provincial secretary's salary superseded by that of Huntington. In the latter instance the Tories Marshall, Crow, Smith, and Elkanah Young joined the Reformers to carry the motion by 27 to 20. Ibid., Mar. 20, 1844.
28 The Tory C.B. Owen told him that "*when he got upon a road* he was apt to *lose his way*," to which Howe retorted: "You must acknowledge that that is a very bad point in a *Leader*." Ibid., Apr. 3, 1844.
29 Because his bill contained a reference to another statute which recognized the superiority of the Church of England to the other denominations. Ibid.
30 Eight Tories deserted him. See *JHA*, Apr. 8, 1844, pp. 134–5.
31 See letter of Thompson in *Morning Post*, Mar. 9, 1844.
32 *Morning Chronicle*, Mar. 6, 1844.
33 *Morning Post*, Feb. 8, 1844.
34 See *Morning Chronicle*, Mar. 6, 1844, for Annand's views on the resignation of Thompson and the appointment of Crosskill.
35 Ibid., Mar. 13, 1844.
36 Collectively the three issues of the *Chronicle* contained the same material as the weekly *Novascotian*. Both Howe and Annand were listed as editors on the mastheads of the two papers.
37 *Novascotian*, May 6, 1844. In mid-March Howe had got an inkling of his

popular support when 2,000 persons met in Mason's Hall to acclaim the retired councillors and serenade him to his home.

38 Ibid.
39 See Howe's speech of Feb. 13, ibid., Feb. 24, 1845. Later Howe would identify him by name. See below, p. 309.
40 Ibid.
41 Chester Martin, *Empire and Commonwealth* (Oxford: Clarendon Press, 1929), p. 217.
42 See Howe's speech of Feb. 13, *Novascotian*, Feb. 24, 1845.
43 See Martin, *Empire and Commonwealth*, p. 215.
44 Speech of Feb. 13, *Novascotian*, Feb. 24, 1845. Falkland was a former lord of the bedchamber to William IV.
45 Ibid., June 17, 1844.
46 *Morning Post*, June 27, 1844.
47 Ibid., Sept. 19, 1844.
48 Ibid.
49 *Novascotian*, Jan. 22, 1844.
50 Ibid., Aug. 19, 1844. This was only one of a number of "political" trials in these years in which the Reformers alleged that local Tory officials were rigging the jury lists against them. For editorials on the *McCoubrey v. Annand* trial see ibid., Sept. 9 and 16, 1844.
51 Ibid., Nov. 25, 1844.
52 Speech of Feb. 13, ibid., Feb. 24, 1845.
53 Ibid.
54 Ibid., Dec. 2, 1844.
55 Ibid., Dec. 23, 1844. Of the December squib, Johnston said that "the language ... was so indecent and scurrilous that it was scarcely fit to allude to on the floor of the House, and could not have proceeded from a gentleman." Speech of Feb. 12, ibid., Feb. 17, 1845.
56 Martin, *Empire and Commonwealth*, p. 217.
57 See Howe's speech of Feb. 13, *Novascotian*, Feb. 24, 1845.
58 Uniacke was to have the solicitor-generalship he had given up in December. The appointments would have increased the council to twelve, in accordance with the permission granted by Stanley earlier in the year.
59 *Novascotian*, Aug. 5, 1844.
60 Ibid.
61 Falkland to Stanley, Aug. 2, 1844, PANS, RG 1, vol. 118, doc. 261, pp. 37–8.
62 Ibid.
63 Ibid.
64 See Chisholm, 1: 480–1.
65 Ibid., pp. 481–2.
66 Falkland to Stanley, Jan. 2, 1845, PANS, RG 1, vol. 118, doc. 284, p. 73.
67 See above, pp. 277–8.
68 Martin, *Empire and Commonwealth*, p. 219.
69 See editorial in *Novascotian*, Feb. 10, 1845.
70 Speech of Feb. 13, ibid., Feb. 24, 1845.
71 Ibid., Feb. 10, 1845.
72 Speech of Feb. 12, ibid., Feb. 17, 1845.
73 Speech of Feb. 13, ibid., Feb. 24, 1845.
74 Rev. John Sprott to Howe, Feb. 14, 1845, JHP, vol. 1, pp. 118–20.
75 Howe to half-sister Jane, Mar. 8, 1846, PANS, "Howe Letters," p. 53.

76 Speech of Feb. 13, *Novascotian*, Feb. 24, 1845.
77 The ailing Tory John Creighton had been unable to resume his seat.
78 *Novascotian*, Mar. 3, 1845.
79 Howe to half-sister Jane, Mar. 8, 1845, PANS, "Howe Letters," p. 53.
80 *Morning Post*, Feb. 27, 1845.
81 Ibid., Aug. 30, 1845.
82 See summary of debate of Feb. 25, *Novascotian*, Mar. 3, 1845.
83 Speech of Feb. 13, ibid., Feb. 24, 1845.
84 Speech of Feb. 6 in Mason's Hall, ibid., Feb. 10, 1845.
85 *Morning Post*, Feb. 14, 1845.
86 Ibid., Sept. 4, 1845.
87 Quotation from Howe's speech in Falkland to Stanley, PANS, RG 1, 1845, vol. 118, doc. 322, pp. 103–11.
88 Speech of Apr. 11, *Novascotian*, Apr. 21, 1845.
89 Howe to Buller, Feb. 28, 1845, JHP, vol. 33.
90 Buller to Howe, Apr. 3, 1845, ibid., vol. 1, pp. 126–8.
91 Certainly Falkland had not intended his permission to cover the wide-ranging area that Howe asserted it did.
92 Speech of Feb. 17, *Novascotian*, Feb. 24, 1845.
93 Ibid.
94 Howe to [?], Mar. 8, 1845, reel 23.
95 Speech of Feb. 24, *Novascotian*, Apr. 7, 1845.
96 Speech of Feb. 5, ibid., Feb. 10, 1845.
97 Ibid.
98 In the heated debate on sectarian colleges late in the session Howe took little part, although he did support Huntington's unsuccessful efforts to repeal the permanent grant to King's College, and to declare it unwise to support sectarian colleges from the Treasury. He did comment, a little resignedly, on the strange combinations that were formed to carry the college grants, noting that even George Young, the advocate of one college, had succumbed in order that Pictou Academy might get its share of the money.
99 Speech of Feb. 14, *Novascotian*, Feb. 23, 1846.
100 Falkland to Stanley, Nov. 17, 1845, *JHA*, 1846, App. 48, pp. 159–61. The "respectable Gentlemen" included J.W. Johnston, S.B. Robie, and T.N. Jeffery. On the basis of William Young's letter to the freeholders of Inverness published in the *Novascotian* of Mar. 9, 1846, it would appear that any offence the Youngs may have committed was much less serious than Falkland had made it out to be.
101 Gladstone to Falkland, May 5, 1846, PANS, RG 1, vol. 85, pp. 179–81.
102 Falkland to Gladstone, June 17, 1846, ibid., vol. 119, doc. 44, p. 29.
103 See Howe's "Letter to the Freeholders of the County of Halifax," *Novascotian*, Feb. 23, 1846.
104 Ibid. Although the words were spoken on Feb. 20, this is the version that appeared in Johnston's resolution the following day. See *JHA*, Feb. 21, 1846, p. 449.
105 By its action the House broke its own rules that words complained of in debate were to be taken down and dealt with immediately.
106 *Morning Post*, Feb. 23, 1846.
107 Ibid., Feb. 25, 1846.
108 Ibid., Mar. 3, 1846.
109 Ibid., June 29 (mistakenly June 26), 1846. In contrast, one of Howe's

friends in London wondered how "that infernal piece of humbug called a 'Censure'" came to be passed. "What a paltry, debased spirit in 'children of a free soil' to sacrifice their claim to common sense for the muddy pride of a man [Falkland] whose highest feeling is to laugh at their folly in quarrelling with *each other* for the sake of a passing stranger." R.B. O'Brien to Howe, Apr. 2, 1846, JHP, reel 23.

110 See Howe's "Letter to the Freeholders of the County of Halifax," *Novascotian*, Feb. 23, 1846.

111 The governor was pleased that the legislature had authorized him to use any funds he saw fit for the contingencies of the militia service (Falkland to Stanley, Mar. 31, 1846, PANS, RG 1, vol. 118, doc. 15, p. 178), while the *Times* (Mar. 24, 1846) saw an increase in the government's strength, especially in the vote of censure on Howe.

112 *Novascotian*, Apr. 6, 1846.

113 Howe to Thompson, Aug. 28, 1846, PAC, John Sparrow Thompson Papers, MG 24, C4, vol. 2.

114 His open letter to the governor appeared first in the *Morning Chronicle* (date not ascertainable) and later in the *Novascotian*, Mar. 16, 1846. It was republished in Chisholm, 1: 601–6.

115 Ibid.

116 Ibid.

117 Ibid.

118 Ibid.

119 *Morning Post*, Mar. 11, 1846.

120 Ibid., Apr. 20, 1847.

121 Chisholm, 1: 607.

122 Ibid.

123 Falkland to Gladstone, May 1, 1846, PANS, RG 1, vol. 119, doc. 33, p. 16.

124 *Novascotian*, Aug. 3, 1846.

125 Howe to Kent, Nov. 28, 1846, JHP, vol. 6, p. 97.

126 Martin, *Empire and Commonwealth*, p. 217.

127 See "Provincial Politics, no. 1," *Novascotian*, May 20, 1844.

128 Falkland to Stanley, May 17, 1845, PANS, RG 1, vol. 118, doc. 318, pp. 94–9.

129 Falkland to Fairbanks, Nov. 14, 1845, ibid., doc. 352, p. 143.

130 *Novascotian*, Nov. 24, 1845.

131 See speech of Feb. 5 and 6, ibid., Feb. 16, 1846.

132 Ibid. For Wilkins's speech, see ibid., Feb. 9, 1846.

133 *Morning Post*, Feb. 11, 1846.

134 Falkland to Gladstone, Mar. 2, 1846, PANS, RG 1, vol. 118, doc. 14, p. 176.

135 Stanley to Falkland, Nov. 15, 1845, *JHA*, 1846, App. 14, pp. 41–2.

136 *JHA*, Jan. 29, 1846, pp. 407–8.

137 *Times*, Feb. 3, 1846.

138 See speech of Feb. 5, *Novascotian*, Feb. 16, 1846.

139 Falkland to Gladstone, Apr. 2, 1846, PANS, RG 1, vol. 118, doc. 18, pp. 79–80.

CHAPTER EIGHTEEN

1 Chisholm, 1: 490.

2 Ibid., p. 492.

3 Ibid., p. 496.

4 Howe to half-sister Jane, Sept. 22, 1844, PANS, "Howe Letters," pp. 44–7.
5 Falkland lost no time in reporting the strengthening of his ministry to the colonial secretary. Falkland to Stanley, Apr. 29, 1845, PANS, RG 1, vol. 118, doc. 305, p. 86.
6 Howe to Fraser, Apr. 25, 1845, JHP, reel 23.
7 Novascotian, July 28, 1845.
8 Ibid.
9 Ibid.
10 Wilkins had agreed to attend the meeting because of Howe's taunts.
11 Novascotian, Oct. 6, 1845. Howe suggested that Wilkins was "not satisfied with a reasonable quantity [of wind] – he b[r]ought a gale."
12 Morning Post, Oct. 11, 1845.
13 Novascotian, Oct. 6, 1845.
14 Morning Chronicle, Oct. 28, 1845.
15 Howe to half-sister Jane, Nov. 21, 1845, PANS, "Howe Letters," p. 54.
16 Ibid.
17 Howe to Leishman, Spring 1846, JHP, vol. 6, pp. 108–12.
18 Howe to John Thompson, Aug. 28, 1846, PAC, MG 24, C4, vol. 2. The family had continued to grow with the birth of Sydenham in March 1843 and John in May 1846. The last child, William, would not be born until July 1848.
19 Sun, June 19, 1846.
20 Morning Post, June 17, 1846.
21 Sun, Oct. 14, 1846.
22 Ibid.
23 Buller to Howe, Sept. 10, 1846, JHP, vol. 1, pp. 151–2.
24 Chester Martin, Empire and Commonwealth (Oxford: Clarendon Press, 1929), p. 228.
25 W.R. Livingston, Responsible Government in Nova Scotia (Iowa City: University of Iowa Press, 1930), p. 201.
26 Martin, Empire and Commonwealth, p. 291.
27 For Howe's letter published in the Montreal Pilot, May 15, 1844, see Chisholm, 1: 482–9.
28 Morning Post, July 6, 1844.
29 See "The Government Scribes, no. 5," Novascotian, July 15, 1844.
30 Howe to Isaac Buchanan, Aug. 31, 1844 (private), JHP, vol. 6, p. 73.
31 Ibid.
32 Adam Fergusson to Howe, Mar. 10, 1845, ibid., vol. 1, pp. 122–3.
33 Novascotian, Sept. 1, 1845.
34 Morning Post, Sept. 4, 1845.
35 Hincks might have shuddered even more if he had known that Howe described Egerton Ryerson as "a man after my own heart." Howe to Buchanan, Aug. 31, 1844 (private), JHP, vol. 6, p. 74.
36 Novascotian, Oct. 6, 1845.
37 Empire and Commonwealth, p. 229.
38 Ibid.
39 Kent to Howe, July 22, 1846, JHP, vol. 1, p. 146. The letter could not have been persuasive in any case, since it went in error to Halifax, England, and Howe did not receive it until November.
40 The always reliable Leishman had already set the party's organi-

zational machinery in motion. Leishman to Howe, Sept. 5, 1846, ibid., vol. 2, pp. 762–5.

41 Memorandum of Harvey to Howe, Doyle, and George Young, Sept. 14, 1846, ibid., vol. 1, p. 159.

42 Doyle and George Young to Harvey, Sept. 12, 1846, enclosure no. 2 in Harvey to Grey, Sept. 15, 1846 (private and confidential), CO 217/193, 249–51. There is a discrepancy in dates in this exchange of correspondence.

43 See JHP, vol. 1, p. 158, for Howe's endorsement of Harvey's note.

44 Howe to Harvey, Sept. 15, 1846, enclosure no. 3 in Harvey to Grey, Sept. 15, 1846 (private and confidential), CO 217/193, 252–4.

45 Ibid.

46 Although Harvey agreed with the Tories' opposition to party government, he confessed to Grey that he had already begun to distrust the Tories and their leaders, while with the Reformers the reverse was true. Harvey to Grey, Sept. 15, 1846 (separate; private and confidential), CO 217/193, 222–9.

47 Howe to Buller, Sept. 16, 1846, JHP, vol. 6, p. 76.

48 See Chester Martin, "The Correspondence between Joseph Howe and Charles Buller, 1845–8," *Canadian Historical Review* 6 (December 1925): 318n3.

49 See Grey to Harvey, Nov. 3, 1846 (private and confidential), CO 217/193, 229–45.

50 Buller to Howe, Nov. 16, 1846 (confidential), JHP, vol. 1, pp. 177–81.

51 Howe to Buller, Sept. 16, 1846, JHP, vol. 6, p. 76.

52 Chisholm, 1: 613–4.

53 Ibid., p. 622.

54 Ibid., p. 623.

55 Ibid., p. 631.

56 Howe to Buller, Oct. 28, 1846, JHP, vol. 6, p. 83.

57 Howe to Grey, Oct. 28, 1846, ibid., p. 89.

58 Howe to Buller, Oct. 28, 1846, ibid., pp. 81–2.

59 Livingston, *Responsible Government in Nova Scotia*, p. 209.

60 Grey to Harvey, Nov. 3, 1846 (private and confidential), CO 217/193, 241, 243.

61 Buller to Howe, Nov. 16, 1846 (confidential), JHP, vol. 1, pp. 175, 181–2.

62 Ibid., p. 182.

63 Uniacke to Howe, Oct. 19, 1846, ibid., pp. 172–3.

64 *Novascotian*, Nov. 16, 1846.

65 *Times*, Nov. 17, 1846.

66 *Morning Post*, Nov. 21, 1846.

67 Howe to Kent, Nov. 28, 1846, JHP, vol. 6, pp. 97–9.

68 Executive Council to Harvey, Dec. 4, *JHA*, 1847, App. 16, pp. 65–6.

69 Harvey to Howe, Dec. 3, 1846, JHP, vol. 1, pp. 186–7. No less enigmatically, but apparently referring to Buller's letter of November 16, Howe replied that he too had received "a very interesting letter by the Packet which put [him] in possession of the views taken at home, of affairs here – it is satisfactory to find that we shall have aid, but no obstruction from that quarter." Howe to Harvey (undated), ibid., vol. 6, p. 101.

70 Harvey to Howe, Dec. 9, 1846, ibid., vol. 1, p. 192.

71 Ibid., Dec. 10, 1846 (private), pp. 201–2.
72 See Howe's "Memo of what took place in 1846, on offer of Coalition, which was declined," PANS, "Howe Letters," pp. 83–4.
73 Martin, *Empire and Commonwealth*, p. 232.
74 Memorandum of Reformers to Harvey, Dec. 17, 1846, *JHA*, 1847, App. 16, p. 72.
75 Ibid., p. 71.
76 Harvey to Howe, Dec. 17[?], 1846, PANS, "Howe Letters," p. 69.
77 Memorandum of Executive Council to Harvey, Jan. 28, 1847, *JHA*, 1847, App. 16, pp. 73–81; memorandum of Executive Council to Harvey for submission to Grey, Jan. 30, 1847, PANS, RG 1, vol. 119, pp. 74–80.
78 Martin, *Empire and Commonwealth*, p. 232.
79 *Times*, Jan. 26, 1847.
80 Kent to Howe, Jan. 29, 1847, JHP, vol. 1, pp. 216–8.
81 Fergusson to Howe, Jan. 12, 1847, ibid., p. 206. Fergusson added: "If I had an hours chat with you, you would concur with me in denouncing Lord M. as the greatest curse ever sent to Canada."
82 For his part, Harvey made certain that the council could not complain of its treatment at his hands; among other things, he let it see his private and confidential correspondence with Earl Grey.
83 *Novascotian*, Feb. 8, 1847.
84 Speech of March 26, ibid., Apr. 5, 1847.
85 Ibid.
86 Speech of March 26, ibid., Apr. 13, 1847.
87 Howe to half-sister Jane, Apr. 22, 1847, PANS, "Howe Letters," p. 88.
88 The Tories had first become annoyed with Bishop Walsh in August 1846 when he refused to sign their address to the departing Falkland.
89 *Guardian*, Feb. 5, 1847.
90 *Times*, Feb. 23, 1847.
91 *Standard and Conservative Advocate*, Apr. 30, 1847. John English, a Catholic, edited the *Acadian Recorder*, while Ritchie and Nugent, both Catholics, edited and published not only the *Sun* but also the *Irish Volunteer*, devoted to Irish causes, and the *Cross*, primarily religious. In confronting Howe at Bridgetown on June 17, Johnston upbraided the Liberal newspapers for not replying when the *Irish Volunteer* scorned their faith. "This I charge against them." *Novascotian*, July 12, 1847.
92 See letter of "Hengist" in *Acadian Recorder*, July 31, 1847.
93 Speech at Preston, date uncertain, *Novascotian*, May 10, 1847.
94 See issues of July and August 1847. Howe replied in the *Novascotian* on July 5 and August 2. Johnston also raised the question at Musquodoboit on June 3, ibid., June 14, 1847.
95 That did not prevent McGregor from asking: "What would be thought of a criminal on his trial for murder, to urge the court and jury, as his defence and claim to be acquitted, that A.B. had also committed a murder in the County of Lunenburg." See McGregor's third letter, *Standard and Conservative Advocate*, Aug. 6, 1847.
96 See memo of T.A.S. DeWolf in McGregor's third letter, ibid.
97 Speech of Johnston at Bridgetown on June 17, *Novascotian*, July 12, 1847.
98 See letter of Howe, ibid., July 5, 1847.

99 Ibid.
100 See Howe's speech at Bridgetown on June 17, ibid., July 5, 1847. Later, because of Johnston's denials, the *Novascotian* (July 19, 1847) published two affidavits which alleged that the passengers of the "grog vessel," who included W.A. Johnston, the attorney general's son, had distributed "Meall, Tobacco and Rum, for the Men, Tea, Sugar and Calicoes for the Women and Frocks for the Children."
101 See Howe's speech at Preston, ibid., May 10, 1847.
102 Ibid., May 10 and 17, 1847.
103 *Acadian Recorder*, May 15, 1847.
104 Howe to Susan Ann, May 12, 1847, JHP, reel 23, item 146.
105 Ibid.
106 Allegedly because he believed that Howe was busy elsewhere. See Howe's speech at Bridgetown on June 17, *Novascotian*, July 5, 1847.
107 Howe to Susan Ann, May 12, 1847, JHP, reel 23, item 146.
108 Johnston's speech at Bridgetown on June 17, *Novascotian*, July 12, 1847.
109 See Howe's speech at Bridgetown on June 17, ibid., July 5, 1847.
110 Ibid.
111 *Morning Post*, June 29, 1847.
112 *Novascotian*, Aug. 2, 1847.
113 *Sun*, Aug. 9, 1847.
114 Howe to Harvey, Aug. 4, 1847, JHP, vol. 6, pp. 180–1.
115 Thomas Bourke (Harvey's secretary) to Howe, Aug. 4, 1847, JHP, vol. 1, pp. 247–8.
116 See letter of "Publicola," *Acadian Recorder*, July 31, 1847.
117 *Morning Post*, Aug. 2, 1847.
118 The results were:

County		Township	
Howe 1,530	Gray 1,079	McNab 873	Uniacke 676
Mott 1,510	Lawson 1,077	Doyle 818	Grassie 655

But the Tories' electioneering tactics apparently worked in Preston, where the blacks gave them sixty votes to the Reformers' forty-one.
119 *Times*, Aug. 17, 1847.
120 This time Howe designated him by name.
121 *Novascotian*, Aug. 16, 1847.
122 Quoted from the *Post* in *Standard and Conservative Advocate*, Aug. 20, 1847.
123 *Times*, Aug. 17, 1847.
124 *Sun*, Aug. 20, 1847.
125 Ibid., Aug. 11, 1847.
126 Ibid. S.B. Chipman, Johnston's opponent in Annapolis, told Howe that "the Catholick have not obeyed there Priest's as well as the Baptist did ... I reduced [Johnston's] majority ... [but] the Screw was laid on so strong that I suppose 100 of my votes stayed at home from fear." Chipman to Howe, Aug. 23, 1847, JHP, vol. 1, pp. 249–50.
127 Howe to half-sister Jane, Aug. 28, 1847, PANS, "Howe Letters," p. 88.
128 As contrasted with 1843, the Reformers gained three seats in both Hants and Lunenburg, and single seats in the township of Halifax, and Colchester and Guysborough counties. They exchanged seats with the

Tories in Pictou, and lost single seats in Richmond county, and the townships of Amherst, Argyle, Londonderry, and Shelburne.
129 Howe to half-sister Jane, Aug. 28, 1847, PANS, "Howe Letters," p. 89.
130 Ibid. Howe was so pleased with Lunenburg county that he attended a political picnic of mammoth proportions in Mahone Bay in September. "Cart loads – yes, reader, cart loads! – of pumpkin pies, were brought, for a top-dressing." *Novascotian*, Sept. 27, 1847.
131 Howe to half-sister Jane, Aug. 28, 1847, PANS, "Howe Letters," p. 89.

CHAPTER NINETEEN

1 Howe to half-sister Jane, Aug. 28, 1847, PANS, "Howe Letters," p. 90.
2 *Novascotian*, Sept. 27, 1847.
3 Howe to Buller, Sept. 2, 1847, JHP, vol. 6, p. 182.
4 Ibid., pp. 183–4.
5 See comments of Yarmouth *Herald*, Sept. 6, 1847.
6 Uniacke's contribution to the Reform victory consisted largely of winning his own seat.
7 Grigor to Howe, Oct. 11, 1847, PANS, "Howe Letters," p. 91.
8 Ibid., Dec. 21, 1847, p. 94.
9 *Novascotian*, Jan. 17, 1848.
10 *Acadian Recorder*, Jan. 22, 1848.
11 Speech of January 22, *Novascotian*, Jan. 31, 1848.
12 Ibid.
13 *Times*, Jan. 25, 1848.
14 Speech of Jan. 25, 1848 in *Novascotian*, Feb. 7, 1848.
15 All members voted except the Liberal Speaker, William Young, and the Tory solicitor general, E.M. Dodd, who was absent because of illness. Yet the assembly *Journals* (Jan. 26, 1848, p. 15) show Dodd as being present and record the vote as twenty-eight to twenty-two.
16 Johnston looked so dejected and jaded that even the *Acadian Recorder* pitied him. *Acadian Recorder*, Jan. 29, 1848.
17 For some inexplicable reason Johnston expressed pride in the dispatches, even though he had done everything he could to defeat the principles they expounded. *Novascotian*, Jan. 31, 1848.
18 *Sun*, Jan. 31, 1848.
19 Uniacke, Howe, Huntington, McNab, George Young, Bell, Doyle, DesBarres, and Michael Tobin.
20 *JHA*, Feb. 7, 1848, p. 42. The amount was to be increased by £160 stg if George also retired as registrar.
21 An act would have required the consent of the Legislative Council which was by no means assured.
22 *JHA*, Feb. 7, 1848, pp. 42–3.
23 Howe to Harvey, Feb. 5, 1848, JHP, vol. 6, pp. 186–7.
24 See summary of debate, *Novascotian*, Feb. 14, 1848.
25 Howe to Buller, Feb. 12, 1848, JHP, vol. 35.
26 Howe defeated his opponent Logan by 1,547 to 715; Uniacke, who ran in the Halifax township seat which McNab had vacated to enter the Legislative Council, won almost as decisively. DesBarres trounced Marshall badly in Guysborough.
27 Howe to half-sister Jane[?], Mar. 15, 1848, PANS, "Howe Letters," p. 99.

28 Ibid., Aug. 28, 1847, pp. 89–90.
29 Grigor to Howe, Oct. 11, 1847, ibid., p. 91.
30 Ibid., Nov. 13, 1847, p. 93. This letter referred to an event that symbolically pointed to the fall of the Tories. Grigor told Howe that T.N. Jeffery, the collector of customs, had left a pitifully small estate, and that Mrs. Jeffery would be forced to sell her house. "What an end for a great man (?) for one who scoffed at the poverty of the Liberals. What an end to a long road!" Ibid.

Note on Sources

The basic Howe records are seventy volumes of original papers held by the Public Archives of Canada, which are available on twenty-one reels of microfilm in the Public Archives of Nova Scotia. Other original papers of Howe are in the Harvard University Library and are available on reels of microfilm (reels 22, 23, and 24) in PANS. Usually considered as an integral part of the Howe record are the George Johnson Papers, held in PAC and available on a single reel of microfilm in PANS. A large selection of Howe's writings and speeches up to 1848 is to be found in the first volume of Joseph A. Chisholm's two-volume edition of *The Speeches and Public Letters of Joseph Howe*. Some private letters are available in PANS in a typewritten collection by Joseph A. Chisholm, here designated "Howe Letters." Limited use has been made of the William Young Papers, especially box 732; the George Young Papers, especially box 720; the Burgess Collection; and the Waterman Papers (all in PANS); and of the John Sparrow Thompson Papers (in PAC).

Of the newspapers the one consulted most was the *Novascotian*, which covers the whole period of Howe's adult life. Together with its companion paper, the *Morning Chronicle* (dating from 1844), it provides not only news stories and editorial comment from the Liberal point of view, but also substantial reporting of the legislative debates over all these years. At times, after 1834, the Tory Halifax *Times* accompanies its strongly anti-Reform editorials with extensive coverage of the debates. Of considerable use throughout the period were the editorials of the Liberal *Acadian Recorder*. Howe's own paper, the *Acadian*, provides the basis for the chapter dealing with the year 1827. In the late 1820s and early 1830s Jotham Blanchard's *Colonial Patriot* (Pictou) and Edmund Ward's *Free Press* (Halifax) reflect, respectively, radical and conservative points of view. After 1837 the Baptist outlook is conveyed by the *Christian Messenger*; in the 1840s the *Register* (Halifax) presents Catholic views; and the *Pictou Observer*, the *Morning Post* (Halifax), and the *Standard and Conservative Advocate* (Halifax) present Tory views. Scattered use is made of the *Halifax (Royal) Gazette* and the *Halifax Journal.*

Most widely used of the government documents were the *Journals* of the Legislative Council and the House of Assembly, and the *Minutes* (and memoranda) of council. The correspondence of the governors, especially to the secretaries of state (colonial secretaries), is to be found in PANS, RG 1, vols. 114–19; the correspondence from the secretaries of state (colonial secretaries) to the governors in PANS, RG 1, vols. 69, 72, 79, 83, 85; CO 217/175 and 193; and PRO G series, especially 184. Papers relating to the Courts of Sessions and the Grand Juries for the county of Halifax are contained in PANS, RG 34-312; reference is made to documents in PANS, RG 1, 237, 252, 312, and 412 on a variety of subjects.

The book relies largely on primary sources. The only biography of Howe which it seemed fitting to draw upon was that of James A. Roy, *Joseph Howe: A Study in Achievement and Frustration.* Used to advantage were the *Collections of the Nova Scotia Historical Society.* By far the most useful secondary source was Chester Martin's *Empire and Commonwealth.*

Index